S0-EPW-373
A00855531001

F395.M5S55 1974

1287633

T.C.J.C.-S.C.

SOUTH CAMPUS LIBRARY
TARRANT COUNTY
JUNIOR COLLEGE
FT. WORTH, TEXAS 76119

DEMCO

*The Mexican American*

# The Mexican American

*Advisory Editor*
Carlos E. Cortés

*Editorial Board*
Rodolfo Acuña
Juan Gómez-Quiñones
George Fred Rivera, Jr.

# ANGLO-AMERICANS
AND MEXICAN AMERICANS
IN SOUTH TEXAS

Ozzie G. Simmons

ARNO PRESS
A New York Times Company
New York — 1974

Reprint Edition 1974 by Arno Press Inc.

Copyright © , 1974, by Ozzie G. Simmons
Reprinted by permission of Ozzie G. Simmons

THE MEXICAN AMERICAN
ISBN for complete set: 0-405-05670-2
See last pages of this volume for titles.

Publisher's Note: This dissertation was
reprinted from the only available copy.

Manufactured in the United States of America

**Library of Congress Cataloging in Publication Data**

Simmons, Ozzie G
    Anglo-Americans and Mexican Americans in south Texas

    (The Mexican American)
    Reprint of the author's thesis, Harvard, 1952.
    Bibliography: p.
    1. Mexican Americans--Texas. I. Title.
II. Series.
F395.M5S55   1974     301.45'16'8720764    73-14215
ISBN 0-405-05689-3

ANGLO AMERICANS AND MEXICAN AMERICANS IN SOUTH TEXAS

A Study in Dominant-Subordinate Group Relations

by

Ozzie G. Simmons

A thesis submitted in partial fulfillment
of the requirements for the degree of
Doctor of Philosophy in Sociology in the
Department of Social Relations

Harvard University

1952

CONTENTS

| Chapter | | Page |
|---|---|---|
| I | THE RESEARCH SITE AND METHOD ............... | 1 |
| | The Setting ............................. | 1 |
| | Method and Techniques ................... | 6 |
| II | ASPECTS OF A SYSTEM OF DOMINANT-SUBORDINATE GROUP RELATIONS ........................... | 24 |
| | The Problem of Dominant and Subordinate Status ................................... | 24 |
| | Factors Conducive to the Ascription of Subordinate Status ......................... | 30 |
| | The Mechanisms Employed for the Maintenance of Subordinate Status ..................... | 40 |
| | The Types of Reactive Adjustment to Subordinate Status ............................. | 46 |
| III | THE MEXICAN AMERICANS ...................... | 59 |
| | The Family .............................. | 60 |
| | Adult Sex Roles ......................... | 74 |
| | Patterns of Interpersonal Relations ..... | 79 |
| | Religion and Related Aspects ............ | 84 |
| | The Use of Leisure ...................... | 104 |
| | Some Aspects of Basic Personality Type .. | 109 |
| IV | THE PATTERNS OF INTERGROUP CONTACT ......... | 124 |
| | Residence ............................... | 124 |
| | Education ............................... | 132 |
| | Recreation .............................. | 137 |
| | Commercial and Professional Services .... | 143 |
| | Religious Worship ....................... | 153 |
| | Informal Social Intercourse and Intermarriage ................................ | 159 |
| V | THE OCCUPATIONAL STRUCTURE ................. | 166 |
| | The Agricultural Economy ................ | 167 |
| | General Aspects of the Occupational Structure and the "Wetback" .................. | 180 |

| Chapter | | Page |
|---|---|---|
| V (Cont.) | The Labor Role | 186 |
| | The White Collar Role | 207 |
| | The Business Role | 213 |
| | The Professional Role | 227 |
| | Aspects of Employer-Employee Relations | 231 |
| | Motivational Aspects | 254 |
| | Occupational Structure and Dominant-Subordinate Group Relations | 265 |
| VI | SOCIAL ORGANIZATION: POLITICS | 270 |
| | The Tradition of the Machine | 270 |
| | The Mexican Vote | 274 |
| | The Controlled Vote and the Political *Jefe*. | 279 |
| | The Mexican American Candidate and Office-Holder | 296 |
| | The Anglo American Candidate and the Mexican Vote | 315 |
| | Patterns of Political Action and Dominant-Subordinate Group Relations | 324 |
| VII | SOCIAL ORGANIZATION: CLASSES | 339 |
| | Introductory Remarks | 339 |
| | Anglo American Classes | 342 |
| | Mexican American Classes | 353 |
| |     Class Divisions and Occupation | 353 |
| |     The Middle Class | 358 |
| |         1. The Determinants of Status | 358 |
| |         2. Distinctive Middle Class Patterns | 366 |
| |         3. Attitudes toward the Lower Class | 379 |
| |         4. The Lower Status Group | 385 |
| |     The Lower Class | 392 |
| | Anglo American Dominance and the Mexican American Class Structure | 398 |
| VIII | THE STEREOTYPE AND PATTERNS OF DISCRIMINATION | 405 |
| | Visibility Symbols | 405 |
| | The Stereotype of the Mexican American | 409 |
| | Discrimination against the Mexican American | 438 |
| |     Residence | 440 |
| |     Education | 446 |
| |     Recreation | 450 |

| Chapter | | Page |
|---|---|---|
| VIII (Cont.) | Commercial Services .................... | 457 |
| | Religious Worship ..................... | 458 |
| | Voluntary Associations ................ | 460 |
| | Law Enforcement ....................... | 464 |
| | The Nature of Subordinate Status ....... | 468 |
| IX | REACTIVE ADJUSTMENTS TO SUBORDINATE STATUS. | 475 |
| | Conceptions of Subordinate Status and Role ....................................... | 475 |
| | Conceptions of the Dominant Group ....... | 483 |
| | Types of Reactive Adjustment ............ | 492 |
| |    Aggression against the Dominant Group.. | 492 |
| |    Aggression against other Subordinate Groups ................................. | 504 |
| |    Aggression within the Mexican American Group .................................. | 507 |
| |    Accommodation through Isolation ........ | 516 |
| |    Accommodation through Assimilation...... | 524 |
| | Leadership and the Association .......... | 532 |

Appendix A. A Note on Other Studies of the Spanish-Speaking Group in the United States ................. 552

Appendix B. Statistical Tables ..................... 560

Selected Bibliography .................................. 570

Numbered Footnotes ..................................... 578

\* \* \*
\* \*
\*

Chapter I

THE RESEARCH SITE AND METHOD

## The Setting

The Lower Rio Grande Valley of Texas is a delta, rather than a valley, about 105 miles long and 35 miles wide, stretching along the Mexican border from Brownsville, on the Gulf of Mexico, to Rio Grande City in semi-arid Starr County. The Valley embraces four counties, Hidalgo, Cameron, Willacy, and Starr, with a total population of 249,000 people.[*] Its rapid growth from 1920 on, when irrigation was developed extensively, is indicated by the fact that it doubled its population size from 85,861 in 1920[**] to 176,452 in 1930, then jumped to 215,803 in 1940. The lush agricultural development of the Valley is a recent phenomenon, and all of its towns and cities, with the exceptions of Brownsville, Port Isabel, and Rio Grande City, came into being after 1900. Brownsville is the largest Valley city, with a population of 31,000; Harlingen, near the center of the Valley, has 20,206 inhabitants; and McAllen, 65 miles west of Brownsville,

---

[*] This is a 1947 estimate prepared by the U. S. Department of Commerce and published by the Valley Chamber of Commerce. Other population figures cited here for individual cities are 1947 estimates made by local chambers of commerce.

[**] All population figures prior to 1947 were obtained from the U. S. Census.

has an estimated 17,500.* The Missouri Pacific Railroad and the main highway run the length of the Valley, passing through twelve of its twenty-two towns and cities. Distances between towns are usually very short. McAllen's eastern neighbor, Pharr (population 9,750), is only four miles away, and its western neighbor, Mission (population 10,678), is five miles away. Eight miles to the north lies Edinburg (population 12,000), the seat of Hidalgo County. McAllen and the Valley are connected with San Antonio (population 365,000), 250 miles to the north, by two highways and the Southern Pacific Railroad. One of these highways runs through McAllen and south to Mexico City. Brownsville is a scheduled stop for major airlines, and a local airline offers thrice-weekly flights between San Antonio and McAllen. Driving south from San Antonio, one passes for hours through vast expanses of monotonous brushland and grazing country and then suddenly comes upon acres of citrus groves, rich farm land teeming with vegetables and cotton, and long rows of palm trees. This is the "Magic Valley", an oasis in the semi-desert country of South Texas.

Physically and culturally, McAllen is much like the other new cities and towns of the Valley.** It has little

---

\* For a more detailed breakdown of the McAllen population derived from the city directory, see Appendix B. On the basis of this breakdown, the Mexican American percentage of the total population is calculated at 56.4.

\*\* See Chapter IV for a detailed physical and ecological description of McAllen.

spring and autumn, and a long sweltering summer of seven months relieved only by a steady but faint Gulf breeze. From April through October, the normal maximum temperatures range from 87.6 in early April to 98.4 in August, the hottest month, and back to 87.9 in October. From November to March, the "winter months", the normal minimum temperature seldom drops below fifty degrees. The heaviest rains fall in September, the normal precipitation being 3.79 inches at that time, but there is a small amount of rainfall during every month of the year. Relative humidity is highest in December and January, the average for the thirteen year period from 1934 to 1946 being 80.2 and 81.5 during these months.

McAllen's first building was constructed in 1905, the year after the completion of the St. Louis, Brownsville, and Mexico Railroad.[1] By 1920, it had 5,331 inhabitants, which increased to 9,074 in 1930, and 11,877 in 1940. The advent of the railroad marked the beginning of an economic development that had been previously hindered by a century of border warfare, and facilitated Anglo American immigration to the Valley. Prior to this time, the Valley had been inhabited largely by Mexican ranchers who maintained large *haciendas* in the traditional Mexican style based on the peonage system. For the most part, their ownership of land could be traced back to the old Spanish grants, or *porciones*.[2] In Starr County, where the Anglo American immigration has been very small, many of the *porciones* are still undivided, and it is estimated that at least fifty percent of them remain in the names of the original grantees.[3] In Hidalgo County, however, most of the *porciones* are now divided into large and small tracts of land owned by Anglo Americans who obtained them through purchase and less legitimate means.[4] Much of the land owned by Anglo Americans today had never been utilized by the original Mexican owners, and was reclaimed by means of irrigation development and with the aid of farm machinery. Although the old Mexican American land-owning families in Starr County still retain much of their traditional prominence in the affairs of the local society, in Hidalgo and Cameron Counties their position steadily deteriorated with the economic development carried out by the ever-increasing numbers of Anglo Americans, and today they are, with a few exceptions, completely overshadowed by the dominant Anglo Americans, who have taken over their social and economic position in the community.

The Anglo American immigration into the Valley was paralleled by that of Mexicans from across the border, who were attracted by the seemingly greater opportunities available for farm labor created by the economic development and agricultural expansion. Actually, there was a small but steady flow of Mexican immigration into South Texas from across the border that long antedated the Anglo immigration. Part of this was seasonal, part permanent. As early as the eighteen-nineties, Mexicans from both sides of the Rio

Grande were following the cotton harvests on foot into East Texas, returning to their homes in Mexico and South Texas after an absence of four or five months.[5] No figures are available on the growth of the Mexican American population as opposed to the Anglo American, but some idea of the increase in Hidalgo County of the number of immigrants from Mexico can be gained from the U. S. Census figures on the foreign born element of the county's population. The startling decrease indicated for 1930 is undoubtedly due to the forced repatriation of Mexican nationals to Mexico in 1929 and 1930 as a result of the Depression.

| Year | Total County Population | Total Foreign Born | Foreign Born from Mexico |
|---|---|---|---|
| 1900 | 6,837 | 2,380 | 2,366 |
| 1910 | 13,728 | 5,340 | 5,202 |
| 1920 | 38,728 | 15,547 | 14,601 |
| 1930 | 77,004 | 1,316 | 152 |
| 1940 | 106,059 | 15,981 | 14,939 |

This table indicates the rapid population growth in the county, as well as the negligible number of foreign born other than Mexican in the total population. In McAllen, in 1940, 1,715 of the city's 1,888 foreign born were of Mexican descent.

Due to the limitations of the study, the "Anglo American" group will be treated residually as consisting of those of McAllen's residents who are not Mexican American. However, it should be kept in mind that, although the number of foreign born is very small. McAllen's Anglos have emigrated to the Valley from all parts of the United States and Texas, and represent a wide variety of regional cultural backgrounds. On the basis of field observation, the native Texans seem to be distinctly in the minority, while the Middle West and South are most heavily represented.

## Method and Techniques

The original purpose of the study, developed before entering the field, was to investigate intergroup relationships between sedentary Anglo groups and a migratory Mexican group with a view to examining the role played by the Mexican's migratory patterns in determining the structure of intergroup relationships. The McAllen area was selected as the initial site for this study due to an offer made by the director of a social service project there to provide lodgings and initial contacts at the farm labor housing center where the project was based. The original plan had to be abandoned due to a number of practical difficulties which need not be discussed here. Instead, it was decided to undertake the study of intergroup relations within the context of an established community where both Anglo and Mexican elements were well represented. Practically all Valley communities seemed to be equally suitable for carrying out the study, but McAllen was selected because this enabled the writer to retain the labor center lodgings, located close to the city, and to take advantage of the initial contacts already made there. The major focus of the investigation was that of intergroup relations, and at no time was a full community study either contemplated or attempted. However, in order to render intelligible the data collected on this subject and place it in its proper context, it proved necessary to gather basic ethnological data as well as information on a variety of matters not directly related to the problem under consideration. Actually, a consistent attempt was made to record the field experience as completely and in as great detail as possible.

The principal technique utilized in the research was that of modified participant observation. The writer joined various Anglo American voluntary associations and participated in their activities; attended the meetings of organizations in both the Anglo and Mexican communities, as well as all sorts of formal and informal social functions and gatherings; taught classes in English to Mexican American farm laborers; at times worked with Mexican American field crews in the harvesting of citrus and vegetables; and in the early stages of the research regularly frequented the bars in the Anglo and Mexican communities. In addition, a great deal of time was spent in securing Anglo and Mexican informants of many types in different groups and strata.

With many of these, a considerable number of hours were spent in "passive" interviews at their places of work, in a restaurant or bar, and in their homes or that of the writer. These situations were always defined as casual and "social", never as formal interviews. With a few exceptions, the research objectives were never disclosed either wholly or in part no matter how intimate the relationship with an informant became, nor were notes taken in the presence of informants. All data were recorded as soon as possible after leaving the field situation, striving for verbatim reconstruction of conversations and to recapture the total context in which they occurred. No set questions or systematic cross-examination were utilized, and direct questioning was minimized as much as possible. Where questions were asked, they were recorded in the field notes along with the responses. In McAllen, two Anglo Americans were taken into the writer's confidence because they were potentially strategically useful in facilitating access to Anglo informants and other sources of important data, a move which turned out to be quite justified. In San Antonio, the research objectives were disclosed to three Mexican Americans, aside from life-history informants, for similar reasons.

For the purpose of explaining his activities and justifying his presence in the community, the writer posed as a teacher of Latin American history and "customs" on a sabbatical leave from a university for the purpose of learning about "Latin" life at first hand and learning Spanish. This role, used for both Mexican and Anglo Americans, was usually acceptable to the former as an explanation of the interest and curiosity manifested in their ways and activities. Quite apart from the role definition, one of the greatest difficulties in the way of establishing effective relationships with Mexican Americans was the writer's membership in the Anglo group. Their first reaction was usually one of suspicion and constraint since their experience with Anglos who manifested a desire to associate with them voluntarily was exceedingly limited, and most had no such experience at all. The role selected by the writer was relatively less successful with the Anglo group, for many of whom the extended "vacation" and apparent command of inexhaustible leisure became somewhat suspect after the novelty of the relationship wore off. The role definition had its limitations in that it was not always possible to be regarded as a genuine participant in the activities and interests of the community by all its members. At times and in certain situations it was possible to be defined as a participant much like other members of the community, but often the fact that the writer was an outsider with no visible stake in the community and only temporary ties with it remained a predominant consideration in the minds of certain informants, and in these cases there were no other available roles the writer could assume to minimize this. The principal disadvantage, then, that ensued from the use of the participant observation technique stemmed from the difficulty of role assumption experienced by the writer. Disclosure of research objectives would have eliminated the problem and have provided the writer with a tangible "occupation" such as those pursued by other community members, regardless of the fact that his was considerably different from theirs. Another disadvantage of participant observation was the necessary sacrifice of a certain amount of uniformity in the collected data.[6] By the very nature of the approach, it was not possible to systematically gather strictly comparable data from large numbers of informants. However, every effort was made to check what was learned from a particular informant by observation and by indirect questioning of other informants.

Despite the problems posed by the difficulty of selecting effective roles, the use of the participant observation technique had its compensations, primarily because it permitted minimization of the distortion that inevitably results from the introduction of the investigator as a new element in the situation to be studied. It may be stated categorically that no informant, with the exception of those taken into the writer's confidence, ever offered information with the idea that he was being "studied" or that what he said would "go into a book". The use of the technique also permitted the writer to avoid creating new or special situations, although his presence and activities undoubtedly altered many going situations in one way or another, sometimes subtly, and at times obviously.[7] Striving for participation also resulted in extensive contact with a wide variety of aspects and situations of the going society that permitted a much more substantial amplification of the range of data collected than would have been possible through direct interviewing of selected informants. Moreover, participation afforded the opportunity to observe the informant in "action" in his society, thereby giving much wider play to observation as a technique for the collection of data and reducing the writer's dependence on "what people say" as his principal source of information.

Including both McAllen and San Antonio, the writer established extended relationships with approximately eighty informants, Anglo and Mexican Americans, and transient contacts with about 130 other informants. The extended relationships consisted of a minimum of three to four hours of "passive" interviewing, but in many cases totaled hundreds of hours by the time the research was terminated. In McAllen, the principal Mexican American informants included agricultural and packing shed workers,[*]

---
[*] For definitions and explanations of the occupational categories cited in this discussion, see Chapter V.

crewleaders, various skilled workers such as mechanics and carpenters, store and office clerks and salesmen, bartenders, businessmen, a few independent farmers, schoolteachers, two lawyers, a social worker, and a civil engineer. The principal Anglo American informants were farmers, farmer-businessmen, businessmen, fruit and vegetable packers, a newspaper editor, a woman reporter, a Protestant minister, real estate brokers, a lawyer, public health nurses, a social worker, store and office clerks, skilled workers, and two crewleaders. Among the principal Mexican American informants in San Antonio there were unskilled workers in the meat-packing plants and military bases, skilled workers such as barbers and carpenters, businessmen representing a variety of commercial and industrial activities, real estate and insurance salesmen, social workers, schoolteachers, lawyers, and doctors. In view of the limited time spent in participant observation research in San Antonio, most of the extended relationships there were developed with Mexican Americans, but about ten Anglo Americans were numbered among the principal informants, including a bond broker, a private secretary, a Protestant minister, a Catholic priest, a female schoolteacher, a college professor, and a few businessmen. Although most of the principal informants were male, it was often possible to use wives and female relatives as informants also. Aside from husband-wife pairs as informants, independent relationships were established with five Mexican American women in McAllen and three in San Antonio.

In McAllen, most of the Mexican American political and civic leaders were numbered among the principal informants, and in San Antonio, although the proportion of the leader group with whom extended relationships were established was somewhat smaller, practically all were personally known to the writer.

In view of the size of the communities studied and of the gulf that exists between Anglo and Mexican groups, it was possible to associate extensively with both groups without much awareness on the part of either of the relationships maintained with the other. In any event, Mexican Americans of course took it for granted that the writer would associate with Anglo Americans as well. There was always the potential danger, however, of loss of prestige and confidence enjoyed with Anglo Americans if they were to know of the intimate contacts maintained with Mexican Americans. Fortunately, the danger did not materialize to any significant extent.

From October, 1947 to June, 1948, six months were spent in field work in McAllen. In July, 1948, the writer moved to San Antonio for four months, terminating the research in October, 1948. The decision to include San Antonio in the investigation was largely motivated by the desire to obtain comparative data on a situation involving

Anglo-Mexican relations on a much larger scale than that which was obtained in McAllen. In San Antonio, the major part of the field work was devoted to the Mexican American community, and access to informants was greatly facilitated by a few Mexican Americans who aided the writer substantially in this task. Lodgings were secured in a settlement house directed by a Mexican American and located in the heart of the Mexican community. Of the research period of four months, the last seven weeks were devoted almost completely to recording the life histories of four Mexican Americans, each of whom gave four to five hours a week to the interviews. In the case of these informants, the research objectives were disclosed, of course, and verbatim notes taken in their presence. For the last half of the research, a wire-recorder was used, making it possible to cover much more ground in each of the two-hour sessions, as well as attain greater fidelity in recording. Interviewing was of the undirected type as much as possible, but a prepared schedule was used to obtain desired data that could not be secured through the undirected interview. The interviews were held in the homes or offices of the informants, and always in private. Three of the informants were male and one female, and all held middle class status in the community. Three of them, however, came from lower class backgrounds, and their life histories provided a number of insights into the process of class mobility. The Thematic Apperception Test was administered to each informant in the final sessions. The material collected in these interviews was used as freely as the data gathered by other means in the preparation of this report, but is by no means to be considered the principal source of the information on which this study is based.

In order to provide the reader with a more concrete idea of the procedures followed in collecting field data, the method of inquiry employed by the writer in gathering data used to support particular empirical generalizations that appear in the study may be illustrated by a few examples. This description of method will be concerned only with the sources and manner of collection of the data on which the generalizations are based. To arrive at the generalization itself as it appears in the text, another step was required, that of structural-functional analysis of the data with reference to the wider contexts in which the problems referred to by the generalizations are involved. In the case of the first example, the wider context is that of patterns of Mexican American political action in relation to Anglo American dominance, and in the second, the caste and class structures of Anglo-Mexican society. Although the data on which the generalizations selected here are based are part of larger bodies of materials collected concerning these wider contexts, it is possible to describe how the specific data bearing on these generalizations were gathered.

In the discussion of political action, the statement is made that Mexican American political leaders view their political power as a means of increasing their own prestige in the Anglo world and of insuring themselves at least a measure of acceptance by the Anglos, with whom they are brought into contact by their political activities. Many informants provided bits of information that could be utilized in establishing this generalization, but the most substantial evidence was obtained from the following: In McAllen, four Mexican American political leaders, two of them farmer-businessmen, one a lawyer, and one a businessman were the principal informants. Seven Mexican Americans who were politically active but not of the leader group also contributed important information in this connection. This group consisted of two housewives, two salesmen, a schoolteacher, a lawyer, and a civil engineer. Anglo American informants included a lawyer who was a political leader, and a newspaper editor and a businessman, who were politically active. In San Antonio, five Mexican American political leaders, all lawyers, and six Mexican Americans who were politically active gave useful data. Of this latter group, one was executive secretary of a <u>colonia</u> organization, one a schoolteacher, one a lawyer, and three were businessmen. There was only one important Anglo informant on this subject, a Protestant minister who was a political leader.

In describing and evaluating their political activities, the political leaders, both consciously and unconsciously, placed the greatest emphasis on the personal advantages they could secure from the dominant group through pursuance of such activities. In the interviews held with them, they dwelt at length on the intimate relationships they had been able to establish with the Anglo American leaders, indicating that their mutual form of address was by first name, that they were invited to Anglo social affairs, that Anglos had to come to them for favors, and that in general they had achieved a frequency of interaction on an equal status basis to an extent exceedingly rare in Anglo-Mexican relations. Interviews with politically active Mexicans confirmed and amplified the data collected from the political leaders on the motivational basis of their political behavior. The stereotype of the Mexican political leader, which dwells only on this aspect of the leader's activity and interprets it as a "sellout" of the Mexican American group, is documented not only by the data collected from politically active Mexicans but by the comments obtained from a wide variety of Mexican informants who consistently expressed an atitude toward Mexican political leaders characterized by suspicion and cynicism. The interview materials obtained from the Anglo informants indicated above tallied with those obtained from the Mexicans. They were most familiar with the Mexican political leaders and referred to them as "friends", knew little about any other members of the Mexican group, advised the writer to see those particular Mexicans if he wished to "learn" anything about the Mexican group, and in general indicated that the Mexican leader's most desirable quality was his political utility.

Further documentation of the Mexican political leader's motivational patterns was obtained through observation of types and frequency of interaction with Anglo Americans. Observation of patterns of intergroup contact revealed that, with few exceptions, only Mexican American political leaders participated in commensalism, home visiting, and "friendships" with Anglo Americans. Mexicans who were ranked high in the community's class structure on the basis of such criteria as occupation, income, and/or education had few opportunities for such joint participation with Anglos unless they also enjoyed political power or were at least politically active. At political rallies and barbecues, it was observed that Mexican political leaders received most respect and attention from Anglo Americans, that their relatively free and easy relationships with Anglos in these situations contrasted sharply with the treatment accorded Mexican Americans attending these functions who might qualify for high status on bases other than political power. Another contrast was provided through observation of interaction between Anglos and Mexicans at the meetings and social functions of the businessmen's organizations of which both are members. In these situations, Anglo-Mexican interaction partook of the constraint and formality that usually characterizes intergroup contacts.

Other pertinent data were obtained by observation and study of the events of political campaigns, particularly of the ways in which alignments were made between Anglo and Mexican politicians, and this was checked through interviews with the chief participants in the campaigns as well as by careful examination of Anglo and Mexican press accounts and campaign speeches and literature. The political careers of the principal Mexican American leaders were reconstructed by the writer from accounts by informants, from autobiographical material obtained from the leaders themselves, and from perusal of local newspaper files and local literature where available. Finally, it may be stated that the writer's findings check with those presented in the studies dealing with Mexican American participation in South Texas politics cited elsewhere in this report, although the present analysis attempts a more thorough treatment.

The method of inquiry may be further illustrated by description of how the supporting data were collected for another empirical generalization, one about the lower status group of the Mexican middle class. In the discussion of class, it is stated that members of this lower status group occupy an ambivalent position in the class structure in that, like the upper status group, they are oriented to vertical mobility, but, like the lower class, they are still attracted to the orientations and values characteristic of the latter as well. Many informants in McAllen contributed directly and indirectly to the data used in establishing this generalization, but the most substantial information was obtained through extended relationships with nine individuals, all of whom held white collar occupations and came from lower class families, and from five family groups where both white collar and labor occupations were represented. Of the nine individuals, two were female, a five and ten cent store salesclerk and a clerk-typist employed by a county agency, and seven were male, including a collector for a loan agency, two department store salesclerks, two office clerks, a salesman for a wholesale produce company, and a grocery clerk. In San Antonio, four informants of the white collar category provided supporting evidence, and the life history materials obtained from three middle class informants who came from lower class families pointed up and confirmed the data on lower status group ambivalence toward middle class and lower class orientations collected by less intensive techniques.

Through interviews, the occupational history of each of the McAllen informants was obtained by means of which it was possible to trace a shift from labor to white collar occupations or to discern a pattern of consistent avoidance of labor occupations from the time the individual became gainfully employed. Interviews also elicited the goal orientations attendant on these action patterns, both on the level of immediate wants and on that of ultimate ends. Interviews with the several members of the family groups concerning intrafamilial relationships revealed that the major strains and conflicts that characterized interpersonal relations within these particular families stemmed from differing points of view regarding status aspirations and traditional obligations, complicated by the fact that the mobile members of the family were still in part oriented to the traditional obligations.

Through observation, pertinent data were gathered on the style of living of these informants, which helped to buttress the information obtained by other means on their status aspirations and other goal orientations. Where possible, inventories were made for comparative purposes of house furnishings, clothing, and so on, and of the types of expenditures made most frequently by informants. Participation in their extra-work activities provided the opportunity for recording the relative frequency of their interaction and attempts at interaction with members of the upper status group and with those they recognized as occupying a status equal to theirs. Such participation also permitted the observation of where and under what conditions they avoided or attempted to avoid interaction with lower class members, including the variations introduced into these action patterns by kinship ties with lower class Mexican Americans, observation of their organizational affiliations and participation, and of their avoidance of behavior defined by the upper status group as typically lower class, such as attendance at public dances and frequenting of bars.

The research was neither initiated nor carried out with reference to a conceptual scheme specially prepared for the project, but a set of basic questions, prepared on the basis of the writer's theoretical orientations and professional preparation, were used to guide the research throughout. These basic questions were modified and added to as the field work progressed. The conceptual scheme used to organize the field materials and to orient their analysis and interpretation was devised after the termination of field work, but is a direct outgrowth of the field experience and findings.

Other sources of information, aside from those already mentioned, used in the preparation of the study include data obtained through examination of school enrollment statistics, district and corporation court dockets, marriage licence records, county health unit records and reports, daily clippings from local newspapers, U. S. Census materials, local and other pertinent literature, the minutes and membership lists of voluntary associations, and a statistical breakdown of the McAllen city directory by ethnic membership for population percentage, sex ratio, family size, occupations, commercial services, and place of residence.

The terms "Anglo American" and "Mexican American" have been selected to identify and distinguish between the two groups whose relations are the subject of this study, and they are used interchangeably with the terms "Anglo" and "Mexican" throughout the discussion. "Spanish-speaking" or "Spanish-name" are perhaps less objectionable terms, but are less specific in that they can also refer to many individuals who cannot be identified with the "Mexican American" group defined in the following chapters. The use of the terms "Anglo American" and "Mexican American" in a scientific report may be legitimately questioned, but they have been borrowed from popular usage for lack of more exact terminology and for the sake of convenience. All of the people discussed in the study are really just "Americans", of course, and the terminology adopted here should not be construed as a sanction by the writer of the separatism it connotes.

## Chapter II

## ASPECTS OF A SYSTEM OF DOMINANT-SUBORDINATE GROUP RELATIONS

### The Problem of Dominant and Subordinate Status

The investigation is centered on a social system wherein may be discerned certain patterns of interrelations between two groups by virtue of which one group occupies a subordinate status with respect to the other. The basic task of the study is to examine the nature and role of the various factors which have been conducive to the development of subordinate status for one of the groups, to explore the mechanisms by means of which the system is maintained, and to delineate the types of reactive adjustment made by the incumbents to their subordinate status. The approach to be employed will be that of institutional analysis, focusing on the structures of occupations and stratification as the contexts within which to study the factors determining subordination, the mechanisms, and the reactive adjustments.

The term subordinate status, as it will be used in this conceptual outline, will refer to the relatively lower position one group, as a group, occupies with respect to the other in the system of differential ranking which governs the relations between the two groups. Conversely, the term dominant status will refer to the relatively higher position one group, as a group, occupies with respect to the other. The domination and subordination involved is expressed in the type of system of differential ranking which is operative in the relations between the two groups. These types may range from caste at one extreme to open class at the other. Caste is commonly distinguished by the criteria of endogamy, prohibition of movement from one status to the other, and unequal distribution of rewards and privileges between the dominant and subordinate statuses in favor of the former. Class permits the practice of both endogamy and exogamy, does not prohibit movement from one status to the other, and also involves the unequal distribution of rewards and privileges. At any point on the continuum between the caste and class poles, dominant and subordinate status are _initially_ ascribed rather than achieved, and ascribed on the basis of birth into a particular racial, ethno-racial, ethnic, religious, or kinship group. To the extent that birth remains, throughout the life of the individual, the sole basis of status determination, which derives its stability from the practice of endogamy and prohibition of movement from one status to the other, the type of system of differential ranking will approximate the caste pole. To the extent that other attributes of the individual awarded mainly on the basis of achievement acquire a status-determining function along with birth, the type of system of differential ranking will approach the class pole, where the possession of some combination of those other attributes may lead to a change in the status of the individual since movement from one status to the other is not prohibited, and the primacy of birth as a status determinant is further weakened by the permissible practice of exogamy.

At the caste pole, the significance of birth for the determination of status derives from the fact that it is birth into one of two or more solidary groups whose members share distinctive physical characteristics, a distinctive cultural and social tradition, or both.* Either one or both of these factors may function as a symbol of visibility by means of which differential ranking on a group basis may be greatly facilitated. In fact, without such visibility symbols, it would be exceedingly difficult to ascribe hierarchichal status on a group basis. At the class pole, the significance of birth for the determination of status derives from the fact that kinship groups are treated as units in the system of differential ranking.[1] Here, however, the role of birth as a status determinant is limited by the fact that other attributes acquired through achievement may possess status-determining functions as well, so that membership in a kinship group is not the primary status determinant and is confined to providing differential access to opportunities whereby the other attributes can be achieved, which in itself may of course be of great significance. Racial and/or ethnic origin may also continue to play a role as a status determinant, but unlike the caste type case, it does so only in combination with other status-determining attributes, which are acquired through achievement.

Employing the typology outlined above, ranking in the concrete social system which is the object of this study is

---

* Birth into a group characterized by occupational specialization may also be significant for determination of caste status, as in India. Thus, there may be racial or non-racial castes.

determined by a combination of approaches to both the caste and class polar types. When one is looking at the relations <u>between</u> the two groups who compose the social system, it can be seen that the type of system of differential ranking which is operative in those relations approaches the caste pole. On the other hand, when one is looking at the relations <u>within</u> each of the groups, the type of system of differential ranking operative approaches the class pole. The former will now be examined to determine its degree of approximation to the caste type. The subordinate group in this concrete social system may be designated as an ethno-racial group in that its members, possessing continuity through biological descent, share a distinctive social and cultural tradition and distinctive common hereditary physical characteristics. These factors make the group easily vulnerable to treatment by the dominant group as symbolically appropriate for ascription of subordinate status and in fact are the basis of such ascription. This does not mean that the subordinate status of the group can be explained in terms of visibility characteristics, physical or cultural, nor can the latter explain why subordinate status is ascribed to this particular group rather than some other. If the ascription of subordinate status to a particular group is to be practicable and enduring, the group must possess visibility characteristics of a fairly obvious nature which distinguish it from the group doing the ascribing. It is in this sense that birth into the group possessing visibility characteristics is the basis of ascription of subordinate status, in that it provides the necessary condition for such ascription. The analysis of the factors which have led to the development of subordinate status for our ethno-racial group is one major aspect of the basic task of this entire study, just as the study will attempt to capture the dynamics of such status and will, as a whole, represent the definition of that status.

The key criterion for classifying the type of system of differential ranking operative in the relations between the ethno-racial group and the other group, which will be residually defined as including all members of the social system who were not born into this particular ethno-racial group, is the degree of freedom of movement between the relative statuses occupied by the groups as a whole. Compared to the case of the Negro, the rigidity of the line between the group statuses under discussion here is mitigated by the belief, held by the dominant group, in the possibility of the assimilation and amalgamation of the subordinate group, although the materialization of this possibility is placed in the dim future. The existence of such a belief makes possible loopholes in the unalterability of the subordinate status in the sense that those individuals who are regarded as having attained the "state of assimilation" may move from the subordinate to the dominant status. Concretely speaking, the vast majority of the subordinate group members are not defined by the dominant group as even approaching this state and so, in their lifetimes, subordinate status may be regarded as unalterable. Similarly, taking up the criterion of endogamy, which is a special case of the larger criterion of movement between group statuses, it may be stated that those members of the ethno-racial group who are defined as approaching "assimilation" are permitted the practice of intermarriage with members of the dominant group without condemnation by the latter. The fundamental significance of prohibition of movement from one status to the other, and of the practice of endogamy becomes clear when consideration is given to the third of the criteria employed to distinguish the caste type of stratification, that of unequal distribution of rewards and privileges in favor of the dominant group. In the case of the ethno-racial group under consideration it may be stated that certain disabilities are imposed by the dominant group on the former which define its subordinate status, and that among these disabilities are limited access to the rewards and privileges of the society, as compared to the access enjoyed by the dominant group. These disabilities are imposed on the basis of membership in the ethno-racial group, and may be escaped only by those who can approximate the definition of "assimilation" held by the dominant group.

In effect, then, the type of system of differential ranking obtaining between the two groups may be classified as semi-caste,[*] which means that the subordinate status occupied by our ethno-racial group is a semi-caste status. This is not a very precise term, but is the only one suitable in view of the fact that it is possible for ethno-racial group members under certain conditions to move from subordinate to dominant status, to

---

[*] The writer follows the usage adopted by Ruth Tuck, who selected the term "semi-caste" because it "reflects an appreciation of the fact that permanent group disabilities for Mexican Americans are less severe and easier to escape than those for Negroes and Orientals." See Not with the Fist, New York, 1946, reference footnote 6, p. 44.

practice exogamy with the dominant group, and to escape the disabilities imposed on incumbents of subordinate status. Actually, it is probably most correct to conceive of the subordinate status as a continuum defined at one extreme by full caste, and at the other extreme by escape from modified caste into the open class system of the dominant group. In short, the caste is open at the top for those who can get there.

## Factors Conducive to the Ascription of Subordinate Status

The factors which are conducive to the ascription of subordinate status are to be found in the sources of conflict between groups. If, e.g., the intergroup conflict is one of interests, subordination of one group by the other may enable the latter to secure differential advantages in access to scarce goods. Similarly, if the conflict is one of values, subordination of one group by the other may enable the latter to limit its contact with the former and thus minimize the potential threat to its own system of values.* One extreme form of conflict is the employment of physical violence. From this pole there is a gradual transition through peaceful competition to the opposite pole where there is still some form of resistance on the part of one group to acceding to the will of the other.**

---

\* An assumption required by this discussion which should perhaps be made explicit at this point is that one group is in a sufficiently advantageous position, due to the prior monopolistic acquisition of such scarce values as economic resources, prestige, and power, to enable it to ascribe subordinate status to the other group.

\*\* Complete submission on the part of one group to the demands and requirements imposed upon it by the other is the limiting case where conflict disappears.

The degree of conflict obtaining in the concrete case is interdependent with the degree of subordination. A high degree of intergroup conflict will call into play the attempt by one group to subordinate and thereby exclude the other group, while the thorough subordination of the latter may result in the minimization of actual conflict, although not necessarily the potentiality of conflict.

As was stated above, distinguishable differences between the two groups, which can acquire symbolic functions, are necessary for the ascription of subordinate status. This requires the possession of visibility characteristics by one of the groups, characteristics which are not shared with the other. These visibility characteristics may take the following forms:

1) Physical appearance - skin color, hair form, stature, head shape, lip form, and so on.

2) Language - a language different from that of the dominant group which is the only one used or which results in an accent when using the language of the dominant group.

3) Gesturing and motor habits - when these differ noticeably from those of the dominant group.

4) Social and cultural patterns - in so far as they function as obvious visibility characteristics. Some examples are a distinctive diet, religious affiliation, and hygienic standards. Visibility characteristics are one of the elements which make the group symbolically appropriate for ascription of subordinate status.

The factors conducive to the ascription of subordinate status will be defined by outlining the types of conflict which may exist between groups.* These factors are to be accorded the status of variables as determinants of the patterns of dominant-subordinate group relations. The value of each in a concrete case will be in part dependent upon the form each assumes, the number of them operative, the manner in which they operate to interlock and mutually reinforce each other, and their articulation with the institutional structure and the realistic situation in which both groups act. Thus, in accordance with the basic task set for this study, the empirical data which is the primary informational source of the investigation will ultimately be subjected to analysis in an attempt to isolate these variables and examine their nature and role.

Tensions and insecurity within a group may be an important source of intergroup conflict. The thesis that such internal tensions and insecurity are generated within a group primarily but not solely in relationships with parents and other socializing agents, that the resulting aggression cannot be overtly expressed against these agents because it is not socially approved, and that it is consequently "repressed" and seeks indirect expression which often takes the form of displacement on a symbolically appropriate "scapegoat", has been extensively investigated and analyzed.** This primary source and pattern of deflected

---

* The formulation of types of conflicts set forth here has been substantially influenced by those of Talcott Parsons and Robin M. Williams. See Talcott Parsons, "Racial and Religious Differences as Factors in Group Tensions". In Bryson, Finkelstein, MacIver (editors), Approaches to National Unity, New York, 1945, and Robin M. Williams, The Reduction of Intergroup Tensions, New York, 1947.

** See, e.g., John Dollard, "Hostility and Fear in Social Life" Social Forces, Vol. 17, pp. 15-26 (1938-39), and Talcott Parsons, "Certain Primary Sources and Patterns of Aggression in the Social Structure of the Western World", Psychiatry, Vol. 10, pp. 167-181 (1947).

aggression will not be investigated in the case of the dominant group which forms part of the object of this study, due primarily to a lack of adequate data in this respect and the need for delimiting the scope of the investigation. Rather, the major focus here will be on sources of conflict involving direct aggression, taking it as given that displaced aggression accompanies the latter and increases its strength. However, this point may be qualified by stating that the extent to which these intragroup tensions and insecurity are aggravated by frustrations deriving from other than the primary sources mentioned above which may also be classified as indirect relative to the intergroup conflict, will certainly have to be taken into account as one of the problems with which the study will deal. An example of such a source would be the instability introduced into the local agricultural economy by such factors as its dependence on a capricious physical environment and a market not under local control. Other examples of such sources would be the strains imposed upon dominant group members in the performance of their functional roles, or frustrations of satisfactions incident to maintaining a desired standard of living where these can not be directly (or rationally) attributed to relations with the other group.

A second factor conducive to the ascription of subordinate status is to be discerned in cultural conflict. This may be conceived as focusing on two analytically distinct levels of social and cultural structure. First, where differences in the idea and action patterns of the two groups result in misinterpretation and misunderstanding. The definitions and expectations of one group, patterned by its social and cultural tradition, may be of a different order from those of the other group. Consequently, either or both groups may come away from situations in which they interact with feelings of frustration and moral indignation. Some examples of complexes in the social and cultural tradition where such conflicts might focus are the following:

The status of women, child training, cross-sex relationships including pre-marital and post-marital patterns.

Codes of obligation and propriety relating to hospitality, manners, reciprocities, "honor" or the definition of insult, friendship, and duty.

Conceptions of individual integrity, "pride", masculinity, emotional stability, dependence and independence, initiative, and self-reliance.

Conceptions of time.

Language, aside from its function as a visibility symbol, in the sense that it is a means of categorizing experience for its users.

On the second level, cultural conflict focuses on differences in what may be termed the ultimate value systems of the two groups concerned, i.e., values which are considered by those oriented to them as ends in themselves. On this level, values may be in basic disagreement with each other in the sense that even when each group is mutually fully informed as to the content and import of the ultimate values adhered to by the other, they may still consider the differences as conflicting and irreconcilable. These values may function to orient action in strategic aspects of the institutional structure where the effective functioning of institutional patterns depends for support on values shared in common, at least to some extent, by those individuals who together perform the necessary institutional functions, whereas on the first level differences may not have such direct implications for the stability of the social system. The conflict may focus not so much on differences in values, as on differences in the hierarchical order each of the groups accords the components of its ultimate value system. For example, if one group's hierarchy of values places occupational achievement at the apex while the other group places it lower in the scale or is relatively indifferent to it, yet both groups function in the same occupational structure, there is a potential occasion for conflict in the failure of the latter group to live up to the standard of performance expected by the former group. Similarly, to take an extreme case, if one group places a high ultimate valuation on unlimited acquisition whereas the acquisitive motivations of the other are limited to maintaining a subsistence level, a potential occasion for conflict is provided.

Cultural conflicts focused on the two levels of differences defined above make an important contribution to the evaluations one group develops of the other. The differences, particularly those defined as irreconcilable, may be used by one group to rationalize the inferiority of the other since the latter fails

to live up to the standards and expectations adhered to by
the former. The result may well be ascription of subordinate
status to the group considered inferior. Again, cultural
conflicts may lead to subordination of one group because its
differences are interpreted as potential threats to the "way of
life" of the other group. In the concrete case, the form that
cultural conflict will assume and the role it will play in
the ascription of subordinate status depends, of course, upon
the degree of relative prominence points of difference and
agreement in the conflicting cultural and social traditions
assume in intergroup relations, which is modulated by the
assimilation process; the other variables involved; the manner
in which it is reinforced or inhibited by the other variables;
and its articulation with the going institutional structure and
the realistic situation.

The conflict of basic personality types discloses a
third factor conducive to the ascription of subordinate status.
By personality type is meant the configuration of personality
characteristics group members have in common which fit them to
respond and conform to institutionally defined expectations.
The discernment and documentation of the various components in
such configurations are extremely difficult, particularly in
complex societies comprising large populations, but the value
of such knowledge for the explanation of differences in group
behavior is of course great. The study to be undertaken here
will make no attempt to establish in any systematic way the
basic personality types of the groups under consideration, due

to the lack of sufficient data. However, since certain institutional patterns may be abstracted from the uniformities in behavior which appear on analysis of the data, it is conceivable that the same uniformities may enable the investigator to abstract the contours of certain personality characteristics, at least to a rough approximation. The cautious use of any conceptual tool, such as personality type, is justified to the extent that it facilitates the objectives of the study. Differences in personality types are probably an important point at which conflicts between groups do focus, and such conflicts have been hypothetically stated to be the sources of factors contributing to the subordination of one group by another. Different groups may contain, in their personality types, different proportions of personal aggressiveness, sensitivity to ridicule, sentimentality, romanticism, and so on, which play an important role in determining the relations between them.

A historical tradition of conflict which remains as a precipitate of past intergroup relations and provides inherited patterns which are records of mutual hostility may harbor a fourth factor conducive to the ascription of subordinate status. In itself this variable would probably be a highly unstable factor in the maintenance of the system of domination and subordination due to its lack of intrinsic relevance to the contemporary situation, but it probably can play an important role if some of the other variables are operative with which it may interlock. In particular, it may perform a significant part in defining a group as symbolically appropriate for subordination, and provide a good deal of material for stereotypical conceptions and rationalizations justifying the ascription of subordinate status.

A fifth factor to be defined here has its source in the conflict of group interests. This concerns the acquisition of such scarce goods as economic resources, power, and prestige as dictated by the interests of the group. The range of variation that this conflict will tend to assume in the concrete case, i.e., the points on a continuum marked by employment of physical violence at one extreme and some vestige of resistance by one group to acceding to the will of the other at the other extreme between which this conflict can be located, is dependent upon the uneven degree of incidence with which it may impinge on different levels of stratification within the two groups involved, as well as the interdependence of interests with the other variables operative.[*] For example, in a given case, the upper class of one group may be more directly embroiled in a conflict of interests with the lower and/or upper class of the other group than is the lower class of the former group. On the other hand, there may be a tendency for the upper classes of both dominant and subordinate groups to cooperate in the preservation or further acquisition of the interests of both, either as opposed to what is conceived to be a threat from

---
[*] This statement is applicable to each of the other types of conflict dealt with in this discussion.

lower class subordinate group pursuit of interests or simply
to maintain the subordination of the latter as a necessary condition for the continued enjoyment of their interests.

Since group interests never stand alone but are interdependent with other elements, such as cultural beliefs and
values, the direction group interests take becomes problematical,
depending in part upon the definitions provided by beliefs and
values. When culturally patterned claims to economic resources,
power, and prestige are of the same order and equally strong on
the part of both groups, the conflict of interests may take the
form of active competition. In such a case, there may be a
powerful incentive for one group to ascribe subordinate status
to the other so that the competitive threat of the latter may
be controlled or minimized. However, real or even fancied
competition between groups, or between the classes of the two
groups, need not be the predominant form that the conflict of
interests assumes, although it is probably always an element
in the conflict. To take an extreme case, one of two interacting groups may attach only limited value to the acquisition
of economic resources, may be oblivious to or fail to understand the potential advantages of control of power, or may be
oriented to criteria of prestige which differ in certain
respects from those of the other group. All or any of these
possibilities may be present in the concrete case, thus
mitigating the severity of the intergroup conflict of interests.
At the same time the other group may be oriented to a set of
beliefs and values channeling their interests so as to dictate

the unlimited acquisition of scarce goods, and may avail itself of the accessibility and/or weakness of the other group to use it as a means to facilitating the acquisition. In order to maintain the availability of the former group for this purpose, the latter group might well ascribe it a subordinate status. In the concrete case, the form that a conflict of interests will assume and the role it will play in the ascription of subordinate status is in part dependent upon the other variables involved, and other conditions enumerated in the discussion of cultural conflict.

## The Mechanisms Employed for the Maintenance of Subordinate Status

The major mechanisms employed by one group to maintain the subordination of the other are the group stereotype and group discrimination. A group stereotype is a set of belief patterns which is held to characterize a particular group, involving the exaggeration, distortion, and omission of actual group characteristics. Stereotypical beliefs constitute a partial and inadequate definition of a group, but they seldom refer to characteristics which are not in some way attributable to some members of a particular group. Stereotypes are evaluative, being either favorable or unfavorable. However, it is the latter type which is of interest here. In any system of dominant-subordinate relations, the stereotype is in a state of interdependence with the elements defined above as factors conducive to the ascription of subordinate status. Although its point of departure is probably the visibility symbols, both physical

and cultural, of the group in question, it is nourished by
the various aspects of traditional patterning and intergroup
conflict and in turn reacts upon the latter. Aside from these
sources, there is a tendency for racial and ethnic group
stereotypes to draw upon already established class stereotypes
for material. Apart from their caste or semi-caste status, or
perhaps because of it, the majority of subordinate group
members tend to occupy lower class status in the society and
thus are vulnerable to the stereotyping already employed by
middle and upper class dominant group members in characterizing
members of the lower class. It is this phenomenon which
probably accounts for the partial similarity of all racial
and ethnic stereotypes, since all these groups have in common
not only the incumbency of subordinate status but of lower
class status as well.*

The major function of the stereotype is to rationalize
for the dominant group the discrepancy between its basic value
system and the subordination it ascribes to individuals by
virtue of their membership in a particular group, thus stabilizing and supporting the subordination. One of the fundamental
aspects of the stereotype is that it veils the true situation,
since it operates to increase the solidarity of the dominant
group, while at the same time it sharply differentiates and
excludes the subordinate group. Thus it places the latter outside

---

\* One exception to this generalization would be the Jews, who as
a group tend to occupy middle class status. However, the Jew is
labelled as too industrious and too ambitious, rather than as
lazy and lacking in initiative, as the lower class stereotype runs.

the moral order and makes the act of group subordination subjectively acceptable to the dominant group. By rationalizing the true situation, the stereotype enables the dominant group to preserve some consistency between the treatment it accords the subordinate group and the treatment it ought to accord the latter as defined by the value system. Once the group is indoctrinated by a set of stereotypical beliefs, its members will tend to interpret the realistic situation in such a manner as to document the beliefs. Those aspects of the characteristics of the group subjected to the stereotype which belie the beliefs will not be socially perceived since the beliefs operate to define the situation in a way favorable to their own survival. The stereotype may become so powerfully entrenched that even those who are victimized by it may unconsciously assume the role defined for them. Thus the stereotype may give a powerful sanction to the relative status occupied by the two groups.

Since the stereotype, along with group discrimination, operates to maintain the subordinate group in a status where its contact with the dominant group can be confined to a limited number of spheres of action, the dominant group may encounter little to disturb and undermine its beliefs. Some types of contacts may tend to reinforce various elements in the stereotype, due to the definition of the situation the latter provides as well as the possible presence of the realistic element from which the belief originally took its departure. Even intimate intergroup contact, on an individual basis, which reveals the inapplicability of the stereotype, may be interpreted by the dominant group member as the exception that proves the rule.

The incidence of stereotypical beliefs, in the sense of their intensity, content, and mode of expression, may be uneven among individuals and sectors of the dominant group, depending upon the personal history of dominant group members, as well as the factors defined above. The various beliefs which the stereotype comprises may have different degrees of appeal for different individuals, depending upon the individual's needs, the degree of satisfaction or frustration of those needs, his class status, occupational role, age, and so on.

Group discrimination, the other mechanism employed for the maintenance of subordinate status, may be defined as the denial to individuals of access to equality of opportunity by virtue of their membership in a particular group. As defined here, group discrimination refers to a set of exclusion devices[*] utilized by the dominant group in ordering its relationships with the subordinate group, which may include endogamy, bans on commensalism, prohibitions of "polite" social intercourse, such as visiting and friendships, rituals which fix social distance and govern social intercourse where it occurs, restrictive

---

[*] Following Merton, an exclusion device denotes arrangements and symbols employed by a dominant group to distinguish itself from a subordinate group, while isolation devices are those employed by subordinate groups for this purpose. In this sense, the stereotype is also an exclusion device. See Merton, R.K., "Intermarriage and the Social Structure", Psychiatry, 4:361-374, 1941, reference footnote 22.

covenants, denial of admission to public places, forms of segregation, school quota systems, occupational, legal, and political disabilities, and so on. In short, all impediments to full participation in the life of the society, when based on considerations of group membership, fall within the category of discrimination.

As in the case of each of the other elements discussed thus far, group discrimination occupies the status of an interdependent variable in the system of dominant-subordinate relations. The nature, degree, and scope of the exclusion devices employed in a given case will depend on the role of the other elements involved, just as the form and direction the other elements assume will be conditioned by the effects of the practice of group discrimination. Discrimination may be in part the reaction of the dominant group to conflicts of interests, cultural conflicts, intergroup historical tradition, conflicts of personality type, or it may be the reaction to some combination of all of these. The causative relation between the stereotype and discrimination has been extensively analyzed by a number of investigators.[*] In its simplest form, termed the vicious circle, the effects of discrimination reinforce the stereotype, while belief in the latter reinforces the practice of discrimination. When both

---

[*] See, e.g., Myrdal, G., An American Dilemma, New York, 1944, pp. 75ff. and pp. 1065 ff., and MacIver, R.M., The More Perfect Union, New York, 1948, pp. 68 ff. Neither of these writers, however, relates these two mechanisms to other elements of the system precisely in the manner attempted here.

of these mechanisms are viewed in their relations to the other elements of the system, there emerges a highly unstable complex of forces, all of which together define the nature of the subordinate status ascribed to a given group, and the manner in which it is maintained. Looked at from one point of view, the sources of intergroup conflict provide the "need" for subordination of one group by the other, the stereotype serves to channel the attempts to satisfy the "need", and discrimination provides the channel through which the "need" can be satisfied. Both the stereotype and group discrimination are sets of exclusion devices employed by one group to subordinate and maintain the subordination of another; the latter by imposing disabilities on a given group, the former by justifying the imposition. Thus both operate to differentiate and set apart the subordinate group. In one sense, discrimination is the expression in action of the beliefs which compose the stereotype.

As in the case of stereotypical beliefs, the incidence of the employment of discriminatory exclusion devices, in the sense of the form selected, the degree, and the scope, may be uneven among individuals and sectors of the dominant group, depending upon such factors as personal history, class status, occupational role, age, sex, and so on, as well as upon the other factors dealt with above. The incidence of both stereotypical beliefs and discrimination will also be affected by the degree of internal differentiation of the subordinate group in such institutionalized areas as occupations and stratification to the extent that this blurs or erases the realistic bases from which these mechanisms take their departure. In a concrete case, such differentiation may be closely related to a process of assimilation where those who become most like the dominant group are subjected to the lightest penalizations accompanying subordinate status.

Consideration of parallel mechanisms, or what may be termed isolation devices, employed by the subordinate group to minimize contact with the dominant group leads directly into the final aspect of a system of dominant-subordinate relations to be considered here, the range of reactive adjustments of the subordinate group, of which the employment of isolation devices is but one element.

## The Types of Reactive Adjustment to Subordinate Status

The concept of reactive adjustment will be employed in this discussion in a limited sense to refer to a response which is adjustive for the individual in that it reduces or removes the motivations deriving from his incumbency of subordinate status.* The term adaptive will be used to refer to the survival value, for the individual or for the society as a whole, of a given response as distinct from its adjustive value. The assumption is made that the types of reactive adjustment selected by the majority of subordinate group members will tend to be adaptive as well. Given sufficient cause or provoca-

---

* Suggested by the definitions of "adjustive" and "adaptive" in Kluckhohn, C., Navaho Witchcraft, Cambridge, Mass., 1944, p. 46.

tion, individuals may make responses which are adjustive but not adaptive, of course, but the frequency and pervasiveness of selection of such responses will be relatively inhibited among the component members of a going social system. To the extent that the individual defines the implications of subordinate status as in some manner operating as a barrier to what he desires, in the sense that subordination militates against his personal or material values in some degree, such status constitutes for him a frustration situation which he may adjust to in a variety of ways all of which involve some element of resistance to subordinate status.* The following analysis will attempt to define the range of variation of such reactive adjustments.

Reactive adjustments as contemplated here fall into two broad analytical categories which may be termed aggressive and accommodative. Aggressive subsumes those reactive adjustments to the frustration situation which are the unrestrained expression of direct or displaced hostility, whereas accommodative subsumes those reactive adjustments which are alternative responses to aggression. Some element of aggression is usually present in an accommodative reactive adjustment, but its expression is controlled rather than unrestrained as in the

---

* The possibility that in a given case there may be some subordinate group members who do not perceive their status as in any way constituting a frustration situation should be noted. In such a case the reactive adjustment will take the form of complete acceptance. However, the assumption is made here that most, if not all, of the subordinate group members in a given case will develop some sense of problem with respect to the implications of their status. The definition of types of reactive adjustment attempted here will be based on this assumption. For an example of such an assumption made in the case of the Negro, see Myrdal, G., op. cit., pp. 27-30.

aggressive category. Given the conditions of the dominant-
subordinate situation as they are presented to the subordinate group member, the unrestrained expression of hostility directed toward the dominant group, in so far as that
group is perceived as the source of frustration, may be an
adjustive response, but it has only limited effectiveness as
an adaptive response, i.e., one which has survival value for
the individual. This is due to the fact that, by virtue of
the advantageous position the dominant group occupies in the
power relations which obtain between the two groups, it would
be extremely dangerous for the weaker group, dependent and disadvantaged as it is, to engage in the unrestrained expression
of direct aggression toward the stronger in view of the superior
ability of the latter to retaliate.* Consequently, direct
aggression, where it is employed, will usually assume evasive,
circuitous, or symbolic forms which may be employed against
the dominant group with relative impunity. The boycott, leaving a job without notice or sabotaging it, gossiping about
dominant group members, and aggressive joking are examples of
such forms. By their very nature, however, such devices do not
provide a sufficient basis for long term adjustment to the
frustration situation.

The expression of direct aggression toward the dominant
group does not exhaust the types of reactive adjustment which
can be subsumed under the aggressive category. The aggression
which ensues from the frustration situation may be turned inward

---
\* The selection of this type of reactive adjustment becomes quantitatively significant only in crisis situations, such as race riots.

upon oneself, or upon the subordinate group, or deflected to other subordinate groups if they are available and unable to retaliate. Intragroup aggression as a type of reactive adjustment, where it takes the form of personal violence, may be fostered and facilitated by the fact that a double standard of legal and police protection usually prevails for dominant and subordinate groups which permits the employment of interpersonal violence within the latter group without fear of serious legal and police reprisal. This form of displaced aggression may be an adjustive response, but it is not very adaptive due to the very lack of adequate justice and policing available to the subordinate group. When all subordinate group members are permitted wide latitude in the commission of interpersonal violence, no one may feel safe. Thus there would be a tendency to play down patterns of violence simply as a matter of survival value, aside from the inhibitions deriving from the moral imperatives which function as social controls within the subordinate group.

Intragroup aggression as an adjustive response may assume other forms, however, which may be relatively more adaptive than interpersonal violence. An example of one such form is the employment of gossip and destructive criticism on an interclass basis, where class differentials have developed extensively within the subordinate group. Class differentials do not necessarily result in interclass hostility, but if the dominant group insists on maintaining the assumption of the homogeneity and unalterable status of the subordinate group, as expressed in the group stereotype and discrimination, and severely delimits the outlet of direct aggression, the displaced aggression may be attracted to the area of class relations as an appropriate outlet. Upper class subordinate group members, lumped together with the lower class regardless of their degree of acquisition of criteria which have status-determining functions within the dominant group, may attribute this tendency of the dominant group to the lower class failure to acquire such criteria, and may consequently come to resent their enforced identification with the lower class. The latter, on the other hand, may become jealous of the ability of the upper class to get ahead, especially if its members accept, consciously or unconsciously, the assumption of the homogeneity of their group which is made so insistently by the dominant group. Belief in this homogeneity makes for an expectation of equality which is frustrated by the mobility of upper class aspirants.

The relation of subordinate group solidarity to intragroup aggression as a type of reactive adjustment is a complex problem, just as the role of such solidarity as a factor in the determination of types of reactive adjustment in the accommodative category is complex, but both will be touched on below. In connection with intragroup aggression, however, it is necessary to point out that to the extent such solidarity is valued by the members of the group, intragroup aggression has negative implications as an adaptive response from the point of view of the survival of the group as a whole. In fact, since intragroup aggression may well operate to impede the fulfillment of the functional needs of the social system as a whole, and since the biological and psychological needs of the constituent members are of course included within those functional needs, it is improbable that intragroup aggression on a quantitatively significant scale, at least in its form of interpersonal violence, can be an adjustive and adaptive response for subordinate group members. In the concrete case, the selection of intragroup aggression as a major component of the reactive adjustments made by subordinate group members to their status will probably be limited to what may be termed the "disorganized fringe" of the group, in view of the above considerations.

The considerations dealt with above indicate that the types of reactive adjustment which have been termed accommodative, i.e., alternative responses to aggression, will tend to be selected by subordinate group members more extensively and with greater frequency than those termed aggressive because of their higher adaptive value in the conditions set by the dominant-subordinate situation. Accommodative reactive adjustments are conceived for the purposes of this analysis as varying on a continuum delimited by polar types which will be termed isolation and assimilation. Isolation as a polar type of reactive adjustment will be here defined as orientation to the cultural and social tradition which is distinctive of the subordinate group, whereas assimilation will be defined as orientation to the cultural and social tradition which is distinctive of the dominant group.* In one sense, isolation may be equated with avoidance and assimilation with acceptance.** This does not refer, however, to avoidance or acceptance of subordinate status,*** but to avoidance or acceptance of the terms set down by the dominant group for release from the disabilities which define the subordinate status. These terms set down by the dominant group are characterized by an ambivalence and inconsistency which make the selection by the subordinate group of types of reactive adjustment approaching the isolation or assimilation poles exceedingly problematical. The tendency of the dominant group to lump together all subordinate group members regardless of their differential degree of acquisition of criteria which have

---

\* Although conceived with ethno-racial and ethnic groups in mind, this formulation is regarded as applicable also to racial groups providing they are in process of acculturation to a dominant group, as is the case with the American Negro group. Assimilation is the limiting type where subordinate status, in the sense in which it is used in this analysis, disappears.

\*\* Isolation is not, however, coterminous with physical isolation from the dominant group, nor is assimilation with a high frequency of contact. Those subordinate group members who select reactive adjustments approaching the assimilation pole may at the same time isolate themselves as much as possible from physical contact with the dominant group, while those who select adjustments approaching the isolation pole may seek such contact, as in the case of the Negro. In most cases, however, the isolation reactive adjustments will probably reinforce lack of physical contact with the dominant group, while assimilation reactive adjustments will tend to increase contact.

\*\*\* The assumption has been made that all types of reactive adjustment involve some element of resistance to subordinate status. The alternative of acceptance of subordinate status has been excluded from this discussion. See supra, pp. 46-47.

status-determining functions within the dominant group, and the related tendency to accuse those subordinate group members who succeed in acquiring such criteria of presumptuousness and insolence, operate to push reactive adjustments toward the isolation pole. On the other hand, there is a co-existing tendency for the dominant group to reward by progressive release from the disabilities of subordinate status those individuals who approach dominant group values and standards, which operates to push reactive adjustments toward the assimilation pole.

The cultural and social tradition to which a subordinate group is oriented, after that group has undergone the experience of subordination and residence in the larger society of the dominant group for a period of time, may be expected to be an amalgam of the indigenous background, the effects of the impact of the dominant group cultural and social tradition, assuming it is different, and certain idea and action patterns which are developed as a result of subordinate status as such. In the early stages of such residence, the indigenous cultural and social tradition probably plays an independent role in determining the attitudes of the newcomers toward contact with the dominant larger society in the sense that the indigenous culture provides strong elements of cohesion within the group that carries it, such as nationality, language, and religion, which at the same time may be elements of differentiation from the dominant group having a good deal of separative force. However, aside from the degree of divergence between dominant and subordinate cultures, the ability of the indigenous culture to persist in performing such a role without diminished strength varies with the reception the subordinate group is tendered, and the status which it is accorded. Where the latter are of the type that has been dealt with throughout this discussion, there will be a tendency for the subordinate group to respond by idealizing their cultural and social tradition, glorifying their history, and erecting a wishful mythology all of which make powerfully attractive the retention of indigenous values and standards. Since the subordinate group cultural and social tradition is in process of acculturation\* to that of the dominant group, it may be expected to eventually incorporate elements of the latter and consider them its own, thus accentuating the distortion which the indigenous tradition has undergone. Reactive adjustments approaching the isolation polar type thus function to reduce the motivations deriving from incumbency of subordinate status by compensating for the impugnation of the group's, and thus the individual's, sense of worth, dignity, and integrity which is occasioned by the implications of its subordinate status. The isolation devices employed by the subordinate group in determining its relations with the

---

\* For the purposes of this discussion, the term acculturation will refer to the process whereby cultural elements are transmitted from one culture group to another who are in continuous first-hand contact, whereas assimilation refers to the process whereby one culture group, or individual members of it, achieves a cultural synthesis with another culture group. In this sense, acculturation may take place without assimilation, although it is possible that ultimately acculturation may lead to assimilation.

dominant group, although attributable in large part to the effects of the exclusion devices employed by the dominant group, may have the negative function of contributing to the maintenance of the gulf between the two groups, as well as the positive function indicated above. Insulated within its own semi-autonomous social system, however, that sector of the subordinate group which selects types of adjustment approaching the isolation pole may not necessarily regard its separateness as oppressive or undesirable.

Types of reactive adjustment approaching the assimilation pole function to reduce for the individual the motivations deriving from the frustration situation of subordinate status by increasing the accessibility to rewards and privileges of the larger society and thereby decreasing the degree of subordination the individual is subjected to. The sweeping assumption by the dominant group of the homogeneity of the subordinate group may impede the selection by members of the latter group of reactive adjustments approaching the assimilation pole, but it does not eliminate the adjustive and adaptive value of such responses. To take an extreme case, the Negro, who is explicitly denied the possibility of full assimilation to the dominant group, may make reactive adjustments approaching the assimilation pole. Negroes are accorded differential treatment, although this is modulated by the caste treatment, on the basis of how closely they approach cultural likeness to middle and upper class whites. The Negro who takes on dominant group patterns of ambition, thrift, and impulse inhibition will obtain greater access to scarce values than will the Negro who does not. To the extent that the dominant group does reward extinguishing of difference and acquiring of likeness, the selection of types of reactive adjustment approaching the assimilation pole is meaningful for subordinate group members regardless of how impossible, due to ineradicable physical characteristics which function as **visibility symbols**, full realization of the assimilation polar type may be. In fact, where subordinate group members are convinced of the superiority of dominant group characteristics and the inferiority of their own, they may strive to imitate the dominant group without the incentive of the reward for likeness.

In the concrete case, the reactive adjustments typical of various sectors and strata of the subordinate group will embody varying proportions of all the analytical types depicted here.

This treatment of reactive adjustments has been made more or less *in vacuo*, with only slight reference to the multiplicity of factors which condition the responses of subordinate group members to their status. As a corrective, some of these must at least be mentioned here. In addition, it should be remembered that, contrary to the impression that this analysis may have unavoidably given, the world that subordinate group members live in includes problems and pursuits and pleasures which are not directly associated with the issue of their status, and that the implications of subordinate status are realized by different individuals in varying degrees.

Some of the factors which contribute to differentiation of responses to subordinate status are the nature and intensity of the various exclusion devices employed by the dominant group in subordinating the other group; the type of leadership generated by the subordinate group which functions as an intermediary to the dominant group; the existence in the society of a value system which emphasizes equality of opportunity and the degree of awareness developed by subordinate group members of the contradictions between this value system and the nature of their status; and the factor of age, in the sense that the older generation may be relatively tolerant about the implications of subordinate status while the younger may tend to bitterly resent them. The physical appearance of the individual, sex, and amount of education also play a role. Certain elements of the indigenous cultural and social tradition may have particularly important implications, such as hierarchical conditioning and a religion which stresses later rewards rather than immediate direct action. The personal history of the individual, particularly the parental attitudes toward the issues of subordinate status as transmitted in socialization, and his personality type, will of course be a factor in his reactive adjustment. A major factor is social class position within the subordinate group and the degree of urgency with which the various classes regard the subordinate status issue. At least equally important are the nature of the occupational structure of the society and the various occupational roles assumed by subordinate group members.

The degree of solidarity* possessed by a subordinate group has important implications for the types of reactive adjustment it will tend to make. Aside from the role the indigenous cultural and social tradition can play in generating such solidarity, which has been discussed above in connection with isolation adjustments, the effects of subordination provide an enforced identity of the group. On the other hand, the fact that most of the aggression generated by subordination must be displaced within the group, and the limited access to scarce values imposed by subordination, may make for heated rivalry between group members and envy and jealousy of those who come out on top. Where there is a high degree of group solidarity, attempts by individual members to assimilate to the dominant group may be regarded as treasonable, and passing may be considered a most heinous offense. The isolation adjustment is of course closely related to the degree of solidarity that can be generated, while reactive adjustments of the aggressive category will be in part modulated by the amount of solidarity the group has been able to attain.

---

* Group solidarity may be defined for present purposes as the feeling of identification between individuals by virtue of common orientation to the facts of ethnic and/or biological relatedness, as well as to value systems.

## Chapter III
## THE MEXICAN AMERICANS

The present chapter undertakes to outline and analyze briefly those institutional aspects of Mexican American society and the corresponding basic personality type, as derived from the field data, which distinguish Mexican Americans from the larger society, residually defined as Anglo American. Many of these characteristics have been discerned by investigators of other Spanish-speaking groups in the United States that derive from the Mexican cultural background,* but explicit consideration of the particular variations manifested by the Mexican Americans of McAllen and San Antonio is essential here if the group is to be treated as an entity in this study of dominant-subordinate group relations in which it plays so prominent a part. It is to be regretted that comparable treatment could not be accorded the "Anglo" group, but such a task could not be accomplished within the period of time available for field research. Nevertheless, from time to time, where it is necessary for the purposes of the study, and the field materials provide sufficient documentation, attempts will be made to isolate and define various aspects of Anglo society and thus alter its status as a residual category in a positive direction. It should be kept in mind that the central focus of this study is the investigation of certain

---
* See Appendix A for a comparative discussion of the literature on Mexican Americans.

dynamic aspects of intergroup relations, and that the delineation of Mexican American institutional patterns, cultural values, and basic personality type that follows has been undertaken in an attempt to provide a more meaningful context for the central problem. In view of this, the formulation attempted here should be considered neither definitive nor complete, but simply as an heuristic device employed in carrying out the basic task of the study.

## The Family

The basic unit of family organization is the conjugal family of husband, wife, and unmarried children, although intimate bonds are maintained with the extended family. The conjugal family is characterized by the dominance of the father, who is accorded a great deal of respect and obedience by his wife and children. He in turn is obligated to be the provider, until marriage in the case of the children. The wife is concerned primarily with the duties of the household and the training of children. Her tasks are sex-typed to the extent that the males of the family will seldom lend assistance in their performance. Usually, the wife leaves the house only to attend mass, purchase food, or visit relatives, the latter mostly in the company of her husband.

The pattern of dominance by the husband and the rigid sexual division of labor often persists in those cases where both spouses are relatively well acculturated to Anglo

American patterns in other respects.

> The Ms are both college graduates and well acculturated people, but a rigid division of labor is maintained in the home. I have never seen husband lift a hand to help wife. Saturday evening, e.g., while we were all sitting in the living room, husband asked wife to bring him a glass of water. She brought him the water and sat down again. He said the water was not cold enough, so she took the glass back and put some ice in it. A few minutes later he said he would like some canned fruit, so she got up again and served him. Wife did not object to any of this or complain.

One informant, a lawyer, expressed a voluntary desire to relinquish the traditional male dominance pattern, however:

> I would like for my children to be like I wasn't. Where I would feel that it was a stigma to change diapers on the baby or help the wife, I want them to feel differently. For awhile I found myself not wanting to do anything like that, and I'm afraid I've been unfair to my wife. I want the kids to learn to give and take about things. You see, our Latin concept is that the husband, he earns, he's the breadwinner, and the wife is the one who changes the diapers and looks after the kids and washes the clothes and does the housework. And the man, it's below his dignity to do it. That's the idea I don't want them to get, nor do I want it myself.

The home-centered role of the wife contrasts sharply with the great freedom of movement considered the prerogative of the husband. Men spend the majority of their nonworking hours away from the home, but seldom in the company of their wives. The following comments indicate the male conception of the good wife:

> My wife will do anything in the world for me. If I ask her to get up in the middle of the night to do something for me, she does, and

> she never fusses or quarrels about it. She gets up and does whatever I ask her to, and she's so nice and sweet.
>
> My wife does not say anything when I come home drunk. She is very understanding. And after all, I come home early, I don't stay out all night.
>
> My present wife is ugly, but she is a good woman. She never bothers me, never asks me where I have been when I come in late. Because she acts that way I give her money to send to her mother in Mexico and try to be good to her in other ways.

Wives are not expected to work outside the home, and middle class* women seldom do. In lower class families, however, the need to utilize all the labor resources of the family and the fact that most types of jobs are as accessible to women as to men, with comparable remuneration, has resulted in a goodly number of working wives. This opportunity for wives to obtain independent remuneration has made inroads into the undisputed dominance of the husband. Although the husband's role as chief income producer is not the sole basis of his authority, the fact that in many cases the wife may be earning as much as he has brought into question his position as the source of authority.

> An Anglo social worker who administers ADC** cases stated that he has instituted a new policy in these cases. Where a parent cannot get work and thus cannot support his children, ADC will come to his aid. Formerly informant gave the allotments to the mother or father, whichever came. But now he will give it only to the father because it has become apparent that

---

\* Class terms are defined in chapter VII, infra.

\*\* The state of Texas maintains a program of financial support for aid to dependent children.

> children lose their respect for the father
> when it is possible to identify the source of
> income with the mother. Formerly, when he
> administered relief, in those families where
> the mother collected the money, the children
> came to look to her for support, and the father
> lost the respect of his children and his own
> self-respect. Also, it was easier for women
> to find odd jobs than men, so there were many
> cases where the woman was the actual bread-
> winner. Then the man had to go off somewhere
> to hunt work and in the meantime the woman
> found she could support the family without the
> help of her husband. When he returned, he soon
> found out that his presence was not needed, and
> in some cases not desired. So when he went out
> again to look for work, maybe this time he did
> not return at all. A lot of this still goes on
> in the Valley, informant said.

In some instances the authority of the husband has been impugned by the relatively greater facility of the wife to cope with the Anglo environment, derived from native birth or longer residence, or from unusual opportunities for interpersonal contact with Anglo-Americans.

In Mexico, the dominant position of the husband has favored the existence of a double standard of sexual morality for married couples widely prevalent in the past and apparently still accepted by the wife, despite recent divorce legislation.[1] The fear of loss of financial support and ostracism by the community probably have had much to do with the tendency of women to tolerate their husbands' extra-marital amours. In McAllen, neither of these pressures for tolerance have much strength, and accordingly there are instances of resistance by wives

to the persistence of the practice of this pattern by
their husbands. Increasing awareness of the position
held by Anglo wives and assimilation of Anglo values
in this respect also lead Mexican wives to object to
the amount of time their husbands spend away from the
home in pursuit of recreation even when this recreation
does not include extra-marital relations. One informant,
to indicate her disapproval of her husband's practice
of spending an occasional evening drinking beer at the
cantinas, locks him out when he comes home late, and has
threatened to leave him if he continues his cantina sojourns.
This woman works outside the home now and worked as a clerk
in an Anglo grocery store for many years prior to her
marriage. Informant said she does not believe in showing
one's husband she is dependent upon him, and will not stand
for his going off to seek his own pleasure. A somewhat
different situation is revealed in the following excerpt
from the field materials:

> Mrs. G has evidence that her husband is seeing
> another woman and spending a good deal of money
> on her. When she complained to him, he told her
> she could leave if she did not like it. She
> went home to her mother, taking her child with
> her, but returned a few days later, apparently
> resigning herself to the situation. Mrs. G
> has no independent means of financial support.

In the past a husband who indulged in extra-marital relationships has not been subjected to community censure as long
as he continued to fulfill his other familial obligations
and was discreet about his amours, but there are signs of
increasing opposition to this pattern.

Further insight may be obtained into the husband and wife roles through examination of parent-child relationships and child training patterns. Mexican Americans place a high valuation on the bearing of children, as is evidenced by the census figures. The tendency to control the number of children in proportion to the ability to provide for them or because income is diverted to raising the family's standard of living is foreign to the majority of Mexican American parents. They positively desire large families and feel that somehow they will always be able to provide for another child. Further, among the farm laborers, children are still regarded as economic assets since they are a potential means of increasing family income when they can go to work in the groves and fields.

Mexican American culture in this respect is essentially child-centered, with extremely permissive and indulgent training patterns. Young children receive a vast amount of attention from parents and other relatives, who are usually so engrossed in observing the antics of their children or recounting their past exploits that other topics of conversation are excluded when children are present. Young children are also held and fondled a good deal by all the adults and older siblings present. When older siblings are not available to assume the parental role, mothers will carry the newest infant about with them everywhere, putting the child down only to accomplish some household task.  Baby-sitting seldom appeals to Mexican American parents even when they can afford it.  Children of all ages accompany their parents on visits, to public gatherings such as political rallies and community entertainments, and to the movie theaters, and on these latter occasions are permitted to consume large quantities of soft drinks, ice cream, potato chips, and popcorn vended in such places.  Little restraint is imposed by parents upon children in public gatherings, allowing them to run about, shout to each other, and so on.

No schedule is maintained for the feeding of infants, the mother often breast-feeding the child in public if the need arises, while older children are never forced to take food at regular mealtimes if they are not hungry.  A crying child is attended to immediately, and efforts to quiet him take precedence over anything else.  Weaning is accomplished between the ages of one and one and a half, and toilet training at about the age of two.  The latter is usually a gradual process, and one seldom encounters a case of harsh imposition on the part of the parent or violent resistance on the part of the child.  Children are seldom subjected to a specific hour for retiring, often staying up as late as the adults or falling asleep in a chair or couch.

Despite the prevalence of permissiveness and indulgence, obedience and respect toward parents and other elders are instilled at an early age.  There is little evidence of ordering and forbidding, but failure to obey the rarely-issued orders usually meets with swift and often severe punishment. Every recorded instance of the use of physical punishment, usually spanking, is for an act of disobedience, such as acting without the permission of the parent when such is required or refusing to obey a direct order. There is a tendency for Mexican American parents to believe that young children are not really responsible for their actions and that they should be permitted to do pretty much as they please. Consequently, the number of "wrong" actions a child may commit is considerably limited and the occasions for punishment are few. Children are reprimanded on occasion, but seldom in a harsh or raised voice. A number of incidents were observed where children broke household objects without being reprimanded. The following excerpt from the field materials is representative:

> Informant's three year old son pestered her a good deal while we were talking, climbing on her lap, throwing his arms around her neck, babbling and talking loudly. She did not reject him at any time, even though his presence and actions frequently hampered her in what she was trying to say. He dropped a large drinking glass and broke it, but informant said it was not his fault and took him in her arms to console him because he appeared frightened. Even when he was playing with the screen door, opening it and letting it bang shut, she did not raise her voice to him. She told him to stop, but in her usual conversational voice, although she was using the telephone and had difficulty hearing while he was engaged in his little game.

Patterns of conditional love, extreme emotional dependency on one parent, or arbitrary punishment are largely absent. Parents are not above using "bogeyman" devices for controlling potential unruliness in their children, such as warnings that <u>el diablo</u> or <u>la llorona</u>* may appear to seize them. Physical punishment appears to be imposed mainly by the mother, but there are instances where the reverse is true and others where both parents and relatives participate in the administering of spankings or blows.

Respect and obedience for the father is in part instilled by the aloofness and reserve he displays toward his children once they are past the years of infancy. The lack of camaraderie of any sort between father and children is strikingly revealed in the life-history data. Older informants recalled that they never smoked, drank, or cursed in the presence of their fathers, even at an advanced age, and were expected to kiss their father's hand on occasion, but there is little evidence of the persistence of these devices for displaying respect. Demonstration of affection by the father toward older children is rare, and an element of fear of the father is often present in the filial attitude, judging by the alacrity with which even grown sons will obey a father's order. Mexican American fathers have a keen sense of protectiveness toward their offspring until they marry and sometimes later. They see no particular virtue in children "going on their own" in order to develop a sense of independence. They do send them out to work to

---

* <u>La llorona</u> is the wailing spirit of a dead mother who returns to Earth seeking to be reunited with her children. The legend has many versions.

increase the family income, but this is regarded as a case
of need, and earnings are turned over to the father.
This sense of protectiveness toward older children is
perhaps an extension of the belief that the young child
does not know anything and is not responsible for his
actions. In connection with this belief pattern, there
is a tendency for Mexican Americans to regard the parental
treatment of children as a family affair, and to resent
outside interference. Informants have voiced their resentment
against school authorities in northern states who have
insisted that their children attend school when the families
migrated there in search of work.

> An Anglo informant in Starr County (95% Mexican
> American) said, The janitor at the school here
> in Roma is hired to keep the place clean, but I
> have never seen him do an hour's work there.
> The school is kept clean all right, but the work
> is done by his daughters, and he collects the pay.
> His daughters are young and should be in school,
> but they can't attend because he has them doing
> the work. Some of us have raised a fuss about
> it, but the principal and trustees (Mexican
> Americans) feel the same way he does about it,
> that the man has a perfect right to do whatever
> he wants to with his children, so nothing has
> been done about it.

There are indications that the respect and obedience
accorded the father are being undermined with the growth
to maturity of a second generation possessing a relatively
greater facility to contend with the Anglo environment, a
facility which often leads to a reversal of roles and
exacerbates the usual conflicts which appear to be inherent
between parents and youth.

In general, the relationship between mother and children is closer and intimate. The affection for the *madrecita* may often impose significant limitations on the dominance of the father in that the mother may come to dominate in all matters pertaining to her children. There are recorded instances where grandmothers living in a three-generation household rule the family affairs with an iron hand. The following comments illustrate commonly encountered filial sentiments:

> A male informant said, For some time after my mother's death, I would dream of her every night as long as I was away from San Antonio. As long as I was here, the dreams would stop. Either I would dream I was at home or out with her or something like that. I think maybe it's a mental attitude of my own, maybe a feeling on my part that I was sort of forsaking her by leaving San Antonio where she is buried.
>
> Informant said that he wanted to remain in Mississippi when he went there to pick cotton because the pay is better, the housing is better, and there is no race prejudice. He returned because when one has an old mother and loves her one does not want to be far from her. Here she is only thirty miles away. He has not seen her for fifteen days but already he misses her very much.
>
> C, an engineer, stated that the main reason he returned to Texas was because he was an only son and felt it was not right that his mother should never see him. He was away from home all during his college years and then he worked in Chicago for three years, so he felt it was time to return.
>
> Male informant, speaking of superstition, said, Of course there's a lot of people who believe in spirits and ghosts, but I don't see how they talk themselves into it. If anybody would be liable to come back, it would probably be a mother who left her children here. You would figure that

she would probably want to see them again more
than anybody would want to see anybody else.
But you never hear of a mother coming back
to see her children.

The element of fear and reserve in the relation with the father may heighten the feeling of affection for the mother, as expressed in the following comment:

We had always the feeling that there wasn't
anything else like mother because of the fact
that at home we had no other will and no other
law than my father's word.

Boys and girls are raised differently. Girls are initiated into the household routine as early as possible, and are expected to care for infant siblings when the mother is occupied elsewhere. The indigenous pattern of chaperonage of girls is still in evidence, but with alterations. Groups of girls may attend movie theaters and club meetings without chaperonage, and boys and girls come seperately to the community dances, again without chaperonage, but usually the father or an older brother is waiting at the door when the dance is over. In McAllen a mutual aid society, La Concordia, runs weekly public dances where girls often come accompanied by boys. Many female informants stated that they would not attend these dances because "nice" girls will not be seen there. Chaperonage is not intended as a device to isolate female children, but is employed as a means of controlling a girl's participation in cross-sex relationships. A high valuation is placed upon virginity, and chaperonage is a realistic means of preserving virginity. When girls violate the code and become illegitimately pregnant, rejection by the parents is usually thorough-going. In some cases, a relative will take her in.

Coeducation and financial independence are doing much to destroy the chaperonage pattern, as well as the pattern of the *hermano mayor* as the protector of his sisters.

> A young schoolteacher stated, It was my duty to take my younger sister to dances and tell her whom she could and couldn't dance with. I couldn't take a girl to a dance anyway. But my sister was ruined when she came to the University. I lived in a boy's dormitory and she lived in a girl's dormitory. I seldom saw her. I would meet her on the street with a boy I never saw before and had to feel thankful if she even introduced me.

The strong parental sense of obligation to support the children, where it has not become impaired,* is reciprocated by the children. Many married couples contribute toward the support of their parents even when they are in financial difficulties themselves, and many children have delayed marriage due to the burden of supporting parents. In most cases this is done willingly, with the expressed regret that they cannot contribute more to the support of parents who "have done so much for them". Parents expect this continued support from children, and are ashamed to admit to failures to meet this expectation. The rolls of the local Texas Old Age Assistance program reveal that the majority of cases are Anglo rather than Mexican, although one could reasonably

---

\* There is evidence of a deviant pattern of fathers drinking up the weekly wages, or deserting the family at the opportunities provided by the frequent migratory treks in search of work.

expect the reverse.* The Mexican American social worker who administers the program explained the situation as follows:

> The Latin people are very funny. As long as they have any income from any source they seem to feel obligated to confess it when they come in here applying for old age assistance. I have tried to tell them the right answers to say to the questions, I mean I just out and out coach them, but they're very stubborn. Call it pride or whatever you like, as long as they are getting some support from a son or other relative, they feel that they have to mention it. And of course if they are getting such support they are disqualified for old age assistance. Now the Anglos regard this as a business and try to conceal other sources of income as much as possible. When the Latin Americans find out that they must deny that their children are helping them in order to qualify, they back out.

In general, ties with the extended family are intimate where the larger kin group has not been disrupted by migration. The greater part of informal social intercourse is carried on between relatives, who frequently visit in each other's homes and take a hand in the socialization of each other's children. The three-generation household is usually a temporary affair where married children are waiting to build a home of their own, but when they do build, they usually establish their residences close to those of their parents, on the same lot when possible. Mutual aid and cooperation within the extended family are

---

\* The rolls of the ADC cases indicate a heavy preponderance of Mexican Americans. Estimates of the amount of aid a child is to receive are made on the basis of the objective situation by the local administrator of the program.

practiced wherever possible, such as in times of financial crisis. Truckers, who recruit their own picking crews for field labor, usually give preference to their relatives in hiring workers, and in those rare cases where a Mexican American has risen to the position of "field man", a job which involves hiring truckers, for one of the packing or canning companies, the same preferance is exhibited. The pattern of compadrazgo, or godparenthood, which played an important role in the indigenous culture in bringing two different family groups into the same network of kinship obligations and often resulted in closer ties between compadres than existed between blood relatives,[2] appears to have lost some of its significance in this respect among the Mexican Americans of McAllen and San Antonio. Many informants cannot even recall who their padrinos, or godfathers, are, while others stated that blood relatives were selected as their padrinos and they made similar selections for their children. There are instances where parents have selected compadres according to the old pattern, but the concept of compadre has developed significance in governing quite another set of relationships which will be discussed below.

## Adult Sex Roles

A few general observations concerning adult sex roles are necessary to supplement the picture of the familial roles. A major component of the male role is the emphasis on machismo, or masculinity. Machismo may be in part an outgrowth of the male dominance pattern and in part a reaction to the earlier tendency to identify with the mother due to the prominence of constraint in the relationship with the father. However, the latter is open to question since the relationship with the mother does not appear to take on the features of "momism", or extreme emotional dependency upon the mother. The major adult male attitude toward the mother is one of reverence, protectiveness, and deep affection, rather than one characterized by a severe dependency need. However, machismo, in its essential aspects, comprises adherence to those behavior patterns which most sharply set off the male from the female. The middle class male's machismo may tend to take the form of consorting with a series of mistresses, or in a more permanent form, maintaining a casa chica, a separate establishment, if he is married, but this practice is much more common in Mexico than it is here.[3] Among some segments of the lower class, primarily those who frequent the cantinas, a man may prove his machismo by the amount of beer he can drink, and his ability to fight (occasionally with a knife) and to "take it". Physical stamina in these exploits is an important requisite for building a reputation as "muy macho", as is evidenced by the following:

> Informant said, You know, I used to work over
> near Saltillo Street in the stockyards (in San
> Antonio). It was hard work, but harder for
> those men who drank. To be a man, a big shot,
> a real man, he has to be able to drink at least
> twenty-four bottles of beer. One is puny if
> he stops at twelve bottles or so. And to stay
> up all night and have a wild time, women here
> and there, and not show it at work the next
> morning, or to have the wild time over the
> weekend, and go right on the job Monday morning,
> is something. That is what they talk about at
> work all of the time. They point the big men
> out -- it is a mark of approval.

Maintaining the distinction between the behavior patterns of the sexes extends to church attendance. The church-going man is a relatively rare phenomenon, whereas the woman is expected to attend regularly.

> A Mexican American lawyer said, You'll find that
> the man who is a church-going man is more or
> less made fun of. If he does go, he's more or
> less outside of the group. He's a *rata iglesia*,
> a church rat.

This expectation holds for both middle and lower classes, although there are notable exceptions among the former.

Although *machismo* is an important theme among certain segments of the population, the vast majority of Mexican American males lead relatively less colorful lives. For the latter, the major emphasis is on responsibility for family, both of procreation and orientation, and the problems of getting a living attendant upon discharging this responsibility. Among this larger group, *machismo* is modulated into working hard and producing children, a routine punctuated by occasional drinking sprees.

The primary emphasis in the feminine role is on domesticity, with all the restrictions this implies. The male expectation that the female will focus her attention on the household, the children, and the church, is still the rule, although there are exceptions. Unlike the Anglo case, where the isolation of the conjugal family leaves the mother without children in later life, the Mexican mother's preoccupation with children is a continual one in that her grandchildren tend to fill up the gap. The Mexican male, conditioned as he is to the chaperonage pattern, to the exclusion of women from the night world of the <u>cantinas</u>, and to their general subordination, tends to view with suspicion the woman who attempts to assert her independence in any way. An unaccompanied Mexican American girl or woman walking down a street of the colonia at night will usually be subjected to a barrage of whistling, staring, and occasionally suggestive remarks. To the Mexican male, the unaccompanied woman is "fair game".

The Mexican American girl who strives for a college education is confronted with a number of problems arising out of this male attitude. To begin with, she must put aside the idea of marriage until she has completed her education. Since most Mexican American males marry young, the girl's delay substantially reduces the number of eligible men. The fact that the number of college-educated males is not large further reduces the college girl's prospects for a husband, unless she is willing to accept a man without a

college education.  Moreover, there is a tendency for
college men to shy away from college women because they
are afraid their wives will overshadow them intellectually,
which would hardly be compatible with the male expectation
of dominance.  This being the case, the non-college man will
be more likely to hold the college girl suspect.  The
result is that usually the Mexican American college girl
has considerably decreased her marriageable value, and
if she insists on getting married, must accept a man far
below her level of aspiration.  In two recorded instances
where college girls have married men with little or no
education, they gave evidence of feeling cheated, and tended
to be somewhat ashamed of their husband's occupations and
lack of educational background.

Despite the emphasis on domesticity as the major theme
of the feminine role, there are isolated examples of middle
class Mexican American women who are stepping out beyond
the narrow limits set by domesticity and approximating the
"career woman" pattern.

> Mrs. M., who married an Anglo, is a descendant
> of an "old family" in Rio Grande City.  She is
> a graduate pharmacist who owns and operates one
> of the two drug stores in town.  She is presi-
> dent of the PTA, an active member of other or-
> ganizations, and the only female trustee on the
> town school board.  She has become a powerful
> political figure through her activities in con-
> nection with the New Party, a political faction
> which recently broke the power of the long-
> ruling county political machine, and was recent-
> ly elected county treasurer, the first Mexican
> American woman to hold a county office.

In McAllen, a Mexican American woman has become an active political figure with a discernible influence, mainly as a

result of her impressive speaking ability, and the extent of her connections with voluntary associations approximates the Anglo "clubwoman" pattern. Both of these women attempt to fulfill their obligations as wives and mothers at the same time, although they spend many evenings away from home in attending meetings.

In the lower class, it is possible that many women have worsened their lot by taking outside employment, a situation seldom of their own making, since they must now perform their occupational duties in addition to their household duties. From another point of view, however, independent remuneration has generally improved the position of women relative to that of the male.

## Patterns of Interpersonal Relations

As indicated above, the Mexican American family continues to play an important role in organizing the total complex of social relationships of the group members. The majority of adult males spend most of their waking hours on the job, while women are confined to the home or working in the fields with the men. Sundays and other non-working days are usually devoted to visiting relatives, to the extent that social relations are largely subsumed under kinship relations. Cross-sex relationships among the younger people are controlled by the chaperonage pattern, where it is still effective, although the school and the neighborhood have provided the opportunity for the establishing of same-sex and cross-sex relationships which are often outside the family. In those cases where _compadrazgo_ has retained its significance, it has provided the basis for an extension of social relationships outside the immediate family. _Compadres_ who take their role as such seriously often develop strong intimate friendships with each other, as do _comadres_, although less frequently. The beliefs traditionally associated with _compadre_ relations, notably that _compadres_ should be interested in each other's general welfare all through life and that they should help each other in times of crisis aside from the obligations to the godchild, have come to govern friendships between Mexican Americans which are not based upon _compadrazgo_ at all. _Compadre_ has become a term loosely applied to any individual with whom one may develop a close friendship, and appears to be an effort to cement the friendship by transferring to it the mutual obligations associated with the _compadrazgo_. Despite the fact that friendships are more or less standardized as family or _compadre_ relationships, non-kin friendships do exist, primarily among Mexican American males. Those Mexican Americans who have lived in the community for a number of years are able to identify most of the members of their group, although they usually claim only slight acquaintance. The _cantinas_, or "beer joints" as they are popularly called, are frequented at one time or another by most lower class males, and provide a setting conducive to the development of friendships. The stability and permanence of such relationships are often questionable, however, since they are born in beery conviviality and may die in sobriety. In connection with this, it may be stated that the principal locale of intragroup violence is the <u>cantina</u>.

The idea and action patterns governing interpersonal relations and "polite" social intercourse in general are worthy of mention. Mexican Americans consistently exhibit an extraordinary courtesy and politeness in their relations with others. The conventional phrases of greeting and gratitude are constantly on the lips of the people. The following recorded observations of occasions when the word <u>gracias</u>, or thanks, is used are indicative:

> Informant introduced the stranger as her brother. When I gave him my name, he thanked me, the usual pattern I have found here.
>
> Informant, a crewleader, was paying off his workers for the two days they worked this week. Each man said <u>buenos dias</u> when he came up and <u>muchas gracias</u> when he was paid.
>
> Accompanied county nurse on her rounds in Mexicantown as she obtained stool cultures from all the children in selected blocks. Cordial and polite reception accorded us by parents in every case. None of them objected, and most said <u>gracias</u> when we left.
>
> We stopped at a filling station to get a can of gas for informant's car. The Mexican American attendant did not have a can, said <u>muchas gracias</u> as we drove off. Informant laughed and said, that's just like a Mexican, he thanks us for nothing.

The extent of patterns of hospitality in the recent past is hinted at in the following reminiscence of an elderly informant:

> The only thing is my father never knew the value of a dollar. He made everyone welcome. A man would come and stay at our house and we never thought anything of it, and then we would go and visit him. When we went to Laredo, we always thought of my uncle's house as our house. In those days there seemed to be room for everybody in a two room house. Now we have a five room house, and it doesn't seem as though there is enough room for anyone.

The extension of hospitality to house guests on a large scale no longer appears to be practiced, just as the conventional phrase, *mi casa es suya*, my house is yours, is tending to die out of popular use, but Mexican Americans may still be characterized as a strikingly hospitable people.* In the course of the field work, the investigator was always invited in when he approached a Mexican American home, and observed that the same treatment is accorded to others, even salesmen and solicitors, providing an adult male member of the household is present. On first acquaintance with Mexican Americans visiting from other towns, the investigator was invited on a number of occasions to visit their towns and stay in their homes. Three Mexican Americans who own ranches in Mexico invited the investigator for sojourns there. This ready hospitality is less apparent in San Antonio, however.

The immediate proffering of food and drink to visitors is institutionalized among Mexican Americans. Refusal to

---
\* Other formal phrases of hospitality which were recorded are as follows: A host greets a visitor when he arrives with, "*Venga Vd. en su casa*", come into your house, and when he leaves, "*Vuelva a su casa*", return to your house. When one is introduced to a stranger on the street, one says on parting, "*Ya sabe Ud. que tiene una pobre casa*", now you know that you have a poor house to come to.

partake meets with emphatic insistence. If the visitor comes at mealtime, he must participate in the meal. Spontaneous giving is a pervasive pattern among the people, whether it be food or something more substantial. This spontaneity tends to become submerged in a system of fixed reciprocity, however. For every gift received, the Mexican American makes a point of returning something of equivalent value, and if there is no opportunity to reciprocate at the time the gift is received, he will carefully remember to do so at a later time. This reciprocity is most strikingly evident in the _cantina_ relationships. When two or more men are drinking together, each man pays for a round of drinks, never for just his own. When the session is over, each man has usually paid for the same number of rounds. Again, when a man sees an acquaintance drinking with a group he cannot join because he has come in with other companions, he will often instruct the waiter to serve that group with a round of drinks. In a few moments, the waiter is back with a round of drinks for the original giver and his friends - the acquaintance has reciprocated. At Christmas and other occasions when the investigator presented some of his informants with gifts, something of equivalent value in return soon made its appearance.

Generosity receives a great deal of formal emphasis among these people. If one admires a possession, the owner is expected to say promptly, "_es suyo_", it is yours. In some cases the recipient is expected to refuse, but if the object

is not of great value, or if its loss would not work any
hardship on the giver, it would be an insult to do so.
An interesting variation of this is the case where one woman
admires the dress of another. The response is usually,
"thank you, you may wear it some time". Under these
circumstances, one would expect to find the parsimonious
individual an object of ridicule and disapprobation, and
such appears to be the case. The appropriate epithet
is codo, which means elbow and refers to the gesture which
signifies stinginess, that of striking one's left elbow
against the table top a number of times or against the palm
of the right hand. The individual who is noticeably reluctant
to share with others or fails to reciprocate gifts of
proffered drinks is codo, and considered somewhat abnormal
by the people.

Other patterns relevant to the functioning of interpersonal relations are best taken up in connection with the
discussion of basic personality type below.

## Religion and Related Aspects

Religion in Mexico may be characterized as a combination of Catholic and indigenous idea and action patterns
which have fused in varying proportions depending upon the
particular region.[4] Christianity did not supplant the
Indian pantheon but supplemented it. The mass conversions
by the priests who accompanied the conquistadores and the
later tendency of the clergy to concentrate in the larger

towns and cities and leave the _peones_ to their own religious devices provided the latter with little opportunity to obtain insight and understanding into the doctrines of Catholicism. In general, the connection between _peon_ and Catholicism, including belief and the Church hierarchy, has remained formal and external. One writer goes so far as to say:

> The Mexican people are not Catholics. Of the fifteen million Catholics who inhabit Mexico, at most two millions are Catholics in the sense accepted in the United States, an equal or larger number are agnostic or indifferent, and the remainder while observing in their worship some of the outward form of Roman Catholicism are in reality pagans. 5

Fundamentally the Mexican has failed to become incorporated into Catholicism; this does not deny that his religion, the combination of the indgenous and the new, has played a vital and powerful role in the shaping of his idea and action patterns. As a folk individual, the Mexican's religion has been meaningful and significant to him only on a local basis, while the Church as a religious organization, with the priest as the agent transmitting its doctrines, has been distant, vague, and somewhat incomprehensible. On the local level, with the patron saint (who embodies the attributes of his local indigenous predecessors as well as the Catholic definition) as the central religious figure to which he is oriented, the Mexican's religion has been inextricably bound up with the other aspects of his culture. Redfield, describing the folk culture, says:

> The village Mexican does not merely rest upon the land; he and his ways of life are a part of the land ... It is not too much to say that the culture of the more isolated of these communities is so closely articulated with the local valley and hills that it cannot exist apart from the local site. The saint is not really movable; his rituals function only where they are at home ... The saint is patron of this village and of these villagers; he does not exercise his guardianship or perform his miracles for men who belong to other villages or other valley communities.[6]

In this local religion, the community social life, which is based on the Church festal calendar and ceremonials dating from an indigenous religion, is integrated with the seasonal agricultural cycle and intertwined with attachment to a particular geographical region, and could be carried on without the assistance of a priest.[7]

National sacred shrines, such as Guadalupe and Chalma, serve as integrating master symbols which balance the tendencies to localism engendered by worship of the village patron saint. The Virgin of Guadalupe, who miraculously revealed herself for the first time in Mexico to Juan Diego, an Indian, appears as a *morena*, or dark-skinned, in the images of her to be found throughout Mexico. The universal recognition and worship of the dark Madonna is indicated by Brenner:

> Countlessly, every day, Guadalupe is on the lips and in the thoughts of all Mexico. The peak of society and clergy, and the serfdom, share her. City and village, mountain and plain, north, south, and center, turn to her intensely. Her ballads are added by thousands; her shrines can never be numbered. She rides printed on cards in taxis, fastened to sombrero-

crowns and saddles. She smiles behind glass in salons, painted on tin in the kitchen, carved into cradle-boards. She is reminisced and reaffirmed in plaster, marble, wood, stone, clay, cake, candy, cloth, tissue-paper; beaded, embroidered, baked. A pistol and a medallion of Guadalupe - this is any Mexican youth's birthright.

The vast majority of Mexican Americans of McAllen and San Antonio are Catholic in the sense that their rites de passage are sanctified within the Church. Beyond this, however, religious feeling and Church adherence are a matter of indifference to most of the Mexican American population, particularly the men, who retain only a nominal bond with the Church. Male informants, with a few exceptions, stated that they had not attended mass for years, and it was evident to the investigator that religion plays no significant role in their daily lives. One of the priests at the Catholic church in the Mexican American community of McAllen had this to say:

> There are about 10,000 Mexicans in McAllen. If we get 1800 of them out to mass on a Sunday we are doing very well. Everybody has the idea that when it comes to deep faith, nobody can beat the Mexican people, but it's just not true. Of course we have a few whose faith is so deeply embedded that they will never lose it, but most of these people don't even begin to measure up to my idea of what faith should be. They tell me it's too far to come to mass if they live ten blocks away from the church, but that's ridiculous because they will go downtown every day, to the stores or to the movies. Yet they won't come to church because it's too far away. I get all kinds of answers when I talk to them about it. And they have very peculiar ideas of what faith is. One will tell me, yo soy muy catolica, and when I ask them when they were in church last, they say, tres o cuatro anos pasados. And yet they still believe they are muy catolicas. Some say, mi toda famila es muy catolica, although none of them have set foot in the church in years. We are lucky if we reach

10% of the men and 25% of the women. I don't
believe these people were ever very religious.
They are so matter of fact about their faith.
Most of them won't even feel that it's necessary
to have a church marriage. I have had cases of
people who came to me and asked me to tell them
what the church marriage would be like. After
I would explain it to them, they would say, well,
we'll go get married by the judge because we're
not satisfied with the church marriage. They
think of it as two alternatives, either a church
or a civil marriage, when actually there is no
alternative, there is only the church marriage
for those who believe. I think that most of
those who do go through a church marriage just
do it because they like the ceremony of it and
want to be married in the church.

In view of the fact that the Mexican's religious life in Mexico was tied to the land and the agricultural economy, it is not surprising that his religion should lose its vitality and intensity in this country, where for the most part he has no personal stake in the success of the crops he grows and harvests, and where continued participation in organized religion would require an intimate knowledge and understanding of the church doctrine and hierarchy, in its universal aspects, which he never possessed.[*] In addition, many of the immigrants came to this country with some background of anti-clericalism, with the idea that "all priests are wolves", or at least with the conviction that the priest and the church are not necessary for the practice of one's religion. The pattern of non-attendance

---

[*] Writing in 1930, Manual Gamio observed, "It is clear that a large part of the Mexican immigrants abandon Catholicism". op. cit., pp. 117-118.

has become so pervasive that, in the words of one informant, "The undercurrent is too strong against the man who is very church-going. They look on him with distrust - people wonder why he is going to church. He must have done something, his conscience must be bothering him."

Despite this pervasiveness of religious indifference, there is evidence that certain of the more deep-seated of the Mexican American's religious idea and action patterns have persisted in retaining at least part of their significance. In those homes where crucifixes and other religious paraphernalia are still displayed, an image of the Virgin of Guadalupe is prominent among them. One Mexican American informant, a lawyer, commented on the Virgin as follows:

> There's a deep relationship between the Catholic religion, as we know it, and Mexican traditions because of the Virgin of Guadalupe, <u>la virgen morena</u>. The fact that the Mexican people, or <u>la raza</u>, has had divine recognition, that the virgin would have bothered to cast her attention on the Mexican people - it's a great symbolic thing. It bolsters up your faith. I guess every race, every people, wants to feel itself the chosen people, and of course there's nothing worse than to be made to feel that you're nothing, or that you're inferior. I think that's been a great source of consolation to many of these people, particularly the humble, who after all see that the Virgin took the shape of an olive-complexioned woman. In those churches (San Antonio) where the largest part of the congregation is the humble Mexican, a lot of emphasis is placed on the virgin, and you see the images of Our Lady of Guadalupe everywhere.

The pattern of making a promise to do something for a saint if he will fulfill a request was observed in a number of instances.* One family in McAllen held a <u>posada</u> for nine consecutive nights prior to Christmas, a ceremonial re-enacting the odyssey of Joseph and Mary in seeking a lodging each night on their way to Bethlehem. Although the <u>posada</u> is rarely performed by Mexican Americans now, this one was the result of a promise made to a saint by the family that <u>posadas</u> would be held for three years if the sons came home safely from the war. In another case, a woman, who an informant told of, promised the virgin of Guadalupe she would dress her son in female clothes until he was 23 years old if the virgin would grant some request or other, and the investigator was assured that she actually fulfilled the promise. The following comments by a Mexican American barber indicate the changing attitude, at least in urban San Antonio, toward the pattern of <u>la promesa</u>, however:

> You take these people who make promises to the saints if <u>los santos</u> will make such and such a thing come true. I think that's a lot of bull, because they would never keep the promises if they didn't have the money to keep them. A lot of my people made money during the war, and they had made promises to the saints that if their sons came home all right or if they had a good cotton-picking season, they would make a trip to Mexico City to visit the shrine of the saint. They really wanted to make that trip, but they pretended they didn't want to go. They would tell their friends, Oh, I have to make a trip to Mexico City because of the promise I made to the saint. But all the time they wanted to go because they didn't know what else to do with their money. If they didn't have the money, they wouldn't even think of making such a trip.

---

* "As elsewhere in the Republic, vow and pilgrimage are the most personal and the most vital expressions of the whole religious system; people go on pilgrimage who seldom go to mass. Once undertaken, any religious function is thought of as a promesa which if broken will bring disaster. E. G. Parsons, <u>op. cit.</u>, p. 303.

> But this way they can make an impression on
> all their friends and neighbors that they're
> going to make a trip to Mexico City.

The pattern of *la promesa* has retained its prominence in connection with the development of folk cults among Mexican Americans, which is discussed below.*

With regard to Protestantism, Mexican Americans in general are opposed to conversion, despite their own tenuous bonds with the Catholic Church. There is a tendency to think of the Mexican American who converts to Protestantism as a renegade, perhaps due to a connection of Catholicism with Mexican nationalism. The Mexican Protestant is considered "an anomaly", who has converted because "there is something in it for him." This view may be in part derived from the indoctrination of the priests, who are granted a ready ear when it comes to matters such as this. Interviews with Catholic priests elicited the following comments:

> There are a lot of Protestant churches which
> have sprung up around here, but the people go
> to them because they give away food and money.
> Their belly becomes their God.
>
> You take this business of the Protestant churches.
> There are little Methodist, Baptist, Lutheran,
> and *aleluya*** churches springing up all through
> this section of town. There must be at least
> ten of them altogether. I don't like to run
> down the Protestant churches, but the truth of
> the matter is that they get only our scourings.

---

* In connection with the pattern of *la promesa*, it should be noted that the reason usually given for the return of the dead in the form of spirits is that the deceased failed to fulfill a promise made before he died, and that he returns to do so. The promise may have been to burn a candle to a saint or make a pilgrimage to his shrine or it may have been an unpaid debt or failure to reciprocate a favor received.

** The Mexican American term for evangelical Protestant sects.

> They have a lot of money, and the people of little faith run to them for bread and candy and whatever else they will give them. But if one of them gets sick, they call for the priest right away.
>
> Every Mexican is a Catholic. They may go to the Protestants for their swimming pools and other recreation, but they're all basically Catholic.

A number of informants expressed the opinion that they "can't see how any Mexican can be a Protestant when for centuries the Mexican people have been Catholic."

Actually, the number of Mexican American Protestants in McAllen and San Antonio is very small. Of the four major Mexican Protestant churches in McAllen, it is safe to say that not one has a membership exceeding one hundred. In the words of a Mexican American Presbyterian, "Mexican Protestants are a minority within a minority, with a large number of tiny churches". The majority of the Mexican American Protestants encountered by the investigator appear to be preoccupied with the "Protestant Ethic", placing emphasis on this worldly achievement and material success, extolling the virtues of sobriety and thrift.

> Informant, Mexican American director of a Protestant settlement house in the Mexican Community of San Antonio, stated that the members of his church are very puritanical-minded. They are strongly opposed to beer-drinking and other 'loose habits' of the people in the community. Informant himself has to be careful what he does and where he is seen. If he goes into a <u>cantina</u> looking for someone he wants to see, it is sure to get back to the faithful <u>pronto</u>. Informant said that most of the members of his church are trying to get ahead and feel that it is

necessary to raise the standards of the whole
group in order to do this. He mentioned a
little Methodist church nearby where 50% of the
members are professional people, doctors and
lawyers primarily.

As evidence of the mobility of these people, the remarks of one of the other Mexican American Protestants may be cited:

Informant stated that she belongs to a small
Presbyterian church here in the Mexican community
of San Antonio. However, almost none of the
members of her church live in this community
but they still continue to attend this church.
Originally, all the church members lived near
the church, but then they got better jobs and
moved into other neighborhoods, just as her
family did.

As the remarks of the priests quoted above indicate, the Catholics tend to characterize the activities of the Protestant churches mainly in terms of their welfare and recreational work. The major agency employed for the performance of these functions is the Protestant settlement house, and the greatest bone of contention between the Catholic and Protestant groups occurs in the area of settlement house work, where there is overt hostility between them and much open rivalry.

Patterns of the folk religion persist among Mexican Americans in both McAllen and San Antonio. The following newspaper description of the site of a folk shrine near McAllen is illustrative:

## HUMBLE WORSHIPPERS FLOCK TO COTTAGE SHRINE IN HIDALGO COUNTY COMMUNITY

Alamo, -- Five miles north of this city on the Alamo road a small Latin American community has sprung up. Its first settlers, being practical people, named it "Los Tres Cheques" - "The Three Checks" - not only because those water gates were the most conspicuous objects in the neighborhood but also because they were the most familiar ... The real heart of the town is a tiny vinecovered house belonging to the family of Lisando Saenz.

By twos and threes, by family groups and singly, the townspeople come daily and gather in what used to be the bedroom.

Now it is a shrine to the "Virgencita de Los Tres Cheques" - "The Little Virgin of the Three Checks".

In 1940 while working in the fields, Mrs. Saenz found a broken mosaic of the Virgin and immediately decided to install it in her home and do it appropriate honor. Word of this beginning of a shrine spread and neighbors came to see the image.

Over the years the shrine has grown. New pictures have been added. Vigil lights have been lit. Candles have been set about the room. Tinsel and decorations have accumulated. Little altars have been placed around the central figure. So many gifts have been showered upon the Virgin that the original little mosaic is almost lost among them ...

In the war years local citizens called to the service brought offerings and parents came to pray for the safe return of sons. Veterans returned to give thanks and left their uniforms as gifts to the Virgin.

Today the room is always crowded with humble worshippers and truly the center of the village.[9]

In San Antonio, a sceptical informant gave the following account of a folk shrine located in the Mexican community which has had a successful existence for many years:

> My father used to peddle fruits and vegetables from door to door. He used to sell lots of fruits and vegetables to a Mrs. Rodriguez who runs this place on Ruiz Street where she set up a shrine for a saint. She really has a good business there. Someone will come in and make a promise to the saint that if the saint gives him such and such, he will buy a gold ear or eye or toe for the saint. Then if the saint does what the man asks, the man will buy a gold ear or whatever he promised the saint. He buys that ear from Mrs. Rodriguez for $15 or $20. Then he hangs the ear on the saint, prays for about three hours, and goes away. Then Mrs. Rodriguez takes down the ear and sells it to somebody else. If the man comes back and asks what happened to the ear, she says she took it down so nobody would steal it. Then the man says, "Oh, that's all right, thank you very much. If someone comes in to buy the ear or toe and hasn't got $15 or $20, Mrs. Rodriguez will ask him how much he has. If he says $7, she will say, That's all right, for now, you can pay me the rest when you have it. Yes, she does very well there with all those poor ignorant people.

In both cases cited, the folk pattern of votive offerings to the saint has no official sanction from the formal Church organization.

Many informants indicated a knowledge of, if not actually an adherence to, magical belief patterns. The usual procedure was to preface one's remarks on this subject with the disclaimer, "I don't believe these things, but many Mexicans do." The most commonly encountered belief concerned mal de ojo, or the evil eye. One who possesses mal de ojo need not be aware of it, and may cause injury by means of his power without the slightest intention of doing so. Infants are most

susceptible, but older persons may also be victims. Among
those who believe in mal de ojo, it is always necessary
to touch a child after admiring it or looking at it
directly to prevent possible ill effects if one is un-
wittingly a carrier of mal de ojo. A middle class
female informant said of her mother:

> She was supposed to have the evil eye all
> her life. She had to be careful about what she
> looked at, and if she looked at it admiringly,
> she had to touch it. Sometimes she forgot to
> touch things, and something happened to them
> right away. We had some plants on a table in
> the living room, and she looked at them admiringly
> without touching them. The next day the plants
> withered away. We had a beautiful pair of
> parrakeets in a cage, and she killed them by
> looking at them.

Another female informant told the story of an acquaintance
whose husband was consorting with another woman. The
jealous wife obtained a stocking of her husband's paramour,
stuffed and shaped it into the form of a small doll, stuck
it with pins, and then burned it, hoping by this act to
cause her rival's death by burning. Informant said the
peculiar part of the story is that the wife herself died
by burning shortly after this when her dress caught on
fire from a cooking fire, and the intended victim is still
alive. This story is representative of a number of cases
of brujeria, or witchcraft, which the writer encountered.
It should be emphasized that the extent of adherence to
and practice of magical beliefs is unknown to the writer,
that there are many sceptics as well as believers, and that

many of the believers confine their adherence to one or
two particular magical beliefs, rejecting many others
as "superstitious".

Among the life history informants, all of whom are
middleclass, beliefs in the predictive value of dreams
were recorded. One male informant stated that if he
dreams he catches an edible fish, he knows he is going to
get good news. If he catches something he cannot eat, or
a fish that turns into an animal, he knows he will get bad
news. Informant proceeded to cite a number of cases where
events have worked out precisely as his dreams predicted.
Informant said he pays particular attention to this type
of dream since he read that he was born under the sign
of Pisces. Another informant stated that just before
Pearl Harbor he had a dream in which all of his brothers
were taken into the armed forces, and that he himself was
in uniform walking through a long vault full of human
skulls and bodies. He awoke convinced that war would break
out soon and so it happened. Both of these informants
insisted that they are not superstitious, but that they
must believe in these dreams because they actually had
predictive value.

Medical idea and action patterns of the Mexican American
group also reflect the impact of residence in the United
States in that they represent a mixture of the persistence
of the indigenous elements and the infiltration of the
American elements. Mexican Americans show little reluctance

to avail themselves of the services of public health clinics and of the use of patent medicines. The fact that Mexican American babies are usually delivered by midwives or an experienced neighbor while Anglo babies come into the world with the aid of a physician may be attributed to the scarcity of physicians in both McAllen and San Antonio and the high fees (high for the average Mexican American income) available physicians charge.*

Among those who believe in the folk medical concepts, home remedies, consisting of either herbs and/or magical rites, are employed if the individual has some previous experience with a particular illness, otherwise the afflicted one may go to a <u>curandera</u>, or curer, who is usually a woman. The latter also employs herbs and magical rites, and may perform evil as well as good magic. According to informants, two of the major causes of illness are <u>mal de ojo</u> and <u>susto</u>, or fright.** Since these are folk conceptions of illness, the tendency is to seek

---

\* See Appendix B for a comparison of types of obstetrical care employed by Mexicans and Anglos and of mortality rates of the two groups.

\*\* That sickness may be caused by any kind of fright, <u>espanto</u>, is quite a general belief in Mexico. The symptoms are everywhere much the same - sleeplessness, dreams, heaviness on awakening, apathy, or listlessness, no ambition, loss of appetite. These symptoms rarely develop at once, but in a month or two, or even in a year or two." E. C. Parsons, <u>op. cit.</u>, p. 120.

out a _curandera_ for a cure if home remedies are of no
avail, since modern medicine does not of course recognize
these folk categories. The major symptom of _mal de ojo_
is a pain or infection in whatever part of the body the
possessor of the evil eye admires or looks at, as is
illustrated by the following excerpts from the field
notes:

> Informant stated that he possessed hair until
> he was five years old, when a girl admired it
> but did not touch it, so it all fell out includ-
> ing his eyebrows. Said he was taken to big
> doctors in San Antonio and other cities, but
> they could do nothing for him. Finally he was
> cured by a Mexican doctor who covered his face
> with tin foil to protect it, and then turned
> a lamp on his head. After a few treatments, all
> of his hair grew back. This occurred when in-
> formant was eight years old.
>
> Informant said she had a neighbor and never knew
> what color his eyes were. So one day when she
> was visiting his house, she looked closely to
> determine the color. The next day her neighbor
> came home with some sort of swelling around
> his eyes. His mother came over and told the
> informant about it. Informant said jokingly that
> maybe she gave him the evil eye because she
> looked at his eyes yesterday. The old woman
> insisted informant come over and touch her son's
> eyes. Informant refused, said she does not
> believe in such things, but the old woman in-
> sisted. So informant went over and touched her
> neighbor's eyes, and shortly after he was com-
> pletely well.

In those cases where the possessor of the evil eye is
not known, an egg may be placed under the bed of the
afflicted one and left overnight. In the morning, if
the yolk has become long, the offender was a woman, if
it is short, a man. Where the offender cannot be located

and hence is not available to effect the cure by touching the afflicted spot, a *curandera* may be enlisted to exercise the malady by means of herbs or various rituals.

An individual who is *asustado*, frightened, will generally display such symptoms as paleness and trembling, stomach pains, and general "nervousness". In the words of one informant:

> You go to a *curandera* when you're afraid, *cuando tiene miedo*. When you get scared of something or somebody, you have a *susto*, and can't get over it. If you have a big surprise, you become *asustado*. It can last a year or more because of its effects on your stomach. When you get scared, the gastric juice shoots out of your bile and makes you sick, so you feel it for a long time. But lots of people don't know that you have to go to a doctor to get cured, they think only a *curandera* can fix it. They think it's in their souls. People still have to learn a lot about the human body. I was just talking to a man today who went to a *curandera* this morning to be cured of a *susto*. During the war his wife made a promise to a saint she prayed to when she lived in Guadalajara. She promised the saint that if her husband wasn't drafted into the army, she would come and visit her. About a year ago she and her husband made the trip on a bus that had to climb mountains. The road was very steep and dangerous and one of the wheels came loose, but that bus kept trying to get to the top of the mountain. Then one of the wheels came off, and the bus slid for awhile before it came to a stop. This man said all the passengers were scared, and his wife has gotten over it, but he hasn't. He still suffers from the *susto*, can't eat or sleep well. So this morning he went to a *curandera* and she gave him a cure. Of course, he doesn't know yet whether it will do him any good. He'll have to wait and see, he hopes pretty soon he won't be *asustado* anymore.

The curious mixture of scepticism and belief reflected in the above passage runs throughout the data collected on magical and medicinal idea and action patterns, and characterizes the relations of many Mexican Americans with the public health agencies.

> On a round of home visits in the Mexican community with a county nurse, we visited a tubercular patient who is an advanced case. A number of children playing near his bed. Nurse asked patient where he deposits his sputum. He held up a can which is kept on the floor. Nurse said she had told him to deposit sputum in paper and then burn it, but patient continues to disregard her instructions. Apparently believes sputum can do no harm. County health unit supplied this patient with a portable one-room unit so that he could be isolated from his family. However, patient gave this unit to his mother and moved back in with his family. Said he became lonesome.
>
> At weekly VD clinic maintained by county health unit, a Mexican American woman came in for a blood test and complained of not feeling well. Said she had aches and pains, and had a record of previous visits. Nurse told me that many Mexican Americans come in for a blood test just because they are not feeling well. They have so little contact with doctors and medicine that they come to think of the blood test as a universal panacea. Nurse said that many of them actually do not know what the blood test is for, but think of it as a treatment. They say that their troubles are due to bad blood and the blood test cures this.
>
> In Starr County, a social worker stated that many of the people would not submit to the TB X-Ray service which was recently provided here free because they were afraid they would find out they had TB. Chief county nurse in Hidalgo County has told me the same thing about the Mexican Americans in McAllen.

In the first two instances cited it is evident that Mexican Americans partially acknowledge the validity of modern medicine since they accept some of the community health services, but at the same time folk beliefs persist. In the third instance, the people acknowledge the ability of the X-ray to prove the existence of TB, but at the same time entertain the idea that if they do not know they are tubercular, somehow the disease cannot affect them.

This section may be concluded with a reference to the Mexican American conception of death. On the Day of the Dead, November 2, Mexican Americans in both McAllen and San Antonio distribute a booklet entitled, "La Calavera", or "The Skull", which contains the photographs of most of the well-known members of the colonia, accompanied by witty epitaphs imagining the manner of their death.* The graves of the departed are adorned with flowers, and many kinds of food are brought to the cemetery for the dead to partake of. After the dead have eaten, the living consume the provisions, in a sort of picnicking atmosphere. In Mexico, vendors appear with sweets for the children prepared in the form of toy skulls, coffins, skeletons and other objects with a funereal significance,[10] but this latter practice has apparently been discontinued in this country. This ostensible flippancy or familiarity with death is, in the writer's

---

\* In San Antonio, La Calavera has become a commercial enterprise since only those who pay for the "privilege" appear in its pages.

opinion, really expressive of the Mexican's intense desire for life. By treating death in this cavalier fashion, the Mexican is perhaps attempting to conceal his very real concern with it, and at the same time attempting to control it. One Mexican American informant, defending his group against what he called the Anglo notion that Mexican Americans hold life cheap, had this to say:

> For the Latin American, life is just as precious as it is for anyone else. Even though he suffers a lot, he enjoys life, it is still dear to him, and when someone dies it is a great tragedy for those who are left behind. The Latin American takes these things very hard. There is no possible recompense for one who is lost. Informant gave example of a girl in Rio Grande City who was burned to death in a steam boiler in the place where she worked. Her parents made no attempt to make a settlement with the company because they felt that nothing the company could do would ease the loss.

Another informant stated that her sister lost a son in the war and would not accept the government money offered because she said it could not take the place of her son, and besides, if she took the money she would feel that it would be the same as selling her son.

These instances reveal, then, that although the generalized attitude toward death may represent an attempt to show indifference toward it, on the occasion of personal loss the Mexican American mourns his bereavement deeply and inconsolably.

## The Use of Leisure

Among the Mexican Americans of McAllen, leisure activities are for the most part of an informal nature. There is no counterpart of the Anglo American plethora of voluntary associations,* nor of "planned" social events. After work hours and especially on Saturday nights, the "main stem" of the _colonia_ in both McAllen and San Antonio is alive with groups of people who have encountered each other by chance or who customarily drift together on a particular corner every evening to discuss the events of the day, with people who are simply out for a stroll or lean in doorways or against lampposts to see and be seen, and with people who patronize the many restaurants and _cantinas_ in which the "juke-boxes" raucously grind out a never ending stream of polkas and _corridos_. The _Calle principal_, or Main Street, has become the locale for the street life, important in its own right, which in every Mexican town and city characteristically centers in the plaza and adjacent areas.

Despite the fact that the brief space of time available to most people for leisure activities is frequently devoted to visiting and associating with relatives, there are other pursuits which should be mentioned here. Although elderly informants reminisce of _bailes_, or dances, as frequently-held

---

\* In San Antonio the Mexican Americans do approximate this pattern, however, a phenomenon which will be discussed in a later chapter, where the role of voluntary associations in the organization of leisure can be dealt with.

spontaneous community gatherings where the younger people danced under the watchful eyes of their mothers while their fathers sat outside drinking and talking, the dances of today are no longer spontaneously arranged. They are either affairs sponsored by clubs and organizations, frankly commercial enterprises, or a combination of both. Weekly open-air dances are promoted in McAllen by the two mutual aid societies in the <u>colonia</u>, dances which are looked at askance by parents adhering to the chaperonage pattern since "all kinds of people come, and they drink, and then there are fights". The two or three young people's clubs in McAllen occasionally sponsor an invitational dance which is well provided with chaperones, and in San Antonio each of the many social clubs arranges a number of fund-raising dances each year open to the general public in order to finance one free invitational affair.

Drinking is an activity which far exceeds dancing in popularity. Total abstinence is rare, except among Protestant Mexican Americans, but participation varies from the occasional consumption of a bottle of beer to the heavy drinking of more potent beverages. In the lower income group, beer is by far the most popular beverage since it is the cheapest,* but for those who have transportation,

---

\* It should be noted, however, that Texas liquor laws permit the sale of only beer and wine in bars and restaurants. "Hard" liquor must be purchased by the bottle in "package stores".

nearby Mexico offers _tequila_, _mezcal_, and rum which can be purchased as cheaply as beer sells for in Texas. Many informants spoke of the money they manage to withhold from the family exchequer as "beer money". _Cantinas_ are as plentiful as grocery stores in the _colonia_, and are supplemented by the many restaurants which dispense beer as well as food.

Listening to the radio is indulged in widely by all age groups. In McAllen, even the humblest _jacales_, or huts, have radios which are tuned at all hours of the day to the Spanish-speaking stations in Mexico broadcasting Mexican music and interminably long commercials. In San Antonio, Mexican Americans have their own radio station, also Spanish-speaking, which has some value as a means of communication and education, but which also devotes most of its time to recordings of Mexican music interspersed with commercials. Music occupies a prominent place among the leisure activities of Mexican Americans, through active participation as well as passive. The number of informants encountered who play the guitar and have developed the ability to sing in harmony is extremely high, and provides some basis for the highly romanticized conception of the "Mexican love of music". The most popular music is still largely of folk origin, the _corridos_ and other _ranchero_ tunes, but the polkas and the more sophisticated _boleros_ and _canciones_ of urban origin are gaining in popularity.

Unlike Mexican music, which appeals to all age groups, the Spanish-speaking movie theaters, two in McAllen and four in San Antonio, draw mainly the older generation. Teen-agers and younger adults prefer the Anglo theaters, with a decided preference for Western pictures. Spanish-speaking pictures are imported mainly from Mexico. This same age pattern is evident in the attention accorded Spanish-speaking newspapers. Despite the retention of Spanish as the primary spoken language by the vast majority of second and third generation Mexican Americans, they are seldom able to read and write it. Consequently, the circulation of McAllen's tiny Spanish-speaking weekly and San Antonio's long-established daily is confined to the older generation. The San Antonio paper is oriented primarily to news of Mexico with some local news occasionally injected, another reason why it fails to interest those who are not of the immigrant generation. Nearly everyone, including those of the immigrant generation who can read English, reads the English-speaking dailies, but little else insofar as could be determined. The children, and some adults, avidly read comic books, but there was little evidence of more widespread reading.

The life history materials indicate that Mexican Americans participate in baseball, basketball, and football during adolescence and early manhood as much as Anglos do.

The investigator's own observations tend to confirm this. In both McAllen and San Antonio, teenagers spend a great deal of their leisure time engaging in sports, provided facilities are available, or following with interest the activities of the local semi-professional teams. Even some of the immigrant generation will watch a sandlot game on occasion, although the whole world of sport appears meaningless and somewhat childish to most of them. For those who can afford the time and the money, fishing and hunting are popular sports.

At children's birthday parties and at picnics, no attempt is made by adults to organize the play of the children into games, and this pattern holds to a large extent for the activities of adults when they gather socially. The major activity at such gatherings is conversation, sometimes accompanied by drinking or singing or both. Many Mexican Americans participate in mild gambling such as bingo parties sponsored by the church or in private homes. In the lower class, a few of the Mexican card games persist, but if middle class males play cards, the game is usually poker. In San Antonio, a "small businessmen's" club has established a large recreation center which has a bar, pool and billiards, and tables for dominoes, the game most popular among this group. This recreation center is well-patronized, as is the "middle class" restaurant in the <u>colonia</u>, where there are also facilities for dominoes and where the non-players come to see and be seen. After a dance, a club meeting, or movie, many Mexican Americans patronize this restaurant for a late snack and to catch up on the latest gossip.

## Some Aspects of Basic Personality Type*

One component of the Mexican American personality type may be designated a "personalistic" sense of loyalty and obligation. The emphasis placed on concrete personal relations, primarily on those which carry a great deal of positive affect, as delimiting the sphere of significant loyalties and obligations is the key consideration here. In the development of "self-hood", the process of assimilation of love objects to the identification of self does not usually go beyond the inclusion of those who are most intimately linked to the individual, i.e., family and friends. These love objects are identified with the self in a possessive and protective sense so that they constitute an integral part of the "front" the Mexican

---

* The brief treatment of basic personality type components which follows is included since the writer considers it essential for rounding out the definition of the Mexican American group which has been the objective of this chapter. The interpretation is primarily applicable to the adult male of the "unassimilated" lower class, although it will serve for the middle class to a large extent as well. The implications of this basic personality type for dominant-subordinate relations and its role in the development of types of reactive adjustments Mexican Americans have made to their subordinate status will be dealt with more fully in the later chapters. Also reserved for later treatment are the Mexican American cultural values which are implicit in the following analysis.

presents to the world, so that their fate (their treatment by others, their general welfare) is bound up with that of the self and with the "honor" or *orgullo*, pride, the Mexican feels compelled to protect. Any attempt by an outsider" to share in or possess love objects thus assimilated is interpreted as an attack upon the self. Consequently, the individual cannot tolerate the idea that any part of the positive affect of a love object may be diverted to others. This is reflected, e.g., in the intense desire of Mexican males for wives who are "untouched", not only in their demand for virgins, but for wives with no previous history of cross-sex relations at all,\* and in the attempt to safeguard their fidelity after marriage by confining them to the home whenever possible. The protective attitude of parents toward children which persists beyond adolescence and which is intolerant of outside interference, is also illustrative.

It is taken for granted that one's basic loyalties and obligations should be directed toward those social entities which are "personalized" by assimilating them to the self, by making them *una y carne*, part and parcel, of the "honor" which one has to protect. Obligations within this inner circle are typically unlimited and unconditional,

---

\* The Anglo pattern of "dating" has no parallel among Mexican Americans.

subject only to the relative priorities accorded the various members, usually on the basis of the degree of "intimacy". Toward the person, group, or thing which has not been personalized, one feels no diffuse sense of obligation nor does one feel he can claim any rights from these in the sense that he conceives of rights and obligations with respect to the members of the inner circle. Under these conditions, the general expectation is that everyone will take care of his "own" and that the conferring of such benefits as jobs, gifts, praise, and so on, will be denied the individual if he has no personal claim on the one who is in a position to distribute the largesse. To the extent that the individual receives such benefits from the "outsider", an obligation is incurred which must be reciprocated as a palpable means of acknowledging the benefit received. Both parties tend to regard the benefaction as an unusual act. The giver does not wish his generosity to be taken for granted, and the receiver, in response to this, feels obligated to reciprocate the generosity to assure the giver that he does not take it for granted. In this case, unlike the diffuse sense of obligation which prevails in the "inner circle", reciprocity is on the basis of equivalence - value returned for value received." The

---

\* The santo, the patron, and the political jefe may be personalized in part by the Mexican American in the same way that more intimate love objects are, but in these cases obligations are not nearly as unlimited and unconditional. One incurs obligations to these authority figures in proportion to the benefits conferred by them, and must reciprocate such benefits, as exemplified by the pattern of la promesa with respect to the santo. Since these figures have been personalized, however, a relationship has been established which involves the continual functioning of mutual rights and obligations, and thus the reciprocity is not on the basis of exact equivalence.

receiver is expected to be <u>muy agradecido</u>, very grateful, regardless of the size or worth of the favor received, since the emphasis is placed on the act of giving rather than what is given. A Mexican housewife will "test the character" of a new neighbor, e.g., and determine her future relations with the latter, by the device of presenting her with a gift of food and observing the manner in which the gift is received. If the gift is not received well, i.e., if the receiver is not sufficiently <u>agradecido</u>, and does not reciprocate the gift, the giver will never send another, nor will she have anything further to do with her neighbor. To be scorned or disdained in this fashion is regarded as a deep affront, <u>tal persona no es digna del favor</u>, such a person is not worthy of the gift.

The compulsion to reciprocate is reinforced by the Mexican's conception of "honor" since the failure to reciprocate is a reflection on one's "honor". This is even extended to the payment of financial obligations. As one informant put it: "<u>Aunque sea pobre, yo pago mis cuentas, y asi conservo mi honor</u>", although I am poor, I pay my bills, and thus preserve my honor.*

---

\* A number of the Anglo physicians in both McAllen and San Antonio prefer Mexican American patients because they believe the Mexicans pay their doctor bills more readily than do Anglos. Similarly, an Anglo iceman in McAllen who serves both Anglos and Mexicans said, "I'd rather do business with the Mexicans than the white folks any time. It's very seldom that one of them tries to do me out of any money."

The importance of this personalistic sense of loyalty and obligation in determining the Mexican American's orientation to his occupation and political participation, in addition to the role it plays in his interpersonal relations, particularly with employers and group leaders, will be taken up in the proper contexts below.

A second basic personality component is extreme sensitivity to insult. The example cited above of the housewife who rejects all further relations with the neighbor who scorns her is a case in point. The failure to reciprocate a favor or a gift, a fancied or real slight, a shaft of ridicule, the questioning of ability, an unfavorable criticism - any of these may result in a grievance on the part of the individual on the receiving end which may be nursed indefinitely. The following illustrates this:

> Informant, a Mexican American businessman, said, There is something about the Mexican people, they are so liable to get mad and pull out for almost any reason. We just hate to be proven wrong. We take all issues personally and just pull out of an organization never to return if we feel insulted. If, during a meeting, someone said to a speaker, 'you don't know what you're talking about - sit down', the speaker would just get up and leave and never come back, and he would hold the remark against the man who said it forever. Even if someone made a politer remark to a Mexican making a suggestion, like 'we will think about it and let you know if your suggestion can be used', the Mexican would want to know right away what is wrong with his suggestion, would want something done about it right away, and would not stand for it being pushed off into a corner.

The adult individual produced by a child-centered culture will tend to have feelings of considerable self-importance and to take himself quite seriously. Socialized in an environment where tolerance of individual behavior is high, beyond the inculcation of such moral imperatives as obedience to parents, the distinction between mine and thine, and the sense of obligation and loyalty discussed above, the Mexican American has little opportunity to question himself, to feel vulnerable because he has committed a "wrong" action. The indulgence and protectiveness of which he is the recipient during childhood, and which often persist into early adulthood, undoubtedly have positive advantages, but do not develop a high resistance, the ability to "take it", for later life situations where the individual's favorable conception of himself may be questioned by those who are in no way committed to feel indulgent and protective toward him. Similarly, the inflated sense of machismo, masculinity, which helps to build the feelings of self-importance and which is fostered by the favored position of the male and seldom challenged until the individual emerges from the environment dominated by the socializing agents, may also be questioned in later life situations.

Rosenzweig's contention, that "insufficient frustration 'spoils' the individual so that he is later unable to withstand frustration adequately,"[11] is applicable in the case of the Mexican. When he tests out the world beyond the family, primed with the expectation that the former will accord him the same treatment he has received from the latter and psychologically unprepared for the failure of his expectation to materialize, the experience is certainly a traumatic one, the reaction to which includes a range and depth of sensitivity to insult prominent enough to function as a major component of the basic personality type. The suspicion of the "outsider" thus engendered, the outsider who comes to be generalized as a potential threat to the individual's favorable conception of himself, reinforces and is reinforced by the dichotomy indicated above between those entities which are personalized and those which remain outside the personalized sphere. The individual is thrown back heavily upon this personalized sphere for recognition and approval as the one sure means of protecting the self. Correspondingly, insults directed by outsiders against one's family and friends are received as directed at the self, and are deeply resented, as are insults directed against any other individual or thing which has been personalized. El orgullo y honor Mexicano, the Mexican pride and honor are closely bound up with the personalistic sense of obligation and loyalty, to the extent that if one does not live up to the latter, it is a reflection on the former. The Mexican American uses a term which recognizes deviance from the pattern of sensitivity to insult, _lomudo_, broad-backed, which means that an individual can absorb a great deal of insult without rushing to the defense of his honor. For those whose _machismo_ will not allow them to accept any insult, _el lomudo_ represents the stereotype of the timid man, but for the majority he is no more than an anomaly.

A third basic personality component may be labelled submissiveness and a sort of passivity. There are, however, important limitations to this submissiveness since aggressiveness will be manifested in certain types of situations.* The usual reaction to an "insult", as indicated above, is withdrawal rather than a hostile impulse to strike back, to hurt the offender in turn. The individual's sense of honor and pride demands that he acknowledge the fact that he has been insulted, but this is accomplished by withdrawal and refusal to have further contact with the offender, rather than by overt aggressiveness. In short, overt aggression as a form of retaliation is seldom resorted to. Aggression in the sense of pushing forward one's own interests by self-assertion or in response to an overweening "drive for power", is also noticeably absent among Mexican Americans.

A great deal of this submissiveness may be traced to the child training patterns. The careful, constant attention

---

\* See _infra_, pp. 492 ff.

to the needs of the child which characterizes these patterns tends to produce passive forms of adaptation since there is little need for aggressive techniques as a means of obtaining need satisfaction. Moreover, the parental goal of instilling absolute obedience in children to the parental commands and requests, despite the fact that it acts as a limitation on the permissive and indulgent attitudes toward the child, further reinforces submissiveness since it requires compliance on the part of the child if he is to remain on good terms with the parents, the sources of need satisfaction. The price of accessibility to the permissiveness and indulgence of the parents is unquestioning obedience. To disobey or to exhibit overt aggressiveness is to forego the parental rewards and invite punishment. The heavy emphasis on courtesy and politeness in relations with others which is evident even among the younger children is an indication that overt aggression toward others, in addition to the parents, is frowned upon. This should not be construed to be a tendency to "turn the other cheek", a kind of tolerance which is not evident among Mexicans, but is rather a tendency to eliminate at least overt aggression as a socially approved form of reaction to frustration in a wide variety of contexts.[*] However, in those cases where

---

[*] This does not mean, of course, that aggression is completely inhibited just because its expression is not socially sanctioned. The covert channels through which aggression tends to flow, such as gossip, aggressive joking, and so on, are best left for later treatment.

machismo has been elevated to a degree of prominence where there is a compulsive need to "prove" one's masculinity, as indicated in the section on sex roles above, the individual's sense of honor is of the "touch-me-not" variety, and overt aggressive retaliation against the fancied or real frustrating agent is not only expected but mandatory if the individual is to retain his sense of honor and his reputation as muy macho intact.

The expectation of rewards, in the form of indulgence and protection, which the child develops in his relations with the parents on condition that he remains obedient and submissive, is later transferred to other authority figures, such as the patron, or employer. As long as his patron is paternalistic, i.e., is indulgent and protective, the individual remains obedient and submissive, a tendency which is reinforced by the Mexican's sense of obligation, of according loyalty to those from whom one receives benefits. From this pattern, Anglo employers derive the idea that "as long as you take care of them, they will do anything in the world for you". On the other hand, harshness, prohibition, disdain, contempt, and so on, on the part of the patron, will be reacted to by withdrawal,* since these play no part in parental

---

\* If goaded enough, and if he develops an awareness of exploitation and defines the patron as the source of exploitation, the Mexican may react with overt aggression. Mexico's violent history, and the rash of strikes of Mexican laborers in California, Colorado, and New Mexico in the thirties provide evidence of this. The significant exceptions encountered by the writer to the above generalization that withdrawal is the dominant pattern will be treated in other contexts below.

attitudes, and are defined as insults to one's sense of honor.

There are important concomitants of the Mexican's submissiveness which should be indicated here. Since obedience is the price of rewards, and since the Mexican automatically expects rewards if he is obedient, he does not develop a sense of responsibility for his own fate, nor a belief in the efficacy of action by the self. *Sea por Dios*, it is the will of God, is the explanation and justification of the contemporary state of affairs accepted by even those Mexicans who are not religiously oriented. Consistent with this, the Mexican will explain and justify the *borracho*, or drunkard, with the phrase, *asi lo hizo Dios*, God made him thus. Faults or weaknesses are not subject to the will of the individual, but are determined by the world of uncontrollable forces symbolized by the word *Dios*. Here can be found an extension of the parental belief that young children are not really responsible for their actions and an explanation of the high tolerance of variation in individual behavior the Mexican American manifests.

*Sea por Dios* expresses a fatalism and a resignation which are further dimensions of the Mexican's submissiveness. The Mexican tends to ignore his own manipulative powers and to wait for whatever developments the uncontrollable forces may bring. The Mexican says, "*A ver que sale*," let's see what comes of it, and since the unknown and unexpected may alter life for the better as well as for the worse, there is not much point in worrying about the future.

Another basic personality component is best described as the "primacy of the mood", which refers to the **tendency** of the Mexican American to be oriented largely to immediate situational factors, to act in accordance with the first flush of their effect upon him and without much regard for the ultimate consequences of these actions. This does not mean that the Mexican is opportunistic or unprincipled, but rather that he tends to spontaneously respond to stimuli of the immediate situation in such a way as to fully exploit its dramatic and affective potentialities. At a political rally, a patriotic _fiesta_, or an organizational meeting, e.g., there is a quick and heartfelt response (which may increase to a high pitch of excitement) to the speaker who plays upon such highly emotionally charged symbols as _la patria_, the fatherland, _la raza_, the race, _yo soy Mejicano_, I am Mexican, _la familia_, the family, and so on. To cite one case which can stand for many, at a meeting of LULAC[*], the president asked for volunteers to sell advertising in a hurry for a forthcoming issue of the organization's periodical, adding that those who volunteered would be working for the welfare of LULAC. A number of members arose in turn and expressed florid and lofty

---

[*] The League of United Latin American Citizens. See _infra_, pp. 537 ff.

sentiments regarding their loyalty to LULAC and their concern for its welfare (exhibiting an emotional intensity which seemed to the writer to be far out of proportion to the actual task in hand), ending with a pledge to bring in a page or so of advertisements. Each speaker received a round of hearty applause. At the following meeting, the chairman of the advertising committee reported that he had been forced to secure all the advertisements himself, but neither he nor the other members made any mention of what had transpired at the previous meeting. To the Mexican, the discrepancy between the word and the deed here exhibited is not necessarily an indication of insincerity since there is no general expectation that the performer in such situations will follow through with the promises he makes at the time.

A sense of the histrionic is a major element of this component. The opportunity to make a grand gesture, to strike a lofty pose, to perform for the group, to show oneself to advantage, is always exploited by one or many of the individuals present, and often one will try to outdo the other, but the failure of the performer to consistently follow through what he has begun is seldom if ever condemned. Rather, it is taken for granted that he will not do so. All present enjoy the spectacle for what it is, and may take a turn upon the stage themselves. Both performers and audience apparently believe in the performance _at the time_, but it does not commit anyone to a future line of action. Oratory for its own sake is highly valued by Mexican Americans. The able speaker, who can touch upon the right symbols and commands a forceful and dramatic technique, is greatly appreciated even though he may not have a particularly significant message to put across. For the Mexican, a good speaker is a spectacle worth travelling to enjoy.

The "primacy of the mood", or emphasizing the impulse of the moment as a guide to action, manifests itself strikingly in the Mexican's conception of a "good time" at a *baile* or *fiesta*, where he proceeds to enjoy himself with an intensity and abandon seldom approached by equivalent affairs among Anglo Americans. This exploitation of the mood of the moment determines and is determined by the Mexican's time conceptions, that life is to be lived now while the opportunity to do so is present, and that *mañana es hoy o nunca*, tomorrow is today or never. Since the future is determined by unknown and uncontrollable forces, there is no point in taking a chance on the vague and altogether undependable benefits it may hold. The only reality is the present, and *mañana* is an indefinite and remote time which may never materialize.* One consequence of this is the vagueness of the Mexican's chronology, his consistent disregard of the clock. No one expects a scheduled event

---

\* The absolutism of paternal authority in childhood and the fixity of status and extreme poverty to which most Mexicans are subjected in adulthood probably play important roles in the development of such a conception of the future.

to start on time, nor anyone to keep an appointment in accordance with a prearranged time, although the event will eventually take place, and the appointment will usually be kept, if one can wait patiently. The Mexicans jokingly refer to this pattern as "Mexican Standard Time", or *la hora mejicana*, the Mexican hour.

Chapter IV

THE PATTERNS OF INTERGROUP CONTACT

The present chapter is devoted to a description of the static aspects of the dominant-subordinate system of intergroup relations, and attempts to do no more than indicate the extent of intergroup contact, apart from consideration of the idea and action patterns governing such contact, in a number of significant areas which will not receive the sort of extended treatment reserved for the spheres of occupations, political action, and stratification. The dynamic aspects of the system to be examined in succeeding chapters within the contexts of these latter spheres can be more clearly seen against the backdrop of the relatively static, purely phenomenological description which now follows. It should be noted that the patterns of intergroup contact described here will again be taken up in the analysis of the mechanisms of subordination in the attempt to explain these patterns as resultants of the functioning of the mechanisms.

Residence

From Brownsville, situated near the Gulf of Mexico, the Missouri Pacific Railroad, paralleled by Highway 83, locally entitled "The Longest Street in the World", bisects twelve major towns and cities of the Lower Rio Grande Valley on its route westward to Rio Grande City, 103 miles from Brownsville. In McAllen, following the official zoning terminology, the "residential" areas of the city lie north of the railroad and highway, while the "business" and "industrial" areas occupy the southern portion of the city, fringed on the east and west by tiny "residential" areas. The zoning map of McAllen, however, is an extremely unreliable guide to actual residence patterns since it cannot indicate the fact that the heaviest concentration of Mexican American residences lies within the areas designated "business" and "industrial". Southwest McAllen is variously referred to as "Mexiquita", "Mexicantown", and "little Mexico" by the city's Anglos, and as the _colonia_ by the Mexican Americans. From north to south, the _colonia_ is bisected by the Southern Pacific Railroad, which connects McAllen with San Antonio and the world beyond. To the west of this railroad, Mexican Americans share their living space with the packing sheds, canneries, and other industrial enterprises which border the railroad; to the east they are sandwiched between the business street of the _colonia_, and the main business section of McAllen.

With but a few exceptions,* the _colonia_ is inhabited only by Mexican Americans,** most of whom live in close proximity to

---

\* The twenty to twenty-five Negro families of McAllen. About eight of these live in a cluster at the southern edge of the _colonia_, but the rest are scattered throughout it.

\*\* With the City Directory as a guide, the writer has plotted the location of each Mexican and Anglo American household on a detail map of the city, thus obtaining a fairly reliable picture of the degree of concentration of Mexican and Anglo residences in separate areas.

each other on tiny lots, often no larger than 25 by 100 feet.
Lots of this size usually contain one house fronting the
street and another one in the rear. Larger lots are covered
with as many houses as there is space for, the rear houses
either arranged in a square facing a central clearing, or
huddled together in no regular pattern. Many of these rear
dwellings house married children and their families or other
relatives, while others were erected to serve as income
property.* The "typical" <u>colonia</u> house is constructed of rough
planking with a thatched or tar-papered roof and cardboard or
canvas nailed over the cracks in the walls, consists of one
or two rooms, has a plank floor or none at all, and is furnished
with a bed or two, floor pallets made of rags and blankets, a
table and chairs, and boxes for groceries and clothes. It also
contains a kerosene or wood-burning cook stove and, during the
cold season, an open tub of coals for heating purposes.
Although the house may have a window and electric or kerosene
lighting, its only source of illumination may be the single
entrance. Most of McAllen's one thousand outside privies are

---

\* A tabulation of the listings in the City Directory reveals that of the 1700 Mexican American householders listed, 1029 own their homes. These homeowners usually own the lot the house stands on as well, and build rear housing for rental purposes. Of the 2119 Anglo American householders listed, 1256 own their homes. It should be remembered, in comparing these figures, that the typical Mexican American house can be constructed for only a few hundred dollars, whereas Anglo American houses are in general much more expensive. An examination of the construction permits authorized by the City Building Inspector and published in the <u>Valley Evening Monitor</u> of McAllen during the period of the study revealed that the average Anglo American house cost around $5000 and consisted of 5 rooms while the average Mexican American house cost $200-$500 and consisted of two or three rooms.

said to be located within the colonia. There is no discernible "middle class" residence area within the colonia, although one occasionally encounters larger houses of better construction and with better furnishings interspersed among houses of the type just described.

West of the Southern Pacific tracks, the colonia extends northward across the highway and Missouri Pacific right-of-way to the northern limit of the city. In this area, one can find a sprinkling of Anglo American families, living in clusters of three and four in an otherwise solidly Mexican American neighborhood. Adjoining the Southern Pacific tracks on the east is a narrow oblong "mixed" area two blocks in width, one of two such in McAllen. Here Mexican and Anglo Americans live side by side in housing which varies from sub-standard to fairly good in quality and size.

The rest of North McAllen, an area approximately equal in size to that occupied by the colonia and its northern extension, is inhabited completely by Anglo Americans with the exception of 17 Mexican American families. Its appearance is in sharp contrast with that of the colonia. North McAllen's streets are paved, whereas in the colonia all of the streets, with the exception of the calle principal, and a few others, are surfaced with dirt or gravel. The street drainage system is effective enough throughout most of North McAllen to adequately cope with the heavy Fall rains, but in the colonia many streets remain submerged until the hot sun has evaporated the rainwater. North McAllen's houses, never more than one to

a lot except in the small portion designated "residential B",*
are set back at least thirty feet from the sidewalks, and
fronted by spacious, usually well-kept lawns. The majority
of the lots are at least 50 by 140 feet in size. From
North McAllen, its streets lined symmetrically with tall,
slender date-palm trees, the city derives its title of "City
of Palms", a name featured insistently in Chamber of Commerce
literature and the local newspaper. This area is genuinely
residential, totally free of the industrial and commercial
establishments which crowd the colonia.

North McAllen's "typical" house is white stucco or brick
often with the Spanish red tile roof, one-storied, consists of
at least five or six rooms, and is furnished in the conventional
middle class American manner, complete with refrigerator, plumb-
ing, and an attached garage. Many houses, particularly in the
newer "additions" near the northern city limit, are more lavish
than this, with two stories, sun decks, seven to ten rooms, and
more spacious grounds.

---

\* A Mexican American informant, a former member of the McAllen
Zoning Board, provided the following information:
- Residential A - only one-family dwellings may be built on each
  lot in this zone. Garage apartments are permitted in
  addition, but only for use of family members or as
  servant quarters, never for rental purposes. Not even
  churches are permitted in this zone.
- Residential B - two-family dwellings, churches, and apartment
  houses may be built in this zone.
- Residential C - small stores and barber shops are permitted
  in this zone.

The major portion of North McAllen, the Anglo community, is
designated Residential A, the rest of it is Residential B. The
northern extension of the colonia is in a Residential C zone, and
the colonia proper, as indicated above, lies in the Industrial and
Business zones.

Seventeen Mexican American families reside in this section of the city, scattered throughout the area. Of these seventeen, ten are prominent in the affairs of the Mexican American group, while at least five of the ten perform strategic roles in the ordering of intergroup relations. For the present, using occupation as a first approximation to the criteria of class status, it may be said that fifteen of the total number (the occupations of two of the family heads could not be ascertained) occupy middle class status. The occupations of these family heads include two lawyers, one dentist, two wholesale grocers and ranchers, one wholesale grocer, one retail grocer, two ranchers, the Mexican Consul, one realtor, the owner of a cleaning and pressing establishment, a roofing engineer, an oil company employee, and the owner of a night club and the largest bar in the _colonia_. This is by no means a complete roster of the Mexican American middle class, as will be seen later, but it represents a substantial number of those with top status.

Besides North McAllen, Anglo Americans have congregated in two tiny areas adjacent to the southern side of the highway, one located at the eastern limit of the city, the other just west of the _colonia_ proper. Mention of a second "mixed" area, approximately equal in size to the one described above, completes the residential picture presented here. This area is located in the southeastern portion of the city, and is separated from the _colonia_ by McAllen's main business section.

Here Mexicans and Anglos live on the same streets, often as neighbors in the same blocks.

Along the irrigation canals on the fringes of the city, and in the open country between McAllen and the Mexican border eight miles to the south, one occasionally comes upon settlements of field laborers and their families, many of them "wetbacks", or illegal entrants from Mexico, living in tents and hovels lacking even the most rudimentary conveniences. These settlements have no recognized existence and have no access to the city's public service facilities, usually obtaining their water from the open irrigation canals. Two miles north and west of McAllen is a "Labor Center" of eighty-five single and two-family dwellings, each containing four rooms, which were constructed during the recent war by the U. S. Department of Agriculture to provide cheap, adequate housing for field laborers. This Center was recently leased by the City of McAllen, and continues to provide housing for a small percentage of the local labor supply.

In concluding this section, a brief summary of residence patterns in San Antonio may be presented. The West Side, despite the fact that it embraces a large Anglo American neighborhood, connotes "Little Mexico" or the "Mexican Quarter" to the majority of San Antonio's citizens. The West Side is, in fact, the principal home of San Antonio's Mexicans, and in the area where the _colonia_ is located, about four square miles, the population is about 95% Mexican American. On the western edge of the _colonia_, and at the points where it borders the West Side's Anglo community, one may see adequate little homes occupied by Mexicans, but for the most part the _colonia_ has been one vast slum, consisting of interminable rows of one and two room shacks almost touching each other, varied occasionally by _vecindades_, or _corrales_, as they are often called. A _vecindad_ is a large, square, one-storied structure, open in the center, containing up to twelve one and two room units, each housing a family, and facing the inner "court". A federal housing project of 1183 two to four room units, completed in 1940 over the opposition of the property owners, now covers ten city blocks in the heart of the _colonia_, erected on the site where an equivalent number of slum dwellings, now razed, formerly stood. In 1939, half of San Antonio's 75,677 families were living in substandard housing, and of this half, 56 per cent, or roughly 21,280, were Mexican Americans.[1*]

Not all of San Antonio's Mexican Americans live on the West Side. The _colonia_ has sent out offshoots to form "mixed" neighborhoods in areas which were originally all Anglo American, thus pushing back the Anglos. Segments of the Mexican American population now live in southwest, northwest, and even east

---

[*] A survey of households in a section of the West Side conducted by the Pan American Progressive Association of San Antonio in 1948 revealed the following information: Of 1949 Mexican American families sampled, 857 or 68.6% owned their homes, 315 or 25.2% rented, and 77 or 6.2% did not reply. With regard to access to public service facilities, of 1220 families sampled, 64.5% had water, 60.5% had electricity, 6.2% had gas, and 2% had sewer facilities.

San Antonio, in areas of "second settlement", away from the stockyards, railroad sidings, poorly paved and ill-lighted streets, industrial and commercial enterprises, and wretched huts and *vecindades* which characterize the *colonia*.

The North and South sides of San Antonio are populated predominantly by Anglo Americans. The further north one goes from the center of the city, the more expensive and elaborate become the homes, and the more spacious and well-kept their environs. In the north-eastern section of the North Side are located the suburban communities of Alamo Heights, a prosperous area with excellent homes, and Olmos Park, where the wealthy oilmen and retired cattle ranchers live. The South Side houses San Antonio's Anglo lower and lower middle classes, and the East Side provides housing for the city's Negro population.

Education

For any child in American society, formal schooling occupies a prominent place in his socialization and consequent assimilation to the culture into which he was born. When the child is a member of a group as well insulated and excluded as is the Mexican American, the potential role of the school in providing opportunities for intergroup interaction and access to Anglo American idea patterns assumes inestimable importance. The Mexican American child spends his pre-school years in a community of his own ethnic group, learns Spanish as his primary language, and comes to the school experience with no conception of the Anglo world beyond that imparted at second hand by his socializing agents. The school thus provides the first opportunity, one of the few opportunities as will appear later, for contact with the Anglo group. For the majority of Mexican American children this first contact consists not of relationships with Anglo American children but with an Anglo teacher as the sole representative of an ethnic group other than their own, a relationship which is the prototype of later relationships with Anglos in that the Mexican is subordinate while the Anglo is dominant.

Of McAllen's seven schools, two, the Roosevelt and the Sam Houston, are located within a few blocks of each other in the southeastern corner of the _colonia_. The Stephen F. Austin school is situated in the heart of the northern extension of the _colonia_, while the Lamar and Wilson schools are to be found a block from each other in the center of Anglo North McAllen. The Lincoln school and McAllen's high school are on the same campus a block south of the highway not far from the main business section and one of the "mixed" residence areas. The physical plant and equipment of the _colonia_ schools do not appear to be inferior to those of the other schools. The following figures indicate the Anglo and Mexican scholastic populations of each school:[2]

| School | Anglo American | Mexican American |
|---|---|---|
| Roosevelt | None | 1,369 |
| Sam Houston | None | 342 |
| Stephen F. Austin | None | 359 |
| Lamar | 330 | 100 |
| Wilson | 253 | 10 |
| Lincoln | 430 | 49 |
| High School | 428 | 261 |
| Totals | 1,441 | 2,490 |

It is apparent from these figures that over four-fifths, 2,070 of McAllen's Mexican American scholastics, attend a school where no Anglo American children are present. The distribution also reveals that school separation is an extension of the residential separation indicated in the previous section. The fact that there are a number of Mexican Americans in attendance at the two North McAllen schools rules out the possibility of deliberate segregation.* The majority of these children probably live in the northern extension of the _colonia_, and represent an overflow from the Stephen F. Austin school. The Mexican students in attendance at the Lincoln school live in the nearby "mixed" area. The figures also reveal that, despite the fact that the Mexican American scholastics greatly outnumber the Anglos as a whole, they in turn are outnumbered almost to the same extent in the high school. Many Mexican Americans drop out at an early grade in primary school, and of the rest, knowing only the "Mexican school", as

---

\* Exclusion devices employed by the dominant group, such as school segregation and restrictive covenants, will be analyzed in a later chapter dealing with the mechanisms by means of which the dominant-subordinate system is maintained. See pp. 438 ff.

it is referred to by both Mexicans and Anglos, many cannot face the adjustment required in entering the "mixed" high school.

The 1948 school census figure for McAllen is 5,408 scholastics, based on a headcount of all children in the city over six and under eighteen years of age.[3] This total exceeds the number of scholastics actually enrolled by 1,477. The majority of these 1,477 children who do not attend school at all are probably Mexican Americans who have either dropped out of school at an early age or never enrolled at all,[*] usually because they are needed to supplement the family earnings.[**]

---

[*] The findings presented here are consistent with the school situation in the state of Texas as a whole, according to the following data reported in a state-wide survey conducted in 1942-43:
1) Only 53 percent of the Mexican American children in Texas, six to seventeen inclusive, enrolled in the public schools.
2) 72 percent of those enrolled were in the age-group six to twelve, inclusive.
3) 68 percent of these children, ages six to twelve inclusive, enrolled in the public schools were in the first three grades.
4) Slightly more than 52 percent of all Mexican American pupils, ages six to seventeen inclusive, enrolled in the public schools were in grades one, two, and three. That is to say, it appears that the greater portion of the 53 percent who do enroll in the public schools never go beyond the third grade.
5) Over-ageness is a dominant characteristic of all grades among Mexican American children.

See Wilson Little, Spanish-Speaking Children in Texas, The University of Texas Press, 1944.

[**] A study of children of agricultural workers in Hidalgo County (McAllen's county) indicates that of 482 children not enrolled in school in 1940-41, 279, or 57.9 percent, were reported by their families as needed as wage earners, Publication 298, U. S. Department of Labor, Children's Bureau, 1943, p. 40.

With reference to the attendance of those who are enrolled, it should be stated that at the time of the study there were thirty half-day classes in the McAllen schools, eight of which were conducted at the Stephen F. Austin school, and the other twenty-two at the Roosevelt school.[4] These half-day classes have existed for over ten years, but construction of new school buildings to eliminate the overcrowding was under way at the time the writer left McAllen.

The San Antonio school situation is similar to that of McAllen in most respects. In this case also there is school separation of Anglo and Mexican children based on residential separation resulting in "Mexican schools" with little or no Anglo student populations. There are also a number of Mexican American students, living in the mixed areas, who attend predominantly Anglo schools. However, in San Antonio, the colonia is large enough to have a high school of its own, which means that the majority of Mexican Americans who attend high school do so in one which has an almost one-hundred percent Mexican American scholastic population. The pattern of dropping out of school in the early grades exists also in San Antonio.[*]

---
[*] " The principal of Sidney Lanier School (the West Side high school) estimates that 'there are about 3,000 Mexican children of school age who have never entered school.' On the basis of his experience in this school where the attendance is almost 100 percent Mexican he further estimates that 'of 200 Mexicans who enter primary school, only 100 graduate from the 5th grade, 90 enter Junior High School (6th to 8th grade), 45 finish the 8th grade, 36 enter Senior High (9th to 11th grade), 22 graduate from high school, and one enters college.'" " Public Welfare Survey of San Antonio," op. cit., p. 90.

Unlike McAllen, the physical plant and facilities provided for West Side schools in San Antonio are generally regarded as inferior to those enjoyed by the predominantly Anglo North and South Sides. Using figures compiled by the West Side School Improvement League,* the following comparisons can be made:

> The West Side has 58 schoolrooms of wooden frame construction whereas there are only 18 similar rooms in all other parts of the city combined.
>
> The total scholastic enrollment for the 43 primary schools in the San Antonio system is 25,637. Of this total, 25 schools on the North, South, and East Sides account for 10,413. The West Side alone, with 18 schools, accounts for the 15,224.
>
> The North Side high school has 33 acres of playground to serve 1,730 students. Of the two South Side high schools, one has 19 acres for 1,769 students, and the other has 75 acres for 1,018 students. The West Side high school has $2\frac{1}{2}$ acres to serve 1,691 students.

Recreation

McAllen's facilities for group recreation are somewhat limited, as are such facilities in the majority of American towns and small cities. There are no nearby lakes to retreat to for relief from the fierce summer heat, and but one park, an area a block square located in the center of the city, equipped with a few benches and a bandstand erected above the subterranean city library. Outside of the city, there are a few wooded areas which serve as picnic grounds. McAllen has

---

* A Mexican American protest organization which will receive later treatment. See pp. 545 ff.

a country club, situated a few miles south and east of the city, which is complete with golf course, swimming pool, tennis courts, and clubhouse containing a dining room, a bar, and a palatial lounge large enough for dances. According to an Anglo informant who is a member, two of the fifty charter members, each of whom contributed $2,000 to finance the club, are Mexican Americans. One of these is the only Mexican American physician in McAllen, the other the only dentist. Later members have been invited to join at a $300 fee without property rights, and all of these are Anglo American so far as could be determined.

McAllen has no playgrounds with the exception of those attached to the schools. During the period of the study, one of the Anglo Protestant churches erected a well-equipped community recreation center in North McAllen, but the *colonia* has no counterpart of this. Its facilities are enjoyed mainly by Anglos, but the few Mexican Americans who are members of YMCA organizations can occasionally be found there since the YMCA carries on most of its activities in the center. There is a privately owned swimming pool, located about a mile south of the country club, which is open to the public for an admission fee, but Mexican Americans are not admitted.*

---

\* The segregation policy of the pool owner, consistently maintained for a number of years and accepted as part of the nature of things by McAllen, finally precipitated a crisis during the period of the study which will be described in the chapter on the mechanisms of subordination. See pp. 453 ff.

Like many other border cities, McAllen has access to the "night clubs" provided for tourists in the border town directly across the river, and consequently has few of its own. All of these places offer alcoholic drinks,* elaborate dinners, floor shows, and dancing at prices far lower than those on the American side. The steady flow of automobiles every evening across the International Bridge connecting Mexico with McAllen eight miles to the north, which becomes a torrent on Saturday nights, is evidence that a large number of McAllen's inhabitants, both Mexican and Anglo, are greatly attracted to the pleasures of the Reynosa night clubs, and the extensive brothel section, aptly named the "Bull Pen", to be found there. El otro lado, the other side, appears to provide a sort of moral immunity for many of the Anglo patrons from McAllen. Many drink excessively and indulge in rather spectacular behavior rarely encountered at the usually sedate social affairs in McAllen. In the words of one indignant Anglo informant, "We got a river here that makes a world of difference. The Anglo Americans can cross the river and then they do anything they damn please and nothing will be said about it on this side. But if the same thing took place on this side, people wouldn't stand for it. If a man is seen in McAllen with a Latin American woman, he is completely ostracized, but if he takes her over to the other side, it's all right to be seen with her." The careful avoidance which characterizes patterns of intergroup

---

\* The peculiar liquor laws of Texas permit an individual to buy his liquor in bottles at a "package store" and then carry it to a bar or restaurant where he may purchase a "set up", soda and ice, and mix his own drink. Bars, however, are permitted to sell only beer and wine.

contact becomes somewhat mitigated on the "other side", where Anglos and Mexicans eat at neighboring tables and dance on the same floor, although seldom actually mingling. There are no night clubs of this sort in McAllen, probably because of the impossibility of meeting the competition from the other side, but a Mexican American, the owner of the largest bar in the _colonia_ opened, during the period of the study, a small place for drinking and dancing. The owner aimed at Anglo clientele, since he announced the opening with telegraphed invitations sent to the majority of the prominent Anglos in McAllen. On opening night, the place was full of Anglo couples sitting at the tables and crowding the dance floor. There were Mexicans present also, but all of them were lined up at the long bar and none of them were dancing because they had not brought their wives or girl friends. Later visits to the place revealed the same pattern, Anglo men and women at the tables, Mexican males at the bar or occasionally forming a group by themselves at one of the tables.

There are over twenty-five bars and restaurant-bars in McAllen. The majority of these are located on or near South Guerra Street, the _colonia's_ main business street. A number of them, however, are located on or near Main Street, McAllen's principal business street. One can find both Anglos and Mexicans in the Main Street bars, but seldom drinking together. The writer has observed Mexican and Anglo acquaintances speaking or joking with each other in these bars, but never entering or leaving together. There are a number of restaurants at the east and west ends of the city, situated on the highway, which also serve a "mixed" clientele, and which are well patronized by beer drinkers in the evenings. The pattern of contact described above prevails at these places also. The colonia bars, with one exception, are almost never patronized by an Anglo, and the appearance of one is sufficiently unusual to make him the cynosure of all eyes. The exception is the large bar owned by the Mexican American who opened the night club. In the words of an informant, this bar "is a place where lots of white folks go." However, here again the familiar pattern may be observed of Anglos and Mexicans drinking separately, with acquaintances occasionally having a beer together.

McAllen has four moving picture theaters, two on Main Street and two on Seventeenth Street. The latter two show films in Spanish, made in Mexico and Argentina, the former show Hollywood films. Very few Anglos attend the colonia theaters, if for no other reason than because so few Anglos know Spanish,* but apparently a large number of Mexicans attend the Main Street theaters, especially the younger people who prefer the Western pictures which are a constant attraction at one of these theaters.

The audiences that attend community talent shows and dramatic productions sponsored by Anglo voluntary associations

---
\* The almost universal ignorance of Spanish which is found among Anglo Americans in itself has important implications for the patterns of group contact. Many Mexican Americans of the immigrant generation know little or no English, while those who are bilingual always use Spanish in conversing with each other.

are wholly Anglo, so far as could be determined by the investigator, just as Anglo-sponsored dances, Chamber of Commerce dinners, and other community-wide social functions never attract Mexicans. A "Follies", sponsored by the Junior Service League, was produced with all Anglo talent and attended by a completely Anglo audience, with two or three exceptions. Similarly, an opera company, composed of both Anglo and Mexican singers, was brought from San Antonio through the efforts of one of the colonia associations to present a concert in the high school auditorium. Although the venture was well advertised in advance in the local paper, and although a few Main Street merchants purchased tickets from the club members who canvassed their stores, the audience was almost wholly Mexican with a sprinkling of ten or twelve Anglos. At dances held at the Labor Center, which has a "mixed" population, both Anglos and Mexicans attended, however the Anglos congregated at one side of the hall, the Mexicans at the other, and there was no "mixed" dancing.

The gulf is maintained even in street lounging. One can observe Mexicans and Anglos in groups on Main Street corners, but always separate, never together.

San Antonio recreational patterns differ from the above in minor respects. The city has a number of parks, some equipped with swimming pools and playgrounds, and these are available to Anglos and Mexicans alike. However, in practice Mexicans and Anglos use the parks within or closest to their respective residential areas. The recreational facilities offered by the

settlement houses are used primarily by Mexicans, since
nine of the eleven settlement house districts are well within
the _colonia_ area. The _colonia_ bars are patronized only by
Mexicans, while the "downtown" night clubs and those situated
at the edge of the city are attended by those few Mexicans
who have the inclination to attend Anglo entertainment places
and can afford the prices prohibitive for the majority of
their group. The city's moving picture theaters are attended
by both Anglos and Mexicans, but, as in McAllen, the six or
seven theaters which show Spanish-speaking films attract few
if any Anglos. Anglo-sponsored entertainment programs and
social functions open to the general public are seldom attended
by Mexicans. Similarly, the affairs promoted by _colonia_
voluntary associations draw only Mexicans, with the exception
of the few Anglo politicians and office-holders who receive
special invitations to attend as guests of honor, and who
find it to their interests to do so. San Antonio annually
stages its week-long Fiesta de San Jacinto, commemorating
the anniversary of the battle in which Texas won its freedom
from Mexico. Although the trappings and attire of the fiesta
are in Mexican and western style, the celebration is primarily
an Anglo affair, participated in by a few prominent and "assimilated" Mexicans who provide the necessary "atmosphere".

## Commercial and Professional Services

The contacts which occur between individuals in the course
of obtaining access to necessary commercial and professional

services generally are of a more impersonal nature than those which occur in any of the other areas of contact considered in this chapter. This is because the fundamental separateness of the parties involved in commercial transactions, beyond what is required of them in their roles as buyer and seller to consummate the transaction in the immediate contractual situation, is institutionally positively sanctioned in our society, and claims and obligations which are not specifically defined as part of the buyer-seller relationship are more irrelevant in this area than in any other. Even though this separateness may impose considerable limitations on the potentiality of commercial contacts for extending the depth and scope of Anglo-Mexican relations, the fact that the _colonia_ cannot satisfy many of the needs of its inhabitants for goods and services necessitates a frequency of contact with Anglo Americans the extent of which must be described here to fulfill the objectives of this chapter.

McAllen has two business sections, one centering around Main Street, the other, three blocks west of Main Street, forming the _calle_ _principal_ of the _colonia_. Main Street is the hub of a business section which has overflowed onto adjacent streets and along the section of the highway which runs through the city. In the _colonia_, however, only Guerra Street is lined with commercial enterprises, a business section much smaller than its Anglo counterpart. Guerra Street has equivalents, on a smaller scale, of the Anglo hotels, restaurants, groceries, bakeries, cleaners and tailors, dry goods stores, drug stores, barber shops, and filling stations. However, the department stores, apparel shops, five and ten cent stores, jewelry stores, banks, and various specialty shops which are a vital part of the Anglo business section are lacking on Guerra Street.

The two main Anglo hotels and the many motor courts situated at the east and west ends of town along the highway are patronized mainly by Anglos, so far as could be determined. Lodgings of this sort are generally sought by Anglo tourists and travelling salesmen. Mexicans and Anglos may be seen eating side by side at the counters in Anglo restaurants, or at adjoining tables. For the Anglo who likes Mexican cuisine, there is a Mexican-owned restaurant on Main Street specializing in such food, patronized by both Anglo and Mexican customers. A large number of the Mexican Americans who partake of restaurant food satisfy their needs in the colonia, however, judging by the thirteen restaurants to be found there. There is no evidence that Mexican Americans are refused service in any of the McAllen restaurants, although many Mexican informants related incidents of this nature which they had either experienced themselves in other parts of the state, or had heard about as occurring to others.*

  The _colonia_ contains fifty-six grocery stores, as compared with twenty-five in Anglo McAllen. The vast majority of the former, however, are feeble little enterprises which are run on a shoestring. They continue to eke out a precarious existence because, in contrast to the Anglo stores, they stock items of the Mexican diet not usually found in the Anglo stores, they extend credit to the limit of their capacity, and they are conveniently located for daily minor purchases. A few of the _colonia_ stores do a substantial business, but none of these can meet the prices nor match the variety of foods to be found in the Anglo chain "supermarket."

---

\* The following quotations from Kibbe give some indication of the extent of refusal of service to Mexican Americans in public places for the state as a whole:
"During the first four months of its existence, ending December 31, 1943, the Good Neighbor Commission of Texas received from Mexican Consuls, Latin American organizations, and individuals 117 complaints of 'discrimination'. Some of the reports related to segregated schools, and other alleged conditions of inequality, but at least 110 of them involved refusal of admission to or service in public places of business and amusement . . . Of the total of 117 incidents, sixty-seven occurred in West Texas, four in East Texas, and forty-four in South Texas. A very negligible number were noted along the Border, where there is the heaviest concentration of Latin American population, and the greatest number were from that Plains section of West Texas which has already been described as the most important cotton-growing area of the State . . . It was notable that refusal of service took place, almost without exception, in fourth or fifth-class cafes, beer parlors, barbershops, etc. . . Forty-five of the sixty-nine towns against which complaints were registered, or practically two-thirds of the total, were small towns of less than 5,000 population". Pauline Kibbe, _Latin Americans in Texas_, University of New Mexico Press, 1946, pp. 209-212.
For a partial list of places in Texas where Mexican Americans are refused service, see Perales, Alonso S., _Are We Good Neighbors?_, San Antonio, 1948, pp. 213-223.

Here the majority of the customers are apparently Mexican, many of whom buy in quantities sufficient for a week's needs. Most of the other Anglo groceries obtain some measure of Mexican patronage, but a Mexican is seldom seen in the three largest independent groceries, probably because their prices are somewhat higher than those which prevail at the chain and other Anglo groceries. An Anglo informant stated that one of these three stores refuses to hire Mexican help and discourages Mexican trade. The _colonia_ contains two bakeries and nine _tortilla_ "factories", so the Anglo bakeries, one attached to the "supermarket", the other to the independent store mentioned above, and one independent receive very few Mexican customers.

The five McAllen department stores, four of which are chain stores, stocking mainly wearing apparel and housewares, are all located in the Anglo business section. Their price range is about the same as Sears-Roebuck, and thus somewhat lower than the high-priced apparel and specialty shops in the city. Usually, more Mexican than Anglo customers can be seen shopping in these stores. As for the higher-priced shops, the manager of one of them stated:

> Well, we do have some Latin American customers in the shoe department and in men's clothing. But our women's clothing is priced rather high and so we don't get many of the local people. Our Latin trade is strong from Monterrey (Mexico) and even from Mexico City, but most of the local women can't afford to shop here. I'm sure they buy their clothes at the lower-priced stores.

Mexicans do not purchase all of their clothing on Main Street, as there are six dry goods stores which do a thriving business in the colonia. Five of these are owned by Syrians, the other by a Jew. A number of Mexican informants stated that they prefer to shop for their clothing on Main Street because of the wider selection, however.

The wares of the three five and ten cent stores, also members of chains, attract great numbers of Mexican buyers. No colonia store, or even Anglo for that matter, can compete with the five and ten cent stores in the range and price of merchandise they handle. The writer noticed a heavy preponderance of Mexican girls among the clerks employed by these stores. The inability of many Mexicans to speak English, together with the low wages offered by these stores, accounts for the preponderance. One Mexican employee informed the writer that there is very little mingling between Anglo and Mexican clerks. Other Anglo stores which are dependent upon Mexican trade for a large part of their business also employ at least one or two Mexican Americans to cope with the Spanish-speaking customers. Thus many Mexican customers are waited on by other Mexicans, further minimizing the extent of contact possible between Anglo and Mexican in the area of commercial services.

Two of McAllen's eight drug stores are located on Guerra Street. One of the Mexican American pharmacists apparently performs the services of a physician, diagnosing ills and prescribing treatment for many of the residents of the colonia.

According to one informant, he does so on the basis of an "understanding" he has with one of the Anglo physicians whose practice is mainly among Mexican Americans. Although these two stores are maintained by _colonia_ clientele, the Anglo drug stores get much of the _colonia_ trade, judging by the numbers of Mexican Americans to be seen shopping in them at all times, and sitting at the soda fountains.

The barber shops constitute a commercial service in which there appears to be complete lack of contact between Anglo and Mexican. One never encounters a Mexican American in a Main Street barbershop. The _colonia_ has as many barber shops as does the Anglo business section, and many Mexicans get their haircuts in Reynosa, across the river, where the price is much lower than in McAllen. The refusal of one barber on Main Street to serve a Mexican American veteran was exposed to public scrutiny when the local newspaper published a fiery editorial attacking the barber, an "Anglo" who upon investigation turned out to be a Cherokee Indian from Oklahoma!

Finally, the writer has never observed an Anglo American shopping in a store on Guerra Street. There are no services offered by _colonia_ business men which cannot be obtained in the Anglo business section. It should be noted that all the commercial enterprises in the Main Street district are Anglo-owned, with the exception of the restaurant mentioned above and one of the department stores. Similarly, the vast majority of businesses in the _colonia_ are Mexican-owned. The exceptions are the drygoods stores mentioned above, and one of the two loan companies on Guerra Street. There are eleven other loan companies in McAllen, many of them patronized by Mexican Americans.

There is one Mexican American physician in McAllen compared to twenty-five Anglo physicians. Although this physician maintains his office on Main Street, it is probable that his practice is largely, if not totally, among Mexican Americans. Of the Anglos, only two practice largely among Mexicans, but there is no evidence that the others refuse Mexican patients. The folk concepts of medicine described in the previous chapter, plus the fact that few Mexicans can afford physician's fees, are sufficient explanation of the failure of more Mexicans to employ medical services. No data were obtained as to the extent of dental treatment purchased by Mexican Americans, although it may be noted that but one of McAllen's seven dentists is Mexican American, and his office is near Main Street.

Although few Mexican Americans have the occasion or the money to engage in civil suits, there are three Mexican American lawyers in McAllen. These men support themselves primarily by handling the legal affairs of the few substantial Mexican American businessmen and ranchers, the few minor civil suits which arise, selling legal advice to the colonia, executing estates, and so on. The offices of the Mexican American lawyers are located on Main Street, in the building which houses the offices of the Anglo lawyers. When involved in criminal cases, Mexicans prefer Anglo lawyers in the belief that the latter will carry more weight with the Anglo courts and juries.

McAllen has three undertaking establishments, one of them Mexican-owned and located in the _colonia_. There is no indication that the Anglo undertakers refuse Mexican patronage, but it should be noted that there are two cemeteries in McAllen, one for Anglos, regardless of religious faith, the other for Mexican Americans.

In San Antonio, there is an area of about four square blocks located at the western edge of the city's main business section where the vast majority of commercial enterprises are Mexican-owned. Here one can find hotels, theaters, grocery stores, real estate offices, bakeries, bars and restaurants, printing shops, apparel and drygoods shops, furniture shops, jewelry stores, barber shops, cleaning and tailoring establishments, drug stores, music shops, and filling stations which cater almost exclusively to Mexican American trade. In addition, there are a large number of small groceries, bars and restaurants, barber shops, drug stores, and filling stations grouped in small business sections throughout the _colonia_. With one exception, all of the large grocery stores in the _colonia_, most of which are branches of chains, are Anglo-owned.

In the region where the _colonia_ business section merges into the main business section, there are a number of Anglo-owned department stores which cater primarily to Mexican American custom, offering cheaper merchandise at lower prices than the larger department stores in the downtown area. Downtown San Antonio, however, which dwarfs the Mexican American business section, is always crowded with shoppers from the colonia, attracted by the wide range of merchandise lacking in colonia commercial enterprises. Mexican Americans patronize all of the hotels, restaurants, night clubs, specialty shops, and theaters in San Antonio, subject to the limitations imposed by their incomes of course. As in the case of McAllen, it should be noted that those commercial services which draw considerable Mexican American trade employ a larger percentage of Mexican help than do those dependent only on Anglo patronage.

As regards professional services, there are about twelve Mexican American physicians and seven dentists whose practices are mostly confined to the colonia. According to two of these physicians, this number is far from sufficient to care for the number of Mexican Americans seeking medical treatment. Consequently, there are a number of Anglo physicians whose practice is predominantly Mexican. The latter maintain their offices downtown, usually in buildings close to the colonia business section, but all of the Mexican physicians are located within the colonia, most of them in the business section. Two of them operate extensive private clinics with small hospitals attached, but the rest are situated in two-room suites in the colonia drugstores. One Mexican American lawyer in San Antonio has achieved a reputation as a successful criminal lawyer, and a few others manage to obtain enough civil cases to eke out a living, but the majority have political appointments, or sell real estate or insurance for a livelihood.

There are a large number of undertakers in the _colonia_, some of them with impressive establishments and a fleet of ambulances and hearses.

This section may be concluded with a brief mention of intergroup contact in public services. In both McAllen and San Antonio, Mexican Americans come into frequent contact with Anglos in the post office, office buildings, and on the city buses. In McAllen all of the postal clerks and the majority of bus drivers are Anglo, while in San Antonio the majority in both services are Anglo. As regards hospital contact, the Valley hospitals are staffed by Anglos, and the county records of maternity cases hospitalized indicate that a small number of Mexican American women avail themselves of the hospital services.[*] Parallel information in this respect for San Antonio was not obtained.

### Religious Worship

The separation between Anglo and Mexican is complete and explicit in the area of religious worship. There are twenty Protestant churches in McAllen, sixteen of them located in Anglo neighborhoods, the other four in the _colonia_, and two Catholic churches, one in North McAllen, and the other in the _colonia_. The fact that the _colonia_ Protestant churches consist of all-Mexican congregations is indicated by the names they bear, Mexican Methodist, Mexican Baptist, Mexican Christian,

---

[*] See Appendix B.

and Spanish Lutheran, and by their practice of conducting their services entirely in Spanish. Each of these denominations is represented among the Anglo churches, but there is no contact between the two churches of the same denomination. The First Methodist Church, for example, in effect recognizes the existence of its Mexican counterpart but once a year when its members take up a collection to buy Spanish bibles for the Mexican Methodist Church and for all Mexican Americans who will accept them. The writer attended many Sunday services of the Anglo Protestant churches and never observed a Mexican American worshipper in any of them. The appearance of an Anglo at a service of the Mexican Methodist Church was so singular an event that when the writer attended for the first time, many heads were turned inquisitively in his direction, the preacher called upon him for a "message" in the middle of the service, and many of the male members approached him afterward to shake hands, introduce themselves, and say a few words of welcome.

Thirteen different sects are represented among McAllen's sixteen Anglo Protestant churches. The Baptists, with three churches, and the Methodists, with two, are the largest Protestant church groups in McAllen. The First Baptist Church and the First Methodist Church number among their members most of the Anglos with top status in McAllen. Both have impressive church buildings, and the Methodist Church recently completed construction of a well-equipped community center across the street from the church. In contrast to the Methodist Church's approximately 1100 members with its extra Sunday morning service to take care of the overflow, the Mexican Methodist Church has about 75 to 100 active members, who worship in a small, bare wooden edifice quite different from the excellent accommodations enjoyed by the Anglo Methodist churchgoer.

The separation between Anglo and Mexican Protestants to be observed in McAllen is officially and consistently maintained at all organizational levels of the various churches throughout the Southwest. Mexican Methodist Churches, e.g., are not included in the Southwestern Methodist Conference, but are organized into the Southwestern Mexican Methodist Conference. According to the Mexican Methodist minister in McAllen,

> Mexican Methodists are organized into a separate Conference which covers all of Texas and New Mexico. We have affiliation with the Methodist Church, but are not considered part of the Southwest Conference. It is the same in California, which has a separate Conference, and Florida, which has a mission group. In the North, there are also Mexican Methodist Churches, but they are part of the Anglo American Conference they happen to be in geographically because there are not enough of them to form a separate Conference. Geographically, our Latin American Conference is the largest in the UnitedStates. There is no Anglo American Conference which covers an area as large as Texas and New Mexico.

All of the ministers of Mexican Protestant churches encountered by the writer are themselves Mexican. Many of the ministers who hold higher administrative positions in the church hierarchies are also Mexican American.[5]

The separation between Anglo and Mexican in the Catholic churches of McAllen is not nearly so explicitly acknowledged as it is in the Protestant churches, but it exists in fact. The Catholic Church in North McAllen has a few Mexican American members of the "assimilated" middle class group, who live in North McAllen, but the writer never observed any of these in attendance at the masses at this church. The Anglo Catholic Church building, a one-storied modern edifice, was constructed in 1941, although the Church existed for a few years prior to this time. Since then it has expanded rapidly, adding a large parochial school building and a convent. The _colonia_ Catholic Church, although established soon after the founding of McAllen, has never had the funds to improve the old physical plant or to erect new buildings, although a new and larger parochial school building is greatly needed. The Church has finally obtained enough funds to build an adequate convent for its nuns, however. The writer has observed a few Anglos at the Sunday masses held at the _colonia_ church, referred to by informants as the "Mexican church", but the vast majority are Mexican Americans. One of the two priests at this church, both of whom are Anglo, had this to say regarding Anglo attendance:

> All the members of this church are Mexican, except for three or four American families. I don't know why those few don't go to the other church. You see, we don't have territorial parishes here. We have Mexicans coming here who live within a couple of blocks of the other church, so our parishes are not territorial. We do get many Americans coming to the masses, but they are mostly tourists. As far as the Mexicans are concerned, most of those who go to church, come here.

Both Catholic churches maintain parochial schools which offer instruction through the primary grades. The enrollment in the colonia church school is somewhat larger than in the North McAllen church school, which contains 157 pupils. The only Mexican American children in attendance at the latter are those of the few middle class Mexican families who are members of the Anglo church. According to one Mexican American couple residing in North McAllen, the priest at the Anglo church refused to admit their child to the school there and advised them to send him to the colonia church school.[*]

The pervasive lack of intergroup contact which characterizes patterns of religious worship in McAllen exists also in San Antonio. The colonia has a large number of small Mexican Protestant churches where the congregations are all-Mexican, and the other sections of the city have Protestant churches where the attendance is all-Anglo. In San Antonio, however, those Mexican Protestant churches which are not financially self-sufficient look to the Anglo church of the same denomination for aid. A small Mexican Methodist church and welfare center, for example, located in the heart of the brothel district, receives substantial financial assistance from a number of Anglo American Methodists. The Mexican Christian Church in the colonia, whose minister proudly informed the writer that the church has finally become self-supporting after years of struggle, has received a great deal of aid in the past from members of the equivalent Anglo church in San Antonio.

---

[*] This incident is described infra, p. 459.

From time to time these Anglo donors visit the _colonia_ church to which they have contributed money, but their purpose is to assess the progress of the church rather than to worship in common with their Mexican brethren. At a special Sunday service and dinner held at the Mexican Christian church to celebrate the final liquidation of the church debt, the only Anglos present were the writer and a few of the Anglo social workers from the nearby Mexican Christian settlement house, although invitations had been sent to various Anglo benefactors.

San Antonio's 142,000 Mexican Americans, plus the fact that San Antonio is the seat of an archdiocese, accounts for the large number of Catholic churches to be found there. As in McAllen, the separation between Anglo Catholics and Mexican Catholics is well-nigh complete. The largest Catholic church, and one of the oldest, is San Fernando Cathedral, located on San Antonio's Main Plaza, which divides the downtown section from the _colonia_ business district. Despite its central location, Mexican informants stated that one rarely sees an Anglo at a Sunday mass. Since Anglos never invade the _colonia_ except on sightseeing tours or in search of local color and Mexican cuisine, the _colonia_ Catholic churches are seldom visited by Anglo Catholics. Similarly Anglo Catholics have informed the writer that they never see Mexicans attending their churches although they know of Mexicans who live in their parishes in "mixed" residential areas. About ten years ago,

the Archbishop of San Antonio abolished by decree the
"national", or ethnic, parishes into which the city was
divided by the Church as part of his campaign to bring
together Anglo and Mexican Catholics. At present, the
parishes are called territorial, but the Archbishop's efforts
have wrought little or no change, due in part to the fact
that parishes still remain largely coterminous with ethnic
residential concentrations, and in part to the inclinations
of both Anglo and Mexicans. Even in the "mixed" areas, where
Mexicans now live in the territorial parishes of predominantly
Anglo churches, most of them continue to attend San Fernando
Cathedral or one of the <u>colonia</u> churches.

## Informal Social Intercourse and Intermarriage

The pervasive separation between Anglos and Mexicans
already observed as characteristic in the residential and
institutional patterns described in previous sections is also
to be found in the area of personal relations. Commensalism,
home visiting, intimate friendships, and cross-sex relations
between the groups are not participated in by the majority
of Mexicans and Anglos. The field materials yield many
instances in which Mexican Americans demonstrated inability
to cope with informal social situations in which Anglo Americans were also present due in part to their lack of experience
with such situations. The record of the writer's own first
contacts with Mexican American informants provides the most
detailed and complete account of this pattern. Almost

invariably in first contacts it was apparent that the informant was experiencing feelings of constraint and discomfort, did not know what to do with his hands or his body, searched frantically for something to say, and often displayed an evident desire to escape from the situation. When the encounter occurred at the home of the informant, other members of the family present would sit in silence, occasionally stealing side-glances at the writer, and would respond to remarks directed to them with brief, non-committal replies. Upon further acquaintance, as the sharp awareness of the writer as an Anglo began to fade, the constraint and discomfort would usually disappear, but would reappear upon first contact with the writer's wife or other Anglos introduced into the relationship.

Consistent with the gulf maintained in the recreational patterns described above, there is no evidence of intergroup contact in at-home visiting and entertaining. Within both Anglo and Mexican groups there is a great deal of easy, informal "dropping in" by acquaintances and friends, but this activity is never extended by members of one group to include members of the other. Anglo Americans may occasionally be invited to an "open house" presented by a middle class Mexican family in honor of a child's graduation from college or like important event, or they may be invited to a Mexican American wedding, but there is no indication that similar invitations are extended by Anglos to Mexicans. Where Anglos do attend such affairs, commensalism usually occurs. "Social sets" and "cliques" exist within both Anglo and Mexican groups, but never embrace members of both.*

In view of the lack of joint participation which characterizes the patterns of voluntary intergroup contact described in this chapter, it is not surprising to find that intimate friendships between Anglos and Mexicans are virtually non-existent. The level at which friendships are established between members of the two groups is illustrated by the comment of an Anglo informant who stated, "I have some good friends among the Mexicans, and we get along fine, but I wouldn't associate with them or anything like that because I like to stay in my own class. You can be friendly with them, but that's as far as I want it to go." Occasionally one finds a relationship between a middle class Anglo and Mexican which both refer to as a "friendship", but these appear to be motivated by mutual need and mutual profit, as in the case of professional men and politicians, and will be dealt with below. Such a relationship is limited to the two participants, and does not involve home visiting and commensalism. Contact is usually made "at the office" of over a cup of coffee in a restaurant.

---

\* There is a certain amount of informal social intercourse between Anglos and Mexicans which is a concomitant of contacts in the spheres of occupations, political action, and voluntary associations, and which involves commensalism as well, but these patterns will be taken up in the following chapters.

No evidence could be obtained regarding the extent of extra-marital miscegenation between Anglos and Mexicans, since all such affairs are of course conducted clandestinely. There are Mexican prostitutes available to Anglos in McAllen, but probably very few due to the thriving brothels across the river where the prices are lower. In San Antonio, the city's major brothel district is located in the colonia. As for cross-sex social intercourse between the groups, the rare sight of an Anglo and a Mexican appearing together in public is always an occasion for stares, nudges, and whispered comments on the part of both Anglos and Mexicans.

In McAllen, the writer knew personally of five cases of intermarriage, four of them consisting of Mexican males and Anglo females. Of the four Mexican males, one is the owner of a bar and night club, one is a Methodist preacher, one a member of McAllen's most prominent Mexican American family, and the fourth is a truck driver. In the fifth case of intermarriage, that of the Anglo male and Mexican female, the former is a citrus grove care worker. In addition, the writer learned of the existence of four other intermarriages. In San Antonio, the writer was also personally acquainted with five cases of intermarriage, all of them involving Mexican males and Anglo females. Four of the Mexicans were professional men and one a businessman. Here, too, the writer knew of a number of other intermarriages. The mayor of San Antonio is the product of a union between an Anglo male and a Mexican female, and is himself married to a Mexican American woman.

The following figures represent the totals of licensed ingroup and intergroup marriages for three selected months of the years indicated in the county in which McAllen is located, and provide a rough index of the rate of legalized intermarriage:[6]

|  |  | Ingroup |  | Intergroup |  |
|---|---|---|---|---|---|
|  |  |  |  | Mexican Male | Anglo Male |
| Year |  | Anglo | Mexican | Anglo Female | Mexican Female |
| 1910 | January | 0 | 7 | 0 | 0 |
|  | May | 1 | 5 | 0 | 0 |
|  | September | 1 | 4 | 0 | 0 |
| 1920 | January | 5 | 28 | 0 | 2 |
|  | May | 7 | 34 | 1 | 2 |
|  | September | 7 | 38 | 1 | 4 |
| 1930 | January | 14 | 29 | 0 | 0 |
|  | May | 20 | 55 | 0 | 1 |
|  | September | 15 | 44 | 0 | 1 |
| 1940 | January | 33 | 41 | 1 | 1 |
|  | May | 23 | 47 | 1 | 0 |
|  | September | 37 | 79 | 2 | 5 |
| 1947 | January | 54 | 92 | 0 | 4 |
|  | May | 34 | 119 | 0 | 3 |
|  | September | 38 | 86 | 0 | 2 |

The patterns of intergroup social intercourse in San Antonio do not deviate significantly from the McAllen case. The life history materials reveal that informants established a number of intimate friendships with Anglos during their childhood and school years, but in every case these friendships did not persist into adulthood, nor do the informants have any close Anglo friends at present. In San Antonio, there is an organization whose stated objective is the promotion of social intercourse between Anglos and Mexicans, but its activities are limited to monthly gatherings at the homes of the members, who are middle class Mexican and Anglo Americans.

A really significant deviation from the McAllen patterns of intergroup contact in general is to be found in Rio Grande City, located in Starr County thirty-eight miles west of McAllen, the population of which is ninety-five per cent Mexican American. The small Anglo minority jointly participates with Mexican Americans in all of the areas considered in this chapter, and social interaction is ordered on a class basis rather than an ethnic basis. There exist close friendships between Anglos and Mexicans, home visiting and entertaining, and a much greater amount of intermarriage. Starr County, like Brownsville and Laredo, has a long tradition of inter-mingling between Anglo and Mexican which has undergone certain modifications as a result of the recent influx of Anglos who have migrated there in the wake of extensive oil developments, but joint participation is still a dominant characteristic of the patterns of intergroup contact.

The materials presented in this chapter establish the fact that in those situations where contact between Anglos and Mexicans is voluntary, such as residence, education, recreation, religious worship, and social intercourse, the characteristic feature is separation rather than common participation, and that where intergroup contact is necessary as a result of mutual dependence, as in commercial and professional services, it is held to the minimum sufficient to accomplish the objectives of the participants. In those situations of voluntary contact where the gulf is breached, as in the case of the intergroup "friendships" described above, it was found that the relationship partakes of the character of commercial contacts in that it is maintained by the mutual needs of the participants who profit by the arrangement. The unequal distribution of rewards and privileges between Anglo and Mexican has also been partially demonstrated through the description of differential accommodations and facilities apportioned to the two groups and through the preliminary indication of the relative scale of commercial enterprises owned and operated by the members of each group. The next three chapters will attempt to examine, within the contexts of the occupational structure and selected aspects of the social organization, the nature and role of the dynamic factors which have led to the establishment of the dominant-subordinate system; the succeeding chapter will take up the mechanisms by means of which the system is maintained, focusing on the exclusion devices employed by the dominant group, and the final chapter will undertake a parallel treatment of the subordinate group, focusing on its reactive adjustments.

## Chapter V

## THE OCCUPATIONAL STRUCTURE*

For the purposes of this study, the occupational sphere is the most strategic area for the consideration of dynamic factors of dominance and subordination since the most frequent contact between the Anglo and Mexican groups occurs in the performance of their occupational roles. Thus the description and analysis of the local agricultural economy, characteristics of major occupational role categories, employer-employee relations, and motivational aspects of the occupational system may be expected to throw light on the role of the dynamic factors conducive to ascription of subordinate status. Such a description and analysis should provide insight into the mutual expectations of Anglos and Mexicans in the context of their occupational relationships; into the varying conceptions of Anglos and Mexicans as to what constitute rewards and privileges; and into the principal power relationships and their role in the unequal distribution of rewards and privileges.

---

* The materials presented in this chapter refer primarily to the rural rather than the urban research site. No attempt was made to gather parallel data for San Antonio on the economy and occupational structure because of the relatively greater complexity of these aspects of the urban site and the limited amount of time spent there. However, to the extent that the data permit, significant similarities and differences between the two communities will be indicated.

## The Agricultural Economy[*]

In order to provide a context for the discussion of occupational structure, it will be helpful to describe briefly the nature of the local economy. The development of agriculture in the Valley in the past two decades is graphically illustrated by the following table:

Trend of Annual Farm Cash Income by Selected Products[1]
Lower Rio Grande Valley  (Three Counties)
(In thousands of dollars)

| Year | Cotton | Cottonseed | Eggs | Milk Products | Fruits & Vegetables |
|---|---|---|---|---|---|
| 1927 | 5,731 | 748 | 832 | 658 | 5,171 |
| 1928 | 9,521 | 1,311 | 909 | 684 | 9,845 |
| 1929 | 8,054 | 1,470 | 1,043 | 804 | 12,084 |
| 1930 | 4,988 | 894 | 812 | 923 | 15,712 |
| 1931 | 1,917 | 247 | 562 | 703 | 9,659 |
| 1932 | 1,091 | 93 | 491 | 512 | 10,722 |
| 1933 | 2,433 | 389 | 495 | 614 | 5,953 |
| 1934 | 5,025 | 932 | 666 | 750 | 6,093 |
| 1935 | 2,698 | 545 | 345 | 950 | 7,219 |
| 1936 | 4,465 | 945 | 800 | 1,159 | 11,470 |
| 1937 | 8,261 | 1,531 | 819 | 1,101 | 22,384 |
| 1938 | 5,257 | 1,094 | 762 | 1,526 | 18,523 |
| 1939 | 4,332 | 672 | 699 | 1,382 | 20,031 |
| 1940 | 4,697 | 944 | 775 | 1,532 | 14,938 |
| 1941 | 4,333 | 1,205 | 1,012 | 1,863 | 18,253 |
| 1942 | 8,554 | 1,974 | 1,243 | 2,910 | 34,597 |
| 1943 | 9,784 | 2,238 | 1,393 | 3,318 | 65,221 |
| 1944 | 16,675 | 4,012 | 2,105 | 3,198 | 92,331 |
| 1945 | 25,456 | 6,092 | 1,390 | 3,125 | 98,084 |
| 1946 | 34,408 | 6,185 | 1,470 | 3,414 | 89,256 |

---

[*] All of the facts and figures presented in this first section refer to the county since a consideration of the town alone, which functions primarily as a center of goods and services for the surrounding area, would reveal only the less important aspect of the local agricultural economy. For the purposes of this study, the description of retail trade outlets in the previous chapter will suffice as an indication of the town economy.

In 1940, 687,225 of the 986,240 acres which comprise the approximate land area of Hidalgo County were utilized in farms, a proportion of 69.7% of the total acreage.[2] The 5,094 farms in the county had the following distribution by size in 1940:[3]

| Acres | Number of Farms |
|---|---|
| Under 3 | 3 |
| 3 to 9 | 908 |
| 10 to 29 | 1950 |
| 10 to 19 | 1210 |
| 30 to 49 | 750 |
| 50 to 69 | 335 |
| 70 to 99 | 313 |
| 100 to 139 | 259 |
| 140 to 179 | 157 |
| 175 to 179 | 12 |
| 180 to 219 | 96 |
| 220 to 259 | 66 |
| 260 to 379 | 113 |
| 380 to 499 | 40 |
| 500 to 699 | 26 |
| 700 to 999 | 31 |
| 1000 and over | 46 |

These figures indicate that roughly two-thirds of the county's farms are under 50 acres and that the great majority of these are under 29 acres. For the leading type of farm, the citrus grove, the typical size is 10 to 30 acres, according to informants. As to land tenure, the census yields the following information for the county in 1940:[4]

| | Number of farms | Acreage |
|---|---|---|
| Full owners | 2119 | 319,532 |
| Part owners (portion owned and portion rented) | 663 | 126,775 |
| Managers | 643 | 73,307 |
| Tenants | 1669 | 167,601 |

Proportion of tenancy: 32.8%

The major types of crops of the McAllen area, and of the Valley in general, are citrus fruits, cotton, and garden vegetables, in that order.[5] The citrus crop is considered "the backbone of Valley agriculture", and the grapefruit usually exceeds the orange in volume produced and cash value obtained. The five kinds of grapefruit mature annually between October 1 and December 15, and the three kinds of oranges mature between October 15 and February 1.[6] These dates do not necessarily indicate the citrus harvest time since citrus keeps on the trees after maturity without deterioration. Federal and state fruit fly regulations require that all grapefruit and most oranges be harvested by July 17 of each year, so the grower can pick his fruit any time between maturity and this date. What this actually means is that citrus harvest time extends from October 15 through July 15 of the following year, with the picking activity varying in intensity with price fluctuations and the weather. When prices are high, the grower hastens to "strip" his groves, and when prices are low, he holds off in the hope that they will rise again. The major part of the cotton crop is planted in March and harvested in July and August. Unlike citrus, cotton must be harvested when mature, so the cotton harvest period is one of intense sustained activity. The most important vegetable crops, by value and volume of crops harvested, are tomatoes, cabbage, carrots, beets, broccoli, snap and lima beans, and to a lesser extent, sweet corn and potatoes. There is no off season in the harvesting of vegetables except in late summer and early fall. Some sort of crop is harvested during every month except August, September, and October, as the following chart indicates:

| Vegetable | Crop | Planting Date | Maturing Date |
|---|---|---|---|
| Tomatoes | Spring | Jan. 1 to Feb. 1 | May 1 to June 1 |
|  | Fall | July 15 to Aug. 15 | Nov. 15 to Dec. 15 |
| Cabbage | Winter | Sept. 1 to Oct. 1 | Jan. 1 to Feb. 1 |
|  | Spring | Oct. 15 to Dec. 15 | Feb. 15 to Mar. 15 |
|  | Fall | Aug. 1 to Sept. 1 | Dec. 1 to Jan. 1 |
| Carrots | Winter | Sept. 1 to Nov. 1 | Dec. 1 to Feb. 1 |
|  | Spring | Nov. 1 to Jan. 1 | Feb. 1 to Mar. 1 |
|  | Fall | Aug. 15 to Sept. 15 | Nov. 15 to Dec. 15 |
| Beets | Winter | Oct. 1 to Dec. 1 | Dec. 1 to Feb. 15 |
|  | Spring | Dec. 15 to Jan. 15 | Feb. 15 to April 1 |
|  | Fall | Sept. 1 to Oct. 1 | Nov. 1 to Dec. 15 |
| Broccoli | Winter | Oct. 1 to Dec. 1 | Jan. 1 to Mar. 1 |
| Beans (snap) | Spring | Feb. 15 to Mar. 15 | April 15 to May 15 |
| (lima) | Spring | Feb. 15 to Mar. 15 | May 1 to June 1 |
| (snap) | Fall | Sept. 1 to Oct. 15 | Nov. 1 to Dec. 15 |
| (lima) | Fall | Sept. 1 to Oct. 1 | Nov. 15 to Jan. 15 |
| Sweet Corn | Spring | Jan. 1 to March 1 | April 1 to July 1 |
| Potatoes | Spring | Jan. 15 to Feb. 15 | April 15 to May 15 |
|  | Fall | Sept. 15 to Oct. 1 | Dec. 15 to Jan. 1 |

Other vegetables grown in the McAllen area are celery, chard, cucumber, lettuce, okra, onions, parsley, peas, peppers, radishes, spinach, and turnips. Other fruits are tangerines, lemons, limes, canteloupe, and watermelon.

The harvest dates for citrus, cotton, and vegetables indicate that there is activity almost year round and that the few lulls are filled with crop planting, but the intensity and extent vary greatly in different seasons depending on a number of factors of which the weather is probably the most influential. Generally speaking, the spring vegetable "deal" (in the local idiom all harvests are called deals) is more voluminous and profitable than the winter or fall deals because climatic conditions in the Valley usually permit higher grade products at this time of year. However, the local growers are always apprehensive of unexpected late freezes in February and March (the average date of the last killing frost in Spring is February 1) which can destroy the spring vegetable and the cotton crops, just as early freezes in the Fall (the average date of the first killing frost in Fall is December 21) can affect the citrus crop. The winter crops of cabbage, carrots, and beets require normal "winter" temperatures in October and November for satisfactory growth. If the weather remains warm too long, these crops are hardly worth harvesting. The spring vegetable deal and the cotton deal which follows soon after it require a delicately timed distribution of rainfall (irrigation is discussed below) if both harvests are to be successful. The decisive role played by the weather in the success or failure of various important crops can be effectively illustrated by briefly tracing the progress and fate of the spring tomato deal and the cotton deal during the period of the study. That year (1948), the largest acreage ever devoted to cotton in the Valley was planted during late February and March. Abnormally cold weather during this

period necessitated the replanting of much of the crop
and continuing cool weather delayed growth to the extent
that a late harvest was predicted. There were no freezes,
however, so the tomatoes survived. Growers feared the loss
of both crops when the expected April rains were delayed, but
the rains came during the third week in April and hopes were
again high for a successful season. The rains did not continue, however, and although this did not seriously affect the
tomato deal, the cotton began to deteriorate, and by the
middle of May the growers were gloomily predicting the loss
of the cotton crop if rain did not come within the next two
weeks. Heavy rains appeared during the last week in May, and
the cotton growers were jubilant. Unfortunately, the spring
tomatoes were maturing precisely at this time, and the heavy
rainfall bloated and spotted the tomatoes to the point where
the volume and quality of the crop were reduced severely, the
volume being half that of the previous year. Again the rain
failed to continue, and to make matters worse, June was an
abnormally hot month in the Valley. By the end of June, when
the investigator left the Valley, the cotton growers definitely
knew that as a result of the lack of rain and the high temperatures their yield would be an extremely poor one.

Irrigation has always been the major means of coping with
the inadequate rainfall of the Valley area. Indeed, it was by
means of irrigation that the Valley was transformed from arid
brushland into a highly fertile and productive agricultural
region. However, the incautious and unregulated exploitation

of the waters of the Rio Grande has resulted in recent years in the drastically reduced effectiveness of irrigation as a compensation for inadequate rainfall. In 1940, 4,094 of Hidalgo County's 5,094 farms were wholly or in part dependent on irrigation.[7] The administration of water distribution in the Valley is in the hands of the several water districts which were formed by groups of growers located in a particular geographical area usually coterminous with the area of a Valley city and its hinterland but in no way controlled by the municipal authorities. Each enterprise is cooperative in that the members contribute funds, in proportion to the amount of water they use, to provide the necessary technical facilities and personnel for distribution of the water. There is no overall coordinating authority in the Valley, and each district operates independently without reference to the others. According to an engineer employed by the U. S. Bureau of Reclamation office in McAllen, the system is chaotic and has developed haphazardly, determined by the local problems within a district and without regard to the overall needs of the Valley. Each district pumps water from that part of the river most convenient to the district, and there is no limitation of amount that can be pumped in proportion to the needs of the members of the other districts. The lack of a centralized control of water distribution has thus made it possible for any district to divert as much water from the river as it pleases, and for individual growers whose farms are contiguous to the river to pump their own water and thus even dispense with the services of the district enterprises.

Due to the constant expansion of irrigated land which has occurred during the Valley's short history, the lack of clear definition of water rights as reflected in the system of water use with the consequent indiscriminate exploitation of water resources,* and the lack of adequate storage facilities, i.e. dams, along the whole length of the Rio Grande to preserve water in times of abundance for use in times of scarcity,** the Valley is now facing a serious water shortage which makes irrigation an extremely unstable substitute for rainfall and which threatens to become chronic. To complicate the grower's problems, excessive irrigation has taken its toll in land fertility in that the water table, the surface formed by the water in a saturated soil, in most Valley land has risen to a level where excessive quantities of salts injurious to plant growth have accumulated from the Rio Grande water. Excessive salt accumulations go hand in hand with high water

---

\* Some districts require twice as much water as they should due to poorly lined canals which waste half their contents through seepage.

\*\* At the time of the study, the U. S. Bureau of Reclamation was planning the construction of a huge dam to impound Rio Grande waters a few hundred miles west of the Valley which would also involve the construction of a gravity canal to provide direct irrigation of Valley lands from the dam reservoir, as well as a master drainage system to alleviate the high water table problem. These latter projects required the consent of Valley growers since they would eventually have to repay the costs of construction. This project would not provide the final solution, however, since the dam would provide irrigation for 580,000 acres and there are already 700,000 acres in the Valley requiring irrigation, aside from the expected continued expansion.

tables. According to one local Bureau of Reclamation engineer, "The excessive accumulation of salts has had a profound effect on Valley agricultural incomes. During the period 1925 to 1945, while salt content of the soil more than doubled, it is estimated that losses in income amounted to $400 per acre."[8]

Thus, with regard to the strategically important irrigation facilities, the McAllen grower is subjected to the chronic problem of continuing acreage expansion versus a declining water supply, for which there is probably no permanent solution under the present system. An indication of the tensions which can be generated by the growing realization of this dilemma was provided during the period of the study when one of the Valley's most prominent growers publicly announced that water users with "senior rights" (since there is no system of clearly defined rights this simply meant those derived from long usage) should be protected from those with "junior rights".[9] Presumably the conflict would be joined on the issue of what distinguishes senior from junior rights.

The local growers dispose of their products, still unharvested, to one or more of the many packing and shipping "sheds" and canneries located in McAllen. The division of labor between grower and packer is not always well defined, since some packers own citrus groves or vegetable farms, and in the case of one large Valley-wide cooperative, the grower members control their own facilities for packing, canning, and shipping. The average citrus or vegetable grower has three alternatives for disposing of his products. He can sell his whole crop early in the growing season to a buyer who is willing to gamble on futures. The price he will receive, which is quoted by the acre, is determined by the buyer on the basis of estimates for the season he has obtained as to probable national consumption of the product, the extent of local supplies in major consumer regions, and likely crop yields in Florida, California, and other citrus and vegetable producing areas. If he chooses this alternative for disposal of his crop, the grower's total profits for the season will probably be lower than if he plays the open market, but he has the advantage of being guaranteed a minimum sum and no longer has to worry about crop failure or price fluctuations as the crop is the property of the buyer once the transaction is made. A second alternative is to sell the entire crop to one buyer at any time after the crop reaches maturity, and the third is to sell the crop piecemeal to one or a number of buyers, waiting when prices are low, selling when prices are high. The latter is the method of disposal most frequently employed by the local growers. In the case of citrus, the grower has eight months (November to June) in which to dispose of his crop, and thus has the leisure to withhold his fruit in a down market and dispose of it in an up market. The grower usually avoids the first two alternatives because they mean putting all his eggs in one basket, whereas disposing of his product a little at a time to the highest bidder when prices are going up at least gives him the illusion that he can exert a measure of control on what is usually a highly fluctuating and unpredictable price market. During the early part of the harvest season, if prices are climbing, he will sell only his poorest quality fruit and withhold the rest, and if prices suddenly begin to fall, he will sell some of his crop and hold on to the rest in the hope that the market will improve again.

Since the Valley's most important and lucrative markets are the Eastern and Middlewestern states, freight rates are extremely costly, and are probably the most important single factor contributing to the small margin of profit the grower has to operate on. The large number of middle men between grower and consumer also contribute to this small margin. Growers estimate that it costs $10 to $15 to grow a ton of grapefruit, e.g., each year. Although red and pink grapefruit sometimes bring up to $50 a ton, the grower is usually hopeful that all of his grapefruit will average between $15 and $20 a ton for the season. Actually, for the 1947-48 season, which was characterized by a tremendous drop in prices from the high wartime levels, the general concensus of opinion in the Valley was that the grower did not even meet his growing costs for his citrus. Much indignation was expressed at the fact that grapefruit dropped as low as $5 a ton for a good part of the season.

The fluctuations in prices are often disconcertingly rapid. To select a few random examples which occurred during the period of the study, the market for winter cabbage opened at $100 a ton and slid to $20 a ton within a matter of weeks although the cabbage deal was still young, and in May grapefruit prices were twice as high per ton as they were in April. For winter tomatoes, the price to the grower began at 13 cents a pound, but two weeks after maturity the price had dropped to 8 to 10 cents a pound. Under such conditions, the grower will fight for an additional ½ cent per pound, as is illustrated by the following excerpt from the field notes:

> While we were in town, V's trucker came in to tell him that he had delivered a truckload of tomatoes to a packing shed, but the shed offered only 5½ cents per pound. V phoned another shed and learned they were offering 6 cents, so he told them he was sending them a load. A second load was in the fields ready for hauling. Then V called the shed offering 5½ cents and said he could get 6 cents for the tomatoes already unloaded at this shed. The shed man told him to pick them up. V instructed the trucker to pick up the first load and deliver it to the other shed. We drove back to V's house. At the house, V received a phone call from the shed which had offered 5½ cents informing him that he would be paid 6 cents, so we had to drive rapidly to overtake the trucker who was already on the way to pick up the load. V said the half-cent a pound is important on a big load because with the additional money he can pay for his labor and have the rest clear.

The factors which boost and lower fruit and vegetable prices in the Valley are too complex to be gone into here, but it is probable that the relative success and failure of Florida and California crops, as well as other fruit and vegetable producing areas, have much to do with the fluctuations. Valley growers view these areas very competitively.

A frost or crop failure for any other reason in competing areas is front page news in the Valley, and certainly not regarded as bad news. Aside from selling piecemeal as a means of coping with fluctuating prices, the grower tries to affect the situation by obtaining a better price from the buyer, the only individual he comes in contact with in the chain of disposal between himself and the consumer. Bargaining between grower and buyer is institutionalized. The buyer can always be expected to depreciate the quality and size of the product and the grower to threaten to take his product elsewhere. The insecurity on the part of the grower induced by the price fluctuations sometimes results in a tendency to define the buyer as a generalized cause of his problems, but the real need of the buyer under the present arrangement as a means of disposing of his product sufficiently restrains the grower in this potential conflict.

Beyond providing a setting for the discussion of the occupational structure which follows, this brief presentation of the local economy has brought out two considerations which are significant for the purposes of this study. In the theoretical chapter, intragroup tensions and insecurity were referred to as one of the important sources of potential intergroup conflict.* In this case, the chronic problem of continuing acreage expansion versus a declining water supply has resulted in a potential conflict for water rights between

---

\* See *supra*, pp. 32-33

members of the dominant group, and the strain in the grower-buyer relationship has just been indicated. The second consideration is that the examination of the economy has revealed the instability introduced by such uncontrollable elements as the weather, irrigation problems, and a seemingly capricious market. Although the farm laborer must of course feel some of the insecurity that stems from these sources, it is the grower* who directly bears the brunt of these problems.

## General Aspects of the Occupational Structure and the "Wetback"

Seasonal peaks of harvest activity, governed by variable weather, water scarcity, and fluctuating market conditions, characterize a local economy which has important implications for the occupational structure of the McAllen community. These seasonal peaks of activity are further accentuated by the nature of the local technology, since the preharvest operations of planting, irrigation, and cultivation are largely mechanized, requiring a relatively small amount of labor at periodic intervals. The harvest is the most important single factor in the active functioning of the field worker, the packing shed worker, and the crewleader, who represent the principal levels of the statistically broad labor base

---

* So far as could be ascertained, the vast majority of growers are Anglo Americans, while farm laborer, as will be indicated below, is synonymous with Mexican American. Throughout this discussion, the reference has been primarily to the two-thirds of the county's growers whose farms are under 50 acres in size. The larger landowners, presumably, have a larger capital, and a volume of production which compensates for the narrow profit margin.

of the occupational hierarchy. The peak periods of demand for labor services are during the winter and spring harvests of citrus and vegetables and during the midsummer harvest of cotton. The demand for labor decreases in the late spring and early summer and reaches its lowest point in the annual cycle between August and October. Even during the peak periods, the demand varies considerably on a daily and weekly basis due to weather and prices.

The extreme variability of labor needs places a premium on a labor force which is fluid and flexible in that its members can be hired and fired at will, are always available when needed, and who conveniently drop out of sight with no claims on the employer when their services are not required. This is the ideal, of course, from the point of view of the employer, but nevertheless the latter has come close to achieving it with the advent of the "wetback"[*], or illegal entrant from Mexico. Besides fulfilling these conditions of fluidity and flexibility, the wetback will also work for an extremely low wage, which of course further enhances his attractiveness in the eyes of the employer. Since the presence of the wetback has had important effects on the functioning of the occupational role structure to be discussed below, some explanatory remarks are in order here.

In August, 1942, an agreement was effected between the American and Mexican Governments which provided for the temporary

---

[*] The wetback derives his name from the manner of his arrival in the United States, i.e., by swimming or wading the Rio Grande.

importation of Mexican agricultural workers into the United States to alleviate the labor shortage caused by World War II. In the summer of 1943, although permitting the agreement to continue in other states, the Mexican Government placed a ban on the importation of its laborers into Texas giving as its reason the discriminatory conditions which existed in that state with regard to Mexicans and persons of Mexican descent.[10] The wetback phenomenon resulted from the continuing desire of Mexican workers to enter nearby Texas with its vast agricultural operations and the continuing demand for their labor on the part of the Valley employers.* The ban coincided with the loss of a large percentage of the resident labor pool, part of which was attracted to the higher wages in industry and part drawn off by the armed forces. Local estimates of the average number of wetbacks to be found in the Valley area range between forty and fifty thousand, depending on seasonal requirements. U. S. Immigration officials apprehend and deport wetbacks when they encounter them on the highways or in the towns, but ordinarily do not venture into the fields and brush, where the majority of wetbacks live and work. The immigration Service and Border Patrol with their slender staffs cannot control the brisk traffic of wetbacks across the long river border, even when they want to.

Although the standard wetback wage is only 20 to 25 cents

---

* Illegal entry of Mexicans seeking work has been occurring on a small scale since at least the twenties, however. See Paul C. Taylor, An American-Mexican Frontier, pp. 138-139.

an hour, it is higher than the prevailing wage for unskilled agricultural labor in Mexico, an economic differential which provides the major attraction for the wetbacks despite the fact that higher food costs in the Valley probably cancel out part of the difference. The wetback's illegal status makes him amenable to whatever wages and working conditions the employer chooses to impose. The very real threat of deportation plus the fact that there is always another worker ready to take his place effectively insures the tractability of the wetback labor force. The following comments, the first by an Anglo grower and the second by a Mexican American crewleader, indicate the advantages to be obtained by employing wetback help and illustrate the conditions under which the wetback works:

> My partner and I have a couple of shacks out at the farm and we put up some Mexicans there whenever we need them. There's a Mexican who has a little store down on the highway, and he can get us some wetbacks whenever we need them. That way we only pay for help when we need it. We work them for two or three days at a time, for planting, fertilizing, and irrigation. We've had a couple of boys staying in the shacks during this irrigating we're doing now, and for them the place is ideal because it's four miles off the highway and there's not much chance of Border Patrol cars. In our grove care business it's the same as out at the farm. Whenever we need any help, that is, when we get a job for grove care, my partner just gets in his car, drives down to the canal banks, and picks up as many men as he needs, works them as long as the job lasts, and then lets them go. He knows where and how to get wetback help.
>
> As far as the farmers are concerned, the wetbacks are the best kind of labor to have around here. You don't have to worry about housing them or taking care of them if they get sick. All you do is work them and then forget about them ... The people here don't like them coming because it makes it hard for them. I

can't say anything against their coming because
I need them. These people who own their own
homes and have to pay taxes can't live on $2.50
a day, and that's about all they can make with this other
labor here. It stands to reason that I'm not going to
pay $3 or $4 a day for labor when I can get it for $2.
So the people who live here have to go North in the
summer to make wages they can live on. It's hard on
them, but I don't know what can be done about it. You
know, the people from Mexico will come here whenever
they get a chance because they can't make more than
4 or 5 pesos a day in Mexico. They can get 10 pesos
a day here, which is twice as much.

The second statement indicates the most immediate effect of the presence of the wetback on local resident unskilled labor, the fact that the latter must work for the wage the wetback is willing to accept or choose displacement in the form of migration to other regions for part of the year in search of a better wage. This depression of wages and displacement of Mexican American field labor by the wetback has had substantial repercussions in the functioning of the occupational structure and will be referred to in a number of contexts in the rest of this chapter. Although the wetbacks have infiltrated extensively into the Valley's labor force, the writer made no systematic attempt to include them directly in the investigation and none were used as informants. The Mexican American group referred to throughout this study is the resident group, whose residence in the United States dates back to the great immigration that began in 1910 or to an earlier period.

The various occupations to be found in the occupation system of the McAllen community may be classified into several broad role categories on the basis of common characteristics, such as functional content, required skills, job stability and availability, remuneration, and degree of mobility, which distinguish each group of occupations from all the others. These broad categories may be termed the labor role, the white collar role, the businessman and grower role, and the professional role. Before entering on a discussion of the labor role, which is the most significant in many ways from the point of view of the Mexican American group, one general fact with regard to the occupational system as a whole should be indicated explicitly, a fact which justifies the use of an occupational role classification in this case. In an agricultural society, the labor functions are typically embedded in a nexus of meaningful particularistic relationships in such a way that *in themselves* these functions are only one of many bases for defining the status of the individual. In the agricultural society under consideration, however, as in the American industrial society, the division of labor has developed to such an extent that we find occupational roles and associated exchange relationships almost completely segregated from all other contexts since the performance of an occupational role has become the principal means of obtaining access to status in the larger community as well as to life-sustaining goods and services, and thus has become the central role in the life of the individual.

## The Labor Role

The following table* gives some indication of the relative distribution of Anglo and Mexican Americans in the various occupations which can be classified under the labor role category:

### Labor Role Occupations in McAllen, 1947

| Occupation | Anglo American Male | Anglo American Female | Mexican American Male | Mexican American Female |
|---|---|---|---|---|
| Bricklayers | 9 | 0 | 37 | 0 |
| Building Construction Workers | 50 | 0 | 4 | 0 |
| Butchers | 8 | 0 | 18 | 0 |
| Cabinet Makers | 6 | 0 | 1 | 0 |
| Cafe Employees | 0 | 11 | 11 | 3 |
| Cannery Workers | 0 | 0 | 41 | 10 |
| Caretakers and Janitors | 0 | 0 | 14 | 0 |
| Carpenters | 44 | 0 | 40 | 0 |
| Cooks and Bakers | 7 | 0 | 40 | 0 |
| Dairymen | 3 | 0 | 0 | 0 |
| Domestic Servants | 0 | 11 | 0 | 117 |
| Dragline Operators | 7 | 0 | 0 | 0 |
| Electricians | 22 | 0 | 4 | 0 |
| Foremen | 10 | 0 | 0 | 0 |
| Hotel Employees | 4 | 6 | 9 | 3 |
| House Movers | 0 | 0 | 2 | 0 |
| Laborers | 25 | 0 | 528 | 4 |
| Machinists | 14 | 0 | 1 | 0 |
| Mechanics | 48 | 0 | 35 | 0 |
| Oil Field Workers | 28 | 0 | 1 | 0 |
| Orchard Workers | 5 | 0 | 1 | 0 |
| Painters | 21 | 0 | 40 | 0 |
| Plasterers | 0 | 0 | 1 | 0 |

---

\* The source of this information, the McAllen City Directory, cannot be considered very reliable, but is used because it is the only source available. The Directory census-taker evidently made no attempt to define and impose occupational categories, simply using the term supplied by the informant. The figures enumerated for Anglo Americans may be more or less accurate, but the Mexican American pattern of residence probably discouraged any attempt to enumerate all Mexican Americans. The residence listings in the Directory usually provide only one name for each street address in Mexicantown, yet the writer's observations indicate that there are one to three houses located in the rear of many of the houses facing the street. Moreover, many Mexicans who are engaged in field labor in the McAllen area live outside the city limits and thus were not included in the Directory census.

| Occupation | Anglo American Male | Anglo American Female | Mexican American Male | Mexican American Female |
|---|---|---|---|---|
| Plumbers | 18 | 0 | 3 | 0 |
| Railroad Employees | 17 | 0 | 19 | 0 |
| Service Station Attendants | 22 | 0 | 22 | 0 |
| Shed Workers | 13 | 4 | 137 | 77 |
| Shoemakers | 0 | 0 | 2 | 0 |
| Truckers | 0 | 0 | 149 | 0 |
| Truck Drivers | 13 | 0 | 0 | 0 |
| Welders | 12 | 0 | 11 | 0 |
| Well Drillers | 9 | 0 | 2 | 0 |
| Warehouse Employees | 0 | 0 | 2 | 0 |
| Watchmakers | 3 | 0 | 1 | 0 |

This table reveals that the majority of Mexican American workers in McAllen are grouped in the unskilled labor categories of farm laborer (the term laborer may be taken to mean farm laborer), shed worker, cannery worker, and domestic servant. In comparison, the number of Anglo Americans enumerated in these categories is negligible. The trucker category is in a class by itself and will be dealt with in detail below. The skilled categories have been included in this table to indicate the distribution of Mexican Americans in the trades, but the unskilled categories are far more important as a basis for characterization of the labor role and will be employed for this purpose to the exclusion of the skilled categories. In the latter, although the Anglos provide the majority of the plumbers, electricians, machinists, and construction workers, Mexican Americans are ostensibly well represented in the other categories, such as painters, carpenters, and mechanics, and in some cases outnumber the Anglos. The writer's own observations, however, indicate that many of the Mexican carpenters and painters work for the Anglo carpenters and painters or for the building construction companies, while the Anglos are usually independent or occupy the higher positions in the companies which employ both Anglos and Mexicans. In the automobile service agencies, the writer encountered very few Mexican master mechanics. If the agency employed a Mexican American, it was usually as a mechanic's helper or as a general handyman. Similarly, the equal division of service station attendants in the table does not reveal that in most cases, according to the writer's observations, the pump attendants are Anglo while the jobs of carwashing and greasing are relegated to the Mexicans. In general, the table confirms the fact that the number of jobs held by Mexican Americans in all of the categories here subsumed under the labor role is proportionately much greater than the Mexican American percentage (about 51%) of the adult population of McAllen, and that the great majority of these jobs fall in the unskilled categories.

The operations involved in citrus and vegetable harvesting, which absorb the majority of farm laborers, are few and simple. During the early part of the season, citrus is ring-picked in order to avoid picking fruit under a certain minimum size. The picker places a ring under each piece of fruit and lifts it, and if the fruit goes through, he does not pick it. After a time, the picker can judge the size of the fruit without the ring and can then pick faster. Later in the season, when all of the fruit is mature, citrus groves are "stripped", which means that all of the fruit is picked regardless of size. The picker places his fruit in a wooden field box the size of an orange crate, and loads his filled boxes on the waiting truck.

Care must be exercised in handling the fruit to avoid bruising. To reach the fruit on the higher branches of the tree, the picker must ascend the trunk and pick each fruit individually. In the case of fruit destined for a juice cannery, the picking operation can be faster since careful handling of the fruit is not necessary. The picker shakes each limb of the tree so that the fruit falls to the ground and uses a long-handled hook to detach the fruit which remains after the shaking. Juice fruit is loaded into bushel baskets, carried to the truck, and dumped there.

In harvesting root vegetables, such as carrots and beets, the rows of vegetables are loosened by a mechanical operation in preparation for the work of the harvest crew. The laborer only picks the vegetables from the ground, shakes them free of soil, and ties them into bunches containing the specified number of vegetables. Then the bunches are counted and placed in bushel baskets or field boxes. In harvesting cabbage and broccoli, the laborer uses a small knife to cut the vegetable from the stalk. In picking cotton, the worker performs the simple task of pulling the cotton from the bolls and putting it in his shoulder sack.

Citrus and vegetable harvesting is arduous and much of it is heavy work, as in the transporting of boxes and baskets of fruit from field to truck. In citrus harvesting, the thorns and branches scratch the pickers and tear their clothing, and there is much reaching and stretching involved to detach the fruit. In vegetable harvesting, squatting, bending, and stooping are required in one or the other of the operations involved.

Consequently, in all of these harvesting operations, physical strength and endurance are at a premium. Regardless of the crop, the tasks performed are repetitive throughout the day. Thus the work is extremely monotonous in contrast to the traditional farmer's routine of performing many different tasks in a day. The length of the workday is determined not only by the hours spent in actually working but also by the time spent in waiting and in transportation. Much time is usually spent in waiting for an assignment at the packing shed in the morning, in travelling to and from the fields or from one field to another, and in waiting to be taken home after the day's work. The writer accompanied truckers who went out at 6 a.m., spent an hour gathering their crews, waited one to three hours for their assignments at the packing shed, lost an hour or two in moving from one citrus grove to another located miles apart, and, at the termination of the day's work, spent two hours in a line of trucks waiting to unload fruit at a packing shed, an hour in unloading and finally returned their workers to their homes at 9 p.m.

The great majority of jobs in the packing sheds and canneries are unskilled. The minute division of labor and the degree of mechanization have so simplified the operations that almost any job may be learned in a few days. In packing oranges, e.g., the fruit is carried into the shed from the truck by a mechanical conveyor, passes through a washing machine, and is dropped onto belts which convey it to mechanical sizers which automatically separate the various sizes. In some sheds, the actual packing and crating is done by machinery, in others by hand. In all cases, the loading of crates onto waiting box cars or trucks is done by hand. The packing of most vegetables is similarly mechanized, with the exception of such items as tomatoes, which are too fragile to be packed by machine. In this case, the tomatoes are transported on long conveyor belts to workers who wrap each tomato separately and place them in small wooden boxes to be carried off by other workers. In canning fruit juice, the harvesting trucks dump their loads on conveyor belts which carry the fruit through a washing machine and into the plant where it is squeezed, pasteurized, and poured into cans. The cans are then sealed, labelled, and packed into cartons which are carried off to the loading platform by waiting laborers. All of these operations are mechanized. In general, packing and cannery workers are auxiliary to the machines, watching them at critical points and sometimes feeding them the necessary materials, although even this process is often mechanized. Hand labor is employed mainly in the packing of fragile vegetables, in tying bunches of vegetables, and in crating and loading. This labor is highly routinized, involving the performance of simple, usually repetitive operations, the timing of which is synchronized with the operations of the machines.

A certain amount of labor is employed by growers for planting, cultivation, and irrigation, but the great demand for labor arises during the harvest seasons, for work in the fields, packing shed, and canneries. The irregular, intermittent labor demand necessitates the recurrent recruiting of a labor force. The principal method of recruitment for that part of the labor force that is wetback, is to drive up and down the roads leading to the Rio Grande calling for wetbacks or to visit the various encampments of crude huts in the brushland along the river which have been constructed by wetbacks in hiding from the Border Patrol. Most of the small landowners personally recruit the few laborers they need in this way, but the owners of the large farming enterprises and the packers usually employ a labor contractor who knows the location of wetback "hideouts" to round up such labor when it is needed. The labor used in the packing sheds and canneries is hired and paid directly by the employer, but the procurement of field labor in quantities sufficient for the large-scale harvesting operation is accomplished indirectly through the medium of the trucker or crewleader, who is the key figure in the recruitment, supervision, and remuneration of field labor.

As the table above indicates, the crewleader (referred to as trucker) is almost always a Mexican American. Access to crewleader status is obtained by possession of a truck, an ability to speak English, and a knowledge of where to recruit labor. Without these facilities, the crewleader would have to return to the ranks of field laborers, as the following comment illustrates:

> I bought my truck during the war, and by the time
> I got through fixing it up, it cost me $3000. That's
> a lot of money, but during the war it was easy to make
> money, and I didn't have any trouble meeting the monthly
> payments. I had to do it anyway. Without the truck I
> would have to work in the fields, at $2.50 a day. I
> have no education. All I can do is common labor, and
> I could never make much money without the truck. With
> the truck I make pretty good sometimes.

As has been indicated,* packing sheds and canneries purchase a grower's crop or part of it while it is still unharvested. The job of harvesting, which is the responsibility of the shed or cannery, is turned over to crewleaders, who are paid on a piece rate basis for specified quantities (in the case of citrus, by the ton) of fruits and vegetables. The crewleader recruits his own field laborers, supervises their work, and in turn pays them on a piece rate basis for whatever quantity they harvest. Thus the grower, the packer, and the canner are insulated from any direct relationship with the harvest crews, which make up the vast majority of the Mexican American labor force. The packers and canners employ a number of "field men", whose job it is to locate and buy desirable crops from the growers. Each of these field men is in contact with a group of crewleaders, who are contracted to harvest purchased crops. This contracting system means that technically the crewleaders are not employees of the packer or canner, but in practice many crewleaders work for the same packer or canner year after year. According to the description provided by a citrus packer:

> I myself hire only the labor that works here in the shed. Everything else is contracted. By that I mean that we contract groves out to crewleaders at $3.50 a ton. They furnish the crews, trucks, and everything else. All we provide are the picking sacks the price of which we take out of the first payment due the crewleader. For the most part, we have been working with the same crewleaders year after year. Of course, there is a small turnover, but it isn't large enough to upset anything. All of our agreements with crewleaders are verbal, nothing on paper. All the packers here work on pretty nearly the same arrangement.

A vegetable packer contributed the following information:

> Informant said that truckers hire their own hands to do the harvesting, and these truckers own their trucks. The piece rate paid the truckers is pretty well standardized, all sheds paying about the same. Informant has nothing to do with paying the hands since they are hired by the truckers, but their piece rates are pretty well standardized too. Since the truckers are hired on a piece work basis, the number of days a week and the number of months a year they work are determined by the amount of produce available. In other words, crewleaders work only when informant has produce to be picked.

Since the crewleader is not actually an employee of the company that contracts for his services, his services may be dispensed with at any time and without notice. To compensate for the insecurity involved in this relationship, crewleaders attempt to build up seniority with one company although this sometimes involves refusing temporary contracting jobs with other companies which offer higher piece rates. One crewleader told the investigator:

> I always try to do good work and take care of a man's grove when I work it. Some fellows skin the trees, ruin them after a grower has worked hard for years to build up that grove. They just don't care. You take V, that trucker who lives on your street. I was talking to him just last week. He's worked for three different companies in the last six months. There's no reason for that unless he just doesn't

> care how he does his work, or maybe he just doesn't know how. Now, I have been working for the same company for seven years. My boss, Mr. M (one of the company's field men), came out today and told me I go to work Monday snapping beans. Whenever he's got any work, I know he'll give it to me. It's the same with the other truckers he's got. They're good workers. Mr. M says he wouldn't trade his truckers for any other bunch. There's a cannery in Pharr that's been after me to go work there, and they promised me I would make more than I'm making on this job. But I've been working for this company so long that my boss knows me and what I can do, and that's not something to be thrown away just to make a little more money.

By developing this kind of seniority, the crewleader can offer his crew more steady employment than can less well established crewleaders, and in turn can introduce relative stability in his crew membership. The crewleader quoted above informed the investigator that during slack periods, his workers wait as long as they can while he attempts to obtain work assignments even though there may be work opportunities with other truckers. When they cannot afford to wait, they will often leave another job they have taken and come back to him as soon as he has work. Of course this may be due in part to the fact that crewleaders tend to recruit the core of their crews from their families, friends, and neighbors, but in a situation where underemployment and unemployment are chronic problems for the majority of workers, the possibility of obtaining more employment in the long run by remaining with one crewleader is a decided attraction. Aside from family and friends, one of the crewleader's major sources of labor is the wetback. The fact that he is of Mexican descent facilitates his approach to the wetback, who is always fearful of apprehen-

sion by the Border Patrol (all Anglo), and through his
established contacts with wetbacks, he is kept posted on
the shifting locations of wetback encampments in the river
brushland to an extent that Anglo seekers of field labor can
never achieve.

The role of the crewleader as intermediary between
employer and worker which is described here is a particular
instance of the general pattern of the use of the resident
Mexican American as labor contractor and in other capacities
to facilitate the rapid utilization of Mexican immigrant labor
throughout the Southwest.[11] Large-scale Mexican immigration
to the United States ceased with the Depression of 1929, but
the Valley is undergoing a new wave of immigration in the
form of the wetback invasion. The wetbacks have augmented
enormously that part of the resident Mexican American group
which has never learned English, and which comprises a
significant proportion of the immigrant generation and those
of their children who, although born here, never attended school
This coupled with the lack of ability to speak Spanish which
is characteristic of Anglo Americans in McAllen and the Valley,
has placed a premium on the resident Mexican American's bilingual ability as a principal means of communication between
Anglo employer and Mexican laborer.

The crewleader system, aside from the useful services of
recruiting and supervising of labor it provides, enables the
employer to nominally evade responsibility for such matters as
remuneration and working conditions and at the same time

have at his disposal a sufficient labor force. As one
Anglo informant, a labor camp manager, expressed it,
"You know, they talk about Texans discriminating against
the Mexicans. Most of that discrimination is by the Mexicans themselves. These crewleaders really take advantage
of the men they hire. The Texans have nothing to do with it."
It is true that the crewleader's relation to the laborer is
such that he can easily take advantage of him and sometimes
does, but the ultimate control of wages and working conditions
obviously rests with the employer, not the crewleader at all.
The entire Valley productive area was developed with extremely
cheap labor, and the growers and packers, both large and small,
are apparently obsessed with the idea that cheap labor is
absolutely necessary for successful operation. Growers and
packers are also preoccupied with the constant fear that there
will not be enough labor available to meet their needs at
those times when they need labor. A surplus of labor also
insures the maintenance of low remuneration of course, and
with the pay on a piecework basis, labor costs remain the
same regardless of the number of workers. To meet these
goals, growers and packers encourage the influx of wetback
labor and set a wage rate which forces part of the resident
labor supply to migrate out of the Valley during the summer
months in search of higher remuneration. The piece rate
offered the crewleader by the employer of course determines
the wage the former can pay his crew members, but in addition,
it is to the interest of the packer to actually specify the

piece rate to be paid crew members so that these wages will be in line with the piece rate the packer offers the shed workers whom he hires directly. Since growers also hire labor directly, they too are interested in the maintenance of low piece rates to the harvest crews. In general, hourly rates and piece rates are well standardized throughout the Valley region for field, shed, and cannery workers, whether they be hired by employer or crewleader. Surplus and cheap labor is also to the interest of the crewleader since the larger his crew the greater his load of produce and the higher his daily income on a piece rate basis.

Field laborers who are employed for planting, cultivation, and irrigation work by growers are paid an hourly rate of 25 to 30 cents. All growers and laborers contacted by the writer quoted this wage for this type of work. An attempt at an agreement by the United States and Mexico in 1947 to legalize the presence of wetbacks in the Valley set a wage scale of 25 to 55 cents an hour for field labor with the minimum reserved for unskilled labor and the higher rates for semi-skilled and skilled labor.[12] Since almost all field labor is unskilled, it is safe to assume that the vast majority of field laborers would have worked for 25 cents an hour. In the packing sheds and canneries that pay on an hourly basis a wage-scale of 40 to 75 cents an hour prevails but here too the majority of workers make the minimum wage since the labor is unskilled. At 25 cents an hour, a worker could earn $15.00 a week working 10 hours a day six days a week. However, even during the height of the harvest seasons, as will be indicated below, this maximum work week is seldom attained by the workers. In harvesting, most field laborers and many shed workers are paid on a piece rate basis, but often this does not mean more money than is earned on an hourly basis. Citrus fruit pickers, e.g., are paid 5 to 7 cents a box, and can fill 20 to 60 boxes a day depending on the size and strength of the individual.* The writer accompanied a crew-leader on his rounds on payday after a week in which his crew-members had been able to pick grapefruit for only two days because of bad weather. Each member of the twelve man crew received between $3 and $5.

A Children's Bureau study in 1943 of 342 families engaged in agricultural labor in Hidalgo County reports the following:[13]

> The median earnings of the families from all types of employment came to only $6.90 for the week, and one-third of the families earned less than $5. For the 262 families who worked exclusively in farm labor during the sample week, median earnings were only $5.95... Even at the height of the vegetable harvest, most workers probably averaged about 3 days' work per week ... Even when several members of the family had fairly steady work, their combined labor did not offset the low piece rates ... Two-thirds of the families of agricultural laborers in this study earned less than $400 during the year preceding the interview ... The median earnings for the year were only $340, in spite of the comparatively large number of workers per family (3.8). One out of every eight families made less than $200.

---

* The low remuneration forces most families to utilize even the young children as wage earners.

The following table presents more recent figures on Mexican American family incomes in Hidalgo County, but the source[14] does not indicate the occupations of family heads:

Total Family Income During Past Year, 3,103 Spanish-Speaking Families, Hidalgo County, Texas, 1947-1948

| Annual Income | Number of Families | Percent of Families | Cumulative Percent |
| --- | --- | --- | --- |
| $ 0-499 | 303 | 9.8 | 9.8 |
| 500-999 | 987 | 31.8 | 41.6 |
| 1000-1499 | 828 | 26.7 | 68.3 |
| 1500-1999 | 452 | 14.6 | 82.9 |
| 2000-2499 | 250 | 8.0 | 90.9 |
| 2500-2999 | 86 | 2.8 | 93.7 |
| 3000-3999 | 92 | 2.9 | 96.6 |
| 4000-4999 | 25 | 0.8 | 97.3 |
| 5000-7499 | 9 | 0.3 | 97.6 |
| 7500- | 1 | 0.0 | 97.6 |
| Not stated | 70 | 2.3 | 99.9 |

Figures obtained by the writer from the records of the McAllen Farm Labor Supply Center indicated that for sixty Mexican American families residing there and engaged in agricultural labor, total earnings in 1946 ranged from $160 to $940. Exceptions were six crewleaders with earnings ranging from $1000 to $1400. Those of the group who reported maximum weekly earnings indicated a range of $18 to $35.

Since the vast majority of Mexican American agricultural workers have no other source of income and are entirely dependent on their earnings from field or shed labor for food, clothing, and shelter,[15] it is not difficult to imagine the severity of their struggle for existence.* There are many statements of Mexican Americans in the field materials which bear eloquent testimony to the problems they face in earning a living. The following comment can stand for many:

> I'm a native here and I've lived here all my life and want to stay on living here, but I can't support my family here. That's why I went to Bay City, Michigan this year. I didn't want to go there and leave here, but I had to do it and may have to do it again. You know, it's terrible here now. I'm out working on land, clearing land of brush, and I have to take my older sons with me because all I can make is $2 a day. I have to take them out of school because I can't make enough to feed my eight children. During the war there were lots of jobs and not enough men, and they came around looking for you. Now they don't care if you work or not. And if they give you a job, it's for what I get, 25 cents an hour, and they're doing you a favor. I tell them I can't support a family like what I've got on $2 a day, especially with what groceries cost now. So they tell me they'll raise me to 30 cents an hour, but that's the best they can do. Well, they can keep their nickel. A man with my family needs at least 60 cents an hour. If I can't get it here, I'll have to go back to Bay City next year.

The irregularity of employment and the resulting lack of job security which are the lot of the field and shed worker

---

* "The wages of the peon are seldom paid in money. Ordinarily for his labor he is given a due bill or time check to be negotiated at the store maintained by the hacienda--with obvious results. On the other hand, the actual wage earned is not the only compensation that the peon receives. Certain perequisites, if one might so describe them, have been established by custom, which alleviate the lot of the Indian laborer. Thus he occupies a hut upon the estate without being called upon to pay rent. He is usually allowed a milpa, a piece of land for his own use, and this may provide at least a part of his living. Moreover, while he is forced to resort to the hacienda store, he enjoys a credit there sufficient to tide him over in the event of a general crop failure. Actually, however, so meager is the compensation received by the peon that he is kept in the most abject poverty, and few opportunities of escape from the bondage imposed by the established system ever present themselves. Obviously, this situation has greatly encouraged the emigration of rural laborers from Mexico to the southwestern part of the United States." George McBride, The Land Systems of Mexico, N.Y., 1923, p. 32.

are evident in the material presented thus far, but the explicit treatment of these aspects of the labor role is necessary to realize the extent to which the worker is subjected to these disadvantages. Aside from the fact that wages are actually low, the meager earnings of the worker are due in large part to intermittent employment and underemployment. As indicated, the seasonal peaks of harvest activity mean that during certain periods of the year there is no employment available at all for the major part of the labor force. The dovetailing of crop harvesting and processing and packing means that the major sources of employment, the farms, sheds, and canneries, are active and inactive at the same times of the year. The occasional crop failures extend the inactive periods in some years. Moreover, even during the harvest periods, the worker is subjected to serious underemployment. Unfavorable market conditions will cause growers to postpone the sale of their crops when this is possible, until prices rise, which means no employment for days or weeks. Rainfall is another factor in underemployment since the harvesting trucks cannot haul heavy loads out of the groves until ahd muddy soil dries, nor can harvesting be carried on under such conditions. A third factor in underemployment is oversupply of labor, a situation created by the wetback influx.

The remuneration figures presented above indicate the earnings of resident labor and reflect the presence of the wetback. The following figures, obtained from the records of the McAllen Farm Labor Supply Center, indicate the duration of the total work year of 1946 for fifty resident Mexican American field and shed workers:

| Number of Months Worked | Number of Workers |
|---|---|
| 2 | 2 |
| 3 | 1 |
| 4 | 5 |
| 5 | 6 |
| 6 | 3 |
| 7 | 12 |
| 8 | 11 |
| 9 | 3 |
| 10 | 7 |

The chronic intermittent employment and underemployment keeps the Mexican American worker constantly on the hunt for work opportunities. The pattern of temporary employment is considered by the employer as part of the nature of things, and his expectation is that the worker will always be available for a job, whether it be for a day or a month. When asked by the investigator how many men he employs on his 100 acre farm, a farmer replied:

> I really can't say because it's so different at different times of the year. Right now I employ very few men because all that is necessary is tractoring. Later, when the crops have to be gotten in, I use many more. When I need them, I get them.

Enough has been said to demonstrate that the occupational categories which embrace the majority of Mexican Americans are characterized by lack of skill, difficult working conditions, poor remuneration, and a high degree of instability in job availability and duration. Aside from the ease with which the technical content of these jobs is mastered the standards of performance expected by the employer are not very exacting. No premium is placed on speed and production, e.g., because of the plenitude of labor and the piece rate. At no extra cost, a crop may be harvested as rapidly by putting more workers into the field as by requiring fewer workers to produce faster. Thus the worker is free to proceed at his own tempo. In practice, however, most laborers work as rapidly as they can in order to earn as much as possible before the job terminates. What is expected of the worker is physical endurance, amenability to irregular work, and willingness to accept low wages. Mexican American workers, as a group, are considered indispensable by their Anglo American employers, but not so the individual, who is always replaceable without impeding the functioning of the system.

All of these characteristics make the labor role an undesirable and extremely disadvantaged one. Since it comprises those occupational functions which no Anglo American wants to perform, it is a residual role. A concomitant of this is the identification of the labor role with the Mexican American. Unskilled labor is Mexican labor, not for a "white man", as Anglo informants have put it. Under these conditions the Mexican American has a monopoly and in this sense his labor is non-competitive. Indeed, no displacement of Anglo by Mexican labor has ever occurred. Field and shed labor have been supplied by the Mexicans since the beginning of the Valley's development so that the present division of labor is regarded as partaking of the nature of things. The stigma attached to labor role functions by the Anglo is indicated by the statement of an Anglo packer who said that he could not employ Anglos as shed workers because "these guys are ashamed to work in a packing shed. In a small town like this everyone knows everything, and these fellows are ashamed to have anyone know they work in a packing shed." The Anglo American conception that these occupational functions are peculiarly Mexican reinforces the inability of the Mexican American to get out of them. That unskilled labor is Mexican labor is borne out by the fact that Anglo Americans are always placed in positions which require even slight skill and responsibility. All the checkers and counters of incoming harvest loads and of piece production in the packing sheds and canneries, e.g., are Anglo Americans, as are the semi-supervisory personnel in these places. Similarly, the cashiers in McAllen groceries are always Anglo Americans although the clerks are Mexican, and as indicated,* the same pattern may be observed in many types of enterprises which employ both Mexicans and Anglos.

Given the realistic situation here described, the objective possibilities for rising within or escaping altogether from the labor role status are extremely limited.** Although the

---

\* *Supra*, p. 188

\*\* The attitudes of the Mexican worker toward mobility are best treated in connection with employer-employee relations and the motivational aspects of the occupational structure. See *infra*, pp. 231 ff. and 254 ff.

labor role provides the very broad base of the occupational pyramid, the lack of differentiation of occupational functions within it has prevented the development of a job hierarchy characterized by gradations of skill and/or responsibility through which the laborer can rise. The function of intermediary between Anglo employer and Mexican worker, as exemplified in this case by the role of the crewleader, provides a limited possibility for mobility. However, one becomes a crewleader not through efficient performance of a job but by accumulating enough money to buy a truck and/or by possession of bilingual ability. Other factors which severely limit occupational mobility for the labor role incumbent are the semi-caste barrier, as exemplified by the identification of Mexicans with unskilled labor, and the handicaps involved in obtaining sufficient and appropriate education that would permit a rise in occupational status. The tendency of Mexican American children to discontinue their schooling at an early age has already been described.* The migration to which many of the Mexican Americans are subjected, the need for the work of children to augment meager family earnings, and the generally discouraging conditions involved in the "Mexican" schools determined by residential segregation all militate against the possibility of education as a means of changing the labor role status of the majority of Mexican Americans in the near future.

Since there does not seem to be much possibility of

---

\* Supra, pp. 134 ff.

upward mobility for the labor role incumbent, it would appear that unionization would provide a means of improving his status as long as he cannot leave it. However, no unionization of any sort exists among labor role incumbents in the Valley at this time. Sporadic efforts were made in 1937 and 1938 by the C.I.O. and the A.F. of L. to organize field and shed workers, and locals were established in many Valley towns. Although a few local strikes were won, the unions quickly disintegrated when many of the members who were migratory workers, left for the seasonal migrations.[16] At the present time, the availability to employers of the large wetback labor force would nullify any attempts to organize the resident labor on a local basis. Besides, the old problem of organizing workers, many of whom do not maintain continuous residence in the Valley, still exists.

## The White Collar Role

Perhaps the most striking aspect of the occupations of the white collar category which are held by Mexican Americans in any number is their exemplification of the intermediary function between Anglo and Mexican American. In most instances, Mexicans hold these jobs because of their bilingual ability, and the extent of their incumbency reflects, as in the case of the crewleader, the need of the Anglo for a means of communication with Mexicans in matters touching the interest of the former. Unlike the crewleader case, however, bilingualism is needed in white collar role occupations for communication between Anglo merchant and Mexican consumer rather than Anglo employer and Mexican worker. The following table of the relative distribution of Anglo and Mexican Americans in white collar occupational roles indicates this:

### White Collar Role Occupations in McAllen, 1947

| Occupation | Anglo American Male | Anglo American Female | Mexican American Male | Mexican American Female |
|---|---|---|---|---|
| Beauty Operators | 0 | 32 | 0 | 5 |
| Barbers | 14 | 0 | 8 | 0 |
| Bartenders | 1 | 0 | 3 | 0 |
| Bookkeepers | 23 | 15 | 7 | 4 |
| Bank Tellers | 4 | 2 | 1 | 1 |
| Border Patrol Employees | 32 | 0 | 2 | 0 |
| Bureau of Reclamation Employees | 23 | 1 | 9 | 0 |
| Bus Drivers | 9 | 0 | 9 | 0 |
| City Employees | 10 | 0 | 21 | 2 |
| Clerks | 32 | 30 | 57 | 88 |
| Fruit Inspectors | 4 | 0 | 0 | 0 |
| Grocery Clerks | 7 | 0 | 20 | 0 |
| Immigration Service Employees | 16 | 2 | 0 | 0 |
| Jewelry Store Clerks | 3 | 5 | 0 | 0 |
| Letter Carriers | 2 | 1 | 0 | 0 |
| Newspaper Employees | 8 | 6 | 5 | 0 |
| Oil Company Employees | 36 | 1 | 13 | 0 |
| Police | 10 | 0 | 1 | 0 |
| Postoffice Employees | 19 | 1 | 0 | 0 |
| Receptionists | 0 | 1 | 0 | 2 |
| Seamstresses | 0 | 2 | 0 | 3 |
| Secretaries | 0 | 32 | 0 | 16 |
| Salesmen | 37 | 0 | 39 | 0 |
| Tailors | 1 | 0 | 6 | 0 |
| Taxi Cab Drivers | 13 | 0 | 2 | 0 |
| Telephone Company Employees | 21 | 31 | 4 | 0 |
| State Employment Service | 2 | 0 | 0 | 0 |
| Utilities | 19 | 3 | 21 | 0 |
| Western Union Employees | 4 | 8 | 4 | 1 |

The table reveals that the greatest number of Mexican Americans are to be found in the occupations of clerks and salesmen. Most of these are employed in the department stores, specialty shops, and other commercial establishments that cater to Mexican American trade.* A male informant who works in a chain department store stated that his major duty was to wait on trade from "across the river" and those local residents who could not speak English. A female informant, who works at Woolworth's made the following comments:

> Informant said that they have a few Anglo girls working in the store every now and then, but that the "American" girls do not stay long because the work is too hard and they do not get paid enough. They can get more money at other jobs, so they leave. The problem also arises about language, informant said. Since most of the trade in Woolworth's is Mexican, the "American" girls have trouble. They cannot speak the language and cannot wait on these customers as well as the Mexican girls can. The Mexican girls speak at least enough English to get by on. The manager and assistant manager of the store are Anglo. When asked how she gets along with the Anglo girls at work, informant replied that they get along all right, but do not mingle much.

A few other characteristics of Anglo-Mexican occupational distribution revealed by the above table are worthy of comment. The majority of Mexicans employed by the Bureau of Reclamation, a government agency, are not engineers, as are the Anglos, but unskilled and semi-skilled labor utilized in various projects of the Bureau. Similarly, the relatively large number of Mexicans indicated in the categories of city employees and utilities perform such tasks as garbage collecting, street repairing, maintenance of gas pipes and water mains, and so on, and thus should properly be classed in the labor role category.

There is no need to describe the functional content and required skills characteristic of the occupations in the white

---

* Cf. pp. 147-48

collar role category since they are substantially the same as elsewhere in the United States and have no special implications for the objectives of this study. Among the Mexican informants who performed white collar jobs there were sales clerks in the department, dime, grocery, furniture, and specialty stores; "general utility" employees who wrapped packages, arranged and cleaned stock, and ran errands in all types of commercial establishments; door-to-door salesmen and saleswomen; soda fountain clerks in drugstores; and cooks, bartenders, and waitresses (most of them in the Mexicantown restaurants). None of these jobs require any special skill and can be learned in a few weeks at most. As indicated above, it is evident that Mexican Americans are to be found in the clerk and salesmen groups in relatively large numbers compared to Anglos because the former possess one skill, bilingualism, which is necessary to the successful performance of these jobs, and because they will accept a lower wage than the Anglo.

No statistical data were obtainable with regard to the remuneration received by incumbents of white collar jobs. From informants who can be classed in this occupational category, the following information was obtained: A number of girls who worked in dime stores earned salaries ranging from $15 to $18 a week for an eight hour day. A few who worked in the small department stores received slightly higher earnings. A middle-aged informant with a family earned $35 a week and 3% commission selling a variety of merchandise to retail stores, and he and his friends considered this "good money". A Mexican American woman who worked as a soda fountain clerk made $20 a week. According to the informant quoted above,* Mexican Americans will accept lower-paying jobs as sales clerks than will Anglo Americans. No data could be obtained concerning this nor with regard to differential remuneration of Anglos and Mexicans in the same types of jobs. The writer encountered a general belief among Mexican informants that Anglos are paid more for the same work than are Mexicans, but the supporting data are scanty. One middle-aged Mexican informant, who had worked as a salesman for a wholesale produce company, had this to say:

> Look what happened when I quit working for that company. I worked for them for six years and was making fifty dollars a week when I quit. They hired an Anglo-Saxon at sixty-five dollars a week, and employed a helper for him at thirty-five dollars a week. I had a helper once in awhile, but not steady. And that's the way it is everywhere.

The Anglo manager of one of the smaller department stores expressed the opinion that most of the larger stores pay higher salaries to Anglos than to Mexicans for the same type of work. Aside from the question of differential remuneration, white collar positions are not always available to Mexican Americans. In McAllen, an Anglo-owned supermarket will not employ Mexicans for even the most menial jobs, and in San Antonio several Mexican American organizations claimed that all of the utility companies, some of the agencies of the city government, and one of the largest department stores

---
* Supra, p. 209

adhere to a policy of not hiring Mexican Americans.

According to the writer's observations, it is the younger people among the Mexican Americans, those with some schooling, who occupy white collar occupations for the most part. They have a greater degree of bilingualism and familiarity with Anglo culture than do the labor role incumbents and, unlike the latter group, a definite desire to avoid agricultural work of any kind. Despite the fact that the remuneration for white collar jobs is usually as low and often lower than the wages of the labor role incumbent, there are a number of attractions which more than compensate for this, disregarding for the moment prestige considerations which will be discussed in connection with stratification. Unlike the labor role incumbents, white collar workers enjoy relatively steady work once they get a job since the demand for their services is not so directly tied to the seasonal crop cycle. Moreover, they receive a fixed stipend instead of a wage based on a piece rate, which from their point of view makes for greater security even though it eliminates the possibility of increasing one's income. Finally, the conditions of work are not as arduous, the hours considerably fewer, and the required physical exertion much less in white collar occupations than in those of the labor role category.

The writer did not find a greater possibility of mobility among the white collar workers than among the field laborers and shed workers. There are no Mexican Americans on a supervisory

level in the stores and other commercial establishments in
McAllen, at least in those which are Anglo-owned. Not a single
case was encountered where a Mexican American was in a supervisory capacity with respect to an Anglo American, nor where a
Mexican had even risen from the status of clerk. So far as
could be determined, managers, assistant managers, and section
supervisors were all Anglo Americans. To the extent that
Mexican Americans hold their white collar jobs only because the
Anglo employer needs their bilingualism, the interests of the
latter are served by maintaining the bilinguist in the contact
situation with the consumer public, and there is no like need
to place him in a higher or different position. The identification of the Mexican with a subordinate occupational position may
make for a great deal of friction in the rare cases where the
Mexican becomes superordinate to the Anglo. Two Mexican
informants who had achieved supervisory positions in government agencies during the war, spoke of the resentment and
resistance they encountered on the part of some of the Anglo
clerks who worked for them. In San Antonio, there are three
Mexican-owned businesses, among the largest owned by Mexican
Americans, that cater largely to Anglo trade, and for that
reason employ Anglo Americans in various key positions in their
enterprises. In these cases, Anglos apparently have no objection to working for a Mexican American employer.

## The Business Role

Unlike the labor role occupations, which reveal a predominance of Mexican American incumbency, the ownership of business enterprises in McAllen indicates a near-monopoly by Anglo Americans, particularly in the most substantial and strategic businesses. The following table presents the relative distribution of Anglos and Mexicans in the types of businesses where both groups are represented, and the second table indicates, for comparative purposes, a number of Anglo-owned businesses which have no parallel in the Mexican American group.

Business Role Occupations by Type of Business - McAllen, 1947

| Type of Business | Anglo American | Mexican American |
|---|---|---|
| Auto Parts | 2 | 3 |
| Auto Repairs | 18 | 10 |
| Bakeries | 1 | 2 |
| Beauty Shops | 9 | 5 |
| Barber Shops | 6 | 7 |
| Cafes, Restaurants, Taverns | 26 | 14 |
| Cleaners | 6 | 6 |
| Clothing Stores | 11 | 1 |
| Contractors | 13 | 2 |
| Department and Variety Stores | 8 | 1 |
| Drug Stores | 7 | 2 |
| Dry Goods Stores | 7 | 1 |
| Farmers and Growers | 116* | 10 |
| Feed Stores | 3 | 1 |
| Fruit Stands | 2 | 4 |
| Funeral Homes | 2 | 1 |
| Groceries | 25 | 56 |
| Hotels | 5 | 2 |
| Ice Cream Parlors | 1 | 1 |
| Loan Companies | 12 | 1 |
| Lodgings | 43 | 1 |
| Lumber Companies | 7 | 1 |
| Mattress Factories | 1 | 1 |
| Printing Shops | 3 | 2 |
| Radio Service | 5 | 3 |
| Real Estate Companies | 103 | 5 |

* The actual number of Anglo farmers and growers is considerably greater than indicated here, since many of them live on their farms and therefore would not have been included in the McAllen directory.

| Type of Business | Anglo American | Mexican American |
|---|---|---|
| Service Stations | 17 | 7 |
| Shoe Repair Shops | 2 | 1 |
| Taxi Stands | 3 | 3 |
| Tortilla Factories | 0 | 9 |
| Wholesale Grocery Companies | 1 | 3 |

## Business Role Occupations by Type of Business
### McAllen, 1947
### (Anglo American Only)

| Type of Business | Number |
|---|---|
| Ambulance Service | 2 |
| Automobile Dealers | 13 |
| Aviation (Sales, Flying School, Crop Dusting) | 3 |
| Banks | 2 |
| Beer Agencies | 3 |
| Bottling Companies | 2 |
| Brokers (Fruit and Oil Lease) | 4 |
| Bus Lines | 4 |
| Business Colleges | 1 |
| Camera Shops | 3 |
| Candy and Tobacco Jobbers | 2 |
| Canners | 8 |
| Cotton Ginners | 1 |
| Dairies and Milk Products | 1 |
| Dehydration Companies | 2 |
| Distributors | 4 |
| Drug Companies (Wholesale) | 1 |
| Electric Contractors | 4 |
| Feed Manufacturers | 1 |
| Floor Sanding Contractors | 2 |
| Florists | 2 |
| Furniture Stores | 7 |
| Gas and Gas Appliances | 1 |
| Hardware Stores | 2 |
| Fruit and Vegetable Packers and Shippers | 35 |
| Ice Manufacturers | 2 |
| Insurance Companies | 23 |
| Interior Decorators | 5 |
| Jewelers | 4 |
| Liquor Stores | 4 |
| Millinery Shops | 2 |
| Oil Producing Companies | 8 |
| Motor Freight Companies | 5 |
| Painters and Decorators | 7 |
| Photographers | 3 |
| Second Hand Stores | 4 |
| Shoe Stores | 3 |
| Theaters | 4 |
| Utility Companies | 3 |
| Wholesale Oil and Gasoline Companies | 8 |

These tables establish the fact that all major financial and commercial enterprises are owned by Anglo Americans with a few exceptions. The largest Mexican-owned businesses are the three wholesale grocery companies and the one department store. The wholesale grocery concerns have prospered because of the inordinate amount of Mexican-owned grocery stores to be found in and around McAllen. The largest of these concerns is only one of the enterprises owned by McAllen's wealthiest Mexican American family. The department store is one of a chain of stores in the larger Valley towns. So far as could be determined, these are the only Mexican-owned enterprises in McAllen along with two restaurants, which have any Anglo clientele at all, although the majority of their custom is Mexican American. The Mexican American representation in such types of business as auto repairs, beauty shops, barber shops, cafes and restaurants, grocery stores, and service stations reflect the dominant-subordinate relation in that all of these enterprises are wholly dependent on colonia clientele and were able to develop and survive because of the opportunities presented by a Mexican group concentrated in one area with a certain number of needs not satisfied by Anglo-owned business. The number of Mexican-owned auto repair shops and service stations are a result of the large amount of old model cars and trucks in constant need of repair to be found in the colonia. The owners of these relics usually cannot afford the prices charged by the Anglo sales and services agencies and patronize the small one-man garages

in Mexicantown where the rates are somewhat lower and second-
hand parts can be obtained. The Mexican-owned beauty and
barber shops flourish because the Mexicans do not patronize
these personal services in Anglotown.* Mexican-owned cafes
and restaurants offer Mexican cuisine not available in Anglo
restaurants, and the reasons for the abundance of Mexican-
owned grocery stores have already been indicated,** and will
be discussed in more detail shortly.

For the purposes of this study, both businessmen and
growers may be classified under the business role category.
An explanation of the relationships between these two aspects
of the business role will also serve to define the Anglo American
role performance. The Valley was originally made suitable
for citrus agriculture by real estate companies which introduced the irrigation systems, laid out groves, and planted
the first trees. These promoters set the tone for farming
which prevails to this day in the Valley and which defines
farming in terms of business enterprise, as an easy way of
earning a living by investing a small capital in an already
established farm, usually a citrus grove, and watching it
grow and produce while enjoying the life of the gentleman
farmer. Some of the first settlers were experienced farmers,
but the majority were city folk attracted by the convincing
propaganda and promises of easy money of the real estate agents.

---

\* See _supra_, p. 149
\*\* See _supra_, p. 146

Since citrus cultivation has always been thought of as a financial investment rather than as a farming enterprise with the way of life this traditionally entails, the ownership and/or operation of a citrus grove has never been sharply distinguished from the business enterprise as such of McAllen itself. Real estate, banking, fruit and vegetable canning, and fruit and vegetable shipping are all part of "big business" in McAllen, and most of the important realtors, bankers, canners, and packers are also owners of citrus groves and other types of farm land. Many of the individuals who are primarily known as growers own a large cooperative which was established to can, pack, and ship their fruits and vegetables, thus placing them in the forefront of McAllen and Valley business. A number of the growers own business property in McAllen or one of the nearby towns, and have put up money to finance new business ventures. Local enterprises such as land-clearing or grove care services may have growers or businessmen as owners. A service station owner, e.g., has a half-interest in a grove care business, and a quarter-interest in 200 acres of tomatoes and cotton.

Thus these two aspects of the business role shade into each other. For most purposes, the orientations and interests of businessmen and growers are the same. Citrus groves often change hands speculatively in the same manner as other properties in business deals. The investigator has been told of deals where the ownership of farming property has been exchanged for a "piece" of a hotel or restaurant or other enterprise, and almost anyone who has some idle money is apt to invest it in a grove or vegetable farm even though his major occupational interest may be something else.* For example, two Anglo informants, one a newspaper editor, the other a commercial photographer, both own citrus groves as a sideline, and have a long history of buying and selling groves, just as one buys and sells shares on the stock market. The extraordinary number of real estate firms in McAllen function as the brokers in these negotiations and the same piece of property may pass through their hands many times in the speculative transactions that are constantly occurring. The real estate interests have always played a prominent role in maintaining the speculative and boom atmosphere which envelops McAllen's economy, plus the idea of McAllen and the Valley as the "last frontier" where anyone can get rich quickly if he has sufficient energy and ambition, which is the standard fare disseminated by the Chamber of Commerce, the service clubs, and other businessmen's organizations.

This sort of close relationship between farming and business enterprise is greatly facilitated by the fact that to be a citrus grower does not require many of the skills traditionally associated with farming. In most cases the grower has bought his grove already cleared and planted by the real estate company or the previous owner. Those growers

---
\* Even many Northerners, who regularly spend their winters in McAllen, own citrus and vegetable farms although their major businesses are in Northern cities.

whose main interest is farming may do whatever work is necessary to keep their trees productive, but more often the grove owner hires a few Mexicans to do the irrigating and pruning, or, if he can afford it, pays for the services of one of the grove care companies which supply all the necessary skill and labor. The harvesting is done by crews supplied by the buyer of his crops. Under these circumstances, the businessman or anyone with no previous farming experience can be a citrus grower since these services are available to all. The cultivation of citrus of good quality and a higher yield per acre requires skill, of course, but there is a good deal of evidence that many of the growers do not have this skill or at least do not practice it. Local citrus and vegetable growers and shippers associations waged a campaign during the period of the study exhorting growers to raise the quality of their fruit by banning poorer grades from the market and declared that "quantity and size are the only considerations with quality being completely ignored."[17]

The unfortunate consequences of excessive irrigation described above* are also evidence of the lack of farming skill. The local growers, with their conception of farming as a business enterprise, are oriented more in terms of prices and market demand than of sound agricultural practices. Commenting on a recommendation to the citrus growers by an

---
* Supra, pp.174-75

expert to stop planting new groves and concentrate on improving the quality of the old ones, the editor of a local weekly newsletter said:

> No doubt but what he's got something in this recommendation, but you can never get folks to quit setting out new groves down here. They can see how Reds and Pinks (grapefruit varieties) bring fancier prices than Whites, so they go and plant new Red and Pink groves. Someday, when Whites are scarce, they'll command higher prices than Reds and Pinks, and then everybody will start planting Whites again.

There is one point of conflict between grower and small businessman which centers around the presence of the wetback. Since the wetback is usually a transient resident who saves as much as possible of his small wage to take back to his family in Mexico, and who does not pay taxes, he is viewed as a dead loss by the grocers, drygoods merchants, and other small entrepreneurs of McAllen who depend on Mexican patronage to any extent. Moreover, the wetback affects these people even more severely in that he forces out of the community a considerable number of resident Mexicans who must migrate. The grower, on the other hand, as has been indicated, enjoys the benefits of a more tractable and flexible labor force willing to accept low wages, as well as a release from the moral responsibility of concern for the welfare of the worker, when he employs the wetback. This conflict of interest, however, does not assume significant proportions because of the close relationships that exist between farming and larger scale business enterprise that provide the latter with sufficient other compensations. The small entrepreneur, who probably suffers the most from this situation since he is usually not a grove owner as well, is not powerful enough to cope with the grower-businessman groups who are interested in the continued presence of the wetback.

The largest and most substantial Mexican American businesses in McAllen are the three wholesale grocery companies, one department store, two or three fairly large grocery stores, a few restaurants that attract Anglo customers, and a bar and night club.* The typical Mexican American business, however, is a tiny grocery with a few shelves of stock, tended by the proprietor and his family. These stores have only sufficient patronage to enable them to stay in business, and usually operate so close to the line of subsistence that they are affected directly and immediately by the fluctuations in the local economy. A crop failure or bad harvest season can put a number of these marginal enterprises out of business, and even a period of unemployment may have the same consequence. In order to attract customers who will buy in large quantities, the Mexican grocer is forced to extend credit. The large Anglo chain grocery attracts the majority of Mexicans because it can sell at lower prices and provide a much greater variety of merchandise than the small Mexican grocer, but it does not extend credit, so the Mexican grocer can obtain the patronage of those Mexicans who cannot pay cash for their groceries if he is willing to accept charge accounts. If he does not extend credit, the Mexican grocer must depend on the sale of those

---
* See supra, p. 140.

items of Mexican food which still persist in a partially Americanized diet and which are not available in the Anglo stores, and on the occasional and petty purchases made by families who do their major buying in Anglotown. The additional burden of extending credit makes even more hazardous an already precarious enterprise. In the case of one grocer, outstanding accounts rose to the sum of $1500 and eventually forced him out of business. This informant stated that some customers would fool him by paying their weekly accounts regularly for a time, then would ask for an extension of time because of lack of work or other excuse, and finally would drop out of sight leaving a debt for a month's supply of groceries. In other cases, these small grocers have experienced severe hardships because their customers could not pay their accounts due to an unexpected period of unemployment.

The most striking characteristic of the Mexican American businessman is that he must depend on his own group for his patronage, and that he is even further limited to those enterprises which do not compete with Anglo business or which offer services more conveniently located for _colonia_ residents. Anglo American businessmen, on the other hand, enjoy all of the Anglo patronage and most of the Mexican as well. In San Antonio, where Mexican American business exists on a much larger scale than in McAllen, a glance at the membership list of the Mexican Chamber of Commerce reveals that the same pattern of dependence on the group itself prevails. The most successful Mexican American businessmen in San Antonio are the owner of a Spanish-speaking radio station; a wholesale grocer and a wholesale produce distributor (both of whom supply the large number of small _colonia_ grocers), the owner of a _colonia_ hotel, a real estate agent who sells lots in the _colonia_, an undertaker who serves the _colonia_, and two _colonia_ furniture dealers. There are a few notable exceptions to this pattern, namely a meat packer, the owner of a piano company, the owner of a chain of drive-in restaurants, and a high official of one of San Antonio's largest banks, who since most of their patronage is Anglo, have considerable status in the Anglo business world. Without taking into account San Antonio's main business section, however, the total volume of Mexican American business cannot be much greater than the Anglo-owned businesses which are located in and near the _colonia_ business section and cater primarily to Mexican American trade.

Anglo American mobility in business role occupations is still a reality in McAllen, but there are indications that the ascent and the rate of ascent up the ladder of opportunity is in the process of becoming relatively more restricted and slower at the present time than in the boom times of McAllen's development. The ladder, however, is kept open by such factors as a still rapidly growing population, the availability and low costs of the labor force, and the development of a tourist trade which brings an increasingly larger influx of winter visitors to McAllen every year. The stories the investigator heard of phenomenal rises to wealth are many, but few of them are dated within the last ten years. The D brothers came to

McAllen in the 1920's with "fifteen dollars in our pocket", and have for a long time been considered one of the wealthiest families in the entire Valley and the wealthiest and most prominent in McAllen. The largest landowner in the McAllen area, whose vast holdings have been broken up and sold by his heirs since his death, came to the Valley in the late twenties as a poor druggist. As late as 1937, one of the most successful vegetable packers in McAllen, who also owns a great deal of farm land, migrated there without any financial resources. The last war gave the local economy a tremendous lift,[*] and the rise in the demand for and the prices of citrus and vegetables resulted in a rapid expansion of cultivable land and the mushrooming of new canneries to meet the government's demands for canned citrus juice for the armed services and other needs. The termination of government contracts resulted in the closing of a number of these canneries during the period of the study, including at least one that had existed before the war, but other aspects of business enterprise are still apparently in an expansion stage. Two local citizens opened a supermarket during the period of the study whose only rival in size was the chain grocery; a new chain department store appeared, and a bubble gum factory was established. The latter two enterprises represent outside capital and did not recruit their executive personnel from local sources, however. The increase in the tourist trade is reflected in the opening of new motor courts in McAllen, despite the large number of lodging accommodations already available.

---

[*] See cash income table, p. 167

The ladder of opportunity in Mexican American business enterprise shows no similar promise. Most Mexican Americans in business are still on the lowest rung, with many vacant rungs intervening between their position and that of the few substantial businesses owned by members of their group. Most of those who have climbed the ladder have not done so in recent times, as is illustrated by the following account of the history of the wealthiest and most prominent Mexican American family in McAllen:

> The Bs came to McAllen from the neighboring county of Starr in 1908, and the then head of the family is considered one of the founders of McAllen. In Starr County, the family had a long history of ownership of extensive ranching properties on both sides of the Rio Grande and still owns much of this property. The firm of B and Sons was established in 1913, one of the first businesses in McAllen. The Bs originally dealt in cattle and agriculture, later established a wholesale grocery, and through the years have accumulated extensive ranching and farming properties in Hidalgo County.

Thus this family already had capital with which to found its wholesale grocery before settling in McAllen. The owner of one of the other two wholesale groceries is also one of the early settlers, who established his business in 1913. The owner of the largest Mexican American retail grocery came to McAllen in 1911, was employed for twenty-two years as the bookkeeper and assistant manager of the wholesale grocery of the B family, and in 1934 finally established his independent venture. The most successful Mexican American business men did not experience the phenomenal rise characteristic of Anglo entrepreneurs, but either had the capital before they came to

McAllen or worked for many years before they could establish their enterprises.

In view of the limitations and handicaps to which Mexican American businessmen are subjected, opportunities for expansion and for establishment of new and profitable businesses do not seem promising. There are a few exceptions, however. The owner of one of the restaurants which caters to Anglo clientele started on a modest scale in 1936 and expanded his establishment to more than twice its original size. The owner of the largest bar in Mexicantown has had a similar history of progress and during the period of the study opened the first "night club" in McAllen "at a cost of $50,000."

The Professional Role

As in the case of the Mexican American businessmen, the Mexican American professional must look to his own group for his income. Doctors, dentists, and druggists confine their activities to the colonia; ministers have churches of denominations prefixed by the term Mexican; and schoolteachers, with a few exceptions, are placed in colonia schools. The following table reveals that Mexican Americans are even more lightly represented in professional occupations than in the business category:

Professional Role Occupations in McAllen, 1947

| Occupation | Anglo American Male | Anglo American Female | Mexican American Male | Mexican American Female |
|---|---|---|---|---|
| Accountants | 17 | 1 | 5 | 0 |
| Architects | 14 | 0 | 0 | 0 |
| Chiropractors | 1 | 0 | 1 | 0 |
| Dentists | 6 | 0 | 1 | 0 |
| Druggists | 14 | 0 | 2 | 0 |
| Engineers | 29 | 0 | 0 | 0 |
| Geologists | 7 | 0 | 0 | 0 |
| Lawyers | 23 | 0 | 3 | 0 |
| Nurses | 0 | 38 | 0 | 4 |
| Optometrists | 4 | 0 | 0 | 0 |
| Pastors* | 17 | 0 | 5 | 0 |
| Physicians | 27 | 0 | 2 | 0 |
| Schoolteachers | 8 | 35 | 4 | 2 |
| Social Workers | 1 | 2 | 1 | 0 |

Since the Mexican American professional group is so small in McAllen, it is advisable to include the data on San Antonio to properly evaluate the Mexican American professional. In the <u>colonias</u> of McAllen and San Antonio the Mexican American doctors are included within the top status group, partly because of traditional distinctions and partly because they represent the highest level of educational achievement and competence attained in the Anglo world under Anglo conditions by Mexican Americans. Although they are largely bottled up within their own group, which may have important effects on these individuals personally and professionally, their practice of medicine does not differ sharply from that of Anglo doctors.

The practice of their profession by Mexican American lawyers, on the other hand, is patterned primarily by the dominant-subordinate relationship between Anglo and Mexican.

---

* None of the Catholic priests in McAllen are Mexican American. This is true in San Antonio also, where the majority of the priests are Spaniards or of Irish or Polish descent.

As indicated above,* none of the Mexican American lawyers in McAllen and only one or two in San Antonio can make a living by actually practicing law, one of these as counsel for the Mexican Consulate. Occasionally they may handle a minor civil suit or sell some legal advice, but for the majority the principal source of income is selling insurance or real estate. One of the McAllen lawyers is related to the B family,** and receives part of his income through handling the legal affairs of this family's business and ranching enterprises, but Mexican American business is not ordinarily on a scale large enough to retain legal services on a yearly basis, as is true of Anglo business. This small-scale development of Mexican business, the fact that Mexicans can seldom afford to get involved in civil suits and are suspicious and afraid of the courts, and the tendency of Mexicans to hire Anglo lawyers when they do need such services, help to explain why Mexican lawyers cannot gainfully practice law. One Mexican American lawyer in San Antonio said:

> Even the Mexican clients will seek the services of an Anglo American lawyer. They would be foolish to do otherwise. The jury would be 100% Anglo American, and you can be sure a Mexican lawyer wouldn't have much of a chance. And the law profession itself is very hidebound and conservative. Before a Mexican lawyer would be accepted by his Anglo American colleagues, he would have to Anglicize his name and ways. So the Mexican lawyer has his practice confined to Justice of the Peace cases and a few divorce cases.

---

\* See _supra_, pp. 150-51.

\*\* See _supra_, p. 226.

Despite the fact that they have little opportunity to practice law, the Mexican American lawyers have come to play an important role in an allied field of activities, that of politics. In a group where the general level of education is low and command of English is poor, where notary publics achieve distinction and status because of their professed ability to cope with English, the lawyer has become prominent because of the level of education indicated by his degree, his skill in speech-making and general verbal facility, and the fact that there are few individuals, aside from doctors and lawyers, in the Mexican American group who have professional status. Thus he has been considered peculiarly well-fitted by the Mexican group to serve as intermediary in dealings with the Anglo group, particularly in the area of political action. In San Antonio, the identification between the law degree (but not the practice of law) and politics has been so consistent that some Mexican Americans have gone into law to enhance their political effectiveness and their opportunities for obtaining political jobs. Most of the prominent political leaders of the Mexican group, <u>los defensores de nuestra gente</u>, the defenders of our people, particularly in San Antonio, have been and are lawyers, although in many cases they must depend upon the businessmen for financial support in their political activities. During the period of the study, the only Mexican member of the McAllen City Commission was a lawyer, and in San Antonio, the only Mexican member of the school board, one of the two elective offices in the city held by a Mexican, was a lawyer, while the first Mexican to run as a candidate for district representative in sixteen years was also a lawyer. The lawyers hold prominent positions in non-political organizations as well. The city commissioner mentioned above was also president of the McAllen Latin American Businessmen's Club,* and in San Antonio the president of the Pan American Optimists Club, a service club composed of the most prominent Mexican businessmen, was a lawyer.

## Aspects of Employer-Employee Relations

The analysis of the occupational structure presented thus far indicates that the growers, packers, canners, and businessmen are the principal employers, and that these groups are overwhelmingly Anglo American. It also indicates that the labor group is overwhelmingly Mexican American. Thus for the purposes of this study, employer-employee relations may be considered as equivalent to Anglo-Mexican relations in the occupational sphere. Minor exceptions to this generalization that the employer is Anglo and the employee Mexican are the few Mexican businessmen and farmers who employ white-collar and field workers, and the small group of Anglos who are in an employee status. A more important exception is the Mexican crewleader, who in a limited sense functions as an employer for the vast majority of field workers who in turn make up the bulk of the employee group. The crewleader is only nominally an employer, however, since he himself is dependent on the real employer, the Anglo American, in the important matters of determination of remuneration, working conditions, and the amount of employment, and has

* In the nearby Valley town of Harlingen, the president of the local Mexican Chamber of Commerce was also a lawyer.

only the prerogative of hiring and firing of his crew members.*
The tracing of the interconnections between farming and business
enterprise has provided a more ample conception of the Anglo
employer and his sphere of interests and activities. Anglo
employer-Mexican employee relations thus do not refer simply
to the relation between grower and field worker, but embrace other
groups as well, since businessmen often are directly concerned,
in the role of employer, with the field labor and shed worker
groups as well as the white collar workers they employ in their
businesses. By virtue of this, the analysis which follows is
in many respects applicable to all the employer-employee relations in the occupational system although it is based primarily
on the relation between grower-businessman employer and
agricultural laborer employee.

A prominent aspect of the employer-employee relation is
its impersonal character. A significant variant pattern of
paternalism will be dealt with presently. The degree of personal contact between employer and employee is held to a
minimum by the nature of the work patterns.** As has been
indicated, many farm proprietors are really not farm operators
and thus have little direct contact with the farming process.
The field laborer, on the other hand, is constantly moving from
farm to farm, and on the many small ones remains only a day or
two, sufficient to harvest the crops. Thus there is no

---

\* See *supra*, pp. 196-97

\*\* Nevertheless, intergroup contact in the occupational sphere is more frequent and extensive than that which obtains in any other area of Anglo-Mexican relations.

opportunity for sustained contact even where the farm owner is directly involved with his farm. The most important factor insulating employer from employee, however, is the labor contractor, or crewleader, who does the hiring and firing of workers, provides the transportation and supervision, and gives them their wages.* The casual nature of the employment patterns also contributes to this impersonal character in that the employee only participates in certain phases of the process from planting to harvesting, has no claim or attachment to the land or the products of his labor, and no concern with the efficiency of his work, because of the low level of skill required and because of this lack of significant integration between his role performance and the other aspects of the occupational system. Thus his relation to the job provides no basis for identification with an employer or his enterprise.

Where the relationship between employer and employee is of a sustained nature, there is a tendency for it to be characterized by paternalism and to develop into a "patron-peon" pattern.[18] Statistically speaking, this pattern is not nearly so prominent as the impersonalistic one, but its description is a good departure point for consideration of employee reactions to the dominant pattern. Observation of cases of Mexicans who enjoy year-round work on a farm or in a town business enterprise, where it is possible to maintain a direct and sustained contact with an Anglo employer, reveal the patron-peon

---

* For the relationship between crewleader and Anglo employer, see Supra, pp. 192 ff.

pattern.* There is also a tendency for this pattern to develop in the relationship between worker and crewleader, in lieu of the contact with the Anglo employer.

The following excerpts from the field materials illustrate the patron-peon pattern in both agricultural and business settings:

> At the house of A, a farmer, a short, plump Mexican came to the door, said a few words, and left. A said that the man is Pedro, who has been with him twenty years. Some years ago he gave Pedro a little plot of land not far from here and built a little house on it for him. A said you could not drive Pedro away from the farm. He has been very faithful, watches the A house with a shot-gun when they are away. So they have never been robbed. A said he never asks him to do things like that, the man just takes it upon himself. A said he takes care of Pedro, calls the doctor and buys him medicine when he or his wife are sick.

On another occasion the same farmer said, with reference to the Mexican field laborers he employs on a year-round basis:

> They look upon me as if I were a god sometimes. They bring me all their troubles and expect me to take care of them. I try to help them when I can, but they ought to be able to stand on their own feet, so I encourage it whenever I can.

A Mexican American employed as collector by a loan company had this to say of his Anglo employer:

> B, his boss, is very good to him, and he has worked for him for ten years. His wife died two years ago and B took him in, giving him a room to live in near the office. All he pays for is his food and beer. He even has free transportation. B has given him a motorcycle to use and he keeps it all the time.
> Informant's boss came into the room at that point, and informant introduced him with the phrase, Este es mi patron (This is my patron.) A few minutes later, In

---

\* This pattern also exists in the case of Mexican women in domestic service, but few data could be obtained concerning this relationship.

the presence of the informant and his friend, B addressed the writer as follows: Aren't these wonderful people? You make friends with them, and they'll do anything in the world for you. Why, if I asked E (the informant) to get on his motorcycle and go 100 miles for me right now, he would do it. Wouldn't you, E? (Informant nodded his head vigorously.) If you make friends of them, they'll give their lives for you. Yessir, the Latin American people are wonderful people. I would trust E with anything. We Texans know the Latin people, and we know how to get along with them.

After B left, informant said: Isn't he one hell of a nice guy? Yessir, he's a good boss, and he takes care of me.

That component of the Mexican American basic personality type which has been designated a "personalistic" sense of loyalty and obligation,* provides an important element of the Mexican's expectations in the employer-employee relationship. There are many instances in the field notes of Mexican informants who defined the good employer as he who provided protection and care, and to whom loyalty and good service were rendered by the employee in return. Although there are many exceptions, the field laborer's conception of a "right to work", in general, is weak, and he tends to feel that anyone who employs him is aiding him and doing him a favor. The mere act of hiring him places him under obligation to the employer and begins the process of "personalizing" the latter. If the employer subsequently acts in accord with the Mexican's expectations, that is, paternalistically, the latter's obligation deepens, his dominant attitude toward the employer is characterized by gratitude and loyalty, he tends to be very amenable to the requests and wishes of his employer, develops

---

* Supra, pp. 109 ff.

a feeling of having a stake in his employer's fortunes, and
even comes to minimize and apologize for decisions made by
his employer which adversely affect him.  In view of this,
the depersonalization of the employer-employee relation,
which has been experienced by the vast majority of Mexican
workers, has resulted in much insecurity.  The worker attempts
to compensate by injecting the patron-peon pattern into his
relationship with the crewleader, often the only visible
employer, but, by the nature of the situation, this can meet
with only limited success.  The crewleader cannot fulfil
the expectations which define the patron role because,
relatively, he is as much dependent on the Anglo employer
as the worker is on him, and the worker knows this.  He
cannot guarantee steady employment, and does not have the
resources and the power to provide the protection and care,
as can the Anglo employer, which are part of the patron role.
In fact, the crewleader seeks the same security from the Anglo
employer that the worker does.*  Nevertheless, there is a
tendency for the worker, who feels isolated and insecure in
his impersonal work situation, to personalize the relationship
with the crewleader, to regard him as his _jefe_ or _papacito_.
Since the crewleader performs the role of hiring and paying
wages, there exists the basis for the personalized relationship
from the point of view of the worker.  Furthermore, there are

---
\* See _supra_, pp. 194-95

crewleaders who will tide over their workers financially in slack periods when possible and who, by virtue of their superior knowledge of Anglo culture, provide advice and aid.

The belief patterns held by Anglo Americans which describe their conceptions of the Mexican American as an employee are a revealing source of the nature of employer-employee relations. The dominant theme indicated by the collected data defines the Mexican employee as characterized by a series of traits which are directly opposed to the traditional Anglo conception of the good worker. Many of these generalizations are undoubtedly derived from the general stereotype of the Mexican which has prevailed throughout the period of contact between Mexican and Anglo in the Southwest,* but their present viability indicates their dynamic relation to the contemporary situation. According to the Anglo definitions, the Mexican employee is improvident, undependable, irresponsible, childlike, indolent. The following comments are representative: "Mexicans should not get much money for their work because they wouldn't know what to do with the money anyway." "These people have no ambition, they're very easygoing, everything is mañana. They just go along, taking it easy, not caring about anything as long as they can get enough to eat." "We work them for a few days at a time, for planting, fertilizing, and irrigation. Actually that's the way those Mexicans want it too. They like to work for a few days, make some money, and then go spend it somewhere." "They're indolent and easy-going, never on time for anything, and never take

---

\* "To the early American settlers, the Mexicans were lazy, shiftless, jealous, cowardly, bigoted, superstitious, backward, and immoral." Carey McWilliams, *North from Mexico*, p. 99.

anything seriously except their momentary whims." "They're just like anybody else if you give them the chance. Of course, you have to know how to deal with them. Here in the shed, and even in the fields, they like to gather in groups and talk, and you have to keep after them. They won't work steady unless you watch them, and they're undependable if you put them on their own." "The Mexicans sure have an easy life. Nothing ever bothers them, they don't worry about anything, and they don't have much to do and are able to just sit around and enjoy themselves." "They are so childlike and never learn. On my father's farm, they would never take care of the housing provided or anything else. They would get their pay on Saturday afternoon and by Saturday night it would all be gone. And they would always be moving on if they heard they could get a little more money elsewhere. They were very undependable." "I think it's true that the Latins have less vision, less ambition, that they're more unstable and less dependable than Anglos. An Anglo employee is worth more to an employer because he will be with the company longer, on the average. I think it's only fair to pay the Anglos higher because they have a much higher potential usefulness to the employer."

The beliefs expressed in these statements obviously have their defensive value in that they justify the maintenance of the Mexican in his present occupational status and under the same conditions. If the Mexican has these characteristics, he is well-suited to the type of employment offered by the Anglo employer. There is no need to provide steady work, raise wages, present opportunities for better or more responsible jobs, or feel any concern for the well-being of the worker, since the present employment opportunities and conditions should fit the Mexican's needs and desires adequately. Aside from their defensive value, these beliefs contain the implicit condemnation that the Mexican has failed to live up to the Anglo standards, that he *ought* to have initiative, ambition, and independence, and be thrifty, industrious, and responsible. The Anglo conceives of himself as possessing these traits,* and sees no reason why the Mexican should not have acquired them as well. Since he has not acquired them, the Anglo concludes, at best, that the Mexican is ignorant and lacking the proper education, or at worst, that he is inferior. The Anglo's emphasis on the possession of the traits which he finds lacking in the Mexican is a part of his general preoccupation with the accumulation of wealth and the pursuit of "success".** According to the Anglo, success is the reward of thrift, ambition, and hard work, and this is precisely where he thinks the Mexican has fallen down. However his conviction that the Mexican worker does not possess the desired traits does not prevent him, in the concrete situation, from expecting the Mexican to act as though he does, and he is continually frustrated and indignant when his expectation is not fulfilled. Thus we find that the employer atti-

---

* Whether or not the Anglo himself actually possesses these traits and acts in accordance with them is not important for present purposes. However, the fact that he believes he does is important.
** This preoccupation is implicit in the discussion of the Anglo businessman, *supra*, pp.218ff. For the importance of wealth as a criterion of success, see the discussion of class structure, *infra*, pp. 349-50.

tudes toward the employee are characterized by a pervasive strain of ambivalence: It is extremely convenient and gratifying to have a labor force with characteristics that fit employer needs so well, but at the same time the employer is morally indignant with the employee and contemptuous of him because he has these characteristics.

The Anglo employer makes his evaluations and consequent condemnations on the basis of the assumption that the Mexican worker acts under the same conditions, with the same premises, and is subject to the same motivations as he himself. Thus he concludes that the Mexican is manifestly culpable of having failed to live up to Anglo standards and is therefore justifiably condemned. It may be stated that certain features of the realistic situation in which the Mexican worker acts, as well as cultural and motivational considerations, are conducive to the development of behavior patterns which are amenable to interpretation in Anglo terms as improvident, indolent, and so on, and that the Mexican worker does exhibit behavior patterns which provide a basis for the Anglo generalizations.[*] However, this does not mean that the Anglo's generalizations provide an adequate description of the behavior patterns, or that the invidious evaluations which the Anglo attaches to these generalizations necessarily follow. The available evidence indicates that the Anglo assumption is not in accord with the facts, that the relationship of the two groups to the

---

[*] The degree of exaggeration involved in Anglo beliefs will be discussed presently.

occupational system in which they both function has been asymmetrical in the sense that the conditions of the participation of the Mexican in the system and his conception of that participation have been somewhat different from those of the Anglo.*

Certain features of the Mexican worker's realistic situation, cultural tradition, and motivational structure may now be viewed from the standpoint of their respective roles in the development of behavior patterns which are amenable to the Anglo interpretation and in the inhibition of Anglo-desired traits. Generally speaking, it has already been established that the labor role, although of course essential for the functioning of the occupational system as a whole, is marginal in the sense that its patterning does not provide the worker with the opportunity to articulate himself to the total system of production, or even a significant part of it, in an integrated and consistent manner. His actual role performance is insulated from most of the meaningful complex which constitutes the occupational system in a way that is not true of that of the Anglo employer, whose participation in the total process is much more extensive, intensive, and meaningfully integrated. This alone probably has much to do with the differentiation of the occupational experience of the employee from that of the employer.

---

* The extent to which the differing orientations to the occupational system of the two groups are mobilized in the same direction and contribute to the effective functioning of the occupational system is treated in the next to last section of this chapter.

More specifically, there are at least three features of
the Mexican's realistic situation which evidently have an
important bearing on the problem under discussion:  low
remuneration, irregular employment, and lack of vertical
mobility. The remuneration of the employee is not simply
relatively lower than that of the employer, but is so low
that the former lives precariously close to the margin of
minimum subsistence. This precariousness is accentuated by
the uncertainty of employment. Aside from the fact that, under
the circumstances, saving is hardly possible, the probability
that tomorrow he may have no income induces the Mexican to
enjoy his earnings while he can since what little he could
save would not be enough to tide him over. Thus, since he
tends to spend his earnings rapidly, the Mexican is considered
improvident by the Anglo. Low remuneration and irregular employment also tend to induce patterns of behavior which, according
to Anglo standards, may be interpreted as undependable and irresponsible. There is a tendency for some workers to leave a job,
and without notice because this is less disagreeable than con-
fronting the employer, when they learn of another job elsewhere that pays slightly more or promises steadier employment.
This, incidentally, shows a kind of initiative the appreciation
of which is lost to the Anglo employer in his annoyance with
what he considers the undependability and irresponsibility of
the worker in disappearing from the job *he* has to offer. At the
other extreme, some Mexican workers tend to stay with a job

under any conditions for fear of not encountering something better or because they have developed a personal tie with the employer. For example, a worker may stay with a job that offers lower remuneration than he can obtain elsewhere just because he has been with an employer for a long time and is guaranteed steady employment. The writer has observed a few cases of this sort where, instead of positively evaluating the behavior of the worker as dependable, the employer has negatively viewed it as a demonstration of lack of ambition and initiative. The lack of opportunity for mobility has obvious consequences in stifling ambition in those who may develop it otherwise, since it is unrealistic to be ambitious in the face of the impossibility of improving oneself within the laborer status or of moving out of it altogether to a higher status in the occupational hierarchy.

These brief considerations make it evident that certain features of the realistic situation presented to the Mexican worker in the performance of his occupational role are conducive to the development of behavior patterns which provide a basis for the elaboration of the Anglo beliefs designated above, but that this behavior has a different meaning for Mexicans. These considerations also indicate that these Mexican behavior patterns are not simply a consequence of failure to achieve Anglo standards because of alleged ignorance or inferiority, but that the problems of the Mexican's occupational situation inhibit the development of the Anglo-desired behavior. There is a vicious circle involved here in that the beliefs of the employer help to create this realistic situation for the worker which induces the development of behavior patterns imputed to him by the beliefs, and the development of the behavior patterns strengthens the basis of the beliefs.

A glance at a few aspects of the Mexican American cultural tradition and basic personality type will throw further light on the extent to which Mexican behavior patterns diverge from the Anglo standards and are amenable to the Anglo interpretation. To begin with, there is no particular emphasis in Mexican American culture on the unlimited accumulation of wealth or other material possessions, no pressure to master and control the physical environment as has been evidenced by the Anglos in their development of the Valley, and no stress on working hard beyond the expenditure of effort necessary to maintain a modest living. Mexicans like material possessions, but their desire for such things is limited to those with utilitarian value which are labor-saving or contribute to material comfort, rather than those which enhance prestige in Anglo terms and are accumulated for conspicuous consumption. The following comment by a Mexican worker is a little extreme and not altogether representative, but it expresses these points well:

> If it took $5 a day to buy groceries and live on, I would like to be sure of having that $5 every day. I don't see any sense in working for more than you need. I would like to do just enough work to support myself and my family, and I would like to be able to earn enough to support them without having to work too hard or too much.

The positive emphases in Mexican American culture call for idea and action patterns which are in many respects either at variance with the Anglo standards or place more importance on values of another order. The familial patterns[*] stress the obligation to support one's parents and other family members when this is necessary, and in view of the Mexican's situation this is often necessary. This prevents the accumulation of capital on the part of the individual since extra money is drawn off by family needs, and leaves little room for the realization of individual ambition. Familial patterns also maximize dependency and minimize initiative,[**] and result in behavior patterns the Anglo interprets as "childlike". The pattern of *amistad*, friendship, and its concomitant of drinking[***] also helps to draw off the Mexican's surplus money, as does the emphasis on generosity and hospitality.[/] Even this cursory consideration of Mexican culture patterns reveals a definite tendency in quite a different direction from the Anglo emphases on thrift, independence, ambition, industriousness, and initiative.

The components of the Mexican basic personality type that have been outlined above,[#] also tend to push Mexicans in

---

[*] See *supra*, pp. 72-74 and 76.
[**] See *supra*, pp. 68-69.
[***] See *supra*, pp. 80 and 105-6.
[/] *Supra*, pp. 81 ff.
[#] *Supra*, pp. 109 ff.

directions other than valuation of Anglo standards, and to motivate behavior along lines amenable to the Anglo interpretation of the Mexican as improvident, irresponsible, and so on. The Mexican American defines obligation as due to the employer only when the relationship has been personalized on the basis of benefits received which are then reciprocated by the employee. In other words, when the patron-peon pattern has been established,[*] and the compulsion to reciprocate impels the worker to perform the job even better than the employer expects. When the employer does not act in accordance with the behavior expected of the patron and manifests no equivalent sense of responsibility toward the employee, the Mexican feels no particular sense of obligation and may exhibit behavior which can be interpreted by the Anglo as undependable, irresponsible, and or indolent. The Mexican has no conception of loyalty and obligation to a concept as abstract as the "job", and usually will not feel any compunction about leaving a job, idling, or performing the required tasks indifferently if there is no personalized tie with the patron to give the job meaning.

A prominent element of the Mexican expectation of the patron is indulgent and sympathetic treatment. If such treatment is not forthcoming, the extreme sensitivity to insult

---

[*] See *supra*, pp. 235-36.

of the Mexican is affected, and the typical reaction is withdrawal.* The extent to which the Mexican receives the desired treatment has much to do with the way he will perform a job, and will often determine whether or not he will stay with it. This is illustrated in the following account by an Anglo employer, a service station owner:

> B said he had a night man, a Mexican, whom he caught sleeping on the job, and then it happened again. B said he bawled him out the second time and told him he would be fired if it happened once more. The man never showed up for work again. B met him on Guerra Street one day and asked him why he quit. The Mexican told him that he would not work for any man who spoke to him the way B had because his pride would not permit him to do so.

This Mexican sensitivity to treatment by employers was recognized by a few Anglo informants.** The first quotation is by an Anglo grower and packer, who incidentally expressed a faith (with qualifications) in the Mexican ability to learn rarely encountered by the investigator among Anglo informants.

> There are good ones and bad ones, like in any race. Some of them can learn to do anything if you show them how. Now mind you, I said show them, not tell them. If you tell them, they'll nod their heads to say they understand, and then go out and do it wrong every time. But if you show them exactly how to do it, they'll make as good skilled workers as any other race. And you have to be nice to them. You won't get anything out of them if you holler at them. If you curse at them or threaten them, they'll never do a bit of work for you.

---

\* See *supra*, pp. 116 ff.

\*\* Cf. the following comments by Anglo landowners in Nueces County, Texas: "You've got to make the Mexican working for you feel you're his friend." "Be kind to them. You can't drive them. You can't beat them like the Negro. They are highly sensitive and will leave you if you show you are dissatisfied. They will leave without a dime, and with no place to go." "Don't reprimand Mexicans in front of others. You've got to lead him; you can't drive him like a Negro." "Do little things for a Mexican ... You've got to treat Mexicans square. A new Mexican will watch us like a hawk; then he finds we're all right and pays no attention." Paul S. Taylor, *An American Mexican Frontier*, p. 133.

> An Anglo iceman said, You can be friendly with them, but that's as far as I want it to go. There are a few Mezcans down at the ice plant who will do anything for you if you treat them right, and we get along fine. But some of the white men at the plant don't know how to treat them. They bully them and push them around, and those Mezcans won't do anything for them.

The Mexican American submissiveness, and its dimensions of fatalism and resignation which minimize the potential utilization of one's own manipulative powers,* sets severe limitations to the development of an optimistic cult of success, and of a belief in self-improvement and general progress, to be realized by hard work, saving for the future, and initiative, as in the Anglo American case. The tendency of the Mexican to exploit the mood of the moment, with its concomitant emphasis on the reality of the present and vagueness of the future,** plays a similar limiting role in this context. These components of Mexican basic personality type interlock with the aspects of the Mexican American's realistic situation and cultural tradition, already discussed, in such a way as to mutually reinforce each other. The result, in the extreme case, is a deeply pessimistic tendency that militates against the development of such traits as ambition, initiative, responsibility, and thriftiness, and makes meaningless such goals as self-improvement and success, or any belief that asserts the possibility that man himself, through his own efforts, can change anything for the better. Such an orienta-

---

\* See *supra*, pp. 118 ff.

\*\* See *supra*, pp. 120 ff.

tion may undergo basic changes, however, according to the degree of opportunity for full participation in American society provided by the dominant group.

The discussion has revealed that the behavior patterns of the Mexican employee are the resultants of a series of factors not operative in the Anglo case, and that consequently there is no basis for their invidious evaluation in terms of a deviation from or a failure to achieve Anglo standards. The analysis of the factors which determine the Mexican American behavior patterns demonstrates that, although there is a realistic basis that serves as a departure point for the Anglo American generalizations, the latter are by no means adequate as a description of the patterns since they involve exaggeration, distortion, and omission. Actually, the analysis shows that the Mexican worker acts under different conditions, with different premises, and with different motivations from those of the Anglo American. He is not, therefore, inferior or necessarily "ignorant", since sheer difference does not imply one or the other. He is to be judged, rather, in his own terms and on the basis of his realistic situation, as well as his cultural and motivational structure. If this is done, and the Anglo standards are eliminated as the basis of evaluation of Mexican American behavior patterns, such pejorative terms as improvident, irresponsible, and indolent lose most, if not all, of their meaning. This type of evaluation, however, is not made by the Anglo employer, and the Mexican differences continue to feed the Anglo stereotype.

Even in his own terms, the Anglo American employer tends to exaggerate the Mexican's "shortcomings" much beyond that involved in the actual misinterpretation and misunderstanding of the Mexican's behavior patterns. These exaggerations are unbridled elaborations of the "truth" even as the Anglo sees it, and do not have the excuse of lack of understanding or insight into Mexican differences. They are elaborated to justify and defend the subordination of the Mexican and to obscure the unpleasant facts of his disadvantaged status. This may be demonstrated by a few examples: "The Mexicans wouldn't know what to do with money anyway." This justifies the low remuneration paid Mexican workers and also the payment of differential remuneration to Mexicans and Anglos employed in equivalent white-collar occupations. The Mexican may spend his money in different ways than the Anglo, as required by his patterns of familism, amistad, and generosity and hospitality, but this does not mean he wastes it pointlessly. Furthermore, when he has the opportunity, he purchases material artifacts and gadgets just as Anglos do, as illustrated by this excerpt from a conversation with two Mexican informants, one a truck driver, the other a bus driver:

> (A was explaining why an Anglo now employed on a job he had left received higher remuneration than he did for the same work.)
> A: They think an Anglo-Saxon needs more than a Latin American. An Anglo-Saxon has to have electric lights, a gas stove, an electric refrigerator, a shower, and

>
> so on. But they think that a Latin American can get along with a lot less.
> B: They figure a Latin American can manage with kerosene lamps, an ice box, and can live in a one room shack where he has to carry water in a pail.
> A: Of course it may be that a Latin American is used to less, but that's not right. He's entitled to have everything anyone else has, if he can earn them. I like good things myself.

"They like to work for a few days, make some money, and then go spend it somewhere." "They don't have much to do and are able to just sit around and enjoy themselves." This justifies the intermittent employment and underemployment of the Mexican. The long hours and hard work described as characteristics of the labor role indicate the lack of basis for these generalizations. The analysis of Mexican behavior patterns in the performance of a job just presented defines, in general, tendency rather than literally concrete practice. The need for employment, for maintaining a subsistence level, is in itself a sufficient stimulus for working hard and whenever possible that often supersedes even the minimum Mexican expectations for desirable occupational conditions and relationships.

A few concluding remarks are necessary concerning certain features of the pattern of authority which have been largely implicit in the previous discussion. The Mexican's concept of loyalty and obligation is essentially particularistic,[19] and since he does not distinguish the employer's rights on a functional basis, he does not accept his authority in universalistic terms. He reacts to him as a person rather than as an employer, and accepts his authority only to the extent that he can be assimilated to the relationship pattern of which the familial relationship is the prototype. The Mexican has little conception of the employer as representing an occupational category to which the prerogative of authority is accorded by an institutionalized set of generalized rules, but accepts the latter's authority only if he proves worthy, by his actions in a concrete situation, of assimilation, as an individual, to the diffuse, reciprocal relationships of what has been termed the "inner circle".* Thus there is no definition of the legitimate sphere of authority due to the employer in his status as employer. On the contrary, once the employer is accepted on the basis of particularistic criteria, he is granted a kind of loyalty that permits him to influence the employee almost without limitation to specific spheres so long as he continues to fulfil the particularistic obligations expected of him.

Enough has been said of the disadvantaged status of the worker in this chapter to indicate that the voluntary acceptance or rejection of employer authority is, from a realistic point of view, a choice that the employee rarely has the opportunity to make. The employee represents the helpless, unstable, and shifting element of this relationship, whereas the employer is, by comparison, permanent and stable.

---

\* See _supra_, p. 110-11

There is not even an approach to parity of status, since the employer has the power to determine the method of recruitment, the number of workers, the amount of wages, the frequency and extent of employment, and the nature of working conditions without limitation or modification by the worker. Furthermore, this advantage is preserved by employer organizations, active in attempting to prevent "outside" interference in the form of labor organizers and governmental regulation or legislation.* Where the worker is employed on a relatively permanent basis, he may limit this employer power by his tendency to establish a dependency relationship, and if this fails, he may show his resistance by leaving the job, idling, or lowering the quality of his work. However, the constant economic pressure to which he is subjected frequently denies him the luxury of even this weak protest. The extent to which the employer can provide the type of relationship expected by the employee determines the extent to which he can obtain maximum loyalty and the best

---

\* During the period of the study, the local growers and shippers association sent representatives to Washington to unite with similar organizations in California and Florida in requesting the exemption of packing shed labor from social security regulations on the thesis that shed workers are agricultural rather than industrial labor and thus not eligible for pensions under the social security act. The securing of such an exemption would mean, of course, that employers would not have to pay the minimum of 3% of their payroll as required under the old age pension program. See articles in *Valley Evening Monitor*, February 24 and 25, 1948.

efforts of the employee in the service of his ends. Given the demands of the local economy and the needs of the occupational system as presently constituted, however, the establishment of such a relationship on a wide scale is neither realistic nor feasible from the point of view of the employer, who can maximize the advantages of his status only by adhering to the maintenance of the depersonalized relationship described above. There is thus a pervasive strain placed on employer-employee relations because of differing and clashing expectations on the part of both groups as to what ought to be the "legitimate" behavior of the other. Furthermore, it is evident that the labor role as presently constituted imposes a number of severe frustrations on the Mexican American worker.[*]

## Motivational Aspects

A further dimension of understanding of the nature and extent of the Mexican American's integration with the occupational system can be obtained by the explicit consideration and comparison of Anglo and Mexican orientations to performance of their respective occupational roles as seen in relation to the motivational aspects of the occupational system. There is no one set of goals which integrate the action of both Anglos

---

[*] One attempt by Mexican Americans to increase the strength and security of the worker's status without resorting to the dependency relationship is that of the returned veterans, who, as a group, form the nucleus of a protest movement, as yet poorly organized, aimed at higher wages, better working conditions, and the reduction of the constant oversupply of workers by eliminating the wetback. This veteran protest will be taken into account in the final chapter on reactive adjustments.

and Mexicans in such a way as to provide them with the same directional force in the performance of their occupational roles. There are, rather, two sets of goals, one applicable to the Mexican worker, the other to Anglos and to those Mexicans who are becoming or are already oriented (through acculturation and assimilation) to the Anglo goals. Although Anglos and Mexicans participate in the same occupational structure, differential institutional patterning in other aspects of their respective social systems has channelled motivational forces into responding to different sets of goals that are incompatible in many respects. Each set of goals is generalized in that it mobilizes the motivational forces of the group members in a particular direction, but the directions are different in the case of each group.*

The orientation to success is the most prominent and pervasive generalized goal encountered among McAllen's Anglo Americans. To the Anglo, success is symbolized by the attainment of high occupational status and its commensurate

---

\* The Mexican orientations have already been related to distinctive aspects of the Mexican American cultural tradition, institutional structure, and basic personality type. Unfortunately, the limitations of the field study did not permit extended investigation of corresponding aspects of the Anglo American social system, and so the Anglo orientations about to be presented stand alone, so to speak, without the benefit of the supporting matrix provided in the Mexican case. The delineation of the Anglo orientations themselves, however, is directly based on the interpretation of field data gathered by the writer.

income. For most Anglos, the ideal to aim at is the astute businessman who owns an expanding enterprise, and who uses its proceeds in the development of an ever-improving style of living. Occupational achievement, one of the two important components of the success ideal, is thus focused on business competence. Those who can decisively demonstrate this competence by skillful management of a business enterprise, the evidence for which is provided by the steady expansion (in physical plant, stock, production, and/or profits) of the enterprise and its visible degree of prosperity, and/or by besting competitors in the constant "deals" which are taking place, may consider themselves as on the way to success. A glance at the tables on business enterprises and professions* shows a low differentiation of occupational statuses based on actual technical competence** because the scale of business

---

\* Supra, pp. 214-15 and 228.

\*\* Technical competence here refers specifically to the intellectual mastery of a technical skill. This would include the administrative skills normally encountered in the "business executive" type prominent in large-scale organization, as well as the skills embodied in law, medicine, engineering, and so on. Business competence, on the other hand, refers to the mastery of the empirical skills necessary to play the competitive game of small business and emerge triumphant, and does not involve any elaborate control of a technical specialty. Thus the distinction is not necessarily coterminous with the traditional demarcation of business and the professions. This distinction may not be valid when applied to a broader canvas than the community under discussion, but it is convenient for present purposes in that it provides insight into the quality of achievement prized by the McAllen Anglo, which is in part determined by the lack of large-scale organization and the relative lack of elaboration of professional activities.

and professional activity has not permitted much of an elaboration of business or professional technical specialists. The conception held by the grower of farming as a business enterprise rather than as a skilled technique, which is enhanced by the fact that it is not necessary to be versed in farming techniques in order to be a productive farmer,* means that farming is assimilated to "business" achievement and receives no special emphasis as a type of technical achievement. There is no evidence that the local growers have developed a prestige hierarchy based on varying degrees of farming competence. Successful farming is measured by the scale of the enterprise and the amount of production rather than by the quality of the product or the grower's control of techniques for improving that quality.** A similar pattern is to be found among the majority of packers and canners, although there are significant exceptions, whose achievement is to be measured by the size of their plants and the extent of their sales rather than by the quality of their pack or

---

\* See *supra*, pp. 219-20.

\* The executives of the grower's and packer's associations and others who tend to think of the Valley's agricultural enterprise from a long term point of view are preoccupied with the problem of improving the quality of agricultural products, if only to cope with Florida and California competition and as a means of increasing profits. There is also a small group of growers who have been successful in the development of bigger and better fruit as well as the creation of new varieties. However, this orientation to technical competence, whether its motivation be "disinterested" and/or "self-interested", plays no significant part in the general pattern of expectations which define the grower role, as indicated above, pp.

their canned products.

There is a dominant tendency, then, to evaluate achievement in terms of the standard business criteria, thus skewing the emphasis away from actual technical competence. The latter is by no means depreciated, of course, and provides additional luster where possessed, but relative to business competence it has no prominent role in access to occupational status in the McAllen community, where the vast majority of desirable occupational statuses do not require this technical competence as a condition of their acquisition.

The recognition of the individual's occupational achievement by the Anglo American group as a whole is the other essential component of the success ideal, and this is largely accorded in proportion to the size of income, which functions as an index to the degree of achievement. The size of an enterprise, the number of individuals it employs, and its volume of production in themselves serve to demonstrate the business competence of the owner to the other members of the community, especially since the relatively small size of the latter makes identification of an owner with his business fairly easy. However, the most decisive and indubitable proof of such competence to the community is the amount of income that competence yields. The ability to exhibit wealth, therefore, and the objects that wealth can buy, are extremely important indications of success and of correspondingly high status in the occupational hierarchy.* The most effective way of exhibiting wealth is by one's style of living. Since success is relative in that it provides no definition of what constitutes the ultimate condition of "having arrived", it has its inherently competitive dimension, and requires a constantly "improving" style of living, which includes better housing, a greater number and higher quality of material artifacts, travel, the ability to entertain guests on a greater scale, the higher education of children, and so on.**

The relative lack of elaboration of technical competence as a basis of occupational achievement, and the fact that businessmen are not arranged in any common hierarchy of office but function in their separate enterprises, enhance the prominence of wealth as a criterion of success. It is easier to evaluate the ability and achievement, and consequent relative status, of a businessman by the tangible, direct, and

---

* This discussion attempts only to define the success ideal and its various components in its role in channelling motivational forces in the occupational system, and in providing access to occupational status. The extent to which occupational achievement and wealth are criteria for the status of the individual in the class structure of the community will be taken up in a later chapter.

** Money, of course, is attractive for the access it gives to the enjoyment of the "good things of life", as well as in its role as a recognition symbol and as a means to acquiring other recognition symbols. Thus an improving style of life signifies to the individual a greater opportunity for the enjoyment of its components apart from its value as a status indicator.

convenient means of ascertaining the degree of his achievement as reflected in his income than by the lengthy and uncertain method of comparison of relative size, volume, and so on of business enterprises. Actually, under the circumstances, there is no other common measure of valuation which is nearly as practical or effective. The importance of the wealth criterion, and particularly the access it gives to the acquisition of style of living elements as recognition symbols, is also enhanced by the fact that McAllen has not had a very long history as a community in which to develop such "status stabilizers" as length of residence, family background, and so on, to any great extent.[*] The short period of McAllen's rapid development has been characterized by high mobility and a significant number of newly-rich. This has kept the status structure fairly wide open, flexible, and lacking in rigid definition. The result has been a high proportion of newly-acquired statuses most easily defined in terms of wealth and "conspicuous consumption" in a situation where constant mobility has not permitted other status criteria to become stabilized.

The Anglo American's goal of success, with its achievement and recognition components, is closely integrated with the functioning of the occupational system since it channels

---

[*] The role of these factors as status determinants is considered in the discussion of class structure, infra, pp. 349 ff.

motivational forces into performance of an occupational role as the principal means of realizing success. The Mexican American, on the other hand, is oriented to goals which accord major emphasis to the obligations of familism, friendship, hospitality - all the objects of the Mexican's distinctive definition of reciprocal obligation - and for the Mexican worker, access to status in the Mexican American community is based in large part on the degree of fulfilment of these obligations. Thus emphasis is skewed away from the occupational system and the motivational appeals it provides. Performance of an occupational role is of course essential for the Mexican since it is the only means available to subsistence, and he must work and produce if only as a matter of survival.* Such role performance is also essential to obtain the means for fulfilment of the Mexican's primary goals, but it is not *the* central component of the individual's life as in the Anglo case. The Mexican worker conceives of his occupational role performance as relatively incidental and definitely limited to obtaining the means for fulfilment of his primary goals. In view of this orientation, there is a corresponding lack of differentiation by the worker himself of a prestige hierarchy of the various labor roles. The nature of the labor role occupations reinforces this. They are only minimally differentiated in terms of functional content, required skills,** remuneration and working conditions

---
\* Cf. *supra*, p. 201
\*\* The job itself provides no impetus to do a "good job" because it is not of a sufficiently skilled level to call forth a pride in the work. Moreover, the Mexican is not interested in efficiency because his work has no visible relation to an end product. Thus he would tend to place more emphasis on the process of work as such than on its results.

and thus offer little basis for the elaboration of a prestige hierarchy. The expectation of the labor role group is that a man should be a *buen trabajador*, a good worker, in the sense that he should never shirk work and should make the most of every job opportunity, not because of a work ethnic, but because work is necessary to obtain the wherewithal to fulfil the major obligations. The man who works is accorded a socially respected status by his peers, regardless of the type of labor role occupation he may hold.

With reference to the realistic situation presented by the occupational system the Mexican worker accepts the disagreeable aspects of his role as part of the nature of things, and does not particularly object to the long hours or the physical exertion and discomfort. What he does not accept is the insecurity of the impersonal relationship and its related aspect of uncertain employment because they introduce, aside from other anxieties already discussed, the anxiety that he will not be able to meet the expectation of the good and steady worker, and more important, that he will not have the means for the fulfilment of his major obligations. He also objects to the prevailing low remuneration so long as it is below the minimum he requires for realization of his goals.[*] Thus the Mexican's immediate goal with reference to the occupational system is the modest security of steady employment at a wage sufficient to provide the means for attaining his primary goals.

---

[*] Cf. quotations of workers, on pp. 201 and 244.

Taking into account the total analysis of Mexican American idea and action patterns pertinent to the relationship with the employer and to participation in the occupational system, it may be said that the Mexican worker's major orientations to motivation are to be found in a set of goals quite different from the success goal of the Anglo group, which is functionally related to the occupational system since it provides a directional force for occupational role performance, and, by its nature, emphasizes the continual application of effort in such performance largely to the exclusion of other types of orientation to motivation. The Mexican's goals, on the other hand, are not comparable in the role they perform with respect to the occupational system. Aside from the impetus provided by sheer subsistence motivation, they give some meaning and justification to the Mexican's occupational role performance in that he must work in order to realize these goals, but by their nature, they severely limit the quality and intensity of Mexican occupational participation rather than mobilize all energy and effort in support of the needs and functions of the occupational system as does the Anglo success goal. In an important sense, the Mexican American goals operate to insulate the Mexican from the Anglo conception of role performance as the means for the pursuit of success since they define access to status on other bases. There is, consequently, no motivation to mobility in the occupational structure since equivalent satisfactions are obtained from other sources within the Mexican American group and there is no great dependence on the Anglo American and the occupational system for recognition.*

This discussion of motivational aspects has not touched upon the Mexican business and professional groups and their relation to the situation here analyzed. It should be noted that the delineation of Mexican orientations to motivation and degree of integration with the occupational system here presented is primarily concerned with the Mexican worker, and is at least partially and in many cases totally inapplicable to these other groups, as well as to certain elements of the white-collar group. Members of these groups find the Anglo success ideal attractive and exhibit consequent motivations to mobility in varying degrees. Their orientations to the Mexican and/or Anglo goals are best treated in connection with the definition of their class status and their attitudes toward mobility in the total status structure in a subsequent chapter.

---

* Recognition and/or response from the Anglo American has value only in the patron-peon context, where a relationship can be established on a personal, and therefore meaningful, basis with an Anglo. As has been indicated in the discussion of this relationship, it exists only to the extent that the Mexican can inject it and the Anglo is willing to accept and foster it. However, even this type of desired recognition differs from the type which is a component of the success goal and provides no impetus to mobility.

## Occupational Structure and Dominant-Subordinate Group Relations

This chapter may be concluded with a brief explicit consideration of the factors determining the subordination of the Mexican American as seen in relation to the functioning of the occupational system.

The preceding discussion has shown that cultural conflict has played a significant role in the development of the present pattern of intergroup relations in the occupational system. The differing expectations of Anglo and Mexican as to how the other ought to perform in the occupational situation ordinarily result in conflict situations. Anglo employers unfavorably evaluate the performance of Mexican workers since the latter do not conform to their standards, and the Mexican workers find the Anglo employers wanting because they do not live up to the latter's conception of what a patron should be. Feelings of frustration and moral indignation are engendered on the part of both groups because of misinterpretations and misunderstandings due to differing conceptions of such matters as codes of obligation, pride, dependence and independence, initiative, ambition, responsibility, and so on. The conflict becomes most severe, perhaps, in the area of dominant values, where the success ideal, so strongly emphasized by the Anglo American, is relatively a matter of indifference to the Mexican worker, who is preoccupied with the different values embodied in the distinctive complex of reciprocal obligations on a personalistic basis. The realistic bases of cultural difference between the

Anglo and Mexican cannot be played down in the occupational relationship, which requires joint participation by the two groups on a scale much greater than that which obtains in the areas examined in the last chapter, areas where both groups may exist, for the most part, without much dependence on each other. In the occupational relationship, where both Anglo and Mexican have a great deal at stake and where the performance of each has important implications for the other, realistic cultural differences provide a ready source of conflict between the two groups. Beyond this, however, there is an Anglo tendency to exaggerate and distort the Mexican's differences as he sees them to the point where they provide one of the bases for the motivation of and justification for the subordination of the Mexican group. As has been illustrated, the Anglo stereotype of the Mexican worker expresses this exaggeration and distortion which motivates subordination, and at the same time serves as an effective device for rationalizing the subordination. In concrete terms, the stereotype, by disqualifying the Mexican worker for incumbency of occupational roles other than the lowest labor role, furnishes the rationale for his continued occupational subordination.

As will be seen in the discussion of class, the intensity of cultural conflict experienced by the Anglo with respect to the Mexican group varies according to the class membership of the Mexican. Although this variation on a class basis will be indicated later, it may be said here that the conflict, utilizing the occupational role categories delineated in this chapter, is much more intense between the dominant group and the Mexican laborer than between the former and the Mexican white collar or businessman groups since the latter groups tend to approach Anglo standards and values.* The conflict of interests, primarily those involved in the struggle for control of economic resources, is more intense between the dominant group and the Mexican white collar and businessman groups than between the former and the Mexican laborer, however. As has been shown, the Mexican worker does not in any way compete with the Anglo group, and his values do not define the control of economic resources as a desirable end in any way at all comparable to that adhered to by the Anglo group. In this case, the Anglo motivation to subordinate the Mexican worker stems not from the desire to minimize competition, but from the desire to maintain a fluid and plentiful supply of cheap labor that is always available when needed. However, the Anglo is involved in a conflict of interest with the Mexican worker to the extent that the latter is preoccupied with the problem of acquiring that minimum share of economic resources necessary for survival and beyond that fulfilment of his principal obligations. The Mexican worker's resistance to the low wage is reflected in his practice of leaving a job without notice when he encounters a higher wage elsewhere, and,

---

\* See infra, pp. 368 ff. and 385 ff.

on a larger scale, by complete withdrawal, i.e., migration to the North where wages are higher. The Anglo employer's attempts to maintain the economic and occupational subordination of the Mexican worker are reflected in his practice of hiring wetback labor by means of which he can control wage rates, replacing resident Mexicans who want higher wages with the more complaisant wetback. The Anglo stereotype of the Mexican worker as indicated above, rationalizes the economic subordination of the Mexican by affirming the latter's inability to utilize money even if he had it.

The Mexican white collar group, which may be said to be oriented to acquisition of jobs and remuneration on a level and to an extent approximating that attained by white collar Anglos, and the Mexican businessman group, whose interests and methods of realizing them are the same as those of Anglo businessmen, are in potential competition with the Anglo group. In the former case, the Anglo attempts to retain his occupational and economic monopoly by preventing mobility and by imposing differential remuneration, and in the latter case the competition is minimized by the fact that Anglos do not patronize Mexican businessmen, and by the fact that Anglo businessmen can provide the Mexican group with the same services as its own businessmen can on a much larger scale and more cheaply. The Mexican American group is not made economically self-sufficient by its businessmen, and the Anglo businessman therefore has no need to fear

Mexican competition. By virtue of the situation, the
Mexican businessman's ability to expand is bottled up because he is limited to his own group, which has limited purchasing power and in any event gives him only limited patronage.

Chapter VI

SOCIAL ORGANIZATION: POLITICS*

## The Tradition of the Machine

The history of politics in South Texas from the time of the Civil War until 1920 is the story of a vast region dominated politically by one man and his successor, and the consequent breakdown of this political empire into successively smaller areas controlled by lesser men and their political machines. Before the Anglo American immigration, which only began in significant numbers after 1907, wrought its great changes in various parts of the border country, the sparse population was predominantly Mexican. A New York lawyer named Stephen Powers, who took up residence in Brownsville after a period of service in the Mexican War, was the first individual in the area sufficiently oriented to political power to attempt to organize the Mexican vote. As a lawyer who could lend assistance in the protection of land rights, and later as a great landowner in his own right, Powers acquired tremendous personal influence over the Mexicans in many parts of South

---

\* In order to provide a larger canvas for the discussion of political action, this chapter draws on all the materials gathered on politics and includes data on other Valley towns and on San Antonio as well as McAllen, although, as usual, the latter community receives the major emphasis.

Texas.[1] A young law partner, Jim Wells, took over the Powers empire at the time of the latter's death in 1882, and maintained this widespread power until it was broken around 1920, after the great changes taking place in the area's population composition and economy had time to make themselves felt. According to Weeks,

> Wells's power in certain localities, and particularly in his own personal bailiwick of Cameron County (bordering Hidalgo county on the east), was based upon his ownership of large tracts of land. Elsewhere over the region his leadership was personal, due in part to his professional connections with certain great landholders, but also to the fact that he early made himself well known to all the old Mexican families throughout the territory, which during the greater part of his reign constituted the vast majority of the population. These families knew him not as a boss but as a type of patriarch ... The inhabitants recognized him as their supreme leader socially and politically.[2]

Wells himself described the nature of his leadership as follows:

> The Mexican people, if you understand them, are the most humble people you ever knew ... Their friendship is individual. For instance, you have a great many friends among them, and they would follow your name and fortunes ... The Kings (of the mammoth King Ranch) ruled through friendship and love. The Kings have always protected their servants and helped them when they were sick and never let them go hungry, and they always feel grateful, and it naturally don't need any buying or selling or any coercion - they went to those who helped them when they needed help ... So far as I being boss, if I exercise any influence among these people it is because in the forty-one years I have lived among them I have tried to so conduct myself as to show them that I was their friend and they could trust me ... I buried many a one of them with my money and married many a one of them; it wasn't two or three days before the election, but through the year around, and they have always been true to me; and if it earned me the title of boss, every effort and all my money went for the benefit of the Democratic ticket from president to constable; and if that is what earned it, I am proud of it ...[3]

Wells of course did not rule his entire empire directly, but through leaders in the various counties, who maintained control of the local Mexican vote. This system of control was made possible by the old ranching economy, with its paternalistic, relatively permanent relationships between rancher and ranch hands, and still persists in those South Texas counties where this economy has remained dominant. The displacement of the ranching economy by the agricultural economy and its impersonal mobile occupational relationships in Hidalgo and Cameron counties, and the influx of Anglo Americans which weakened the numerical potency of the Mexican vote,* eventually destroyed the conditions which made possible a county-wide control of the total vote of the Wells variety. Wells's power to deliver the solid vote even in his own county of Cameron was broken in 1920, but the country-wide machine in Hidalgo County lasted well into the thirties. Throughout the twenties, a number of attempts were made by the Anglo newcomers to break up this machine, but the reform movement was not powerful enough to accomplish the overthrow

---

\* A Mexican immigration of equivalent proportions into these counties from 1910 to 1930 did not increase the size of the Mexican vote since the immigrants were aliens of whom the vast majority never became naturalized. The 1940 Census provides the following information: There were 15,038 foreign-born residents over 21 years of age in Hidalgo County in 1940, of which 14,939 were of Mexican descent. Of the total number of foreign-born, 11,717 were still aliens, and no citizenship status is reported for 905 of the remainder. In McAllen, there were 1,888 foreign-born residents over 21 of which 1,715 were from Mexico. This group contains 1,284 aliens, and no citizenship status is reported for 96.

until facilitated by the death of A. Y. Baker, the boss of the machine. According to a local newspaper editor, the Baker machine "hit an all time high here for graft and corruption. Baker and his collaborators practically looted Hidalgo County of everything movable". Starr County, which borders Hidalgo on the west, has a somewhat different political history from that of Hidalgo and Cameron. The head of the county machine there was a Mexican American, who ruled the county under the benevolent direction of Jim Wells, and who established a family dynasty which remained in control until 1946, when the returning veterans finally channelled the discontent which had developed through the years into a successful rebellion against the machine. Starr County has remained almost completely Mexican American in population, and was bypassed by the large-scale irrigation developments and the consequent Anglo American immigration.

Although Wells and his lieutenants apparently maintained their political power by their ability to manipulate the "Mexican vote", there is no indication that the Mexicans as a group benefited from their voting strength either in the sense of having representation through electing Mexicans to office, or by receiving any significant share of the spoils which accrued to the political leaders they supported in power. Nor is there any evidence that Mexican political participation under these machine regimes was more than nominal, or that it left any heritage of political awareness and solidarity which today could provide the basis of a political unification, independent of serving the individual interests of a few political leaders, that could be instrumental in improving the status of the Mexican American group as a whole relative to that of the Anglo.

Although Hidalgo County is no longer dominated by a single machine controlling a decisive bloc of votes, the controlled vote is by no means a thing of the past, as will be seen in the discussion that follows. The real heritage that the machine tradition has left is that of a number of small blocs of votes controlled by various individuals which, in certain situations, can play strategic roles out of all proportion to their actual size in the constant jockeying for power which constitutes an important aspect of the patterns of political action.

The Mexican Vote

There is a stereotype widely held among Anglo Americans that Mexicans do not care who is elected, that they will give their votes to whomever will pay for them or provide free barbecue and beer, and that they are the willing tools of political bosses who herd them to the polls.

Like the stereotypes already discussed, this one has elements of truth, but is far from being an adequate generalization. The role played by a complaisant, easily-influenced Mexican electorate during the era of the powerful political machines certainly was not conducive to the development of a conception of the rights and duties of responsible citizenship since the Mexican's political participation was limited to simply placing his vote at the disposal of the political boss as part of the obligation due him for benefits received.* Nor did the Mexican cultural tradition provide any patterns of genuine democratic participation which could be helpful to the Mexican in his adjustments to the American political system and its ideal pattern of the citizen-voter.** This historic

---

* "When these Texas-Mexicans automatically became American subjects (after the Treaty of Guadalupe Hidalgo in 1848), according to the terms of the treaty, they found themselves unprepared for American democracy. Mexican politics, to which they were accustomed, were politics of the sword and revolution; manhood suffrage was almost unknown to them and certainly never practiced. The vote which had been given to them as by a miracle meant nothing to these newly created American citizens. It was then that bossism originated. It grew as a necessity at first. The need of instructing these new voters was evident, and if to the victors belong the spoils, the votes of these men belonged to those who were intelligent enough to herd the voters together. Here were hundreds of voters who were willing to do as they were bid." Jovita Gonzalez, Social Life in Cameron, Starr, and Zapata Counties, unpublished M. A. thesis, University of Texas, 1930.

** Tannenbaum says of Mexican politics: "The nonexistence of party organization, the lack of any sense of the rights of minorities, the complete absence of democratic habits and practices, made democracy a farce from the beginning. He who had the power won the government, and as soon as he was in power he despoiled, persecuted, and robbed his opponents and contenders for public office. As the group or individual in power was in fact legislator, judge, and executive at the same time, his opponents had no recourse but rebellion. Government was thus a very personal matter among groups of individuals, without serious regard to party politics or party ideals, but with very serious attachment to some individual attempt to make the world safe for themselves and their friends, and, in the process, as uncomfortable and unsafe as possible for their political and personal enemies." Op. Cit., p. 92.

pattern of abject submission to the dictates of the machine has had much to do with the development of the Anglo's stereotype and the consequent tendency to identify the Mexican with corrupt politics. Many Anglos tend to think of the "Mexican Vote" in these historic terms, as a more or less organized bloc of votes at the beck and call of whoever is unscrupulous enough to use it, and as a threat to "clean", "honest" politics which must always be guarded against and nullified. The fact that Mexicans provide fifty or more percent of the population in most Valley towns and about forty percent of the population in San Antonio enhances the potential threat of what might happen if the "Mexican Vote" were to get out of hand.

At the present time, it cannot be said that an organized or unified "Mexican Vote" exists on an extensive basis either in the Valley or in San Antonio, in the sense of a total vote which can be delivered for one particular candidate or ticket, or which is held together by a common orientation of all Mexican voters to the goal of furthering the interests of their group as such. Part of the Mexican American electorate submits to controlled voting, part of it votes independently, and part of it does not vote at all. Actually, this may be said of the Anglo American electorate as well, but the proportion of the parts to each other is probably different in the two cases, and the bases of voting are certainly different. Other things being equal, there is a tendency for Mexicans to vote for Mexican candidates on the rare occasions when they appear on the ballot. Anglo American politicians have always recognized this tendency and have tried to cope with it, when no other means were available, by putting up a second Mexican candidate of their own choosing in order to split the Mexican vote. However, other things are seldom equal, and the considerations which determine Mexican American voting are many and varied. First of all, it should be noted that a large percentage of the Mexican American population, at least those in the labor role category, do not vote at all.* Aside from the one-fifth of the Mexican adult population in McAllen which is not naturalized,** the non-voting element is swelled by apathy and a lack of awareness of or interest in the concept of active citizenship, although political apathy is not confined to Mexicans, of course. Some Mexicans, although American

---

\* Just how large a percentage is not known. No distinction is made in election returns between Anglo and Mexican votes. An analysis of votes by precincts would not yield even approximate estimates since precincts in McAllen and Hidalgo County are not coterminous with districts in which Mexicans reside. That a large percentage of Mexicans do not vote is a widespread belief among Valley and San Antonio informants who are politically active, which is consistent with the writer's own observations and impressions.

\*\* This is a rough estimate based on the comparison of the figures in the footnote on p.272 with the census of the McAllen Anglo and Mexican populations compiled from the City Directory. As for the County, the 1940 Census figure of 11,717 aliens over 21, practically all of whom are Mexicans, looms large when compared with a total potential voting population (which includes both Anglos and Mexicans) of 41,953.

citizens by birth, still tend to think of themselves as Mexicans and of elections as the affair of the Anglos. A number of informants professed disillusionment with all politics and office-seekers and disfranchised themselves on that account, as illustrated by the following, which also indicates one of the techniques used to influence Mexican American voting:

> I won't vote at all because I don't like to be told what to do. Plenty of times when I'm in a beer joint, someone will come up to me and ask me if I have bought my poll tax. When I tell him no, he offers to buy me some beers and tells me he knows someone who will buy it for me if I will vote for soandso. I tell him to keep his beers and his poll tax, I don't want any part of it. I'm so disgusted with this politics business that I wouldn't vote for anyone.

This suspicion and cynicism is a prominent characteristic of the Mexican attitude toward leadership in general, as will be seen below. Finally, an important factor in Mexican non-voting is the required payment of a poll tax which, although a small sum ($1.75), costs the laborer most of a day's wage.

Among those Mexicans who do vote, aside from the group whose votes are regularly controlled, there seems to be a greater tendency to vote on the basis of personalistic criteria than on the basis of issues or the qualifications of the candidates.* Many voters who are "independent", even though they are not subject to the direct pressure of controlled vote bloc leaders, may feel obligated to follow the recommenda-

---

* There are important exceptions to this general statement that will be brought out in the course of the discussion.

tions of these leaders because of small favors received or because they respect the advice of such men. A political leader in Starr County described this pattern as follows:

> Informant said that most Mexicans who vote independently have someone in mind who they go to for advice or who they know can do them a favor, even if the man is not their patron. They usually vote on this man's recommendation. He cited his own case as an example. He would estimate that he controls outright about 50 votes, but he knows that there are about 200 others who will vote the way he votes. These are people who come to see him from time to time to ask him for small favors. Since he grants them without asking for anything in return, the recipients of the favors come to hold him in high regard. Many of them have already come in, although he puts no pressure on them, and asked him how he is going to vote in the coming election. When he tells them he has not made up his mind yet, they say, well, let us know when you do, and we'll vote the same way. Your judgement is good enough for us. Informant said that he knows it is similar in the case of D (the dominant political <u>jefe</u> in a small town near McAllen which is almost completely Mexican in population). D controls directly about 200 votes, but can influence about 800 more. D's directly controlled 200 voters have families with other voters in them, and then D is an important figure and is looked up to in the community, so the way he votes is good enough for many people he does not control.

The discussion that follows will bring out in more detail the nature of these and other patterns of Mexican political participation and leadership, the role of the dominant-subordinate relationship in the patterning of political action, and the contribution in turn which these patterns make to the functioning of that relationship.

<u>The Controlled Vote and the Political Jefe</u>

The one-party system characteristic of Texas and all the Solid South has had important implications for the organization of Valley politics. Hard and fast allegiance to the

Democratic Party is taken for granted because of the lack of Republican rivalry. This means that the struggle for votes and group support may be carried on freely within the Party without the problem of presenting a unified front against the threat of opposition from another party. The Democratic Primary is the crucial election since the nomination is tantamount to election to office, and it is at this point that strategic alliances and bids for support must be made by the various candidates and political leaders. Part of the vote in each Valley town is organized into one or more blocs of controlled votes, and although these blocs are usually independent of each other, they often combine to enhance their bargaining power. The candidate running for a municipal office is usually assured of victory if he can obtain the support of the local bloc or blocs, but the candidate for party nomination to an office in the county government, the state legislature, or the Congress faces the problem of obtaining the support of each of the local blocs within the particular political jurisdiction in order to be successful. On the city level, the local bloc either controls the majority of the vote, or if there are two or more blocs which control the majority between them, they will usually work together to defeat independent candidates. One of McAllen's city commissioners explained the procedure as follows:

> There are four commissioners elected to the city commission, and they are at large, do not represent specific city precincts. Candidates are usually nominated on a ticket

which is made up by a private group that invites the candidate to run. Anyone can run if he submits his name to the election commission, but independent candidates seldom have a chance. Last year there were ten candidates for the two vacant commissioner's posts, but the independents did not even show.

In the municipal elections, the blocs are thus usually strong enough to provide and elect their own candidates.

In county elections, however, no local bloc is strong enough to elect a slate of candidates for all the county offices by itself, although a number of blocs may combine to do so, each taking one or two offices for itself by mutual agreement. Beyond the county level, the local blocs have no direct influence in selecting candidates, but retain an important role by virtue of the votes they can throw to one candidate or another, and are usually courted by all of the latter. Since all of this goes on within the party, the freedom of the blocs to switch their support from one candidate to another in succeeding elections is not limited by any idea of party loyalty which must not be breached, and it is generally expected that the leaders of the blocs will seek alliances and give support where their interests are best served, and that they may shift their allegiances from one election to another. The one-party system has a further significance in that the local bloc has bargaining power only in the race for the nomination, i.e., the primary election. The bloc leaders must select their candidates at this point with care. Since there is no Republican opposition, the candidate who wins the nomination for a post in the state legislature or for Congressional representative no longer needs the support of those blocs which gave their votes to other candidates in the primary, nor need he fear their opposition when he makes the final race. Thus, even though a Democrat will hold office in any event, those political leaders who did not aid him in obtaining the nomination will be ignored in the distribution of patronage just as completely as though a Republican had been elected to office. If there is a runoff election,* those bloc leaders who backed the eliminated candidates will have another chance since the two remaining candidates still need all the support they can obtain.

An examination of the controlled vote bloc as it operates in McAllen, and of the role of the bloc leader, will help to illuminate the connection between politics and dominant-subordinate group relationships:

The leaders, or *jefes* as they are usually called, who control blocs of votes in McAllen are not professional politicians who pursue such activities on a full-time basis or who obtain their principal income from this source. The opportunities for patronage and income afforded by the municipal offices are on too small a scale, as is the share of the spoils

---

\* If no one wins a clear majority in the first primary in Texas, i.e., at least fifty percent of the total vote, there will be a second primary for the two leading candidates to decide the nomination. A candidate who may have had a strong lead in the first primary but failed to gain the necessary majority may lose out in the second primary because the eliminated candidates may give their support to his rival and thus defeat him after all.

obtainable through participation in county and higher politics. During the period when the county was run by one machine there was probably enough to go around for the small group in power, but at present there are many groups who must share in the proceeds. The few political leaders in McAllen are businessmen who own relatively extensive commercial and farming enterprises and who are preoccupied with their business interests primarily and with political activities only secondarily. There are a few lawyers who are also active in municipal and county politics, but they do not control enough votes to become *jefes*, and their activities are limited to serving as candidates and office-holders sponsored by the *jefes*. This is understandable since the principal basis for controlling votes is the power a *jefe* wields by virtue of his status as employer.

The basis of the political power of the *jefe* is of a different sort from that of the boss of the urban political machine in that he does not control strategic elective and appointive offices and through these many minor political jobs, nor does he have a formal political organization with a staff of workers capable of thoroughly canvassing the electorate. San Antonio politics offer approximations to this type of organization, as will be seen, but the Valley *jefes* control votes through the personal influence and power which they exert in their capacity as employers and in other relations maintained through their business activities. Political leadership in McAllen is identified with top business status and has none of the stigma often found attached to it in the case of the machine boss or other type of professional politician. The controlled vote blocs are not considered machines,* and the general concensus of opinion is that city politics are "clean" and fair. This conviction is obviously buttressed by the fact that politics in McAllen are in the hands of individuals who enjoy the utmost prestige because of their high occupational and economic status.

The greatest concentration of controlled Mexican American votes is under the domination of one Mexican American and his associates, a Mexican American who is generally conceded to be the wealthiest member of the Mexican group, and whose business establishment and farming interests compare favorably with those of the more successful Anglo Americans.** His

---

* The idea of the machine has very unfavorable connotations in McAllen, probably because of the alleged fraud and corruption which characterized the county machine overthrown only 15 years ago. No one, apparently, desires a return to the days when Hidalgo County was notorious throughout the state and beyond for its corrupt politics. The threat of "machine politics" was made the dominant issue in the Congressional campaign of 1948 by the local candidate, who was running against an aspirant from Laredo, which is in a county still dominated by one political group in the machine tradition.

** This man is head of the B family referred to supra, p. 226.

political power, as well as his business and farms, were inherited from his father and brothers, who played similar roles in the community before him. The principal basis of his political power is derived as a byproduct of the patron influence he enjoys in his relationships with his employees. The sense of obligation felt by the employee toward the patron is easily extended to doing him the favor of voting for whomever the latter indicates. The procedure used by the _jefe_ is to pay the poll tax of his employees in order to make specific the obligation of placing their votes at his disposal. With the votes of his own employees as a nucleus, this _jefe_ has extended the size of his bloc by obtaining control of the votes in the families of his employees and of the employees of other Mexican American businessmen who follow his lead and who have votes at their disposal also by virtue of the patron-peon pattern. Due to the personalistic relationship he maintains with his employees, most of these votes are granted voluntarily, but beyond this, the fear of losing one's job is a sufficiently realistic threat for bringing recalcitrants into line. A Mexican American professional, a reliable informant, related the story of an attempt by a Mexican American veteran, an employee of the local office of a government agency, to organize a "civic club", a story which illustrates how the _jefe's_ business power can be employed to further political ends:

X wanted to start a civic club made up of veterans, and
had the idea that a club like that could do a job of
educating the people to their rights. He thought they
could have classes and have the members go around to
the people's houses and tell them about their rights
with respect to the police and jobs and so on. He
talked to a lot of veterans and they were all willing
to start a club. We talked to B (the _jefe_) about it,
and he said it was a fine idea and he would support it.
Well, all of B's sons and his son-in-law came to the
first meeting, all of them veterans, and they brought
a whole bunch with them who always hang around with
them. They had decided what they were going to do
before they came. When it came to electing officers,
the B bunch voted one of the sons in as president,
and gave all the other offices to B boys. No one else
had a chance because the Bs and their bunch were voting
together, and some of the others went along with them.
X was so disappointed and angry about the whole thing
that he just cried. They held the second meeting in a
bar of all places, sat around for a while, and dismissed
the meeting. They never called another one. There are
still some boys who would like to start such a club,
but they're afraid to come up against B again. He was
behind the whole thing. Let me tell you what he did.
Soon after the failure of the club, X was called in by
his boss, who told him that he heard he was getting
mixed up in politics, and said that he would have to
stay away from that sort of thing if he wanted to keep
his federal job. He wasn't the only one who felt B's
pressure. B called the fathers of a lot of those
boys and told them he would fire them or have them
fired if their sons tried to get mixed up in politics
by organizing clubs. You see, some of the boys'
fathers worked for B or for people who B could tell
to fire them. He even called the fathers of the other
boys whose jobs he couldn't threaten and told them
that the gringos don't like the organizing of such
clubs and would kill their sons if they kept it up.

The _jefe's_ connections with other local politicians, as well
as with men influential in county and state politics, and
his business status enable him to provide services and
occasionally a job for individuals who thereby become obligated to vote his way even though they are not his employees.
For example, the _jefe_ told the writer of his efforts to

obtain a parole for the son of a local Mexican by enlisting the aid of the state senator and various judges in pushing the petition, and of how he finally had to take the case personally to the lieutenant-governor of the state, a Valley man, in order to obtain the parole.

Estimates of the extent of the Mexican *jefe's* control vary between 30 and 50 percent of the total active Mexican American vote, the rest being considered independent except for those controlled by the Anglo *jefes*. By the very nature of the basis of his power, the *jefe* cannot reach the group of field workers in the harvest crews who represent such a large percentage of the total Mexican American population in the area, nor does he make an attempt to do so. There are a number of considerations which minimize the importance and usefulness of this group from the political point of view for all the *jefes*. The general lack of contact and integration of this group with the town community, the fact that many of them migrate north for part of the year, the expense of paying the poll tax, and the absence of stable relationships with employers who might provide an external stimulus,* largely eliminate this group as a source of independent votes which could threaten the effectiveness of the *jefe's* controlled bloc in the distribution of voting power in McAllen and the county. Those Mexicans who do vote are to be found in the town occupations and among the farm and shed laborers who hold relatively stable jobs. The proportion of this vote controlled by the

---

* It is probable that many of the *jefe's* controlled voters would not vote at all if they were not requested to do so by the *jefe*.

*jefe* has been sufficient to decisively determine the outcome of Mexican participation in elections since the independent vote is ordinarily not organized against him, and thus part of it can be expected to go along with the candidates he supports. Consequently, there is no need to augment the size of his bloc by recourse to the large farm labor group which, as long as it does not vote at all, presents no threat to his balance of power.

The political power controlled by this Mexican *jefe* and his associates makes him a factor to be reckoned with by the Anglo American political leaders in their efforts to "sew up" the situation for their own candidates. As the local newspaper editor said, "He does know everybody in town, and the Anglo candidates feel that he represents a substantial number of votes, even though they do not know how many, so they feel impelled to woo him." The usual procedure is to make a "deal" whereby the *jefe* employs his vote bloc to support the candidates sponsored by the Anglo leaders, and the latter in turn instruct their voters to vote for a candiate put up by the *jefe*. With regard to Mexican office-holders in the city government, this has resulted in no more than a token representation. For many years, the *jefe* himself was the only Mexican American on the City Commission where the mayor and three other commissioners were Anglos, and recently this post has been occupied by a Mexican American lawyer, a relative of the *jefe*. Occasionally the Anglo bloc will ask the *jefe* to select a Mexican for appointment to one of the city's administrative board such as the zoning board, where he will be the sole Mexican member. For example, during the period of the study the _jefe_ made a "deal" with the chief Anglo leader, a leading businessman who had held the post of mayor for years, whereby the _jefe's_ support for this leader's candidates for election to the school board was exchanged for the latter's influence in electing a Mexican candidate sponsored by the _jefe_. The deal proved to be a fiasco, but if the Mexican had been elected, he would have been the only Mexican on a school board of seven members. Such token representation is better than none at all, of course, but its effectiveness can be gauged by comparing relative Anglo and Mexican access to public services and facilities, for example. The _colonia_ suffers from unpaved streets, poor drainage, overcrowded schools, and almost no street lighting, whereas the Anglo residential section does very well in all of these respects.

The use of political power for wresting concessions from the Anglo-dominated city government for the benefit of the Mexican group does not figure as a major orientation to political action on the part of the _jefe_ and his associates in any event. Rather, they view their political power, such as it is, as a means of increasing their own prestige in the Anglo world and of insuring themselves at least a measure of acceptance by the Anglos with whom they are brought into contact by their political activities. Such a motivation limits still further the effectiveness of the representation the _jefe_ can exercise in the city government since it pushes action in the direction of accommodation rather than protest. By virtue of the political role he plays with respect to the Anglo group, the latter finds it reasonable, as well as convenient, to define the *jefe* as **the** leader and representative of the Mexican group in McAllen, and to use him as the principal intermediary in the more important dealings with Mexicans. He and his associates thus monopolize whatever meager channels of communication exist between the two groups.

Given the goal of Anglo acceptance on the part of the *jefe* and his group, and the fact that the present use of their political power is the means of at least partial realization of that goal, the employment of that power for furthering the interests of the Mexican group as a whole is necessarily excluded. Adopting the latter course would mean sacrificing Anglo approval and recognition since it would make the Mexican vote an independent factor not necessarily amenable to Anglo desires. Adherence to the group interest goal would also require mobilizing every possible Mexican vote and initiating programs of voter education. Such efforts are not necessary under the present arrangement since the *jefe* controls enough votes, or at least has the reputation of controlling enough votes, to obtain the limited concessions he requests from his Anglo collaborators, and voter education serves no useful purpose when controlled, rather than independent, votes are desired. Furthermore, the education of Mexican voters in the rights and obligations of citizenship, and the development of their awareness of their potential political power when the high proportion of the population they comprise is considered, would probably encourage independent thinking and weaken the jefe's control of votes.* A Mexican electorate oriented to obtaining more ample and effective representation, whether it be by Anglo or Mexican office-holders, colonia improvements, and other concessions would upset the existing arrangement and undermine the basis of the present adjustment made by the jefe and his group to the Anglo world.

The pattern of the controlled vote is being undermined by a number of factors, the most prominent of which is the coming to maturity of a generation educated in the American schools who attach more importance to the vote than did their fathers, who are taking up white-collar jobs where they are relatively free from the kind of pressure that jefes can exert to control their votes, and who have abandoned or never assumed the tendency to establish the patron-peon relationship and are instead oriented more to the Anglo concept of "independence." Many of this group are veterans who have returned to McAllen and the Valley with broader horizons, a greater awareness of their "rights", and a determined, if somewhat vague, desire to improve their status. A group of these veterans established a Spanish-language weekly in McAllen in which appeared a series of editorials attacking the local organization of Mexican businessmen, which is largely dominated by the jefe and his associates,

---

* The story quoted on page 286 indicates the jefe's awareness of this.

for its failure to provide effective leadership for the
colonia. A number of attempts were made by the club members
to silence the editor of the paper, but this simply stirred
him on to more devastating criticism, including the publishing of the names of the businessmen who tried to silence him,
as well as a description of how they tried to do so. The
criticism was focused on the political practices of these
businessmen, so a few representative excerpts from the editorials
may be quoted:

> It is not possible to create organizations with the
> purpose of being united so that, by means of that union,
> we will be able to realize our rights and claim what
> is in justice due us. I say this is not possible
> because there already exists a club which considers
> itself the representative of our colonia in all affairs
> which are of interest to the latter. But what has this
> club done up to now for the welfare of the colonia?
> Nothing but prepare coyotes who are charged with
> carrying our votes to those who, after the election,
> look at us over their shoulders, and not only that,
> but segregate us like undesirable beasts. It is time
> that our Latin American element, as the Anglo-Saxons
> are accustomed to calling us, make use of their rights
> as citizens, and if tomorrow we wish to vote for a
> cooper, may it be our conscience that tells us to do
> so without the intervention of dirty lunch of barbecue
> and beer with which the inferior politicians are
> accustomed to buying our vote. Let us vote as our
> conscience dictates, then, and not as our friends, who
> are paid by the political machine, tell us.[4]
>
> The unification of the masses is as essential as the
> food that nourishes and fortifies, since the latter
> fortifies the body and unification stimulates the spirit
> to continue fighting for a better environment, for an
> environment free from the defects that afflict us at
> present. Organization will be the bond that will
> unite our Latin American family in an armor that no one
> will be able to destroy, and if tomorrow these inferior
> politicians aspire to continue profiting and making
> themselves influential simply because they shout at
> the tops of their voices that they are the manipulators
> of the Mexican vote, they will encounter the first

barriers that will obstruct the development of the program that they have been practicing for so many years. Then our Anglo American cousins will acknowledge that our race is worthy of consideration like the rest of the races, and not simply as heads of sheep which are only counted in the electoral contests.[5]

Patterns of controlled voting and concentrations of political power are somewhat different in San Antonio and are worthy of a brief description for comparative purposes. San Antonio politics are profoundly influenced by a political machine of the urban variety that has been dominated for years by the county sheriff. The machine controls primarily the county government, but by virtue of the large vote the sheriff has at his disposal, plays a weighty role in city politics as well. The basis of the sheriff's power, as that of any machine boss, is the patronage of elective and appointive offices which he can dispense, the favors he can do for his followers, and the large number of "political jobs", large and small, at his disposal. The fact that, at the time of the study, the sheriff's brother was Congressional representative from the district that includes San Antonio gave him access to federal patronage as well. The machine accounts for a large part of the Mexican vote that is controlled, while other Mexican votes that are controlled can be found among the employees of city and county officials who form semi-independent (i.e., of the machine) political organizations composed of the men who are employed under their jurisdiction. Since the spoils system is direct and simple in San Antonio, these men must vote for and work for the reelection of their bosses if they are to retain jobs.

Unlike the Valley, there are no Mexican American *jefes* in San Antonio who control blocs of votes of a size sufficient to give them the sort of strategic position with respect to Anglo politicians that the McAllen Mexican *jefe* has attained to. The Anglo *jefes* and the machine have built up their own following among the Mexican Americans through the jobs and influence they have at their disposal, and there is no need to make deals with Mexican representatives. There are a number of Mexicans in San Antonio who control tiny blocs of votes which they sell to the machine boss or to the highest bidder at elections, or which they use as a means of bargaining for some sort of political job. These *jefecitos*, little leaders, do not necessarily buy the votes they control, although this is occasionally true. A more effective basis of control is that the *jefecitos* function as intermediaries for the Mexicans in their dealings with the Anglo world. Some Mexicans, because of poor command of English or unfamiliarity with the proper channels, have difficulty in approaching the local governmental or other agencies for obtaining licenses of one kind or another, paying fines for minor violations of the law, and so on. The *jefecitos*, or *coyotes*, as they are derogatorily called, take care of these things for the people and in general are defined by the recipients of their services as performing a protective and facilitating function. In order to discharge the obligation incurred, these people place their votes at the disposal of the _jefecito_, who in turn sells them to the machine or receives some other benefit in payment. Thus the _jefecito_ retains no independence of political action by virtue of the votes he controls; it is purely a commercial transaction.

A few years ago, one of these _jefecitos_ entertained ambitions of becoming a _jefe_ on a grander scale and was apparently on the way to realizing those ambitions when his career was cut short by a conviction to a federal penitentiary for fraudulent participation in political campaigns and voting without having American citizenship. His story as told by an informant who worked with him, is interesting for its contrast with the _jefe_ role in McAllen, as well as its illustration of the techniques employed by the _jefecito_.

> L was the man who organized this organization he called the Club Democratico, in fact he was the Club Democratico because it was a one-man organization. The reason they called him the leader of the West Side was because he took it upon himself to organize most of the political meetings that were held on the West Side every time there was a political campaign, and because most of the time he was able to carry his precinct. He was active enough to go down the line from door to door asking people to vote for the man he endorsed. His favorite dodge was to go out and throw out a few thousand circulars offering all sorts of talent and famous speakers, and as many Mexican artists as he could crowd into the space of a small circular. All of the people in the neighborhood would come most of the time. The majority of them didn't own a poll tax, and didn't intend to pay for a poll tax, but the politicians would see a big crowd, and thought, what a wonderful meeting. The newspapers would come out next day and say, 3000 people at L's rally. They started calling him a leader, the political leader of the West Side. Besides organizing meetings, he would hang around the city hall and the courthouse, he was just a _coyote_. The moment he would hear that some commissioner or some department was going to hire people for any reason whatsoever, he'd run out to the West Side to his constituents, and he'd say, you go over there and talk to soandso, tell him I sent you, and

he'll give you a job. That was the kind of game he'd play ... He was looking after the almighty dollar, and he knew that as long as he kept that club going and had people coming to the meetings, and was able to get them together during the campaigns, he was going to make money. As a matter of fact, politicians would come to his house and bring him money. At each campaign he would get a few hundred here and a few hundred there, and up to $500 from some. He got much more than that from some of the state politicians, who thought that he really controlled the West Side.

There is a great difference, then, between the jefe of McAllen and the jefecito of San Antonio, in motivation, in power, and in status, and in fact they play very dissimilar roles. The Mexican Americans who are prominent in San Antonio politics are primarily the lawyers, who have attempted to obtain political representation on the basis of their own efforts rather than as the result of deals made between Anglo and Mexican jefes, as in McAllen. Mexican businessmen are active in other spheres of leadership in San Antonio, but play no comparable role in political action to that of the Mexican businessmen of McAllen.

## The Mexican American Candidate and Office-Holder

The number of Mexican Americans holding elective office (during the period of the study) was extremely small. One city commissioner in McAllen was Mexican, the other three commissioners and the mayor being Anglo. Of all the county's elective offices, which include judge, sheriff, treasurer, commissioners, and so on, a Mexican American was incumbent of one of the four county commissioners' posts. The local representatives to the state legislature were Anglo, as was the Congressional representative from McAllen's district. A Mexican held an appointive office, that of assistant district attorney, and a few Mexicans were members of various administrative boards in McAllen. This was the extent of Mexican American political representation in Hidalgo County.* During the period of the study, two Mexican Americans ran for office, one for the city school board and the other for county judge, but both failed to be elected. So far as could be determined, no Mexican had ever run for the office of county judge before, the highest and most influential office in local government in Texas. The county's political history reveals that a few Mexicans were county auditors and clerks in the past, but no Mexican ever held a higher office since the Anglos obtained political power.

In San Antonio, Mexicans hold no elective offices in city or county with the exception of one member of the city school board and a justice of the peace.** On the infrequent occasions when

---

\* This should be compared with the Anglo-Mexican population ratio. All estimates of the Mexican proportion of the total Valley population run between 50 and 60 percent. The investigator's census of the McAllen City Directory (1947) gave the Mexicans 56.4% of the city's population. The census also indicates that there are 5,486 Anglos over 18, and 5,523 Mexicans over 18. If the 1,284 aliens (a figure derived from the U.S. Census of 1940) are subtracted from the Mexican total, a rough approximation of the relative potential voting populations of the two groups would be 5,486 Anglos and 4,239 Mexicans, although it should be remembered that these figures include the 18 to 21 age category.

\*\* The Mexicans comprise roughly 35 to 40 percent of the city's population. The best estimates obtainable indicate that about 11,000 Mexicans purchase poll taxes in an election year as compared to about 35,000 Anglos. The number of those who actually vote is usually considerably less.

Mexicans have run for public office, they have always been unsuccessful, with the exception of recently filling the two offices just mentioned. Mexican lawyers have been candidates for the city school board, the county commission, and the state legislature. From time to time, Mexican lawyers have held appointive offices as assistant district or city attorneys, but a membership on the city's civil service commission is the only prominent appointive office held by a Mexican at present.*

The fact that Mexicans have relatively greater political power in the Valley than in San Antonio and thus hold a few more elective offices, and that this power has been concentrated in the hands of Mexican businessmen and farmers, is not accidental. With regard to the question of relative power, scale is an important factor. The control of municipal government in the Valley does not offer much opportunity for dispensing patronage,** the basis of power, and the division of power among many small blocs minimizes the number of offices any one bloc can gain in

---

\* This lack of representation in appointive offices extends to the city's draft boards as well. During the period of the study, the local Mexican American organizations sent a joint telegram to President Truman protesting the fact that of all the men recommended by the Governor for appointment to San Antonio draft boards, "not one was of Mexican descent."

\*\* Every one of the Valley's larger towns has a city manager, which considerably reduces the control of distribution of municipal jobs by the elective officials. Most of the city administration is handled by the city manager, which means that the mayors and their commissioners need only perform part-time. In McAllen, the mayor's salary is $50 a month, while commissioners receive $5 each time the commission meets, which is semi-monthly. Participation in city politics in McAllen is hardly remunerative financially.

the county government and the amount of patronage it can thereby obtain from this source. This has left the road open for the businessmen, whose power as employers have enabled them to control votes, and whose businesses make them independent of the need to utilize politics as a source of income. A few Mexican businessmen and farmers in the Valley have had the resources to participate in politics on this basis just as the Anglos do. In San Antonio, on the other hand, the scale of city and county government provides those who can dominate it with innumerable opportunities for dispensing patronage and thus controlling votes, as well as with a number of lucrative sources of income. The size of the electorate is so much greater than in the Valley towns that the number of votes a businessman could control by virtue of his employer status would never enable him to compete with the machine and the patronage it offers in controlling votes, nor could he obtain the bargaining power and the strategic position that goes with it which is characteristic of the Valley businessman-politician. Since the employer power is the major basis of vote control in the Valley, and since political power is distributed among many small blocs rather than concentrated in a dominant machine, a few Mexicans have been able to profit by the situation to build up controlled vote blocs of a sufficient size to enable them to bargain for political offices and other rewards.

This explains why Mexicans have relatively greater political power in the Valley, and also partially explains why the businessmen are politically active there and not in San Antonio. A further explanation of the latter difference lies in the fact that active participation in politics is one of the roles assumed by several of the most prominent Anglo businessmen in the Valley and thus is identified with high status, while in San Antonio politics are in the hands of "professional" politicians, of the machine boss and his henchmen. In the Valley, politics, on the city level at least, are a sort of honorable avocation, a means of adding luster to a position primarily determined by occupational status, for men who are high up in the status hierarchy of the community, whereas in San Antonio the politician is somewhat suspect, is generally considered a not altogether desirable type who may have nefarious connections.* Thus, in the Valley, politics, because of its associations, has been defined by the Mexican businessmen as a means of improving his status relative to the Anglo group, whereas since Anglo businessmen in San Antonio have kept aloof from at least formal participation in politics, the Mexican businessmen have followed suit, seeing no status advantage to be derived from such activity.

For reasons already indicated,** the Mexican Americans who

---

\* This conception of politics as "dirty" and politicians as corrupt is no different from that encountered in many American cities. San Antonio has a "good government" organization, composed mostly of Anglos but containing a few Negroes and Mexicans, who have banded together in righteous indignation to overthrow the machine and clean up city and county politics. This organization accused the machine boss of being in league with the city's racketeers and of opposing the candidacy of the present district attorney for re-election because he had allegedly fought the rackets.

\*\* <u>Supra</u>, pp. 228-30.

have been most prominent in San Antonio politics, above the **jefecito** level, are the lawyers.* Unlike the Valley *jefes*, however, the lawyers have had no political power, and have participated in politics primarily as independent candidates seeking political office. Since they control few if any votes and have no bargaining power with the Anglos, their pattern of campaigning for office differs significantly from that of the Mexican office-seekers in the Valley, whether the latter are the *jefes* themselves, or the lawyers who are sponsored by the *jefes*. The Valley Mexican who campaigns for a county office** does not make an issue of this ethnic origin, nor does he make a special appeal to the Mexican voter with a promise to represent the Mexican group if elected. This is because he depends on Anglo support as well as Mexican due to the deals that have been made, and he cannot afford to antagonize the Anglos by suggesting that

---

\* Lawyers have been traditionally associated with politics in the Western World, but the Mexican lawyer's relation to politics is at least in part a function of the situation created by the dominant-subordinate relationship. The lack of opportunity to practice law has pushed the Mexican lawyer into political activity, an area which has seemed most appropriate to his training and talents in lieu of practicing law. Moreover, the general lack of education and professional training among Mexicans have placed a premium on the skills of the lawyer and have made him the logical choice of those Anglos who have sought effective intermediaries in their dealings with the Mexicans, as well as of those Mexicans who have felt the need of representation in their relations with the Anglos.

\*\* Very little campaigning is necessary by candidates for municipal office since the deals between the blocs usually determine the outcome of the election.

he represents the special interest of the Mexicans and is in opposition to the Anglos. The Mexican who ran for county judge during the period of the study, e.g., carefully avoided all reference to this issue in his campaign speeches, confining himself to such issues as better farm roads and improved collection of delinquent taxes.

The Mexican candidate running for office in San Antonio does so as an independent without organized support and usually with little funds. He cannot hope for machine support and does not have the money to pay for *jefecito* support. The Anglo-dominated machine has no need to put up Mexican candidates as an attraction to the Mexican vote since it directly controls a strategic section of that vote without resorting to Mexican intermediaries, as in the case in the Valley. The offices most frequently sought by Mexicans (county commissioner and representative to the state legislature) are almost always filled by men affiliated with the machine, so that the Mexican candidate must run against a machine candidate. The Mexican's only hope, therefore, is to capture the independent vote, and although he may hope to attract a small part of the Anglo element, he must necessarily concentrate his major efforts on the Mexican "independent" vote.

Given all these advantages, the Mexican candidate must define his campaign from the start as a crusade for *la raza*,*

---

* A term universally used by the Mexicans to designate their own group. See *infra*, pp. 520 ff. As one informant put it, "When we say *la raza*, we mean the Mexican race, our own people, and when we want to include everybody, we say *la raza humana*, the human race."

emphasizing that his sole purpose in running for office is to provide sorely-needed representation for the Mexican group. He is dependent upon the Mexican businessmen for campaign funds, and although he may promise them various political favors if he is elected, he appeals mainly to their sentiments about _la raza_, arguing that by helping to elect him as a representative of the Mexicans they will be helping themselves. In campaigning, he attempts to secure the active aid and participation of the other lawyers who have come to be known as "political" leaders of the group, as well as of various other prominent Mexicans. This aid and participation are usually limited to speaking at the rallies staged by the candidate in and near the _colonia_. The speeches are always in Spanish, and follow a regular pattern of presenting the candidate as a _defensor de nuestra raza_, defender of our race, who will fight for the rights of the Mexican people, and of glorifying Mexican descent and demonstrating great pride in such descent in an attempt to work up the patriotic fervor of the crowd. At one of these _colonia_ rallies during the campaign undertaken by two Mexicans for the Democratic nominations of state representative and county commissioner in 1948, the speakers included the president general of an interstate Mexican American organization, who happens to live in San Antonio, the two most prominent Mexican lawyers who have been active in politics, and a Mexican American who is a professor at the state university. One of the speakers pointed out that, although the Mexicans comprise one-third of San Antonio's population, they have no political representation on the city, county, or state levels, and that, without representation they are being denied access to the rights which are theirs. He said that the Mexicans need their own representatives so that they will get the respect and attention which is their due, and that the poorly equipped schools, bad lighting, absence of sanitary facilities, and unpaved streets evident in the colonia are the direct result of lack of Mexican representation in government. Another speaker stressed the need for unity among the people and the importance of electing the candidates if the Mexicans are ever to improve their condition. One of the candidates referred to the origin of the United States, to the fact that the basis of the Revolution was a protest against taxation without representation. He stated that this has been precisely the situation of the Mexican people, who are taxed but get nothing for it. He concluded with the words: "What the Mexican people need is a Mexican to work for them, and I am qualified to represent them because I have worked for them all my life. Nothing is more Mexican than my name. My father is Mexican, my mother is Mexican, and my heart and blood are Mexican!"

These candidates did not win the nominations they were seeking, nor were they successful in previous bids for the same offices made some years ago. The man who ran for state representative is a very unusual Mexican American in that he is known to have a prominent status* in the Anglo world. He actually received more votes from the Anglos than he did from his own group. The other candidate ran for county commissioner from a precinct of which the colonia is a major component, yet he failed to obtain as many votes as his Anglo opponent. The previous campaigns of both of these men had similar outcomes. The reasons why Mexican candidates do not obtain a higher percentage of the Mexican vote have already been partially indicated, but it will be profitable to explore a few of these in somewhat greater detail.

Earlier in this discussion, the statement was made that, other things being equal, there is a tendency for Mexicans to vote for Mexican candidates. Mexican candidates organize their campaigns on the basis of this belief, and place their hopes of success in attracting the Mexican vote. However, these hopes have been in every case unfounded. Actually, many of the candidates and leaders, in view of their own feel-

---

* Other Mexican Americans in the Valley and San Antonio have a certain status with the Anglo group, but this is almost always based on political or occupational considerations and does not extend beyond these spheres. However, this man's relationships with the Anglo group have a broader basis, as is evidenced, e.g., by the fact that he is president of the city-wide boy scout council and a trustee of an Anglo Methodist church with high status in the city.

ings of solidarity with their group,* tend to impute similar sentiments of like intensity to the mass of the people. They fail to realize that, although there is a latent solidarity among Mexicans, it is not strong enough to overcome a number of considerations which carry more weight in determining how the Mexican will vote. The tendency of Mexicans to vote for members of their own group is illustrated by the case of a small grocer, who said:

> I vote in every election. In last Saturday's election I voted for all of the Mexican candidates, as I always do. Some fellows offered to give me $5 to vote for someone else, but I don't go for that sort of stuff because I don't think it's right.

Unfortunately for the Mexican candidates, this type of Mexican voter, who is free from occupational pressure and at the same time takes it for granted that a Mexican should receive his vote, is distinctly in the minority.

---

\* The small group of Mexican lawyers in San Antonio who have built up their reputations among Mexicans throughout the state have done so as defensores de la raza. In their writings, speeches, organizational activities, and most of all political action, they have continually stressed the need for unity in the Mexican group, and have expended much of their time and effort, inside and outside of San Antonio, in attempting to build up such unity, although their motivations and results in dedicating themselves to this crusade must be considered apart. The most widely-known individual in this group informed the writer that he will support a Mexican for political office regardless of the issues involved. Referring to an offer he received to participate in a political campaign in South Texas, he said that he refused, as a matter of principle, because there were no Mexican candidates in the race. He was offered money to participate, but that was irrelevant as far as he was concerned, since he never takes money for the speeches he makes. He does not care who wins an election if all the candidates are Anglo, but if there is a Mexican candidate, he will campaign for him regardless of what side he is on, and he will do it at his own expense.

The tendency of Mexicans to use their votes as one means of discharging personal obligations they have incurred,[*] may result in their voting for Anglo rather than Mexican candidates. In San Antonio, e.g., the many small blocs of votes of the *jefecitos* are for sale to the highest bidder. These Mexican votes are lost to the Mexican candidates, who cannot afford to pay for them. A variation of the obligation pattern is to give one's vote to an Anglo politician in the hope of placing him under an obligation. During the congressional campaign of 1948 in the Valley, in which there were three Anglos and one Mexican running for the office of representative, a Mexican in a small Valley town said that he and his friends would normally vote for the Mexican, but how they actually would vote depended on the local Anglo sheriff, since they thought it best to go along with him. He said that the doubtful favors that could be bestowed by a Mexican congressman in Washington were far overshadowed by the small, real favors they could obtain from the sheriff right here at home.

In the Valley, the vote blocs controlled by the Mexican *jefes* are used in local politics to elect Mexican candidates sponsored by the blocs, but beyond the local scene the *jefe* may support an Anglo candidate opposed by a Mexican. In the above-mentioned congressional campaign, the Mexican *jefe* in McAllen and some of those in nearby towns endorsed one or the other of the two Anglo candidates from Hidalgo County. They ignored the Mexican candidate, who was from Brownsville, and

---

[*] See *supra*, pp. 278-79.

the other Anglo candidate, from Laredo at the far end of the congressional district, who based much of his campaign on the advocation of "equal rights" for Mexicans, the only candidate to explicitly do so. The *jefes* supported the Anglo candidates from Hidalgo because they knew these men much better than they did the other candidates and felt they could expect more from them in exchange for their bloc support, and because they are preoccupied with Anglo acceptance.

In San Antonio, the Anglo machine controls a large number of Mexican votes which are diverted to Anglo candidates sponsored by the machine. Aside from the county machine, city officials, who employ Mexicans for most of the labor and some of the white-collar jobs in their departments, control these votes and have access to others which their Mexican employees obtain for them. A Mexican informant active in politics explained this procedure as follows:

> The City Hall controls the votes on the West Side, and that's why X (the Mexican candidate for state representative) couldn't get many votes there. In the street commissioner's department, e.g., they hire a lot of Mexicans, and they all must have their poll taxes. Well, if in one department they have, say, 200 men, with their wives and friends they multiply to about 600 votes. That's quite a bloc on the West Side. The fire and police commissioner does tricks the same way. The firemen, as a rule, are sent out to work politically. They are sent into the houses and they come into my shop. They say that they're working for the city and they'd like to have my help. They say, "My job depends on this." So some people help them out.

The investigator witnessed an incident where a Mexican employee of a county commissioner, who had campaigned actively for him against his Mexican opponent, apologized to the latter's campaign manager after the campaign was over, saying that he was sorry if he had done anything to offend him during the campaign, but that he had to work for the county commissioner because he is his boss.

Another factor which diverts Mexican votes from Mexican office-seekers is a commonly encountered attitude of suspicion and cynicism with regard to the motivations of the candidate.[*] As will be seen, this suspicion of opportunism is a prominent element in attitudes toward all types of leadership in the Mexican group, but at this point only its political implications will be discussed. The stereotype of the Mexican politician which expresses this suspicion depicts him as only interested in his fellow Mexican when he wants his vote, and as desiring political office or power in order to improve his own status

---

[*] "This combination of economic, cultural, and racial conflict, this history of conquest, exploitation, and cruelty, of political chicanery and dishonesty, has left a deep sense of distrust within the mass of Mexicans, especially among the mestizos ... The mixture of bloods has brought with it a cultural by-product that has carried into the small community the bitterness and distrust that have arisen out of the centuries of exploitation and political chicanery. Son desconfiados (they are suspicious) is an almost universal description of the small rural community, especially if the community is of mixed blood. They have been betrayed so often, promises have been broken so many times, that no other result was possible. Disbelief has become natural; it is their most effective, and perhaps, their only, means of defense. The fruits of experience indicate that any promise made will probably not be kept, that any leader will betray, that any undertaking will remain uncompleted." Tannenbaum, op. cit., pp. 101-2.

with the Anglos and/or to line his own pockets. The comments, "One man I won't vote for is X, because he is only a Mexican when election time comes around", and "The Mexican politicians pass by my barber shop every day of the week without saying hello, but before election time they come in and kiss my hand and call me brother", illustrate the first part of the stereotype. A number of informants in San Antonio explained the defeat of the Mexican lawyer who ran for state representative[*] as due to his estrangement from the Mexican community and its affairs except when he decided to run for political office. A Mexican businessman said that the candidate should have won, but actually his defeat should not be a surprise because he is like all the other leaders the Mexican people have had. They do not stay with the people for a long period of time and build up a record which can obtain trust and confidence for them. They pop up as leaders of the people, then go off in pursuit of other interests, then return to take up positions of leadership again. He concluded that it is because they are always looking out for themselves that the leaders have not really been leaders and have not been able to keep the support of the people. Another businessman explained the outcome of the election in similar terms:

---

[*] Supra, pp. 304-5.

I don't think he got as much support from the Mexican people as we thought he would. I don't think he has made a good enough attempt to become well-known among them. He didn't spend much time with the people until he decided to run for office. And you can't fool them. The Mexican people are very sensitive and touchy, and if they felt that he wasn't a good Mexican all the time, they wouldn't vote for him. They don't let those things go by.

Closely related to the idea that the only tie that binds the Mexican candidate to his group is his desire for Mexican votes, is the readiness to believe that he will "sell out" to the Anglos for status or money. "All those fellows are alike. As soon as they get to the top, they forget their people and try to please the Americanos". A Mexican lawyer not involved in politics in San Antonio said:

> The Mexican *politicos* holler to the people, "Elect me and I will protect *nuestra raza*!" Then they go to the Anglo politicians and make a deal. So it is only a matter of time before they end up out in the cold. The Anglo doesn't respect him because he can hire the Mexican to do things he wouldn't do himself, and he loses out with the Mexicans because his promises were spurious in the first place and he had no intention of keeping them.

The extent of the tendency to suspect the motives of political leaders, as well as a glimpse of the reaction of the leader to such suspicion is nicely illustrated by the case of a Mexican lawyer in San Antonio, who, during the period of

the study, was elected to the school board.* In the first
flush of victory, many Mexicans felt that much would be done
to improve the condition of the colonia schools now that the
group had a representative on the school board. Actually, the
Mexican had one vote as opposed to six Anglo votes, and regardless of what tactics he might have employed, the results he
could obtain inevitably would fall far short of the expectations that had been aroused among his fellow-Mexicans now
that they at long last had a representative on the board.

---

\* Since several previous attempts to elect a Mexican as a member of the school board were unsuccessful, this election was enthusiastically hailed by many Mexicans as a great step forward in their attempts to obtain representation, and as an impressive example of Mexican political unity. This was undoubtedly an example of how Mexicans could unite to vote for their own interests on a particular issue, but the victory itself was not necessarily an indication of other successes to come. In this election, for the first time, the group of Mexicans conducting the campaign arrived at an agreement with the Negro political leaders who, unlike the Mexicans, control a large percentage of the Negro vote. The Mexicans agreed to campaign for the election of a Negro candidate to the junior college board in exchange for Negro support for the Mexican candidate. As a result of this combined strength, both candidates were successful, although by narrow margins. It should also be noted that the school board post carries no patronage, and so all Mexicans were free from the ordinary machine and job pressures to vote as they pleased. The primary election in which the Mexican candidates failed to win the nominations of state representative and county commissioner were held some months subsequent to the school board victory, and revealed the same failure to obtain the Mexican vote which had occurred in previous elections, thus disappointing the hopes kindled by the school board victory. There was no alliance with the Negroes in that election, however, since the Negroes had no candidate of their own they wished to elect, and the patronage at stake, as well as the attitudes being discussed here, diverted much of the Mexican vote to the Anglo candidates.

The Mexican school board representative became a sort of "race hero" as a result of his victory, and went off to the Valley to campaign for the Anglo candidate in the congressional race there who was espousing equal rights for Mexicans. Upon his return, he found that he had been attacked from many quarters as a "fence-straddler" on the school board, anxious to please the Anglos, and accused of participating in Valley politics because he had been paid to do so and wanted the publicity he received. In a speech before the members of the local LULAC* council, he attempted to defend himself, pointing out his weak position on the school board and emphasizing that he had gone to the Valley in defense of the Mexican cause since the Anglo he supported was "the only candidate with guts enough to bring into the open the injustices which the Latin Americans suffer in his district." The conclusion of this speech is worthwhile quoting:

> I have not been engaged in politics to get my name in the headlines, nor to make money out of it, as so many people here have been saying maliciously behind my back. My bank account is overdrawn, to be truthful about it. I am about through putting up with the back-biting and back-stabbing I have been subjected to. That is why you people can never keep any decent leadership, because you tear down your leaders when they try to do something for you. If everyone insists that I have been taking money for my political activities, and that I have been a fence-straddler on the school board, well, maybe I ought to do just that. As long as everyone is convinced that I am taking money for what I am trying to do in helping the cause, I suppose I might as well get something out of it for myself. The thing that has really hurt is that my LULAC brethren have not only been ready to believe this vicious gossip about me, but have been active in spreading it themselves.

---
\* See infra, pp. 537 ff.

The suspicious attitude toward the Mexican political leader has a realistic basis in that the Mexican group has actually suffered from a long succession of self-seeking leaders, although this has been true more of the past than the present. The *jefe* pattern in McAllen offers a striking example of the lack of disinterestedness which is the major target of the Mexican's suspicion and cynicism, and is but one case of a persisting tendency to succumb to the temptation of obtaining Anglo recognition at the expense of Mexican group interests. Adherence to a course of disinterested leadership is for many a far less attractive and rewarding alternative than seeking Anglo acceptance, and the pursuit of both courses is often incompatible.* Nevertheless, the readiness to believe the worst of their political leaders is often overdone by the Mexicans, and involves the danger of victimizing leaders who may be sincerely oriented to the goal of group betterment. To cite one example, many of the Mexican lawyers active in politics in San Antonio have established residence outside the *colonia*, which conforms to a general pattern among Mexicans to seek better housing when they have sufficiently improved their economic status. This is not condemned by the *colonia* in the case of businessmen or others who take no part in group leadership, but it has assumed a special significance in the case of these lawyers as sufficient evidence, sometimes the only evidence, that they are trying to pass or have passed into the Anglo group and "are only

---

* See *supra*, pp. 290-91.

Mexicans when election time comes around."[*] Suspicion and cynicism are prominent elements of the Mexican attitude toward leadership in all spheres, and will be taken up again below.[**]

## The Anglo American Candidate and the Mexican Vote

The discussion of Anglo-Mexican political relationships has indicated that the Mexican vote presents no special problem to Anglo political supremacy in McAllen, where the controlled portion is delivered to Anglo politicians and minimizes the potential force of the total Mexican vote by splitting it, nor in San Antonio, where the Anglo machines control enough of the Mexican vote to neutralize that part which is independent. This manipulation of Mexican votes functions smoothly on the municipal level, and to a large extent in county politics as well, but in the wider arena of the Congressional district, the lack of widespread control by any one group or machine and the possibility of competition between a number of Anglo candidates for the office of Congressional representative may upset the equilibrium and

---

[*] This expectation on the part of the Mexicans that the leader must remain closely identified with his group illustrates a sense of "passive" solidarity which, by diverting Mexican votes away from Mexican candidates who are suspected of trying to pass, operates in this context to achieve the opposite effect from that sought by candidates who try to arouse "active" solidarity in their exhortations to advance la raza by voting for them.

[**] See infra, pp. 514 ff.

invest the Mexican vote with a particular importance relatively absent in local politics, where the monopoly of candidates and votes by one machine or group largely eliminates the necessity of campaigning for Mexican votes. The congressional race that took place in the Valley during the period of the study affords a good example of how the Mexican vote could become the object of much vigorous campaigning by Anglo candidates, and of how the "Mexican problem" came into the open in the form of a political issue.

The huge Congressional district* of which the Valley is a part has had only two men as its representative during the past forty-six years. One of these, John N. Garner, held the office from 1903 until he became Vice-President in 1933, and his successor kept the post until 1948, when he decided not to run again. Four men, one from Brownsville, two from Hidalgo County, and one from Laredo at the upper end of the district, announced their candidacies for the vacant office. Due to the nature of the district's population distribution, it was generally predicted that there would be a run-off between the Laredo candidate and one of the Valley candidates since the three local candidates would split the Valley vote,

---

* The district embraces 13 counties stretching along the Mexican border from Brownsville on the east to Eagle Pass on the West and including counties as far north as San Antonio. The Valley, which contains only four of these counties and is but a small part of the total area, nevertheless possesses roughly two-thirds of the district's population. As of 1940, the total district population was 334,616, while the Valley contained 215,803 of this figure. Source: *Texas Almanac*, 1947-48, p. 337.

and that the Valley candidate who got into the runoff would eventually win the nomination by capturing enough of the top-heavy Valley vote to overwhelm the Laredo candidate. This is in fact what happened, but few could predict that the contest would be as hotly contested as it was, or that most of the excitement would be aroused over the issue of the Mexican vote. As has been described, the usual procedure on the part of Anglo politicians has been to obtain direct or indirect control of a sufficient number of Mexican votes so that the rest could be comfortably ignored. For present purposes, the most important aspect of the Congressional campaign under discussion was the manner in which the Anglo candidates found it necessary to diverge from this pattern and the implications of this divergence for the understanding of dominant-subordinate group relations.

During the first stage of the campaign, the candidates followed the usual procedure of maneuvering and bidding for the support of controlled vote blocs within the district. The Laredo candidate had the initial advantage, a substantial one, of support from the only county-wide bloc in the district, his home county, which was counted upon to deliver all its votes to him. It is probable that the Laredo candidate would not have entered the race without this support, along with the support that the bloc could obtain for him in neighboring counties, since he made little progress in winning controlled vote support in the Valley, where bloc leaders found it more to their interest to support one or the other of the Valley candidates.* In the Valley, the three local candidates competed vigorously for the vote blocs similar to the one controlled by the McAllen _jefe_.** All of the controlled vote blocs being committed to one or another of the candidates, the second stage would normally have consisted in campaigning mostly for the more or less*** independent Anglo vote, giving

---

\* See _supra_, p.307-8.

\*\* The writer had the opportunity to witness an attempt made by adherents of one of the Valley candidates to bargain for the support of two blocs of Mexican votes. Unfortunately, this incident could not be described without violating the confidence of informants. Suffice it to say that the rewards offered for support were substantial and attractive. Informants among the _jefes_ described other cases which tallied closely with this one.


\*\*\* No very satisfactory information could be obtained on the extent to which the Anglo vote in McAllen is controlled. Judging by the comments of informants, the answer seems to be relatively little. A Mexican _jefe_, e.g., said: "Those people (Anglos) are too independent to submit to controlled voting. Why, in the same family you find husband and wife voting for different candidates. An Anglo can control at most 50 votes, but they like to think they control more." The type of employer-employee relationship with its corresponding sense of obligation which is the basis of _jefe_ power is alien to the Anglo employee, and it is probable that if Anglo political leaders control Anglo votes in McAllen, they do so on other bases. Much of the Anglo leader's power, aside from his own control of Mexican votes, is afforded by the indirect control granted him by the Mexican _jefe_.

only minor attention to direct efforts to secure Mexican votes that might not have been included in the various deals for controlled votes that had been consummated. The Laredo candidate, however, selected as one of the major issues for his campaign, "equal rights and representation for Latin Americans", thus being the first Anglo candidate in the recent history of Valley politics to campaign on such an issue, as far as could be determined.[*] He made his campaign speeches in Spanish and English, prepared his campaign literature in both languages, and enlisted Mexicans from many Valley towns to speak on his behalf at his rallies. When his supporters began to predict that he would sweep the Mexican vote in the Valley, his two Anglo opponents,[**] as well as other Valley Anglos, took alarm. Such a campaign brought to the fore the latent Anglo fear of a solidary Mexican vote

---

[*] Although evaluation of the candidate's sincerity is irrelevant to the purposes of this study, even if this were possible, the following considerations are somewhat enlightening. Laredo, like Brownsville, has a population roughly 85% Mexican, and the candidate's local support, as well as the vast majority of his campaign workers, were Mexican Americans. Since he speaks perfect Spanish and has maintained close relations with Mexicans most of his life, he was well-equipped to attract Mexican votes. Although the candidate had established a reputation as a champion of Mexican "rights" previous to his present political involvement, the fact that he had much to gain and comparatively nothing to lose in campaigning on the Mexican rights issue in the Valley probably had something to do with his decision. He had little hope of obtaining much of the Valley's Anglo vote, which was sure to go to Valley candidates, so he could concentrate on capturing the independent Mexican vote in the Valley without fearing the consequences of alienating Anglo voters.

[**] The fourth candidate, although Mexican, made no explicit attempt to attract Mexican votes, and indeed hardly bothered to campaign at all.

and all of the unpleasant associations this carried with it.[*]
The fact that the Laredo candidate was prominently connected
with the political machine that dominated his home county, a
machine in which many Mexicans actively participated, made
it possible to define him as embodying the historic threat of
corrupt politics and the unscrupulous use of a complaisant
Mexican vote as the tool of such politics. The Valley candidate who ultimately won the election devoted most of his
efforts in the runoff campaign to what he termed "a fight
of independent voters against the candidate of the Webb County
political machine," conveniently overlooking the fact that he
himself had sought and obtained support from many controlled
vote blocs. To the Valley Anglo, the Laredo candidate thus
came to symbolize the threat of the return of the highly disliked and feared conditions of the machine tradition, corrupt
politics and the domination of a solidary Mexican vote.[**]

Aside from the machine accusation, the other Anglo candidates reacted to the Laredo man's tactics by adopting similar
ones. So as not to alienate Anglo votes, they compromised by
condemning discrimination against Mexicans when they were speaking before predominantly Mexican audiences, and ignoring the
subject when addressing Anglos. They too enlisted Mexicans to
speak on their behalf who questioned the sincerity of the
Laredo candidate, and one of the candidates even attempted to

---
[*] See supra, pp. 274-76.
[**] See supra, p. 283-84.

read part of his campaign speeches, to Mexican audiences, in Spanish. Another reaction consisted of condemning the Laredo candidate for injecting "racial issues" into the campaign and thus seeking to divide the Anglo and Mexican groups in the Valley. Actually, the Laredo candidate at no time during the campaign became very specific about what he proposed to do about Mexican "rights", limiting himself to promising Mexicans equal representation if he were elected, and generally advocating the elimination of discrimination. However, the idea that he was sowing the seeds of racial discord rapidly caught fire among the Valley Anglos, and he was attacked from all sides.* The alarm was rapidly picked up and spread by the Valley newspapers, which were supporting the local candidates. The following excerpts from editorials in two Valley newspapers are representative:

### THAT RACIAL ISSUE

Working under the coldly vicious strategy of "divide and conquer", Laredo's candidate for Congressman is doing a grave disservice to the cause of racial amity in this district. Openly and brutally, in speeches and in street corner conversations, the Laredo man is dragging the racial issue into the campaign. In talks and in campaign literature, he is appealing to Latin American citizens to vote for him as the only true apostle of racial equality, the only active foe of discrimination, the only man who will see that non-Anglos get a fair deal. Such an appeal is ridiculous on its face. There isn't a man in the congressional

---

\* Sample comment from a letter to the editor published in a Valley newspaper: "Any candidate who builds a platform on this foundation (i.e., the racial issue) should not have the support of any citizen, nor should hold public office in any city, county, or district in this state or in this country of ours."

race who hasn't taken a firm stand against racial discrimination, not only for the campaign but in the past. It is a little difficult to see just how Mr. _____, who is not a Latin himself, suddenly conceives that he is the knight in shining armor anointed to quickly and painlessly eradicate all racial feeling, all discrimination....To achieve his personal ambition - a seat in Congress - Mr. \_\_\_\_\_ is seeking to drive a dividing wedge between the citizens of Latin descent and those of Anglo blood in the district. His efforts can only hurt the sincere efforts toward racial harmony in this region. They should be repudiated by all thinking citizens of whatever racial extraction. 6

## IT'S DEFINITELY OUT OF PLACE

As the Congressional race has gained momentum during recent weeks, there has been a growing tendency in some quarters to inject a racial issue into the campaign. This is not only regrettable. It is a development of serious concern. As many of us have had occasion to observe, there is nothing more calculated to upset folks, inflame the passions, nurture the seeds of bitterness, or cultivate hate in the human heart than the arraying of groups of different racial extraction against one another ... In a political campaign clever utilization of the racial theme can oftentimes mean victory, particularly in a region where one group outnumbers the other. It has become evident that along with this racial issue a question of discrimination is being brought into the campaign. That is natural enough since the raising of a racial issue means nothing more or less ... than an implication that discrimination toward one group is being practiced by another. And unfortunately, it is true that people who have never considered discrimination as their lot can sometimes be persuaded that it is if they are told so often enough ... Together they (Anglos and Mexicans) have cultivated the land, built towns and communities, elected their representatives to local, state and national office ... In some counties Spanish-speaking residents far outnumber those who were born of the English-speaking families. But, as in various other areas of our country where people of many origins and tongues have pooled their physical, mental and spiritual resources to make the America of today, the people of the border country have lived and worked together to advance the region. Consequently for any candidate, seeking to represent the people of this district as a whole, to make a division among them as he appeals for votes, to set up one group against another for political gain, is for him to follow a disturbing, an unhappy and an unwise course .......

The conflict thus joined between the Valley Anglos and the Laredo candidate and his followers had its counterpart in a division that appeared within the Valley Mexican group between those who supported the Laredo candidate and those who supported the local candidates. All of the Mexicans in this latter group, regardless of their actual reasons for opposing the Laredo candidate, found it convenient and effective to focus on the "racial issue" as a means of combatting him. The high point in this opposition was reached with the publication of an open letter signed by seventeen Mexicans from different Valley towns in which the "racial hatred campaign" of the Laredo candidate was compared to the techniques employed by Hitler. A Valley Mexican representing the opposite camp responded with an open letter which said in part:

> Hitler tried to destroy democracy; Mr. _____ (the Laredo candidate) is trying to preserve it in its true form. What he is trying to do is to extract the poison of racial superiority from the minds of a few persons ... I personally believe that these persons (who signed the letter) are puppets of so-called big political bosses ... I want to remind my fellow-citizens that a discussion by a candidate of civil rights is an issue and not a subversive movement. By reading the list of signers of the mentioned public letter, I can see that they are and have been supporters of one of the other candidates; that's perfectly legal, but if they are afraid of the winning possibilities of a candidate, they should at least respect his qualities. [8]

The outcomes of the primary and runoff elections agreed fairly closely with the initial predictions, and thus indicated that the Anglo fears aroused by the course the campaign had taken had little realistic basis. In the runoff election, the

Laredo candidate received only two-thirds as many votes as his opponent, losing the nomination by 10,000 votes. He lost most of the Valley vote, obtaining, e.g., only 4,000 votes in Hidalgo County as compared to his opponent's 10,000, and less than half the number received by the winner in the neighboring county of Cameron. In McAllen, where the potential vote is roughly 60% Anglo and 40% Mexican, the winner received 2,769 votes and the Laredo candidate 292.[9]

The implications of the Anglo reaction and of the various divisions which appeared in the course of this Congressional campaign are best treated in connection with the discussion which follows of political participation and the dominant-subordinate group relationship.

## Patterns of Political Action and Dominant-Subordinate Group Relations

An analysis of the idea and action patterns in the political sphere from the point of view of the cultural conflicts and conflicts of interest which they reveal will serve to make more explicit the dynamic interrelations between political action and the dominant-subordinate group relationship. The discussion has shown that, with respect to mass participation in politics, the Mexican's personalistic sense of obligation and loyalty performs a prominent role, just as it does in the occupational sphere. Indeed, it is the functioning of this sense of obligation in the employer-employee relationship that provides the principal basis for the control of Mexican votes. The absence of patterns of genuine democratic participation in the Mexican cultural tradition has meant that the Mexican does not define the significance of the vote in accordance with such participation, and he may therefore use it, with no feeling of impropriety, as a means of discharging obligations incurred in non-political spheres, particularly the occupational. The lack of valuation of democratic participation, or more specifically the absence of a sense of individual voter responsibility, interlocks with the Mexican's orientation to personalistic criteria to invest the vote with concrete significance as a means of fulfilling personal obligations rather than as an instrument for fulfilling the rights and obligations involved in the abstract concept of citizen. Thus, the Mexican may dispose of his vote to his employer or anyone else to whom he is obligated, without involvement in any moral conflict because he has done so. For the same reasons, even when the Mexican voter is independent of the personalistic ties, embodied in the employer-employee relationship, he will tend to view the voting procedure concretely and to cast his vote on the basis of personal considerations rather than as a contribution to the maintenance of democracy which he helps to insure by voting for the "best" man.\*

That the Mexican American cultural patterns here discussed should manifest themselves in a susceptibility to submit to controlled voting is largely due to certain structural and

---
\* Cf. comment of informant quoted above, p. 279.

situational factors.  In McAllen, the fact that the political
leader role is assimilated to the businessman role provides
the incentive for the businessman, in his capacity of employer,
to take advantage of his personalistic relationship with his
employees to ask for their votes, and for the employee to
deliver his vote in accordance with the generalized loyalty which
he feels toward the patron.  If this identification between
employer and politician, which provides the basis for controlling
votes, did not exist, it is possible that the Mexican American
who now gives his vote to his employer would not exercise his
franchise at all.  The Mexican's realistic situation reinforces
this use of the vote in that, preoccupied as he is with job
security, he may improve his hold on his job by turning over his
vote to his employer.  In San Antonio, the fact that the politician,
by virtue of the number of jobs at his disposal, becomes an employer, may mean that his control of Mexican votes is partially
due to the establishment of a personalized relationship with
employees, but the pressure of the realistic situation is
probably the most influential factor since the job that the
Mexican holds is political.  If the politician loses his office,
the Mexican loses his job.  Thus, cultural, structural, and
situational factors combine to produce the Mexican's pattern
of mass political participation.

 A brief comparison of Anglo patterns in this respect with
those of the Mexican reveals a significant difference.  Anglo
American culture defines no sense of obligation and loyalty

which plays a comparable role to that which is characteristically
Mexican.* The Mexican American's tendency to assimilate the
good patron, as well as other key figures who may be appropriate
for such assimilation, to the network of diffuse, personalized
relations that is developed by orientation to his peculiar code
of obligation and loyalty, is not a prominent pattern in Anglo
American culture. An Anglo may feel obligated to his employer
for providing him with a job, and treating him well, but he
will seldom feel impelled on that account to establish a relationship with him of the kind that has been defined as "patron-
peon", much less to grant the employer the kind of loyalty that
would permit the latter to influence him in spheres other than
the one legitimately defined as the employer-employee relationship.
To the extent that the Anglo does feel generalized loyalty of a
type that approximates the Mexican's, he tends to confine it to
such relationships as those of kinship, and does not extend it
to occupational and political relationships, as does the Mexican.
The Anglo's occupational relationships are governed by relatively
more universalistic criteria than are those of the Mexican, and
thus are segregated from the more diffuse relations governed by
particularistic criteria to which the Mexican may assimilate
his occupational relationships. The kind of specific loyalty
the Anglo may develop in his relations with his employer would dis-
courage the acceptance of the latter as a political mentor, or
of his influence in any other capacity outside of that which is

---

\* This is not to deny, of course, that the Anglo possesses a
personal sense of loyalty and obligation. However, as in the
case of most of the Mexican group characteristics defined in this
paper, the difference from Anglo characteristics is a matter
of degree rather than of kind, of emphasis, and of the manner
in which these characteristics combine with one another and with
other aspects of the culture to provide a series of definitions
markedly different from those which prevail in the other culture.

defined as functionally specific to the job.* Moreover, the Anglo's realistic situation does not play a role comparable to that of the Mexican's since the former is subject to relatively less pressure in the matter of job security.

Beyond this, Anglo American culture positively enjoins democratic participation, and imposes an ideal definition, lacking in Mexican American culture, of the individual as a citizen who ought to discharge his responsibility by voting independently. In practice, of course, the Anglo diverges considerably from this ideal pattern, but, for the reasons just described, as well as because of the force of the ideal pattern itself, the divergence does not ordinarily manifest itself in mass political behavior similar to that of the Mexican. His divergence takes the form of political apathy and passivity,** which

---

\* For definition and discussion of particularism, universalism, and functional specificity, see Talcott Parsons, Essays in Sociological Theory, pp. 189 ff.

\*\* The fact that a few Anglo political leaders in McAllen (with the help of Mexican leaders) and San Antonio are able to maintain themselves in power and defeat independent bids for office through the judicious manipulation of what must be a relatively small percentage of the potential voting population points to the existence of wide-spread passivity and apathy in political matters. Although no figures are available for precise documentation, the following figures give a rough idea of voting activity in McAllen and the county: In the 1948 Congressional race, which was said to have called out a record vote, there were 3,061 votes cast in McAllen as compared to a population over 18 years of age of 11,009. For the county, of an estimated total population of 140,000, 23,804 purchased poll taxes, and of this number, 17,098 actually voted. It is not possible to distinguish the relative percentages of controlled and independent votes in these figures, nor the relative number of Anglo and Mexican voters.

involves no direct conflict with the ideal pattern, rather than controlled voting, which would involve such conflict.*

The differences in Mexican and Anglo idea and action patterns with regard to mass political participation, which have been traced to actual cultural differences, provide the basis for a realistic conflict between the two groups since the Anglo tends to use his ideal pattern as a means of evaluating the Mexican's political behavior, and the Mexican fails to meet the standard thus set. Actually, however, this realistic conflict is only the departure point for a series of distortions, rationalizations, and accompanying emotional reactions on the part of the Anglo which serve to support and justify the Anglo domination of political initiative and rewards.

The Anglo American stereotype of Mexican American political behavior** focuses upon the Mexican tendency to submit to controlled voting, but imputes motivations other than those which

---

\* Perhaps it should be stressed that this discussion attempts to define prominent tendencies rather than literal fact. Actually, of course, as has been indicated, many Mexicans also are apathetic, and others vote independently. Similarly, there are Anglos who submit to controlled voting. However, according to the field materials, it would appear that controlled voting is a much more prominent pattern in Mexican American mass political behavior than in that of the Anglo, and the present analysis is concerned with explaining this difference on the basis of cultural and other considerations. Moreover, as will be seen shortly, it is the Mexican's pattern of controlled voting which has been the target of much hostile Anglo sentiment, and this is one of the reasons why the discussion has been so concerned with analyzing this pattern and defining its realistic basis.

\*\* See supra, p. 274.

have been delineated here, and on the basis of these imputations draws conclusions which are out of all proportion to the true situation. Thus, the Anglo believes that the Mexican will give his vote to anyone who will pay for it, that he is the willing tool of political bosses, and that he therefore becomes a ready and accessible means for the corruption of politics. The Anglo evaluates the Mexican's political behavior as immoral because he is applying his own standards, whereas the Mexican, in ceding his vote to his patron, is actually engaged in obeying his own cultural and moral imperatives. The Anglo stereotype comes to the fore when the Anglo feels that his dominance is being threatened by a Mexican vote oriented to its own group interests. One of its functions is to serve as a means of isolating and condemning any _independent_ effort, i.e., independent of Anglo control, direct or indirect, by Mexicans to obtain group representation and political power.*

The appearance of a Mexican American candidate who campaigns for office on the issue of representation for the Mexican group sets in motion an opposition campaign by Anglos who accuse the candidate of stirring up "racial issues" and who try to identify him with corrupt politics. This occurred, e.g.,

---

* There is an obvious inconsistency between Anglo condemnation of Mexican submission to controlled voting and the Anglo practice of exploiting that submission to control Mexican votes. However, the Anglo evidences no strain toward resolving it since, as this discussion indicates, both patterns serve useful purposes. For an inconsistency of precisely the same order in Anglo-Mexican occupational relationships, which serves similar purposes, see above, p. 240.

in the 1946 school board election in San Antonio when a
Mexican American ran for office on the platform of equal
school facilities for Anglos and Mexicans. A prominent Anglo
businessman circulated a letter among the Anglo group which
read in part as follows:

> On Saturday, April 6th, a most important election
> will be held here in San Antonio to elect two
> members of the Board of Education of the San Antonio
> Independent School District. The candidates of the
> BETTER SCHOOL TICKET, John Doe and Richard Roe, are
> running for reelection. They are opposed by another
> candidate, _____, a Latin-American lawyer. It
> is reported he has the support of a Latin-American
> political group on the West Side ... Make up your mind
> right now to vote in this election. The issue is a
> vital one - just as vital as our public schools. Tell
> your employees and your friends to vote, and be sure
> you vote yourself next Saturday, April 6th. Let us
> keep our present School Board uncontaminated by
> destructive politics and politicians.

The Mexican who ran for this office (and lost) was the first
to do so in many years, and so far as could be determined,
had no organized political support, machine or otherwise.
A parallel illustration can be found in the events of the 1948
Congressional campaign in the Valley. In both these cases, a
candidate aimed at rallying Mexican support on the basis of the
latter's own interests. If their campaigns had been successful, they might have affected the existing arrangements whereby
the Mexican vote is neutralized and channeled into acceptance
of Anglo domination and might thus have led to the development
of a Mexican vote oriented to its own group interests. These
independent bids, which present a realistic threat from the
Anglo point of view, are combatted by defining them as attempts

to stir up "racial discord". Moreover, the men who make these bids are pictured as connected with or representing corrupt machine politics,* and as attempting to stir up racial discord in order to capture the votes of the Mexicans, who have already been defined as lacking in voter responsibility and therefore easily corruptible, and use them for nefarious purposes. In view of the imposing size of the potential Mexican vote, the Anglo fears eventual inundation resulting in domination by the Mexican group if any of these bids are successful in defining the political situation for the Mexican electorate as one of Anglo _versus_ Mexican.**

---

\* In the case of the Laredo candidate, the connection did in fact exist. However, it is extremely doubtful if his opponents would have publicized this to such an extent, in view of their own similar connections, if it had not been such an effective weapon when juxtaposed to his direct bid for the Mexican vote. In combining the two, his opponents could conjure up the ever feared image of the corrupt politician riding into power on the basis of the support of the controlled Mexican vote, a power which would threaten Anglo interests because it had been won by promising to further Mexican interests as such.

\*\* This is why the Anglo becomes so emotionally aroused at attempts to introduce "racial issues". Candidates who campaign in the interests of _la raza_ inevitably call attention to the facts of Mexican subordination and the discrimination this entails. This is aggravated by the fact that the opposing candidates are forced to attack discrimination also in order to compete on equal terms. As will be seen, the Anglo tends to take for granted the present dominant-subordinate relationship, and prefers to have no public issue made of it, especially since this may stimulate Mexicans to thinking of themselves as the victims of discrimination, and thus bring on an anti-Anglo reaction. For a good illustration of this, see the second newspaper editorial quoted on page 322 above.

The result of all this is to discredit these independent bids in the eyes of the Anglo electorate, which rushes to the defense of its dominant status, as well as arousing the resistance of those Mexicans who are oriented to the goal of Anglo acceptance, and who consequently wish to avoid "racial issues". This reaction is not evident in those cases where Mexicans run for office who are sponsored by _jefes_ in league with the Anglo politicians because, as has been demonstrated, these Mexicans are at least under indirect Anglo control, and because they do not raise racial issues. The man who makes an independent bid, on the other hand, becomes an "agitator",* who threatens clean politics and Anglo dominance with corrupt politics and Mexican dominance. The distortions and accompanying emotional hostility involved in the development of this simplified dichotomy of good and evil serve the twofold purpose of justifying the subordination of the Mexican American, who, if he were not subordinated, might threaten the Anglo's "democratic way of life", and of providing an effective weapon against attempts to break through

---

\* In the Valley Congressional campaign, the moral indignation of the Anglo reaction was heightened by the fact that the "agitator" was an Anglo, who, by introducing the racial issue, was breaking dominant group solidarity.

that subordination.*

The degree of distortion and emotional overreaction (which mutually reinforce each other) involved in the Anglo's definition of the situation, as opposed to the realistic elements present in that situation, may be estimated by reviewing the data that have been presented in this discussion of politics. It can be seen that, although certain realistic conflicts of culture and interest have provided the departure point for the development of hostility between the groups, the Anglos have

---

\* The following comments, all by Mexican political leaders in San Antonio, indicate the manifestation of the Anglo reaction at the polls: "It never fails that when there is a Mexican running for office, thousands of Anglos turn out to vote who never vote at any other time. For some reason or other they regard it as a threat to themselves that a Mexican may get elected, and so they turn out in force to prevent this. In the last election (in which two Mexican candidates ran for office), I had never before seen such long lines of Anglo voters at the polls."

"You can be sure that when a Latin American runs for office, he is going to arouse the hostility or at least the anxiety of the Anglo American people. There was a case in Dallas where a Latin American ran for some city office, and the Anglo American vote was three times as high as it had ever been before. When the Anglos know that a Latin American is running, many people vote who never vote any other time because they become aroused. In view of this, there is no point in getting the Anglos excited unless we stand a chance of gaining something concrete in the process."

"We have no chance until the Anglos become generous enough to allow a Mexican candidate to win. The Anglo Americans have the majority of the votes, and they do not want any Mexican officeholders, even though all the Mexicans want is one representative in each place to present their case and register a protest vote. But the Anglos will not even let the Mexicans have that. They gang up every time a Mexican runs."

elaborated these sources of conflict much beyond their realistic bases to the point where they provide both the motivation and the justification for the complete political subordination of the Mexican.

The analysis of the various factors that determine Mexican mass political participation, as manifested in both controlled and independent voting, has demonstrated that they militate against the development of unified action in such participation, thus contributing to the strength of Anglo dominance by minimizing the threat to it. One type of Mexican political participation, however, that exemplified by the Mexican *jefe* pattern, plays a positive role in the maintenance of the present distribution of power between the two groups. This type of participation is directly patterned by the dominant-subordinate group relationship and in turn has the effect of reinforcing it. The *jefe* acknowledges Anglo dominance and strives only to associate himself with it. His pursuit of greater frequency of contact with Anglos and equal status with them, although not in fact completely realized,[*] is sufficiently successful as a result of placing his political power at the disposal of Anglo dominance to insure his aid in dissipating any threats to that dominance. Thus, as has been shown, the *jefe* not only carefully avoids the introduction of "racial issues" in the various aspects of his political

---

[*] A closer examination of the nature and extent of this Anglo-Mexican contact is offered in connection with the discussion of class structure, *infra*, pp. 375 ff.

participation,* but will actively oppose any politician who campaigns on this basis, as occurred in the Valley Congressional campaign. The raising of such an issue would imperil Anglo-Mexican harmony and thus affect adversely the type of adjustment the jefe has made to the Anglo group.** The fact that Mexican political leaders in San Antonio have campaigned openly for group representation and have appealed directly to the Mexican voters does not mean that they are necessarily "nobler" or more disinterested than the Valley jefes, of course. As has been indicated, their lack of actual political power does not win for them the kind of consideration and approximation to equal status that the Valley jefe can obtain, and the lack of prestige attached to the politician role in San Antonio eliminates its attraction as a means of improving status relative to the Anglo group. Thus, the Mexican politician in San Antonio has no particular stake in the maintenance of Anglo dominance, and indeed must define himself as a defender of la raza in order to attract votes from the only source open to him. The fact that the Mexican group has often been afflicted with self-seeking political leaders in the past, and the persistent readiness of the people to accuse their present leaders of participating in politics with the ulterior motives of seeking Anglo recognition, good political jobs, and/or money, indicates that a leader may succumb

---

\* See supra, pp. 289-90 and 301-2.

\*\* It should be pointed out that the jefe's adjustment to the dominant-subordinate situation as presented in this discussion does not necessarily signify complacent acceptance of Anglo dominance. In fact, there is evidence that the jefes and others who have made similar adjustments deeply resent Anglo dominance with its accompanying stereotyping and discrimination. However, their principal reaction has taken the form of accommodation rather than protest. The discussion has focused on this aspect of their reactive adjustment to the exclusion of others because of its significant implications for the connection between political action and the ordering of intergroup relations. For a more rounded treatment of the various aspects of Mexican reactive adjustments, see the final chapter.

to the temptation of trading whatever political influence or supposed influence he may have for these rewards while using the screen of fighting for group betterment.

These considerations indicate that it would be erroneous to conclude that the Valley *jefe* is the personification of self-interest and the San Antonio political leader of disinterestedness. The analysis has shown that a more adequate explanation of the differences in their typical political behavior can be made by focusing on the situational rather than motivational differences in the two cases. Actually, both types of leaders have at least one major motivational element in common, the desire to modify or escape from the disabilities imposed by their subordinate status. In the Valley case, the *jefe*, possessing political power by virtue of his employer status, has found that the most effective means of realizing this goal has been through the use of that power to support Anglo dominance and through playing down intergroup conflict. In San Antonio, on the other hand, the political leader lacks such power and hence influence with the dominant group, and so has nothing to lose by adopting the role of defender of la raza, indeed must adopt this course if he is to achieve power at all. This does not preclude the possibility of employment of this power, once it is achieved, as a means of gaining status in the Anglo world, thus ultimately casting the San Antonio political leader in a role similar to that performed by the Valley *jefe*. In both cases, the Anglo's hostile reaction and discrediting of Mexican political action independent of direct or indirect Anglo control has minimized the possibility of integrating the individual goal with the group interest goal, and has made it more rewarding to pursue the former to the exclusion, and frequently at the expense, of the latter. Nevertheless, as indicated, there have been and are political leaders who chose the latter course, although they have been distinctly in the minority. In view of the fact that the success of the Mexican political leader's adjustment to Anglo dominance is largely dependent on the maintenance of his influence with his own group, it is probable that the rising protest against that adjustment among certain elements of the Mexican group\* will exert pressure on the leaders to work more consistently for group interests if they wish to maintain their influence within the group. This would probably necessitate modification of present accommodation adjustments to the Anglo group. The general indifference of Mexican Americans to political participation, as well as other considerations indicated in this discussion, will probably limit the extent to which a widespread protest movement in the sphere of political action can materialize, however.\*\* Rather than an overt political struggle defined in terms of Mexican American versus Anglo American, the result may well be new alignments and arrangements with the dominant group to obtain more effective representation and its ensuing rewards, by the strategic use of the potential political power of the Mexican vote as a lever with which to obtain such concessions.

---
\* See *supra*, pp. 291-92.
\*\* The extent of Mexican-American protest against subordinate status, and the ways in which it is expressed is treated systematically in the final chapter.

## Chapter VII

## SOCIAL ORGANIZATION: CLASSES

Introductory Remarks

The following analysis of class and status distinctions can make no claim to elaborate statistical documentation. However, as will be seen, occupational status is a strategic determinant of total class status, although by no means the only one, and the figures on occupational categories presented in a previous chapter thus provide a rough idea of the size of the various classes although not of the status groups within classes. Beyond this, the analysis is based on data collected from informants, on the writer's own observations, on the perusal of the membership lists of the various voluntary associations of the community, and on clipping files from the local newspapers.

The writer found that each of the two groups of the McAllen community* is characterized by a two-class system with varying subdivisions. When looked at from a regional point of view, i.e., South Texas as a whole, the upper class of each of the two groups of the local community becomes part of the middle class of the larger society, and in order to

---

* The entire class analysis is based on the McAllen data and is considered applicable only to that community. Unless otherwise indicated, all illustrative material is also drawn from the McAllen data.

acknowledge this and maintain a necessary perspective, they will be referred to as the middle classes throughout the discussion. In the Anglo American group, the traditional upper class of the region has been composed of the landholding, cattle-raising ranchers with vast domains, and this class still retains a great deal of economic and political power and influence throughout the state. A newer element in this class, which has in part reinforced the older, is a plutocratic elite based on oil fortunes. Some of the members of this elite are men who rose to fortunes from a moderate economic status through their own enterprise in oil ventures, while the others are the ranchers themselves, whose already substantial incomes have been considerably augmented by the discovery of oil on their properties. Some of the big ranchers still live on their cattle domains, but others, together with the oil operators, practice absentee ownership and have made San Antonio, Austin, and Houston the centers of their activities. Together with a few of the biggest businessmen, they form the upper classes of these cities and of the region of South Texas dominated by these cities. With one or two possible exceptions, no upper class Anglo in McAllen could claim membership in this regional upper class.

The Mexican American case is similar. With the exception of one family, none of the members of the Mexican American upper class in McAllen can claim status in the Mexican American regional upper class. The latter, although small in numbers,

contains at least three distinct elements. One of these
is the remnant of an old land-holding aristocracy in the
hacienda tradition that traces its ancestry and status back
to the Spanish royal land grants or porciones (made in this
area between 1748 and 1821). The power and influence of
this element has waned considerably since the advent of the
Anglo American, but it still commands much prestige in the
regional Mexican American community. A second element consists
of a small group of businessmen, located in the large
cities, whose enterprises are on a much larger scale than
any Mexican American business in the Valley. Their status
is due primarily to personal achievement rather than family
background, as in the case of the land-holding group. A third
element is composed of the professionals, mainly lawyers but
including a few doctors and academicians, who have achieved
top status in the larger Mexican American community primarily
by virtue of their activities as political and civic leaders
of Mexicans in Texas and secondarily as a result of their
professional competence, although there are a few outstanding
exceptions to this order. This element has developed contemporaneously
with the businessman element and also in the
larger cities as a rule. A few of the older men in the professional
group are descendants of the old families who have
buttressed their ascribed status with achievement, while others
are of the immigrant generation who received most of their
education in Mexico. The size of this group is slowly being
augmented by younger men of the second generation who have

completed their education within the last decade.

The regional upper classes will be further referred to only when necessary for the purposes of the study.

## Anglo American Classes

Of the two classes that may be discerned within Anglo American society in McAllen, the middle class has at least three subdivisions which may be nascent classes, but at this point they can only be called status groups since they indicate points on a continuum rather than actual class divisions. The members of the top status group have much in common with the next subdivision, but they may be distinguished from it by the possession of a peculiar combination of characteristics that is seldom found among the members of the latter. They own the largest business enterprises in McAllen are usually in combination with the largest agricultural landholdings in the surrounding area, although there are a few exceptions who are only "big" businessmen or large landowners. They reside in North McAllen, although a few live outside the city on their farms; and their homes are the "showplaces" of McAllen. They take it for granted that their children will go to college, either to the state university or outside the state. The men are the most active and prominent figures in such organizations as the Chamber of Commerce, the YMCA, and the Community Chest, where they are always numbered among the highest elected and appointed officers. They are members of the service clubs, Kiwanis, Rotary, and Lions, but they ordinarily leave the active roles in these organizations to members of the middle status group. Their wives, however, rotate amongst themselves the highest offices in the most prominent women's clubs in McAllen, such as the Junior Service League, and the Garden and Book Clubs. They are usually members of the First Methodist Church, or less often, of the First Baptist Church, and are often referred to by the parishioners as the "powers that be" in the affairs of these churches. They and their wives set the tone for the "social" life of McAllen, through their style of living and their prominent manner of participation in the Country Club activities as well as in the big "social events" sponsored by the "best" clubs of the city. Finally, the political leaders described in the previous chapter are always members of this top status group, although not all the members of this group are politically active. The top status group is small, numbering perhaps 15 or 20 families, and includes one or two outstanding lawyers as well as the businessmen and/or growers.

The middle status group is much larger, and contains the lawyers, the doctors, all other independent businessmen down to the small retailers, real estate and insurance brokers, growers who own their farms, and the better-paid salaried dependents such as the department store managers and the local representatives of large firms in San Antonio and Houston. The top members of this group have relatively high incomes, live in North McAllen and participate in the same clubs, churches, and other organizations as those of the top status group, but with the important qualification that their participation is limited to supporting and following that of the top group rather than initiating action themselves. Although they may dominate such lesser power groups as the service clubs, they play only secondary roles in the organizations mentioned above. This "upper sector" includes members of other religious denominations, such as Presbyterians, Christian Scientists, Jews and an occasional Catholic, as well as Methodists and Baptists, and they play leading roles in their respective churches similar to those played by the top status group in the Methodist and Baptist churches. Most of the families in this upper sector are active in the Country Club, and the wives are members of the Junior Service League, but the latter may also be the most active and influential of women's clubs that do not include top status group women. Here too the expectation exists that children will go to college. The "lieutenants" of the political leaders ordinarily come from this "upper sector", as do the candidates for municipal office.

From this "upper sector" there is a gradual shading off to the small real estate brokers, insurance salesmen, small retailers, and growers with moderate incomes. These people may live in North McAllen but are more likely to live in other parts of town, their homes may be comfortable but in no way pretentious, and the question of college for children is more a hope than an expectation. The men are members of the Chamber of Commerce and of a service club, but they hold no important offices in these organizations. They do hold the leading offices in the local posts of the American Legion and the VFW and in the various lodges, and their wives may be active in the auxiliaries of these organizations. They are members of one of the churches mentioned above, but may be members of the Christian or Lutheran Churches. Their wives provide most of the membership of the women's clubs headed by women of the upper sector, but may be members of clubs that do not include any of the latter. With the exception of upper sector men, none of the members of the middle status group are politically active.

The third and lowest status group of the middle class consists of store and office clerks, civil servants, and most of the occupational group listed above[*] as white collar workers. They ordinarily do not reside in North McAllen and do not always own their homes. They are not members of the Chamber of Commerce, the service clubs, nor of the Country Club, but are frequently encountered in the veteran's organizations and the lodges. They may be members of any of the churches indicated above, but a few adhere to one or another of the evangelistic churches characterized by highly emotional revivals such as the Assembly of God, the Church of God, or the Church of the Nazarene. Their wives may be members of clubs that include women of the middle status group, but rarely a club that includes women from the upper sector of

---
[*] Pages 208.

that group. Educational aspirations for children ordinarily are limited to high school, but may include the local junior college.

Regardless of the differences just sketched, all status groups of the middle class have in common the orientation to the success ideal already described,[*] although perhaps in varying degrees. Thus, all middle class members tend to identify with the world of business enterprise and its values. The lower class, on the other hand, may be said to be composed of those who are outside the competitive world dominated by the success ideal, and indeed, for the most part, outside the community activities that have just been described as characteristic of the middle class. In the town, this class consists of the skilled workmen, the service station attendants, icemen, the Anglos who work in the packing sheds, and a few other semi-skilled occupational groups. In the surrounding area, the lower class would include the tenant farmers, the foremen on the large farms, those grove care workers who are Anglo, and the few Anglo crewleaders. With the exception of church membership, the writer encountered very few of these people in the voluntary associations mentioned above. Lower class members may belong to any of the churches attended by the middle class, but the congregations of the evangelistic churches are drawn almost completely from this group. Very little data were collected on this group, but it is the writer's

---

[*] Supra, pp. 255-60.

impression that it is numerically inferior to the middle class, that it is largely peripheral, and that it is not nearly as well integrated as the middle class since it lacks the latter's various types of associations as mediums for common expression and participation as well as the common goal of success and the ideology this entails.* The relative insignificance of the lower class is in large part due to the presence of the Mexican American group, which has acted to push up into the middle class Anglos who otherwise might still remain in the lower class group, and also to keep out of the community Anglos who might have taken the labor role occupations now so completely filled by Mexican Americans. Thus, for the purposes of this study, only the Anglo middle class is important in defining the class structure of the Anglo community. From many points of view, this is the class that occupies the strategic position with respect to the Mexican group, and the class that stands to gain from maintenance of the present relationship. Lower class Anglos have no competitive bone to pick with the Mexicans,** and little opportunity for practicing subordination.***

---

\* In non-union McAllen, there is little opportunity for the lower class to concretely identify with "labor" and the type of organization represented by unionization that might provide a counterpart to the middle class ideology and its medium for expression.

\*\* With the possible exception of the skilled workers in a few occupational categories.

\*\*\* See supra, pp. 204-5

The terms "top", "middle", and "lower" status groups are those of the writer, and although intended to indicate the nature of the continuum that represents the prestige hierarchy of middle class Anglo society, perhaps tend to convey a more rigid picture of class or status conceptions among McAllen Anglos than actually exists. From the point of view of the people themselves, no matter where they are situated on the middle class continuum, there is a tendency for status distinctions to be clearer and more definite at the top of the hierarchy than at the middle or bottom. All Anglo informants acknowledged the existence of the small top status group, variously referred to as the "powers that be" and the "elect", and its outstanding role in the community is generally recognized. The depiction of the "upper sector" of the middle status group would probably also meet with general agreement, but below this people would tend to place themselves higher than the position allotted them here, and to blur distinctions of higher and lower within and between the middle and lower status groups. As has been indicated,* McAllen still retains a frontier element in its social structure that has prevented the development and stabilization of rigid status distinctions, let alone class divisions. Access to middle class status is fairly easy, and climbing the middle class continuum not too difficult. Nevertheless, distinctions are beginning to emerge, in group participation, styles of living, and levels of aspiration, as indicated in the

---

\* Supra, pp. 219, 224-25 and 260.

above sketch, although these have not yet solidified into definite class divisions.

As should be evident from the preceding discussion, the principal criteria for determining status in the Anglo prestige hierarchy are occupational achievement,[*] primarily within the business world, and income as expressed in style of living. The professionals, mainly doctors and lawyers, are evaluated by the same criteria as the businessmen since their relative "success", measured in terms of the extent of their practices and the amount of their incomes, largely determines their status, although their professional competence gives them added luster and would not permit them to fall below the middle status group in the prestige hierarchy. Such competence, however, taken alone, does not automatically include the professional in the "upper sector" of the middle status group.

Other criteria, such as length of residence and education, have varying importance, but family background plays little or no role at present. The "old settlers", those who participated in the first development of the Valley, have made bids to erect length of residence into a status determinant, but length of residence is a concomitant rather than a determinant of status since only those "old settlers" who took advantage of their early arrival to acquire extensive landholdings or establish substantial business enterprises have high rank in

---

[*] In the special sense described above, pp. 255 ff.

the prestige hierarchy at this time. Their claims for an "elite" based on "old" residence have had no more than a sentimental significance for the many later comers who have equalled or surpassed their achievements and possessions, and who in any case would hardly care to grant acceptance to a status criterion that they themselves can never hope to acquire. Education, in the sense of formal training, is generally respected but not accorded strategic importance by a group whose highest ranking members have attained "success" as "self-made" men with only a modicum of education. Although education is thought of as a "good thing to have", and parents feel that children ought to get as much of it as possible, a man with a college degree has no particular claim to status in the prestige hierarchy at the present time unless he can also show evidence of possession of the principal criteria. Education in the sense of "manners" or "refinement" plays a more subtle and perhaps more important role as a status determinant, particularly in determining degree of acceptance or rejection within the various cliques and circles of the higher status groups, but those who have a firm grasp on the principal criteria may be forgiven much in the way of "manners". Nevertheless, within the upper status groups may be discerned a tendency to value knowing how to behave and how to spend one's money, although this is usually overshadowed by the more evident tendency to indulge in undiscriminating conspicuous consumption of material artifacts as a means to acquiring status. Family background, in the sense of having a well-known name, has no importance as a status determinant in the Anglo prestige structure primarily because of the short history of settlement of the region. The "immigrant" generation is still the dominant generation, and although some of its members may have had well-known antecedents in the communities they came from, this had little carryover value in the new community. A number of families now have well-known names not only locally but throughout the Valley, and a few have received state-wide recognition through election or appointment of one of their members to state and national offices, but this is more a refledtion of the status they hold rather than a determinant of it. Their children, however, may reap the benefit of the prestige to be derived from a well-known name when they begin to acquire their independent status.

Anglo conceptions of distinctions within the Mexican American group will be indicated in the next chapter, but a few preliminary remarks at this point will be helpful in understanding the analysis of Mexican American class structure that follows. The tendency of the Anglo to recognize differentiation within the Mexican group is severely limited by his arbitrary assumption of its homogeneity, which is a cardinal principle of his caste attitudes. The principle, however, is not consistently maintained in practice. From the homogeneous mass of the Mexican group, the Anglo isolates a few who he distinguishes as "high type" or "better type". This distinction is made on the basis of three criteria: degree of possession of the Anglo's principal status determinants, i.e., occupational achievement and wealth, command of Anglo American ways, and light skin color. The last criterion is not essential for inclusion in the "high type" category, but it helps.* The few Mexican Americans who can qualify on these bases are acceptable for membership in the service clubs and a few other Anglo American organizations, for limited "social" intercourse of various sorts, and may even intermarry with Anglos without being penalized or ostracized. Were it not for the semi-caste line, these Mexican Americans would be considered part of the Anglo middle class, most of them fitting into the middle status group, and one or two into its upper sector. They compare favorably with Anglos of these status groups in business and agricultural achievement and in wealth, and they have a high command of Anglo ways. These characteristics are explicitly recognized by the Anglos in their acceptance of the "high type" Mexican in the form just indicated, but the acceptance is not complete in that it does not include access to full social participation of the sort that exists among Anglos themselves. Moreover, as will be seen, in certain contexts and under certain conditions the semi-caste line descends completely, and the "high type" Mexican again becomes part of the homogeneous mass.

---

\* See <u>infra</u>, pp. 413-14.

## Mexican American Classes

### Class Divisions and Occupation

Mexican American class divisions, and particularly relative status within the classes, are drawn on somewhat different bases from those of the Anglo, but occupational status is an important determinant of class status within the Mexican group as well, and may be legitimately used as a first approximation to the definition of the Mexican American classes. There is a high correlation between occupation and class, but there are other criteria that are extremely important in determining relative status within the classes and an understanding of the Mexican class system can only be obtained by a consideration of the differential evaluations of status criteria made by the classes, and of the class variations in behavior patterns, orientations, values, and patterns of participation.

Occupation is a constant criterion of class status in that there is wide agreement throughout the Mexican group as to which occupations can be classified as middle class, and which as lower class. The professions carry most prestige within the group, and the few doctors, lawyers, and other professionals[*] are consistently accorded middle class status. The few large landowner-farmers, and the most substantial[**] businessmen, some of whom are also large-scale farmers, provide

---
[*] See *supra*, p. 228.
[**] See *supra*, p. 222.

the other major component of the middle class. Between this small group, which numbers about thirty-five to forty families, and the lower class, which embraces the great bulk of the Mexican colony, there is a wide gulf, occupied only by the small shopkeepers and the white collar workers. The latter are considered middle class, but, as will be seen, their status is much more ambiguous than either of the other two groups in that, although they have much in common with the upper group, they are closer to the lower one in certain respects. In size, this group does not exceed a few hundred. The lower class consists of the manual workers. At its upper limit there is a thin layer of skilled workers, followed by a small group of crewleaders, but the vast majority of its members are the farm and shed workers, the domestic servants, and those individuals who perform the menial tasks in McAllen's business enterprises.

Although occupational status is a prominent criterion of class status for both Anglos and Mexicans, their conceptions of it are somewhat different. To the Anglo, occupational status symbolizes a certain achievement and corresponding income, and he accords prestige in relation to the magnitude of the occupational achievement of the individual. The Mexican, on the other hand, places somewhat less emphasis on the achievement aspects of occupations, and accords prestige more on the basis of traditional distinctions. The professionals and businessmen in Mexico, although small in number and never accorded a status as high as that of the _hacendado_, were identified with the _gente decente_, the genteel or better people, and never with the _gente vulgar_, the common people, who provided the peasant base of Mexican society.[1] This identification has been consistently maintained by the Mexican American so that the professions and business have been automatically defined as middle class occupations without necessarily involving an evaluation of the quality of achievement and commensurate income as in the Anglo case. Mexican American lawyers, e.g., may be accorded slightly differential status in the prestige hierarchy depending on their possession of the various criteria to be discussed below, but the mere fact that they are lawyers is usually sufficient to place them near or at the top, regardless of the "success" they have attained in the actual practice of their profession, and this is largely true of the other professions as well. In the case of the businessman, although there is an increasing tendency to evaluate his status according to the size of his enterprise and income, the fact that he is a _comerciante_ still receives first consideration while the extent of his achievement is secondary.

For a number of reasons, class lines are much more distinct and sharply drawn within the Mexican group than in the Anglo. The heritage of explicit class distinctions from Mexico, embodied in the terms _gente decente_ and _gente vulgar_ (this term is no longer current, however), still have a great deal of force for Mexican Americans, although access to the former group is on somewhat different bases here than in Mexico, and relatively much easier. This is the opposite of the Anglo tendency to deny the existence of class, which has done much to blur whatever actual divisions exist. The realistic gulf that still exists in the Mexican group between the tiny middle class and the large lower class, comparable to that which existed in Mexico, has contributed much to the development of clear class divisions. The greater mobility available to Anglo Americans in the occupational system, on the other hand, has worked against the growth of clearly-defined class divisions, and has permitted the retention of a relatively fluid status continuum that gives credence to the Anglo denial of class. However, the dominant-subordinate relationship has greatly complicated Mexican class conceptions, playing a two-fold role that has affected each of the classes in a different way. In the case of the middle class, the pressure exerted by the dominant group has operated to strengthen the already existent class divisions, but in the case of the lower class it has tended to minimize them. The huddling of all Mexican Americans into the narrow confines of subordinate status and the Anglo American assumption of the homogeneity of the Mexican group has impelled middle class Mexicans to distinguish themselves as much as possible from the lower class in order to demonstrate the Anglo error in identifying them with the latter group. Although the traditional class distinctions are helpful in providing the middle class Mexican with a relatively secure class status within his ethnic group, that status is by no means as secure with respect to the Anglo group, and he must make a special effort to persuade the latter that he really is different from the lower class Mexican. As will be seen, this necessarily involves the acceptance, at least in part, of an orientation to Anglo standards and an attempt to realize them. The lower class Mexican, on the other hand, is impressed by the fact that the middle class cannot escape many of the disabilities of subordinate status to which he himself is subject, and tends to accept the Anglo assumption of homogeneity for his group. Thus he develops an opposing tendency to minimize the actual class divisions and to expect a sort of equality within the group that makes him resent and belittle middle class pretensions to higher status.

The sections that follow will attempt to amplify and document the generalizations made here.

## The Middle Class

The terms used by middle class Mexican Americans to distinguish the classes from each other provide a preliminary insight into the criteria of status and interclass attitudes. Most commonly used to designate their own group is the Spanish phrase *gente decente* or the English "the better element". Also heard are "middle class", "upper class", "wealthy class", and more rarely, "leader class". Most frequently used to refer to the lower class is the term "*pelado*"[*] but "the common people", "the lower classes", "the poorer (or poorest) class", and more rarely, "the humbler people", are also heard.

### 1. The Determinants of Status

Occupational status is ordinarily sufficient to determine membership in one class or the other, but relative status within the middle class is dependent on a number of criteria in addition to occupation. One of the most important of these is education. Education may have more weight than occupation or wealth, as illustrated by the case of the Mexican lawyers. They seldom practice law[**] but the level of education symbolized by their degrees is sufficient to grant them top status. The title *licenciado*, lawyer, is religiously and ostentatiously prefixed to their surnames, a deference pattern evident in the case of the other professions as well. A schoolteacher, no matter how lowly his job, is always referred to as *profesor* or professor. None of the Mexican lawyers have incomes that can begin to compare with those of the more substantial businessmen, and the most prominent is said to be "rich in debts", but they are all

---
[*] See *infra*, pp. 379-80.
[**] See *supra*, pp. 229-30.

accepted at the very top of the middle class group. The
few schoolteachers, who probably have even lower incomes,
also have high status. Generally, the level of education
attained is important for relative status within the middle
class, but it is possible to have high status without much
formal education, as in the case of many of the businessmen.
However, even they profess much interest in education,
lament their lack of it (when their status is secure enough
on other counts), and accord high status to those who have it.
The paucity of professionally trained people indicates that
interest in, or opportunity for, higher education is a relatively recent phenomenon, but a large proportion of middle class
families are now sending their children to college, and higher
education for children is a generally expressed aspiration
in the middle class. A few of the wealthiest families send
their children to private preparatory schools in San Antonio
and Brownsville, a practice that apparently began in the early
days when there were no adequate Catholic schools in McAllen.
Education in the sense of having good manners and knowing how
to converse and "behave" is also important for high status
and will be discussed more fully in connection with other
criteria. Education has received a great deal of emphasis
among middle class Mexicans as a means of raising the general
level of their ethnic group. Many feel that the stereotyping
and discrimination by the dominant group can be traced to the
low level of education characteristic of the Mexican group. As
will be seen, better education for Mexicans is one of the major

goals of most middle class service organizations.  One
informant, a schoolteacher, said that another generation
or so will see the disappearance of discrimination and
exploitation because "the level of education of the Latin
American group is rising, and thus it will be correspondingly
able to raise its status".  In this connection, middle class
informants stressed formal education, learning "proper
behavior", and "how to act in public".  As one informant
said:

> The Latin Americans are not going to get anywhere
> until they get an education.  They will not re-
> ceive equal treatment or be equal until they
> get as many doctors, lawyers, teachers, and business-
> men as everybody else.  The most necessary education
> is of the Emily Post kind.  That's what the Latin
> American needs most, to learn to act like all the
> others.  When you can't tell him apart, except for
> his skin color, from the others, he will be accepted
> by them.  It is important that the Latin Americans
> change their speech, and manners and bearing.  Emily
> Post isn't exactly what I mean, but you get the idea.

The Spanish-speaking newspapers in McAllen and San Antonio
print long articles extolling the virtues and rewards of
education and devote a great deal of space to the announcement of educational achievements and honors of <u>colonia</u> members.

Family background is a heritage from the traditional
status distinctions that still retains a certain amount of
force as a status determinant.  The importance accorded
family background in Mexico can still be discerned in the
towns of Starr County, where Anglo American culture has only
recently penetrated.  Starr County informants described a
class system based primarily on a distinction between "old

families" or "good families" and "_peones_". The ideal for the old family is the possession of ancestors who received land grants from the Spanish Crown, and many of these families still own at least fragments of the ancestral lands. A member of one of the old families said, "Your family has to be an old one in the County. You have to be able to trace it back at least three generations". Old family status involves more than length of residence of course, since many of the _peones_ can also claim this, and entails ownership of land and illustrious antecedents. The distinctions between old families and peon families is apparently extremely rigid. According to an informant in the town of Roma,

> The old families will not associate with the _peones_ socially and are very strongly against intermarrying with them. For some of the men in the old families here and in Rio Grande City things got so bad that they had to go to Monterrey (Mexico) to look for their brides. They considered all the eligible girls already married, and felt that they would be marrying beneath them if they took a girl from a _peon_ family.

In McAllen, family background is by no means this decisive as a status determinant, but a claim to it enhances status. A few of the top status people in the Mexican group take great pride in their "old family" backgrounds and make the most of them, but access to relatively high status is possible without it, since many middle class families are of immigrant background and humbler origins. There are indications that at least the older generation is still preoccupied with origins, although the younger people do not seem to attach much importance to it. In San Antonio, there is a tendency for middle class Mexicans with humble immigrant backgrounds to be reluctant about revealing them. One Mexican informant, the head of a settlement house, said that a Mexican will always try to give the impression that he comes from a long line of successful people, and that successful Mexicans who come from humble origins try to conceal them. The few members of the immigrant generation who had middle or upper class family backgrounds in Mexico tend to make the most of it. Although most Mexican Americans have dropped the Spanish pattern of using the maternal family name along with the paternal, these men still retain the use of the maternal name in those cases where it was associated with high status in Mexico. Finally, it should be noted that, although family background may be on the wane as a status determinant, contemporary family reputation is important for status. As one informant said, "The important thing is maintaining a certain level of respectable behavior and not doing anything people can condemn your family for."

Interest in the Mexican group and readiness to serve it may be considered a criterion of status. The middle class Mexican places a great deal of emphasis on service to the group, and being known as one who takes an interest in the group "cause" and participates in the various activities organized to foster its betterment, whether as a leader or follower, enhances status at any point in the prestige hierarchy.[2] Pride in being a Mexican, in *la raza*, is a necessary adjunct of service to the group. Such pride in itself cannot serve as a status criterion since lack of it is the exception rather than the rule, but it plays an important role as a negative control in that the man who denies his Mexican antecedents will rapidly lose status despite his possession of any or all of the other criteria. All the men who hold top status within the middle class in McAllen and San Antonio are noted for their participation in one way or another in group betterment activities. There may be much cynical suspicion of their motivations, much criticism of their methods, and much grumbling about the reluctance of the "better element" to devote time to "working for the betterment of the group", but service to the group remains an ideal pattern for both lower and middle class Mexican Americans, although with varying emphases, and top status in the middle class is reserved for those who develop reputations as leaders in this effort. Top status cannot be obtained solely by means of this criterion, but those who lack it, despite their possession of the other criteria, cannot reach the top of the class hierarchy. In San Antonio, e.g., the most successful Mexican physician and the wealthiest businessman were singled out for approbrium time and again by informants for the isolation they maintain from "service" organizations and activities and their failure to contribute funds to community projects although well able to do so. Their notable achievements as physician and businessman are acknowledged, but they are accorded little respect or esteem apart from this. As will be seen, practically all middle class organizations are formally dedicated to service ideals, either for certain groups within the Mexican American community, or the community as a whole.

Money is important in the determination of higher status, and there is a high correlation between wealth and status, particularly among the businessman element. However, as indicated, occupation and education may determine high status without the possession of wealth, and the wealthy man who does not render service to the group cannot achieve high status. Moreover, flagrant violation of ideal patterns that define manners and morals may discredit a man regardless of his wealth. Many informants would insist at first that money was the only determinant of status distinctions, but further conversation elicited qualifications that considerably reduced its importance. When speaking in general terms, there is a tendency for middle class Mexicans to identify the two classes as the wealthy and poor and to say that a member of the _gente decente_ is always a rich man and a _pelado_ always poor. In general, however, middle class Mexicans place relatively less emphasis on the acquisition of money than do their Anglo counterparts. There are outstanding exceptions to this generalization, but they are regarded as exceptions and were often pointed out as anomalies by informants. An informant, himself a well-to-do farmer and businessman, in commenting on the interest in money displayed by one of these exceptions, expressed an ideal which is fairly representative of the middle class Mexican:

> I don't understand that fellow when it comes to money. He's just as tight with it as he can be. He has about fifty times as much as I have, but all he can think about is holding on to it and making more. I just can't understand that. I don't think a man should spend all his time making money. If he just works at whatever he wants to, has enough to eat, can educate his children, and have a little fun, I think he's got everything he could want.

It is possible that such an attitude contains elements of a rationalization of inability to amass large quantities of money and feelings of jealousy of those who have been able to, but it seems to be more positive than this. Higher status in the Mexican prestige hierarchy is not nearly so dependent on the acquisition of money and its ostentatious display as is true in the Anglo case, as consideration of the other criteria has shown.

The last status determinant to be considered here may be termed command of Anglo American ways. The criteria already discussed, although they set a limitation on orientation to Anglo standards by their difference from those standards, must be accompanied by a familiarity with Anglo ways if the individual is to achieve high status. Such familiarity is demonstrated by the ability to speak good English, as unaccented as possible, and to deal on easy, casual terms with Anglo Americans; and by knowledge and practice of a variety of idea and action patterns regarded as peculiarly Anglo. Effectiveness in serving the group presupposes command of Anglo ways, thus making the latter a requisite for acceptance into the leadership element accorded top status within the Mexican group.

A number of middle class Mexicans expressed a desire to "make the best of both ways", to retain the "best" of the Mexican values and accept the "best" of the Anglo, an attitude that helps to allay the ever-present suspicion of the Mexican that the leaders are trying to become Anglos themselves. However, there is an extreme tendency, opposed by those who want to make the best of both ways, to concede the superiority of Anglo standards and values and re-create the Mexican in the Anglo mold,* defining Mexican ways in general as undesirable, inferior, and disreputable. This attitude manifests itself in a wide range of intensity and variation but always involves a higher, more favorable evaluation of Anglo ways as opposed to Mexican, as well as a favorable stereotyping of certain idea and action patterns as peculiarly Anglo.** However, command of Anglo ways has high status value for all middle class Mexicans, regardless of lack of agreement as to the limitations that should govern their acquisition.

2. <u>Distinctive Middle Class Patterns</u>

Mexican middle class status criteria vary somewhat from those adhered to by Anglo Americans, but the difference is largely one of degree of emphasis, with the exception of those criteria that reflect the Mexican's response to his subordinate

---

\* Cf. the comment quoted <u>supra</u>, p. 360.

\*\* The problem of assimilation, and the range of variation encountered in motivations to assimilation, are discussed in the last chapter.

status and thus have no Anglo counterparts, such as service to the group and command of Anglo ways. Although always modulated by retention of pride in Mexican origins, this difference in emphasis is apparently slowly giving way to a fuller orientation to Anglo American standards and values. However, the orientation is already sufficiently well developed as a distinctive middle class characteristic to accentuate Mexican class differences in idea and action patterns with respect to the problems of subordinate status and the attitudes governing relations with the Anglo American group. A consideration of contrasting class patterns in this connection will help to establish the definition of the Mexican middle class which has been attempted here.

Most middle class Mexicans are keenly aware that Anglo Americans basically tend to evaluate them on a group basis regardless of the differences that may exist within the Mexican group. They know that Anglo deviations from this caste attitude occur in practice, but that the Anglo regards these in the light of concessions that may be permitted in certain areas, that beyond this the caste distinctions are applied to all Mexicans, and that under certain conditions even the concessions are ignored by Anglo practices that summarily include them in the tenet that "a Mexican is a Mexican". The middle class Mexican reacts to this Anglo attitude with resentment and indignation, as illustrated in the following comments by two Mexicans, one a lawyer and the other a businessman, who hold top status in the McAllen colonia:

> I think a great deal could be accomplished right now if Anglos could only learn to distinguish between the deserving and non-deserving. Then the whole thing would be on a much more equal basis, and we would have little to complain about. That wouldn't be just a little push, that would be a big push. It doesn't matter what kind of person a Latin American is, to the Anglos all Latin Americans are alike. We're all no good and just here to be pushed around and spit on. I tell you it's a hard subject to discuss coolly and rationally because one gets so mad and upset.
>
> I don't know how it happens. I can see how such people (prejudiced Anglos) feel that way toward me, because I speak broken English. But you take my two boys. They have had better than average upbringing, a better than average house to live in, better than average clothes, and they speak perfect English. Still the Anglos look on them as different. They don't think of them as Americans, but as Mexicans.

A prominent lawyer in San Antonio, discussing possible reasons why Anglos do not like Mexicans, had this to say:

> Differences? They sure talk about the differences between the Anglo Americans and the Mexicans. The Anglo Americans say they cannot understand the Mexicans. But there are no differences. You take the Pan American Optimists (a Mexican American service club), e.g., they are just like any group of Anglo American businessmen. If you attend a meeting of the Pan American Optimists, you will find that they dress the same way, use the same language, and talk about the same things. I think the Anglo Americans make a great deal of fuss about the differences of the Mexican people because they want a justification for rejecting them. They do not reject them because of the differences. (Here informant recounted an incident involving refusal of service in a small town restaurant to a group of high status Mexicans.) This exemplifies that no one is safe. It would be different in the case where an individual is dirty, but the Anglos reject the best Mexicans, so what hope is there.

Regardless of the ultimate limitations imposed by the Anglo caste attitude, middle class Mexicans manifest a great deal of interest in and increasing orientation to Anglo ways and values. In part, this may be due to finding the latter attractive in themselves, but the fact that Anglos, despite their caste thinking, tend to reward the acquisition of such traits[*] is undoubtedly an important consideration. Unlike the lower class, the middle class Mexican is concerned with participation in the larger society and improvement of his status in the system of stratification that embraces both Anglo and Mexican groups. This motivation is reflected in the middle class preoccupation with "changing" Mexican behavior patterns for a set they tend to identify as Anglo, and the conviction that this has already been at least partially accomplished by the "better element" Middle class informants characterized the "better element" as consisting of people "who want to get ahead, who are not satisfied with staying in the same old rut." One informant said that Mexicans are going to have to be forceful, aggressive, and hard working if they want to command the Anglo's respect and make a place for themselves in the larger society. Informant added that Mexicans are going to have to imbibe some of the immigrant boy to president idea. A Mexican American settlement house director in San Antonio, defending his policy of exacting "correct" behavior from the young people who come to the settlement house, expressed himself as follows:

---

[*] See *supra*, pp. 351-52.

It is not so much that these are the standards of the settlement house as they are those of society, and these boys are going to have to eventually appropriate these standards if they are going to make a successful adjustment to society. If the Mexican people are ever going to get anywhere, they are going to have to attain to the behavioral standards the Anglo American supposedly has. It makes no difference that frequently the Anglo American does not live up to those standards himself. The point is he expects the Mexican to do so, and when he does not, then the Anglo American has his justification for keeping the Mexican down. The status of the Mexican will never be raised until the Mexican people, as a group, strive for adherence to Anglo American standards.

The motivations to upward mobility in the total status hierarchy expressed in these comments contrast sharply with the lack of such motivations in the lower class Mexican.\* In accordance with these orientations to mobility, the middle class Mexican tends to emphasize, and to display, certain behavior patterns and aspirations which are generally considered characteristic of middle class America. They include self-reliance, ambition, industriousness, and thrift, all of them patterns commonly associated with "getting ahead", and are precisely those behavior patterns found wanting in the Mexican worker by the Anglo employer.\*\* Moreover, they represent definite departures from the behavior patterns that have been described throughout this study as characteristic of Mexican American culture. The following comment, e!g., was made by a Mexican businessman-farmer:

---

\* See *supra*, pp. 248-49 and 261-62.
\*\* See *supra*, pp. 231-46.

> I don't believe in doing anything for my children. My son A is a good boy and wants to be an engineer. I hope he makes it. I want my children to develop a sense of responsibility and stand on their own feet. I'll help them, but I'm not going to give them their lives on a platter even if I could afford it. I sent L to the University, but when she got married, she went on her own. I want my children to appreciate what we can do for them, but only by showing they remember us with a little gift now and then. I don't want to interfere with their lives in any way or even get in their way.

One middle class informant, a schoolteacher, spoke proudly of her husband's rejection of a disability pension when he was discharged from the Army, saying, "Of course he wouldn't hear of it, and it was for the best because it encouraged him to do for himself." Although he was ill and could not work for a time, he also rejected veterans unemployment compensation since "we both thought it was a downright racket and wouldn't have anything to do with it." Many Anglos accepted these aids without feeling that they were threats to their independence, but this "overreaction", encountered in a few other middle class informants, is indicative of the middle class Mexican's preoccupation with differentiating himself from the lower class pattern of dependence so often singled out by the Anglo in his characterization of the Mexican. The comment of another middle class informant, "The main thing is to work hard, save my money, educate my children, and try to send them to college if they want to go", is representative. The following quotation from the life history of a middle class informant expresses a high valuation of all the behavior patterns under discussion:

My brother went to high school, and although I was working and wanted him to go to college, he didn't like the idea of being helped. After high school it was hard to get a job. He worked at one job and then another. He didn't help us much. We were only too glad he could help himself. He has very good mechanical skill, and when he got a good job with the Government, he got married. He has been promoted and is making good money, and the position is his as long as he wants it. He's hard-working, punctual, and never misses a day. His vacation time piles up on him because he is reluctant to stay away from work. He has a shop at home and does a lot of electric repair work for extra money. He thinks a lot of his children, he says he wants them to have what he didn't have. He has a lot saved and could buy a home for cash if he wanted to, but he thinks building costs are too high now, so he is renting.

The life histories collected from middle class informants contain frequent instances of orientation to the standards and values described here, while the data collected from lower class informants revealed little of it. It should be noted, however, that this characterization of middle class orientations is concerned with tendency rather than concrete fact in the sense that these orientations are given greater emphasis and encountered with greater frequency among those informants who can be defined as middle class, according to the bases already described, than among those who are lower class. Actually, despite the relative prominence of these patterns, there is evidence that middle class Mexicans are still partially oriented to the values embodied in the Mexican American patterns of familism, friendship, and generosity, values that may be considered as predominantly those of the lower class. The white collar and small businessman element of the middle class reflects this double orientation and its resultant conflicts most clearly and will be discussed separately below.

The various types of attempts made by Mexican Americans to mitigate the disabilities of their subordinate status will be systematically treated in connection with reactive adjustments, but such attempts are ordinarily confined to middle class Mexicans and may be briefly considered here as a distinctive middle class pattern. For present purposes, the desire to mitigate his subordinate status may be thought of as motivating the middle class Mexican in two directions, somewhat opposed to each other. One of these is toward the development of interclass solidarity across the semi-caste line, the other toward the development of intragroup solidarity across Mexican class lines. These opposing goals are a direct reflection of the ambivalence involved in the Anglo principle of regarding all Mexicans as composing an undifferentiated group but at the same time recognizing differences in practice. Both Anglo and Mexican middle classes derive some very real benefits from the maintenance of a solidary relationship that protects and furthers their class interests as opposed to those of the lower class. The fact that middle class Mexicans possess a monopoly of whatever political and economic power exists in the Mexican group places them in a position to provide the Anglo middle class with a number of substantial services. The political advantages the latter receives by extending its cooperation to the Mexican leader group have already been described in detail and require no further elaboration here. The interclass solidary relationship enables the Anglos to keep their contacts with the subordinate group at a minimum, restricting them to the cooperation necessary with the small Mexican middle class. Moreover, the relationship provides the Anglos with a readily available source of intermediaries who can be used most effectively in manipulating the subordinate group and siphoning off its potential protests and antagonisms. For the Mexican, middle class status in itself, to the extent that it represents possession of Anglo status criteria and command of Anglo ways, is a means of alleviating the rigidity of subordinate status because of the Anglo tendency to single out the "high type" Mexican for special consideration. Participation in a solidary relationship with Anglo Americans, limited though it may be to certain areas, is a general step forward for the middle class Mexican in realizing his goal of higher status in the prestige hierarchy of the larger society, but he also derives some specific material benefits. Combining his political resources with those of the Anglo buttresses his political power, as has been shown. Without Anglo support, the independent Mexican vote could be much more troublesome. Furthermore, although the writer has little documentation on this point, it would seem that such cooperation ought to give the middle class Mexican claims on special favors and protection that facilitate his business interests, such as exemptions from zoning ordinances and other municipal regulations that control business enterprises.

The most important benefit to be derived from the cooperative relationship, however, is the prestige garnered from increased opportunities for joint "social" participation with Anglo Americans. Actually, the attraction of such participation for the Mexican lies not so much in the desire for increased interaction with Anglos for its own sake, since he ordinarily has enough interpersonal relationships in his own group to satisfy his "social" needs, but in the symbolic value of the joint participation and its role in breaking down the semi-caste line. Political cooperation as an aspect of the interclass solidary relationship provides a good example of how such cooperation can foster joint participation of a sort that approximates equal status relationships, including commensalism, home visiting, and other activities that are ordinarily carried on separately within each of the two groups. The relationship of the Mexican political *jefe* and his associates with their Anglo collaborators is characterized by an easy familiarity and intimacy that is not evident in most other aspects of intergroup relations. They visit each other's offices, pause to chat or enter a nearby restaurant for a cup of coffee together on the occasion of chance encounters in the street, and on a number of occasions, the writer has been present at a public gathering or meeting when an Anglo politician has taken the initiative in approaching a Mexican colleague in order to greet him. The Mexicans apparently take great pride in the fact that they can address all of the Anglo political leaders by their first name no matter how high their status and that the latter observe the same practice with regard to them. The free use of given names is apparently an impressive symbol of equal status relationship since the Mexican political leaders often stressed it in conversations with the writer. As one Mexican informant said, "B (the *jefe*) was a city commissioner for many years, a big politician, and he got to know all the big boys in Austin, and he became a part of the bunch that has always run McAllen. He calls them all by their first names. He's a big man around here." The most substantial experience of social equality occurs on the occasion of political rallies and barbecues. Both types of event enable the middle class Mexican to display publicly the intimate nature of his relationship with Anglo leaders, but the barbecue is the more impressive of the two. Barbecues may be public affairs staged at a local park as an adjunct of a political rally or as the high point of a political campaign, or they may be offered privately by Anglo or Mexican political leaders at their homes for their political confreres. The writer attended one of the latter type given by a Mexican political leader where the guests included all of the major and minor county and municipal officials, Anglo and Mexican, as well as all of the Anglos and Mexicans prominent in local politics who did not hold public office. The guests mingled freely without regard to ethnic membership, ate and drank together, and engaged in most of the easy familiarities usually indulged in among peers.

Another example of how political cooperation with Anglos may provide an avenue to social mobility is afforded by the case of a middle class Mexican American couple in McAllen who wield an appreciable amount of informal political influence among the Mexican electorate. In the Valley Congressional campaign described elsewhere, this couple gave their support to one of the local Anglo candidates. During the campaign, the woman, who is the more politically active of the two, freely associated with Anglo middle class women working for the same candidate, was invited by them to teas where campaign strategy was planned, and in general travelled and worked with these women in their campaign activities. As a result of this collaboration, the Mexican couple established a few friendships among the "upper sector" of the Anglo middle class which they expected to maintain permanently after the campaign was over, and spoke of inviting these Anglo friends to their home for dinner. As one of them said, "If nothing more, at least we were able to make some reliable, fairly powerful friends among the Anglo Americans through our support of D (the Anglo candidate) in this campaign. People like the Smiths, who will be able to come to our aid when we try to get something for the Latin Americans."

The joint participation on an equal status basis described here is ordinarily limited to the political sphere, although the above discussion indicates that it may spread to other areas on occasion as a result of the stimulus provided by political collaboration between the Mexican and Anglo middle classes. Similar opportunities are available to middle class Mexicans through their cooperation with middle class Anglos in the area of economic interests, although these do not seem to be as extensive as those just described. Membership in the Chamber of Commerce and the service clubs enable a few Mexican businessmen to participate with Anglos in the semi-informal weekly meetings (the service clubs have luncheon meetings) and the social affairs sponsored by these organizations. However, as described elsewhere,* the dominant pattern, even between middle class Mexicans and Anglos, is consistent separateness in matters of informal social intercourse, joint participation on an equal status basis being the exception.

The interclass solidary relationship is of course limited and controlled by the Anglo caste principle of the homogeneity of the Mexican group. The principle itself provides a formidable barrier which the Mexican finds difficult to penetrate, and manifests itself in action frequently enough to humiliate and insult the middle class Mexican and act as a constant reminder that he is after all a member of the subordinate group. Such experiences serve to throw the middle

---

\* See *supra*, pp. 159 ff.

class Mexican back on his own group in search of a means for modifying the rigidity of the semi-caste line. He becomes convinced that the Anglo caste principle retains its force because of the "undesirable" behavior patterns of the lower class, and that the only way of ultimately breaking the principle is by "raising" the entire group to the level of his own standards.* The motivation for Anglo acceptance pushes him, on the one hand, in the direction of interclass solidarity with a corresponding weakening of intragroup solidarity, and ultimately sends him in the direction of intragroup solidarity on the other.

### 3. Attitudes toward the Lower Class

Middle class attitudes toward the lower class still partake of the traditional class distinctions that are part of the Mexican cultural heritage, and although it might be supposed that in the normal case the distinctions would have been considerably blurred by contact with the tendency in Anglo American culture to deny class differences and "middle-classify" the total society, the Anglo caste attitudes toward Mexican Americans have instead operated to reinforce the traditional distinctions in a number of ways. The term "pelado" used most frequently by the middle class to refer to members of the lower class, is very expressive of middle class attitudes.** At best, the word simply means a penniless

---

* Cf. the comments quoted supra, p. 370.

** There are a number of middle class Mexicans who do not hold the attitudes about to be described, but, as usual, the discussion is concerned with major trends and tendencies.

person,* but as used by the middle class Mexican, it has definite perjorative connotations, signifying an individual who is not only poor, but also uncouth, ignorant, and so on. As one middle class informant put it, "_Pelado_ means low class, poor people without much education who talk loudly and do a lot of cussing." Another said, "_Pelado_ always means the low class of Mexican who does little or nothing for a living." However, a few middle class informants used the term to refer to anyone who displays "undesirable" traits regardless of his class status.

This traditional attitude has been nourished by the tendency of middle class Mexicans to accept the Anglo stereotype of Mexican behavior patterns as true of the lower class. In their descriptions of lower class behavior, they too stress improvidence, indolence, and ignorance. In part, they tend toward this evaluation because of their increasing orientation to Anglo standards. The identification of these behavior patterns with the lower class also reflects the constant middle class attempt to demonstrate its difference from the lower class and the consequent inapplicability of the stereotype in its case. As was just indicated, the middle class Mexican perceives the necessity of intragroup solidarity and unity, but this does not prevent him from resenting his enforced identification with the lower class and from condemning the lower class failure to adopt Anglo standards as the cause of

---

\* This is its long-established idiomatic meaning. Technically, _pelado_ means peeled or plucked.

his own inability to gain complete Anglo acceptance. The following comment, made by a middle class informant protesting against the constant influx of wetbacks into the Valley, is illustrative:

> To the Anglos, a Mexican is a Mexican, regardless of how different he may be from the mass. For everyone that tries to improve himself, there are one hundred more to take his place because of the kind of immigration system we have. If we could find some way to prevent any more Mexicans from coming here, in twenty-five years you wouldn't be able to tell the difference between a Mexican and an American except by the name Garcia or Lopez, which wouldn't mean anything any more because the Mexicans would be American in everything else. But the person who does strive to improve himself gets lost in the shuffle since there are so many who are ignorant and primitive because of where they come from. As long as we have them as they are, they will be pointed out as the example of the Mexican, and there will be no hope for those who are not like them.

In their descriptions of lower class behavior, middle class Mexicans tend to ignore the large number of orderly, hard-working families in the lower class[*] and focus on the "disorganized" element characterized by family instability, direct expression of aggression, and the apathy and hopelessness born of severe economic hardship. They stress the behavior patterns of this element as typical of the lower class, just as the Anglo tends to apply his stereotype to all Mexicans regardless of differences. They deplore the "loose" behavior and excessive drinking habits[**] of the

---

[*] See the discussion of the Mexican American family in Chapter II and especially pp. 76-77. The patterns described there are considered applicable to the majority of lower class families. See also pp. 261-62.

[**] Middle class Mexican Americans are not all teetotalers by any means, but they ordinarily drink at home and only occasionally visit a *cantina*. They do imbibe publicly, however, and in some cases to excess, at dances and other social functions.

lower class, and often explain the former as due to the latter. The following excerpt from the San Antonio field notes may be quoted in this connection:

> Informant (a Mexican American lawyer) lamented the existence of the vast number of cantinas in the colonia. He said this number will have to be cut down. He is a tolerant man, but it is too much. The decent-minded Mexicans have to get together to demonstrate their disapproval. All the violence takes place in cantinas. The police and the courts do nothing because they think they are satisfying the Mexicans by leaving them alone. Informant thinks they should be handed stiff sentences. If you give a few of the Mexicans life imprisonment and hang a few, the violence will diminish. This violence is a terrible shame for the Mexican people, and does not occur among the Negros or the Anglo Americans.

One middle class informant, a Mexican American farmer-businessman, had this to say about the lower class:

> Most of the workers sure like to drink their beer and have their fling while they can. They never think about trying to improve themselves a little. They get their pay, buy groceries and some candy for the children, and then go out and buy beer and go around with women until they have spent the rest of their money. They sure like to have a good time. Every week it's the same story. They get together in a bunch and go out looking for women, or just stay by themselves and drink beer.

On another occasion, this informant, explaining why Mexicans lost out economically to Anglos in the Valley, said:

> Maybe it is because the Latin Americans are so lazy. They just want to get their food and a few extras, and then they're satisfied to let the other fellow do all the work. So they stay behind, and the others get ahead. I think education is the answer.

The following remarks, by a Mexican businessman in San Antonio illustrate the middle class anxiety for differentiation from the lower class as well as preoccupation with "raising" its standards.

There's a big job to be done to teach the people how to behave, not only education, but -- I don't know how to say it -- but also moral education, you know, better habits. The people go out and work and make money, but then they spend it all on beer, and there's nothing left for their families. And you see the girls out late at night here. If I had a girl, she certainly wouldn't be doing things like that. I have only one boy, but even he doesn't stay out late at night. If I want him to grow up to be a good boy, I have to set an example for him, not be delinquent myself. My son knows I don't run around with other women and stay out nights and get drunk ... The Anglos object to the dirtiness of so many of the Mexican people, and their spendthrift habits. I believe the Mexicans could correct that. There are many men who migrate to the North and make a great deal of money. But when they return, instead of fixing up the house and buying better clothes, the Mexican spends it all for beer.

There are a number of indications in the field data that middle class Mexicans tend to keep joint "social" participation with the lower class at a minimum, but further investigation would be necessary to adequately document this. In general, as indicated elsewhere,* social relations are largely subsumed under kinship relations for lower class Mexicans, and thus participation across class lines is ordinarily a matter of indifference to the lower class. In both McAllen and San Antonio there are a few colonia restaurants which cater primarily to Anglos and middle class Mexicans, although lower class Mexicans are served, of course. Conversely, middle class Mexicans almost never frequent any of the other colonia restaurants. The paucity of voluntary associations in McAllen's colonia made it impossible to observe interclass

---

* Supra, p. 79.

participation in this area, but a comment by the Anglo priest of the colonia's Catholic Church is interesting in this connection:

> It's very obvious that Mexicans are conscious of being high class and low class, and they talk about it very openly, in a matter of fact way. For example, we have a society here in the Church called the Dominus Catolica, and the members all consider themselves high class. I have been present at meetings where they have discussed the application of some person for membership, and have turned it down because they decided that the person was low class. The rich keep themselves apart from the others, being careful never to associate with them.

Weekly dances in the colonia sponsored by the mutual aid societies have already been mentioned as places where the "best people" do not go.* The following comment was offered by a middle class female informant in explanation of why she would not attend these dances:

> I refuse to lower myself by dancing at a place like that. It's a business dance where everybody comes, including street walkers, and I don't feel that I should put myself in the same class with people like that. Someone told me the other day that I must think I'm better than they are. Well, that is right, I do think I'm better than they are. Maybe I'm wrong, but that's the way I was brought up and that's the way I look at it. I don't have any respect for girls who work as waitresses in beer joints or even restaurants. They're in the same class as street walkers as far as I'm concerned. Girls who have any self-respect don't have to take jobs like that. They can do better for themselves, and if they don't, I think I'm better than they are. After all, I have a good education and a good upbringing, and they entitle me to better than association with low class people.

The owner of a colonia moving picture theater in another Valley town, Brownsville, himself the product of a Mexican-Anglo intermarriage, volunteered this piece of information:

---
\* See supra, pp. 71 and 105.

> Informant asked me if I have noticed any discrimination among the Latin Americans themselves. I asked him what he meant. He said: Well, there's a small group of Latin Americans here who won't come to my theater because they say I admit all the riffraff. They say these people are dirty and noisy and shouldn't be admitted to the theater. A few of them have told me to raise the admission price to 75 cents or a dollar so these people will stay away. I laugh at them and tell them that I'm in business to make a profit. I couldn't get enough of their kind at a dollar a piece to make it worth my while.

In San Antonio, the Mexican American director of a colonia settlement house provided some enlightening remarks on mutual class attitudes in the process of describing the dilemna his position places him in as a result of those attitudes:

> The trouble with me is that I am too accessible, and the professionals and businessmen among the Mexicans don't like it. The trouble with being as accessible as I am means that I lose the respect of both the upper class and the lower class. The upper class Mexicans think that because of their education and money they have to keep themselves apart from the lower class, and the lower class thinks it only proper that the upper class do so. If I become too accessible to the lower class, that is, I mean that anyone can see me and ask me for something whenever they want to, they lose respect for me because I have in some way failed to live up to their idea of how a member of the upper class should act. He is supposed to maintain a distance between himself and the masses which most of the businessmen do maintain.

### 4. The Lower Status Group

This discussion of the middle class has dealt primarily with the group of professionals and businessmen who form the upper level of the Mexican American status hierarchy.* The description is largely applicable to the white-collar and

---

\* See supra, p. 354.

small businessman group as well, but their situation involves special features, marking it off from both the upper status group and the lower class, that require separate consideration. The lower status group, like the upper status group, is characterized by orientations to mobility and to acquisition of middle class criteria, but with the important difference that, whereas the upper status group is preoccupied primarily with mobility in the status hierarchy of the larger society, the lower status group is primarily concerned with rising in the class structure of the Mexican group itself. This is because the status of the upper group is secure <u>within</u> Mexican American society and insecure only from the point of view of its struggle for acceptance in the Anglo world. The lower group, on the other hand, must concern itself primarily with acquiring and stabilizing its status with reference to the upper group and is relatively less preoccupied with the problem of Anglo acceptance. This does not mean, of course, that the lower status group does not feel pressure to orient itself to Anglo standards and values. Aside from the general Mexican middle class tendency to consider the acquisition of Anglo ways as in themselves desirable, a premium is placed on such acquisition in according relative status within the middle class as has been noted.

In its struggle for middle class status, the lower status group tends to be very determined about avoiding whenever possible those occupations that are unmistakably lower class, such as farm or shed labor and domestic service. The writer encountered a number of cases in which individuals in this group had turned down labor jobs for clerking jobs in stores although the former offered higher remuneration.* Once the individual has held a white-collar job, he definitely feels he is lowering himself by taking a job as laborer or domestic servant, as the following case illustrates:

> A girl whose entire occupational history consisted of clerking in stores lost her job at Woolworth's, where she earned $16 a week, and was offered a job as a housemaid at $20 weekly plus room and board. She refused the job, considering it "beneath her station". A friend of hers, a graduate beauty operator whose small independent venture had recently failed, accepted the job because she needed money very badly. However, she attempted to conceal her place of work and the fact that she was working as a housemaid from her friends.

In their drive to secure middle class status, members of the lower status group, like those of the upper group, also manifest orientations to the patterns necessary for "getting ahead" and attempt to differentiate themselves from the lower class by avoiding joint participation with lower class members. However, their situation is much more complicated and relatively more difficult than that of the upper status group in these respects since they are ordinarily the first generation removed from lower class status, they still retain many ties with their lower class families, and are still partially embedded in the Mexican American orientations and values that the upper status group is leaving behind in its increasing adherence to Anglo ways. They are concerned with thrift, ambition, and so on,

---

\* For the various reasons why white collar work is considered more attractive, aside from its prestige value, see *supra* p. 212.

but they are also oriented to the distinctive Mexican American patterns of generosity, friendship, and familial obligations and all they entail, and their close relations with the lower class makes it difficult to avoid the claims made on them for compliance with these patterns. Their ordinarily low economic status makes it extremely difficult to save and "get ahead" since whatever surplus they may have is absorbed by adherence to the old patterns. Similarly, the expectation of aid from children held by Mexican parents,[*] effectively frustrates in most cases the desire, where it exists, for education as a road to mobility. In general, the demands made on the individual by Mexican American culture are not very compatible with orientations to mobility, as has been noted,[**] Members of the lower status group place a great deal of emphasis on middle class standards of morality, and seem to be even more preoccupied than are upper status group members with the ideal patterns of strict marital fidelity, chaperonage for unmarried girls, sobriety, and control of aggression. This emphasis on the ideal patterns of middle class morality reaches its acme in the small groups of Protestant Mexican Americans.[***]

In matters of participation, lower status group members encounter perhaps their most acute problems in striving for middle class status. The small merchants and a few of the clerks in this group may be approached by the upper status group when the latter is conducting a membership drive for the

---

[*] See supra, p. 72.
[**] See, e.g., supra, pp. 245.
[***] Cf. Supra, pp. 92-93.

Latin American Businessmen's Club or soliciting funds for some community project, but ordinarily contacts between these two groups are intermittent and casual. The lower group has no share in the economic and political power controlled by the upper group, and its material condition and style of living has little in common with the upper group. From the point of view of the latter, the objective situation of the lower status group is only slightly better than that of the lower class as a whole, and its possibilities of bettering that situation are severely limited,* so there is no greater basis for joint social participation with the lower status group than with the lower class. Inability to increase participation with the upper status group is aggravated by the existence of the close familial and other personal ties with the lower class that do not permit lower status group members to minimize their contacts with the lower class even when they want to. Despite these considerations, increasing participation with the upper group and decreasing it with the lower class is felt to be essential for improving one's status.

> L, a woman who holds a responsible clerical job in one of the county offices, due to the housing shortage, lives at the Labor Center where almost all the residents are farm and shed laborers. She has asserted that she is only interested in meeting one kind of people, those who can do her good socially. She said that the people here in the Center are all right, but they certainly cannot help her to better herself.

There is some evidence that members of the lower status group

---
* See supra, pp. 212-13.

exert pressure on their fellows to conform to this pattern. One member of a family with middle class pretensions protested against this pressure and told the writer that he has many so-called friends in McAllen, but they are not the kind of people he wants for friends. Informant said they are middle class and all they can think about is making money. Anybody who does not look at things the same way they do is not accepted by them. They have told the informant that he is hurting himself by the kind of people he is associating with because they are low class.

The situation of this informant is typical of a number of cases encountered by the writer of conflict within families of the lower status group where one member persisted in adhering to one or a number of lower class behavior patterns and the others were afraid he would lower the family status by doing so. In this family, the deceased father, an immigrant, had been a brick mason, managed to buy some property, and educated his children through high school. One son opened a small grocery store, and when this failed, undertook a course of training at the local business college so that he could qualify for "office work". A daughter was trained as a beauty operator and opened a small shop in the colonia. Both children, and the mother, exhibit the behavior patterns that have been described as characteristic of the lower status group, and tend to avoid joint participation with the lower class although they have relatives and old family friends within the latter.

The youngest son, the informant just quoted, is a deviant from the family pattern in most respects. He would not go beyond grade school, despite his family's urgings, tended to avoid work when he could, and spent most of his time in the cantinas drinking to the point of drunkenness. Even the deviant had no desire to become identified with the lower class to the extent of accepting a lower class occupation, since his ambition was to work in a store or as a hotel clerk, but in most other respects his behavior was typical of the "disorganized" element of the lower class. He was in constant conflict with the other members of the family, who were determined to retain their middle class status, and they complained about his deviances, ridiculed them, and manifested a great deal of anxiety about them. In another case, the wife was striving for middle class status while the husband, a crewleader, was content with membership in the lower class. She herself had a job as a salesclerk and enjoyed friendships with a number of lower status group people. She constantly objected to her husband's association with the men he worked with and his habit of frequenting the cantinas, complained of his lack of ambition, and goaded him to work more and harder and to change his occupation for one of the middle class. These conflicts between family members who manifest differing class orientations and behavior are paralleled by the internal conflicts of the lower status group individual who is constantly being torn between status aspirations and familial and other personal obligations.

## The Lower Class

For the purposes of this description and analysis of Mexican American classes, the previous discussions of Mexican American culture* and of the Mexican American worker** present orientations, values, and behavior patterns that may be considered characteristic of the lower class. In view of this, it will not be necessary here to treat the lower class in nearly as great detail as the middle class, and the discussion will be limited to placing lower class patterns in their proper perspective with relation to those of the middle class in order to round out the discussion of class.

Lower class Mexicans most frequently use the Spanish term, <u>senores</u> <u>grandes</u>, and in English, "big men" or "bigshots", to refer to the Mexican middle class. The more specific terms, <u>ricos</u> and <u>comerciantes</u>, or "businessmen", are also employed to designate the upper group. The phrase <u>la</u> <u>raza</u> is ordinarily used as a designation for the entire Mexican group, but when speaking of themselves as distinct from the "bigshots", lower class Mexicans use it to refer to the common people. Less frequently, they call themselves <u>los</u> <u>pobres</u>, or in English, the "poorer people".

In general, lower class Mexicans concede the validity of middle class status criteria in determining class membership, but accord them no significant role for differential ranking within their own class. In part, this is due to the fact that

---
\* See Chapter III.
\*\* See Chapter V.

their possession of these criteria is minimal, of course, but more important is the lack of interest in upward mobility, characteristic of the lower class, which makes unimportant the issue of relative status <u>within</u> the lower class group and eliminates the need for criteria designed to measure such relative status. On an occupational basis, e.g., the professional and the businessman are unhesitatingly granted the prerogatives of high status, but for reasons indicated elsewhere,[*] occupation in itself means little for access to status within the lower class. The skilled worker, by virtue of his skill, is referred to deferentially as <u>maestro</u>, and the crewleader, by virtue of his delegated authority, accrues some added prestige, but in neither case is this sufficient to place the incumbents of these occupational roles on a separate and higher status level differentiating them from the mass of the lower class. Similarly, education, wealth, service to the group, and command of Anglo ways are considered important for defining the middle class Mexican and are included as a matter of course in lower class expectations of the attributes a "bigshot" should possess. As has been described, acceptance by one's fellows and incumbency of a socially respected role in the lower class depends on the more diffuse criteria of fulfilment of familial and other personal obligations and observance of the morality defined by

---

[*] <u>Supra</u>, pp. 261-64.

Mexican American culture in its ideal patterns. The lower class Mexican will, however, dissociate himself from those who do not measure up to these standards and will definitely relegate them to a lower level. He may attach no particular importance to the independence, ambition, and thrift so prized by Anglos and middle class Mexicans, but he rejects the "loose" morality, the uninhibited aggression, and the excessive drinking of the "disorganized" element, which conflict with his own standards. The "lower" element itself may attach positive prestige values to the patterns embodied in unbridled machismo,[*] but the bulk of the lower class has little respect for these people, although they are more tolerant of them than are Anglos and middle class Mexicans.

The limited possibilities open to the lower class Mexican for rising in the occupational hierarchy have already been described in connection with the discussion of the labor role,[**] as have the cultural and psychological factors that militate against the development of orientations to mobility in the lower class Mexican.[***] However, lack of orientation to mobility, as a distinctive lower class pattern in relation to middle class patterns, merits a few further comments here. Lower class Mexicans are not unaware of the mobility-success pattern of the Anglos and middle class Mexicans, in fact may even admire it, nor do they condemn thrift, ambition, and other traits involving self-denial and impulse inhibition. The

---

[*] See *supra*, pp. 75-76.
[**] *Supra*, pp. 255-7.
[***] *Supra*, pp. 241-51.

success stories of the Anglo Americans and of the few middle class Mexicans who have achieved their present status by mobility are well-known among lower class Mexicans, who give them credit for what they did and are willing to acknowledge the benefits they have accrued by doing so. However, this does not mean that the lower class Mexican is willing to subscribe to this set of values, since he considers his own more attractive and important. The latter enable him to obtain his rewards outside the occupational and class systems, and insulate him from the mobility escalator and the frenetic competitive race for success. His peers judge him and accord him status according to his ability to fulfill the traditional obligations and not his ability to advance himself. In view of this, the ends defined by middle class patterns, even if the opportunity were present for realizing them, would not justify the means. The positive advantages that the lower class Mexican enjoys now as recipient of concrete and personal response and recognition from his group by virtue of his incumbency of a socially respected status within it far outweigh the vague, remote, and impersonal benefits he might obtain by entering the stressful world of competitive mobility, with its concomitant necessity for self-denial and renunciation. The middle class Mexican, on the other hand, partially oriented to Anglo standards and desirous of Anglo acceptance, conceives of the success ideal as desirable in itself and as a means to that acceptance, and is willing to make the necessary sacrifices to realize it even though the rewards he craves from the Anglo group are not always forthcoming. In any event, his efforts do result in the achievement of power and prestige within his group, as well as the limited rewards from the Anglo group that have been described, results which may seem attractive to the lower class Mexican, but not attractive enough to pull him away from the satisfactions he receives from another quarter. The lower status group of the middle class perhaps gains less and suffers more than either the group above it or the class below it. Lumped by the Anglo Americans with the lower class, largely ignored by the upper status group, and subject to a series of conflicts because of its attempts to sever affiliations with the lower class, its members nevertheless hold to the middle class ideal, despite the lack of substantial rewards and the limited sphere of opportunity available to them.[*] The very existence of this group, that has emerged from the lower class, indicates that lower class Mexicans are not unalterably committed to their present orientations and values, and that increasing acculturation and assimilation, if it goes hand in hand with elimination of the caste barrier and improvement of the basic material conditions of living, will eventually push more and more lower class Mexicans in the direction of the middle class ideal.

This section may be concluded with a brief description of lower class attitudes toward the middle class. The lower class

---

[*] See supra, pp. 212-13.

tendency to acknowledge the prerogatives of higher status and to give the middle class Mexican his due has been implicit in the previous discussion. The recognition of the *gran senor*, the "bigshot", as such, is legitimated by the traditional distinctions between an upper and lower class and is substantiated by the realistic gulf that exists at present between the classes. The informant's comment quoted above[*] is expressive of this. The categorical treatment of the Mexican group by the Anglos has somewhat modified the lower class tendency to take the superior status of the middle class for granted, however, and has led to the development of expectations of equality which prompt the negation of a superiority formerly accepted without question. The resentment engendered by awareness of the invidious evaluations directed at his group by the middle class tends to reinforce the lower class Mexican's sensitivity to middle class pretensions to superior status. This sensitivity was most often verbalized by lower class informants in such phrases as, "The big shots forget about the little people and always think about the next step up", and "They think they're too good for us."[**] One middle class informant, attempting to describe the lower class expectation of equality, had this to say:

> The *pelado* is so used to being ignored and exploited by an upper class that he has come to take it for granted that the Mexican leaders have no intention

---

[*] Supra, p. 385.

[**] This attitude is tied up with the suspicion and cynicism that has been described elsewhere as a prominent element in attitudes toward group leaders, and will be described more fully in the final chapter.

of doing anything for him. This he does not mind so much. What he does mind is any attempt on the part of the leaders to establish superiority over him. He does not mind particularly if the professionals and businessmen do not do anything for him, he is used to that, but there is quick resentment if he becomes aware that the leaders think they are too good for the masses. The pelado wishes to draw everyone down to his level, he is anxious to thrust his equality upon you and make sure you understand that he knows you are no better than he is.

## Anglo American Dominance and the Mexican American Class Structure

This chapter has attempted to show the pervasive effects of Anglo dominance on the patterning of Mexican class structure. The prominent role of the dominant-subordinate group relationship in determining criteria for status in the Mexican middle class, in creating distinctive middle class patterns, and in coloring interclass attitudes within the Mexican group is clearly evident. Moreover, the subordination of the Mexican is reflected in the relative size of the Mexican classes, the lower class providing the broad base for the slender middle class spire, while the large Anglo middle class overshadows its small lower class base. With regard to status criteria, the emphasis placed on command of Anglo ways and assumption of a leadership role required by the criterion of service to the group, as attributes of high status in Mexican society, are for the most part functions of the pressure of Anglo dominance. Anglo standards and values are becoming, to an increasing extent, the standards and values of the Mexicans in determining relative status within their own group, and only those who can approximate to Anglo ways are eligible for high status. The prominence of service to the group as a criterion of status testifies to the importance attached to the leadership element in the attempts of the Mexican group to cope with Anglo power. Since Anglos limit their significant contacts with Mexicans to dealing with a few representatives of the group, and since the latter's need for leadership in the face of Anglo dominance is overwhelming, those men who assume the liaison role with Anglos merit top status, whereas those who may be expected to serve the group in this capacity or in community projects for group betterment but are reluctant to do so find it difficult to reach the top. This marked emphasis on leadership and service to the group as a requisite for top status has no counterpart in the Mexican cultural background nor is it to be found in McAllen's Anglo society to anything like the same degree, and is apparently a resultant of the Mexican's subordinate status.

The role of the dominant-subordinate group relationship in the development of internal differentiation within the Mexican group needs little further discussion here. The major differences between middle and lower class orientations and behavior patterns are those involving differential reactions to Anglo dominance. Resentment of Anglo caste attitudes, the drive to develop Anglo traits and acquire Anglo values, and preoccupation with minimizing and eliminating the disabilities imposed by Anglo domination are predominantly middle class patterns, as described, and demonstrate the desire for

Anglo acceptance and the prestige accorded by the middle class Mexican to the dominant group's way of life. Interclass attitudes and participation within the Mexican group also bear the unmistakable stamp of Anglo dominance. The middle class Mexican, in order to further his goal of Anglo acceptance and to escape from subordinate status, attempts to differentiate and isolate himself from the lower class, which he thinks of as the major barrier in the way of realizing his goal. He utilizes the Anglo evaluations in characterizing lower class behavior and in devaluating certain Mexican ways which he tends to identify with the lower class. The lower class, on the other hand, tends to accept the Anglo's categorical treatment of his entire group and as a result tends to minimize the distance between the classes and to resent middle class attempts to widen it.

There are a number of factors that make for identification between the Mexican classes that should be mentioned here as a corrective to the emphasis that has been necessarily placed upon middle class attempts at exclusiveness throughout this discussion. One of these factors is the dependence of the middle class on the lower class as the source of its economic and political power and authority, which are important bases of middle class status. As the previous chapters have shown, Mexican American businessmen and professionals are almost completely limited to their own group for their clientele, and their political strength depends on ability to control and influence relatively large numbers of Mexican American votes. In view of this, middle class Mexicans cannot afford to emphasize too much their difference and separateness from the lower class, since the latter provides the basis of their class status in a number of important respects. The Anglo tendency to treat the Mexican group categorically may be considered a second factor since it forces the middle class Mexican to identify himself with the lower class and pushes him in the direction of intragroup solidarity if only as a means of ultimately raising his own status by raising that of the entire group. A third factor that should be emphasized is that middle and lower class Mexicans, despite increasing middle class orientations to Anglo standards, still share a common culture and that the gulf created between them by class differences is after all much narrower than that which exists between Anglos and Mexicans. There are few middle class Mexicans who do not express pride in their Mexican origins regardless of how preoccupied they may be with acculturation and assimilation to Anglo ways. This pride in origins is a powerful force for voluntary identification with the Mexican group and makes for a feeling of responsibility for group welfare that often endows group leaders with disinterested as well as self-interested motivations and nourishes their

---

\* Like the Anglo, the middle class Mexican tends to interpret his difference from the lower class as superiority. The increasing tendency of lower class Mexicans to resent middle class pretensions to superiority must also have some restraining effect on middle class attempts to mark itself off from the lower class.

common bonds with the lower class. Finally, the personalistic ties of loyalty and obligation that characterize the patron-peon relationship, to the extent that the relationship still functions in the traditional manner, operate to bring middle and lower class Mexican closer together on an individual basis and to minimize interclass hostility.

In terminating this discussion of class, explicit reference should be made to the role of conflicts of value and interest in determining differential treatment by Anglos of the Mexican classes. The degree of intensity of cultural conflict, which appears to be more prominent than the conflict of interests, experienced by Anglos in their relations with the two classes is directly related to their readiness to grant acceptance and alleviate the rigors of subordinate status. Notwithstanding their principle of Mexican homogeneity, Anglos tend to reward in practice those Mexican Americans who are most like themselves in idea and action patterns, and thus accord better treatment and greater acceptance to the middle class Mexican, whose increasing orientation to Anglo ways and values progressively eliminates the basis for cultural conflict between the dominant group and the Mexican middle class.\*
The cultural conflict between the Anglo group and the Mexican

---

\* Unlike the Negro case, the Mexican does not seem to run the danger of being considered presumptuous by the dominant group when he assumes Anglo patterns. As the next chapter will show, Anglos basically believe that Mexicans can and will be eventually assimilated, and there is no counterpart in Anglo-Mexican relations of the emphasis on "place" that exists in the Negro case. Since the Mexican's "place" is not nearly so well-defined as that of the Negro, the Mexican who acquires Anglo ways is seldom thought of as "uppity" by Anglos.

lower class has not abated, however, since cultural differences remain prominent, and differences in values are substantial. The continuing cultural conflict with the lower class Mexican supports and reinforces Anglo motivations to subordinate the Mexican group. Anglo stereotyping takes its departure from lower class patterns and discrimination is applied directly and consistently to this class, whereas the concessions made by the dominant group apply only to the middle class Mexican.

With regard to the conflict of interests, the Mexican middle class is more directly involved with the dominant group than is the lower class, as would be expected. Middle class Mexicans actively compete with Anglos, although on far from equal terms, for wealth, power, and prestige. This realistic conflict of interests between Anglo and middle class Mexican is partially submerged in the interclass solidarity whereby the interests of both groups are furthered by mutual alliance at the expense of the Mexican lower class, and the cooperative relationship in itself helps to promote Anglo acceptance of the middle class Mexican. Although muted by such devices, the conflict exists in fact and feeling, however, and helps to explain the Anglo ambivalence toward middle class Mexicans as expressed in the opposing tendencies to recognize the inapplicability of the stereotype in their case and at the same time categorically lump them with the lower class. The insistence on Mexican homogeneity provides the Anglo with a weapon for subordinating the middle as well as the lower class. The conflict of interests between the dominant group and the Mexican lower class is much less intense. The different values of the two groups channel their interests in different directions, and there is no direct competition between Anglo and lower class Mexican for wealth, power, and prestige. Nevertheless, the furtherance of Anglo interests depends upon the maintenance of the present economic, occupational, political, and social subordination of the lower class Mexican, both as a means for realization of Anglo interests and of controlling a potential competitive threat from this group.

## Chapter VIII

## THE STEREOTYPE AND PATTERNS OF DISCRIMINATION[*]

The discussion thus far has been concerned with the description and analysis, within a series of institutional contexts, of the nature and role of the various factors that have motivated the Anglo American to subordinate the Mexican American, and of the patterns of intergroup relations that have developed in the process of establishing Anglo dominance. Although the principal focus of the discussion was that of investigating the sources of conflict between Anglo and Mexican to discover the Anglo's "needs" for subordinating the Mexican, it was also necessary, in the discussion of intergroup relations in the spheres of occupations and politics, to pay some attention to the mechanisms employed by the dominant group to maintain the subordination of the Mexican, and to relate these to the conflict factors. The present chapter undertakes to treat these mechanisms in a relatively more systematic fashion, demonstrating the range of variation of forms they assume when considered from the point of view of their role in the functioning of the total system of dominant-subordinate group relations.

### Visibility Symbols

Before examining in detail the idea and action patterns

---

[*] For a theoretical statement of the nature and function of the stereotype and discrimination, see pp. 40-46.

involved in stereotyping and discrimination, it is advisable to consider briefly the symbols selected by Anglo Americans that enable them to readily define the Mexicans as a distinctive group and provide a practicable basis for the categorical treatment of the latter, in terms of easy visibility. Perhaps the most frequently utilized visibility symbol is skin color. Some Anglo informants consistently made a distinction between white and Mexican when referring to the two groups; others occasionally lapsed into this terminology. Anglos tend to equate Mexican with Indian,[1] and to think of all Mexicans as dark-skinned. The skin color of Mexicans actually ranges from dark brown to white, but the Anglo conviction that Mexicans are very dark is so strong that when an Anglo meets a light-skinned Mexican who can be identified as Mexican on other counts, he will often insist that the latter is Spanish rather than Mexican, according to the experiences cited by a number of Mexican informants. Anglos also commonly believe that all Mexicans possess straight, black hair, and as one informant stated, "I have been told that I must be Spanish because I have curly hair rather than straight hair." The Anglo insistence that a light-skinned Mexican is of Spanish rather than Mexican descent is meant to be complimentary, and is a special instance of the general tendency to define as "high type" those Mexican Americans who approach the physical and cultural characteristics of the Anglo himself.[*]

---

[*] For an important qualification of this tendency, see *infra*, pp. 413-14.

The Anglo preference for light skin color is strikingly illustrated in the life-history material gathered from one Mexican informant who happened to be the only light-skinned member of his family, and who described a number of instances where he had received preferential treatment from Anglos in comparison with his dark-skinned brothers.

Language provides another means of readily identifying the Mexican's group membership. With few exceptions, Spanish is the primary language of Mexican Americans in the Valley and San Antonio, and ordinarily results in accented English. Even in the case of those who speak unaccented English[*] there is a tendency to lapse into Spanish whenever in the company of another Mexican. Speaking Spanish or accented English results in immediate identification as Mexican, and where there is no desire or need on the part of the Anglo to be complimentary, this will occur regardless of skin color. In most of the cases of refusal of service in public places known to the writer where the Mexican was not easily identifiable by skin color, his group membership was established by the fact that the Anglo proprietor or employee overheard him speaking Spanish or accented English. One very light-skinned middle class informant who speaks unaccented English said that she is often taken for Anglo American at first sight, but that on

---

[*] There are a number of Mexican Americans, particularly in the professional group, who speak English with no trace of an accent. Nevertheless, Anglo informants expressed the belief that "you can always tell a Mexican by the way he talks."

one occasion, when she was engaged in a conversation in Spanish with a clerk while shopping, an Anglo woman overheard her and attempted to hire her as a maid because she was looking for a "nice-looking Mexican woman".

The distinctive Spanish surname is another characteristic of Mexican Americans which is readily utilizable as a visibility symbol. Although this characteristic plays no role in identifying the Mexican at sight or in most casual contacts, it provides an unequivocal means of identification in a wide variety of social situations. In San Antonio, for example, the election of a Mexican American to the office of justice of the peace was explained by Mexican informants as due in large part to the fact that he had an Anglo surname.

The combination of dark skin color, accented English, and Spanish surname apparently provide the Anglo American with sufficient means for distinguishing Mexican Americans as such. It should be noted, however, that they are not infallible in identifying Mexicans since, as indicated, there are light-skinned Mexicans who speak unaccented English, and the surname is not always available. To cite another variant, one informant, who was dark-skinned and spoke unaccented English, maintained that Anglos associate poor dress with Mexicans, and this association may take precedence over dark skin in making identifications.

> Any man who has a dark skin and does not dress
> neatly is immediately assumed to be a Mexican.
> A light-skinned man wouldn't have any trouble
> in most places, but I, unfortunately, would be
> challenged in many places where he wouldn't be
> questioned. If I am dressed in old clothes
> when I go into some places, because of my dark
> skin I am informed that I am not wanted. If I
> am dressed as I am now, they assume that I am
> Greek or Italian. These people (Anglos) don't
> believe there can be any such thing as a well-
> dressed Mexican. Of course, anyone who speaks
> Spanish is immediately considered to be Mexican
> even if he is well-dressed.

## The Stereotype of the Mexican American

In previous chapters, a number of the Anglo American's stereotypical beliefs about Mexican Americans were presented and analyzed with reference to their specific function in the ordering of intergroup relations in the spheres of occupations and politics. The present discussion will be concerned with those beliefs that serve the general function of explaining and justifying the total system of Anglo dominance. The beliefs to be examined here have a wider application in that they sanction the exclusion and subordination of the Mexican American on general principles rather than necessarily serving this purpose for one specific aspect of dominant-subordinate group relations.

The separation of Anglo and Mexican and the subordination of the latter by the former that prevail in practically all aspects of intergroup relations are ordinarily thought of as part of the natural order of things by Anglo Americans. It is believed that the Mexican and Anglo live together in perfect harmony, each occupying the place for which he is best fitted, and each satisfied with the present arrangement, which is the outcome of the operation of natural forces. Actually, one could live in Anglo McAllen for a considerable period of time, participating in all the activities of the community, without hearing a single reference to the existence of the Mexican group. The writer regularly attended church services and meetings of a number of service clubs and other organizations in the Anglo community where various types of community problems came up for discussion at one time or another, but there was never any mention of a "Mexican problem". The lack of formal techniques for subordination of Mexicans lends credence to the belief that there is no Mexican problem and no "racial issue". There is no legal segregation of Mexicans that can act as a constant reminder of separation as a deliberate policy of exclusion practiced by the dominant group. There are no legal restrictions on physical and social contacts, and no legal, residential, and educational segregation. There is no elaborate conventional etiquette of intergroup relations of the sort that prevails between Negroes and whites in the South that would require Anglos and Mexicans to be constantly on the alert to insure that the latter render deference to the former. Unlike the Negro case, where this is "the common denominator" of dominant group attitudes,[2] there is no sacred dogma of anti-amalgamation which requires the constant protection of "white womanhood" and the erection of elaborate barriers to prevent the possibility of intermarriage that would make for a constant state of tension between Anglo and Mexican regardless of the degree of active hostility present in the relationship between them. Finally, as will be seen in the next chapter, the Mexican reactive pattern of withdrawal and the lack of significant organized protest minimize the "problem" the Mexican constitutes for the Anglo and thus reinforce the Anglo tendency to believe there is no "Mexican problem" at all.

This stereotyped belief that the dominant-subordinate group relationship is a natural phenomenon is of course belied by the evidence presented in preceding chapters to show that Anglo Americans have had to devise various techniques for imposing and maintaining the subordination of the Mexican. If the relationship were as stable as the belief claims, there would be no need to employ these techniques, and if it were "natural", there would be no need for the rationalizations developed by Anglos to make subjectively acceptable the Mexican's subordination. The belief, however, is comforting to the Anglo, and serves, like the other rationalizations, to obscure the true state of affairs. In a relationship characterized by little overt hostility or open aggression on the part of either group except for rare crises, where the relative lack of rigidity of restrictions and prohibitions by the dominant group is usually matched by a reluctance or indifference on the part of the subordinate group to test the semi-caste line where it does become rigid, the belief that there is no Mexican problem and no "racial issue" can retain its plausibility for the Anglo under ordinary circumstances. The belief is far from adequate as a total rationalization of Anglo-Mexican relations, however, and is discarded, although often with great reluctance, for a mass of other rationalizations when challenged.

The racial beliefs of the Anglo American as applied to the Mexican are of strategic importance in determining the rigidity of the semi-caste line. Again unlike the Negro case, these beliefs are characterized by a pervasive ambiguity that has left a number of important loopholes in the caste line. Anglo Americans have traditionally made a distinction between "whites and Mexicans" and often express the view that Mexicans are "practically the same" as Indians, but surprisingly enough those who make the distinction often stop short of drawing the clear-cut conclusion that Mexicans belong to a different race, and some who use the phrase "whites and Mexicans" may refer to the latter as Caucasians in the next breath. This inconsistency about the Mexican's racial membership has made for uncertainty with respect to the nature of his "inferiority", i.e., as to whether it is inherent or not. There are not lacking those who hold steadfastly to the belief that Mexicans are of a different race, that they are biologically inferior because of their racial origins, and that amalgamation and assimilation, now or ever, is consequently completely unacceptable. Nevertheless, it has been of strategic importance that the racial beliefs about the Mexican have been predominantly ambiguous, and that this has not permitted the racial doctrine to assume the status of a sacred, unalterable dogma adhered to by all Anglo Americans and consistently applied to the Mexican group.[3]

The fact that the racial inferiority and anti-amalgamation doctrine has not played a dominant central role in the development of beliefs about the Mexican has left a loophole in Anglo caste thinking to the extent that the amalgamation and assimilation of the Mexican group is admitted as a possibility. Despite the fact that the realization of the possibility for the Mexican group as a whole is usually placed in the dim future, the very admission of assimilation as a possibility had had important implications for the treatment of Mexicans here and now. Anglo attitudes toward the assimilation of the Mexican are most strikingly revealed in the concept of the "high type" Mexican. As already noted,[*] Anglos define as "high type" those Mexicans who demonstrate Anglo idea and action patterns and possess high status attributes according to Anglo valuations. Dominant group members manifest preference for physical likeness to themselves as well by favoring

---
[*] Supra, pp. 351-52.

light-skinned Mexicans for inclusion in the "high type" category. It should be emphasized, however, that skin color does not necessarily play an independent role in determining Anglo acceptance of the Mexican. The general Anglo penchant for light skin color is not constant since it may be outweighed by cultural likeness and the possession of Anglo high status attributes. Not all Mexicans who are defined by Anglos as "high type" are light-skinned, and in McAllen particularly, of those who are most accepted by the Anglo group, a few are very dark-skinned.

Mexicans who are defined as "high type" are acceptable for intermarriage, judging from the intermarriages encountered by the writer in the McAllen area and San Antonio. In sixteen cases where data were available, eleven of the twelve Mexican males and the four Mexican females were all of middle class background and of the "high type" category. The eleven Mexican males were professionals or substantial businessmen, nine of them held top status in their Mexican communities, and most of the latter enjoyed particularly high status with Anglo Americans as well. In general, neither Anglos nor Mexicans favor or approve of intermarriage, but there is no severe condemnation of it where it occurs, let alone ostracism of the marriage partners by either group. In the cases indicated, intermarriage has not adversely affected the status of the people involved with regard to either the Anglo or the Mexican groups. Border cities such as Brownsville and Laredo, and Starr County, where the Anglo population has always constituted a small minority, have been noted for their high rate of intermarriage between the middle class elements of both groups, and in Brownsville particularly the <u>colonia's</u> "old families" are said to be very much bound by marriage ties with the Anglo community.

The Anglo's ethnocentric concept of "high type" manifests the belief that Mexicans are assimilable, and provides an avenue of at least partial escape from the disabilities of subordinate status. However, Anglos apply it sparingly, and although they are willing to concede the eventual assimilation of the Mexican American group, they do not want it to come too fast.[*] This is the principal function of the belief in the homogeneity of the Mexican group. The maintenance of the homogeneity principle serves the Anglo American as a brake for controlling Mexican American assimilation, and provides the principal basis for the rigidity of the semi-caste line. The average Anglo American may classify Mexicans as "high type" and "low type" and at the same time believe that "a Mexican is a Mexican". Both beliefs serve his purpose, depending on

---

[*] In fact, the belief in assimilation may itself serve as a justification for the maintenance of the status quo. As one Anglo informant said, "It has to come gradually, and with no attempt to force it. It's got to be natural, or it isn't going to work. Once you start forcing it, you have nothing but trouble". This informant, like many others, thought of amalgamation as included in assimilation.

the situation.

Regardless of the distinctions the Anglo may make within the Mexican group and of his uncertainty as to whether or not the Mexican may be biologically inferior, most of the Anglos used as informants for this study* believed that the vast majority of Mexicans are inferior _now_, and their beliefs are concerned with describing aspects of this inferiority. Mexicans are generally believed to be a "backward" group and inferior in most respects to the Anglo. This inferiority is held to be self-evident, demonstrated by the very status the Mexican occupies. To be Mexican and inferior is synonymous. As one Anglo woman phrased it in a letter to the local newspaper, Mexicans are inferior because "they are so typically and naturally Mexican". Since the Mexican is so

---

\* It should be noted that not all Anglos hold the same beliefs about Mexicans, nor with the same degree of intensity. Some do not adhere at all to the beliefs discussed here, some are more "liberal" than others, some have greater need for "hating" or for displacing their aggression onto Mexicans, and, in general, stereotypical thinking will vary with background and experience, as well as other factors. The "Anglo group" itself is of course far from homogeneous despite the fact that the treatment it has received in this study may tend to give the contrary impression. However, it was not possible to take the variations into account given the limitations of the study. The beliefs and practices presented here as characteristic of the Anglo group were selected as such because they appear to be the most heavily patterned, and the most decisive in determining the status of the Mexican American group.

obviously inferior, his present subordinate status is appropriate and really his own fault. There is a ready identification between Mexicans and humble and menial labor, and a number of rationalizations for justifying this, as the discussion of occupations has demonstrated.* If the Mexican is fit only for the most simple labor, there is nothing abnormal about the fact that most Mexicans occupy a labor role, and the fact that most Mexicans are labor role incumbents is sufficient proof that they belong in that category. The belief in the inferiority of the Mexican of course conveniently ignores the fact of the existence of a middle class group that represents all levels of business and professional achievement. That their number is still relatively small may be explained in part by the limitations imposed by the dominant group.

A prominent component of the general stereotype is based on what may be called fear of inundation by the Mexican group. The belief expresses the idea that the Mexican group

---

* "The Mexican is specially fitted for the burdensome task of bending his back to picking the cotton and the burdensome task of grubbing the fields". Hon. Carlos Bee, Congressman from Texas, Hearing before the Committee on Immigration and Naturalization, Sixty-sixth Congress, 1920, p. 19. Testimony before the same Committee in 1926 when the desirability of admitting seasonal laborers from Mexico was being considered presented the idea that Mexicans are the best workers for harvesting sugar beets because "they are much smaller in stature than Americans and more wiry." A Mr. Smith, lobbyist for a sugar beet company, stated that "Not only can (Mexicans) do (this work) better than anybody else, but there is scarcely any other work they can do as successfully." Hearings, Sixty-ninth Congress, pp. 225-226.

is overwhelming and submerging Anglo culture, and that "opening the door" to more than a few Mexicans means that the Mexicans will eventually "take over". Anglos are concerned with the high Mexican birth rate,[*] with the high percentage of Mexicans in the total population, and with what they consider to be the general ubiquity of the Mexican on the local scene. The following excerpt from a letter written by an Anglo to a local paper touches upon a number of the ideas connected with the Anglo fear of inundation:[**]

> When we see cities such as we have here in the Valley run 50 to 80 percent Mexican, both in population and school enrollment, then it behooves every American citizen to fight for a law enforcement that will correct such a condition, and bring into the country only such who are qualified to enter in a legal manner ... A day is coming again, probably sooner than some realize, when unemployment will again become a problem, and we will have a charity list here in OUR VALLEY which will be a real problem. Upstate on my recent trip I was shocked time and again to hear many refer to the Valley as LITTLE MEXICO. Others asked 'do they really speak much English down in the Valley'. Others said 'I understand one can't get a job in the Valley unless he can speak both English and Spanish.' 4

---

[*] "They (the Mexicans) don't vote, but they increase like rats. If something is not done we will soon be shoved out of the picture. There ought to be a law passed that every (white) married couple should have so many children and if they don't they ought to find out why not". - Comment of an Anglo landowner quoted in Paul S. Taylor's Dimmit County study, op. cit., p. 457

[**] Cf. the following letter to the Austin American, October 1, 1948: "I had not been in Austin for several years until last Saturday. People are not likely to notice changes that take place slowly and insidiously. I used to admire the refined and nice looking people one saw along Congress Avenue. Now - perhaps because it was Saturday - I believe it would be conservative to say that 40 percent of them were Negroes and Mexicans. It looks very inconsistent to me for the State to have Jim Crow and segregation laws for the Negroes and spend so much money rather than admit them to our schools - and keep the Indians within our borders on reservations - and then for (state agencies) to be so insistent there must be no discrimination against the Indians from across the Rio Grande, which every observing person can see is what a high proportion of Mexicans really are."

A McAllen barber, complaining about an experience where he had been subpoenaed fo jury duty only to find that of the one hundred people called about ninety-five were Mexican, said, "Why, I'll bet you that if you stood at this door (of the barber shop) and counted the people who walk by, it would average out, over a day, that seven out of ten would be Mexican, and on Saturday night, when they all come out, it would be almost 100% Mexican". Although it has been shown that Anglos know very little about actual Mexican differences, it is true that they definitely feel that Mexicans are "different", and that the Mexican, through sheer numbers, threatens to blot out Anglo culture with his "alien" culture.* The most tangible symbol of this difference, and the one most frequently quoted, is that of language, the constant use of Spanish by the Mexican.** An Anglo waitress, complaining that Mexicans always talk Spanish, said, "My boy friend is Italian, and I have met his friends, but I do not see him breaking out in Wop every time he meets them." The owner of a fruit packing company said,

> In this plant we make every one of them speak English, no Spanish. They are working for us, and getting wages from us, so they should talk our language. Some of the packing sheds here let them talk Spanish, but not here.

---

* Anglos feel that the faster population increase among Mexicans is "wrong" because this is "their" country, and the presence of the Mexican is often regarded as a "foreign invasion". They conveniently overlook the fact that Mexicans were settled in the Valley long before the Anglos came, and that the latter have themselves contributed greatly to the later "invasions" by their energetic recruitment of laborers from Mexico.

** "The use of Spanish in public ranked foremost, far above all other reasons given by Anglo Americans as a cause of friction and ill-feeling between the two populations." Tuck, op. cit., p. 97. Part of the resentment aroused by the Mexican's use of Spanish is undoubtedly due to the Anglo belief that the Mexican uses it deliberately as a means of talking unfavorably about the Anglo in his presence, see infra, p. 429.

The widespread use of Spanish enhances the Anglo's belief that Mexican culture threatens his own, and has become the target of much of the Anglo's resentment and hostility. Curiously enough, hostility is not usually expressed toward the Mexican diet, which also represents a very visible cultural difference. Most Anglos are fond of Mexican food, and a Mexican restaurant on Main Street does a brisk business catering mostly to Anglo clientele. In the Anglo's repertory of pejorative terms for Mexicans one may find such phrases as "pepper-belly" and "chili-eater", but these are rarely heard and are seldom accompanied by the hostility directed at the use of Spanish.

According to the statistical data compiled by the writer,[*] there is some basis for the Anglo contention about the higher birth rate and population ratio of the Mexican Americans, although the figures for the latter given in the comments quoted above are grossly exaggerated. However, the conclusions the Anglo draws from these facts have no basis in reality. Even if the Mexicans were interested in the subversion of Anglo culture and in supplanting it with their own, which they are not, there would be no radical changes. The truth of the matter is that, with the exception of certain very real cultural and personality differences that have been described in previous chapters, the Mexican American culture of today has more in common with American culture than it

---

[*] See Appendix B, tables on record of live births and on census of the McAllen population. See also school enrollment figures, supra, p. 134.

does with the culture of Mexico, and, as has been indicated, there is a tendency, at least on the part of some Mexicans, to merge with Anglo culture that which still remains distinctive. Most of the Mexican American's material culture is already of the same variety as the Anglo's, and ideational aspects become more and more colored by the impact of the dominant culture. Actually, it is Mexican American culture that faces the threat of being inundated and "subverted" by that of the Anglo since the Anglo has all the advantages of his dominant status for demanding likeness to himself as the price of acceptance and release from subordinate status.

This belief that Mexican culture threatens the integrity of Anglo culture and the imputation that Mexicans are bent on making good the threat provides the Anglo with a general justification for the subordination of the Mexican, just as the belief in Mexican inferiority does.[*] The only way of minimizing and controlling the threat is to generally exclude the Mexican from participation in Anglo life and to keep a watchful eye on those who have been accepted on one basis or another lest they open the door for others. Judging by the small extent of intergroup contact as depicted in a previous chapter and by the evidence to be presented in the next section, this aim has been very well realized. The general belief is useful for the justification of discrimina-

---

[*] The procedure utilized here for the analysis of the defensive function of stereotypical beliefs was suggested by that of John Dollard. See *Caste and Class in a Southern Town*, pp. 363-88.

tion against Mexicans in a number of specific areas of intergroup relations, of which examples will be presented below. Such discriminatory practices as refusal of public service, prevention of residential choice, and limitation of membership in voluntary associations can be rationalized in terms of the need to forestall the Mexican invasion of Anglo institutions. Finally, the belief in the inundation of Anglo culture by the Mexican rationalizes the Anglo's failure to develop large-scale programs for the amelioration of the unfavorable conditions under which the majority of Mexicans live. An Anglo college professor in San Antonio made the following observation:

> Informant said he has particularly noted that Anglos engaged in community chest work feel that there is not much use in trying to help the Latin American because there are always more coming, that it is a tide which will eventually overwhelm the Anglos anyway, so why bother to make a contribution to what appears to be a bottomless need. This attitude gives the Anglo a feeling of resentment toward the Latin, as well as feelings of futility and discouragement. Anglos say if you help one, there will be five more to take his place, so there is no point in helping at all.

A general belief directly opposed to the one just described is that Mexicans prefer separation from Anglos, they segregate themselves because "they want to stay by themselves", "they get along very well by themselves", "they are happier by themselves". The function of this belief is of course obvious and needs no comment.* Again, the same person may hold this belief and also believe that

---
\* It is also used to substantiate the Anglo contention that there is no Mexican problem.

Mexicans are bent on inundating Anglo culture since, although contradictory, each has its rationalizing function. As the next chapter will show, Mexican isolation is to a certain extent self-imposed, but the exclusion devices employed by the Anglo group have played a decisive role in fostering this isolation in the first place and continue to do so.

Another general belief accuses the Mexican of being unclean. The examples cited to illustrate this supposed characteristic of Mexicans most frequently refer to lack of personal cleanliness, dirty home conditions, and a high incidence of ailments, particularly skin ailments, which are thought to be due to lack of hygienic practices, and which are actually called "Mexican sores". One female informant, to document her contention that Mexicans are unclean, said that while riding on a bus recently there had been a Mexican woman in the seat directly in front of her with plainly visible bugs crawling in her hair, and a Mexican child in the next seat had a severe case of impetigo. Various Anglo informants indicated belief in the lack of cleanliness of the Mexican, but none were quite as vituperative as the author of the following letter, here quoted in part, to a local newspaper, who was attacking a statement by a State agency deploring the high infant mortality rate among Mexicans in Texas:

Should Texans force the Mexicans to not have too many children and too fast? Should we go personally and feed them each feeding, and supervise the w ter from any mudhole, and shoo off the flies and lice etc. their own parents see no harm in letting them swarm the place! How'd we ever attend to our own business? The same goes for the all too familiar ailments of lice and pink eye ... I'll wager three-fourths of the Latins have them, and if you want to be floored, just attempt telling them how to rid themselves of the pests. You get a look that seems you have hurt their feelings and asked them to part with their best friends. Sore eyes they consider as a natural part of life, and if they don't want to doctor and treat them and prevent them, what can we do? Go and put medicine in their eyes three times a day, personally? And also I guess we should force them to let us wash their hair in kerosene every day for a week! [5]

There are few immigrant groups, regardless of their racial or ethnic membership, to whom this trait, as well as a number of the others included in the stereotype of the Mexican, has not been attributed by the dominant group. The accusation has its grain of truth in that Mexican hygienic standards, like those of most lower class groups, seldom approach the compulsive stressing of cleanliness which is characteristic of most middle class Anglos. Moreover, lower class Mexicans usually do not have access to the sanitary facilities available to Anglos, nor a sufficient wardrobe to change their clothes frequently. Labor in the fields, packing sheds, and in the town occupations performed by Mexicans is rarely clean work, and it is possible that many Anglos base their conclusions on observations made in such situations, or in viewing Mexicans on their way home from such jobs. Cleanliness of the sort demanded by Anglo middle class conceptions is also a matter of economics, as is the treatment of skin and other ailments. The Anglo contention of the high incidence of diseases supposedly due to lack of cleanliness could easily be proved or disproved by investigation, but in any case, the Anglo incidence would tend to be less visible because Anglos have more money for availing themselves of medical treatment than do lower class Mexicans.

The belief that the Mexican is unclean is useful for rationalizing the Anglo practice of excluding the Mexican from any situation that involves close or supposedly close contact between Anglo and Mexican, as in residence, the common use of swimming pools and other recreational facilities, and in various types of social intercourse.

There are other allegations made by Anglos regarding Mexicans that have appeared regularly in the stereotypes applied to other immigrant groups,[*] and which serve generally to justify the subordination of the Mexican and his exclusion from full participation in the life of the community. One of these is that Mexicans are inveterate drunkards. "All this talk about Mexicans being underpaid is not true because if they were paid more they would just drink it up anyway." Mexican drinking patterns have been described elsewhere.[**] The ample patronage enjoyed by bars in the Anglo part of McAllen and the drinking behavior ex-

---

[*] This is true also of the traits attributed to the Mexican worker that were discussed in Chapter V. Aside from serving specific rationalization needs in Anglo-Mexican occupational relationships, variations of those beliefs are often utilized for general justification of subordination.

[**] Supra, footnote, p. 72, pp. 76 and 105-6.

hibited by Anglos when they cross the river to Mexico indicate that Mexicans do not have a monopoly on drinking. It is true that the number of Mexicans arrested for drunkenness is much higher than that of Anglos,[*] but this may be because Mexicans, due to their ethnic group membership and socioeconomic status, are more vulnerable to arrest than are Anglos. Another allegation is that most law violation is committed by Mexicans, and the conclusion is drawn that Mexicans therefore have criminal tendencies. "There is very little crime down here except for the Mexicans." "Look at these knife killings, dope peddlers and what not that appear in the papers. Ninety percent of them are Mexicans. Just keep up with the newspaper and see if I'm not right." "Intelligence, why sure they have ability, but it is a fact that seventy-five percent of the highway accidents in the Valley involve Latin Americans." The samplings of criminal offences collected by the writer[**] demonstrate that with few exceptions Anglo criminal behavior does not differ significantly from Mexican.[***] With regard to traffic

---

[*] See Appendix B, table on Corporation Court Offences.

[**] See Appendix B, table entitled Incidence of Crime. For traffic offences, see table on Corporation Court Offences.

[***] "In view of the man-on-the-street notion, which appears to be widely held, that the Latin-American element is the source of most of the troubles in the community it is worth noting that the Police Department records as well as those of the Juvenile Court and Probation Department show little difference in the contributions made to delinquency and crime between the Anglo - and the Latin Americans." Public Welfare Survey of San Antonio, Texas, American Public Welfare Association, Chicago, 1940, mimeo., p. 84.

offences, Anglos appear to have a much higher incidence than do Mexicans. If Mexicans have a higher incidence of involvement in traffic accidents than do Anglos (which does not appear in the records), it should be taken into account that Mexicans are transported in groups of forty to fifty in one truck to and from their field labor, a pattern in which Anglos do not participate. Valley newspapers no longer label Mexican offenders by ethnic group membership (although they do label wetbacks as "aliens"), but the San Antonio papers still do this on occasion. In any event, publishing of the name always reveals the Mexican's ethnic group membership. It is probable that singling out of drunkenness and criminality as peculiarly Mexican traits are reflections of the Anglo tendency to grasp at all possible types of "evidence" in the consistent attempt to rate the Mexican low and the Anglo high, and both these types of behavior are very "visible".

There are a number of beliefs in the Anglo's stereotype that display marked elements of projection in that they attribute traits and practices to the Mexican which are characteristic of the Anglo himself, or because they manifest fears based on the knowledge that such behavior on the part of the Mexican would be justified in view of the treatment he has received from the Anglo. One of these beliefs is that Mexicans themselves exploit their fellow-Mexicans and discriminate against them when they are in a position to, and that the Mexican variety is much more harsh and severe than that practiced by the Anglo.* Some Anglo informants placed

---
\* For one expression of this, see *supra*, p. 197.

this on a class basis. One said that "discrimination by higher class Mexicans against lower class ones is more vicious than that practiced by Anglos, particularly in the relationship with domestic servants." Others said they never cease to be astonished by the rigid "caste system" that exists among Mexicans, and by the "cruel treatment" meted out to lower class Mexicans by the "upper class".* An Anglo Catholic priest in San Antonio said, "If you really want to know who is doing whatever exploiting there is, it's the Mexicans who cheat the Mexicans." He went on to give a series of examples, stating that the owner of the pecan-shelling plants in San Antonio, which were notorious for their exploitation of Mexican workers,[6] was a Mexican, and that the corrupt government of San Antonio was due to the fact that its mayor was a Mexican.** An Anglo schoolteacher in San Antonio spoke of the time she did charity work among the Mexicans, and cited cases of Mexican doctors who treated their patients inhumanly and would do nothing for them unless they were paid in full. This same informant said of the principal Mexican-owned restaurant in San Antonio that "the

---

\* One Anglo American, commenting on life in Mexico in a letter to the editor of the Valley Evening Monitor, wrote: "The well-educated and travelled Mexican draws the color and class line so rigid that it makes the Jim Crow law look sick."

\*\* The first of these statements is wholly false since the owner was not a Mexican, and the Mexican named did not own any such plants, and the second partially so since the mayor's father was Anglo and his mother said to be Mexican. San Antonio's corrupt government existed long before the present mayor took office.

Anglos get good food and service, but the <u>peons</u>, the Mexicans, get nothing but scraps and these are thrown on the table for them. Besides that, he cheats them on the check, overcharging them, you know. But he doesn't do that to Anglo Americans." The writer was able to check these last charges by personal observation and found them to be utterly unfounded.

Another Anglo belief accuses the Mexican of being deceitful and having a "lower" morality. "They're all alike. I wouldn't trust one out of my sight." "The Mexicans will take white men for whatever they can get, but they don't like them. White men go over to the other side (the Mexican border town across from McAllen), and they'll welcome you as long as you spend money for drinks and things, but when your money is gone, they don't know you. If they can't get something from you, they don't want anything to do with you. It doesn't do any good to give them anything because the more you give them or do for them, the more they want." The following excerpt from an interview with an Anglo bond broker in San Antonio is another illustration of this belief:

> Informant said he would rather work a Negro than a Mexican any time because you can trust the Negro more and depend on him more. The Mexican is always resentful, and you know that when you tell him to do something he is going to do it unwillingly and not at all if you do not keep an eye on him. He went on to say that Mexicans are very shifty and secretive. If they get into a situation where you have to call them down for something, they take advantage of their Spanish and pretend they do not understand English. They will use Spanish to talk to each other so that you will not understand them, and you know they are talking about you, but there is nothing you can do about it. A Negro, on the other hand, will do his work cheerfully and openly, even though he does not always do it too well.

There were other charges of "immorality", most of them directed at Mexican family life, which is thought to be characterized by a "lower" morality than that of the Anglo: Mexican husbands desert their wives regularly, any Mexican woman can be had for the asking, parents do not care if their children die because they can always have more, and "the family feeling is of the kind that a master might feel for a useful dog, but that's about all."

Closely related to the belief that the Mexican is deceitful is the idea that he is mysterious and unpredictable. One Anglo Catholic priest in McAllen said:

> It's a hard job you take on when you try to get to know what kind of people they are. The priests I know who have been working with them for many years say that it's impossible to ever learn their psychology. Just when you think you understand them, they turn around and do something so unexpected that you feel you know nothing and have to start all over again. Their ways are hard for Americans to understand, even after years of experience with them.

Another priest in McAllen characterized the Mexicans as follows:

> These people are very unpredictable. You never know what's going to happen. They have no convictions. They're a great people for convenience. If they want something, they want it now. If they can't have it now, they want nothing further to do with it. They have no conception of waiting years for the fulfilment of anything. That adds to their unpredictability. There is no way of keeping up with let alone anticipating their momentary whims.

Another projective belief imputes hostility on the part of Mexicans toward Anglos, and manifests itself in fear of the Mexican <u>colonia</u>, and to a lesser extent of the Mexican himself. This seemed much more pronounced in San Antonio than in McAllen, however, where it was said that even the police were afraid to enter the _colonia_ after dark. Apparently Anglos do not mind entering the _colonia_ during the day, but feel they must be out of it by sundown. One native San Antonian, a businessman, taking the writer on a tour of the Mexican colony before the research was initiated, insisted on departing before dark because it would be "dangerous" to remain. The Anglo schoolteacher quoted above had this to say:

> They sure can make us feel we're not wanted. You go into some of those places on Santa Rosa and they stare at you in such a way that you just know they want you to get out. The X Cafe is a good place to go slumming, but you only want to stay a few minutes if you know what's good for you. You sure don't want to hang around very long.

When pressed for details, Anglos say that Mexicans do not like to see Anglos in the _colonia_, and may knife them or beat them up. However, no one could cite a case where this had happened. Most Anglos expressed this fear in connection with visiting the _colonia_ at night, and did not seem to expect any aggression from a Mexican when working with him or in any situation that does not involve venturing into the Mexican's "lair" at night. Nevertheless, an Anglo contractor in McAllen told the writer about two Mexicans who have worked for him for a long time, said they are always teasing each other and sometimes this threatens to get serious. He said he is afraid to say anything to them because he sits between them in the truck and is afraid one of them might pull a knife on him if he does. The writer also encountered a related belief in both the Valley and San Antonio imputing fear of Mexicans to Negroes. The fact that there are so few Negroes in the Valley was explained by a number of Anglo informants as due to the Negro's fear of Mexicans, that "they stay away from here because they are afraid the Mexicans will use violence on them." It was explained that Mexicans do not like Negroes and do not want to associate with them. In San Antonio, when the writer visited a State employment office with the intention of hiring an Anglo or Negro cook, the woman in charge stated that it would be very difficult to find an Anglo woman who would be willing to work in the colonia, where the writer was living, and out of the question as far as Negroes were concerned because the latter are always afraid they will be attacked if they venture into the colonia.

Each of these projective beliefs will now be examined briefly to indicate the realistic elements they may contain and the functions they serve in rationalizing the dominant-subordinate group relationship. The nature of the social discrimination that exists within the Mexican American group was described in the previous chapter. As indicated in the discussion of politics, there is exploitation of the Mexicans by the Mexican jefes, and the writer has a little evidence of economic exploitation of workers by Mexican employers. However, taking into account the fact that relatively few Mexicans are in a position to exploit their fellows even if they wanted to, exploitation within the Mexican group is not nearly as systematic or pervasive as that practiced by Anglos toward Mexicans, according to the evidence presented in the discussion of occupational structure. The preoccupation of the Anglo with exploitation of Mexicans by other Mexicans is an obvious attempt to obscure Anglo practice in this respect by projecting it into the Mexican group, and to justify it by stressing that the Mexican variety is worse. To strengthen the justification, the Anglo substantially exaggerates and distorts Mexican exploitative practices, as illustrated in the cases cited above where the charges turned out to be unfounded upon investigation by the writer.

As to the charge that Mexicans are deceitful, it is quite possible that Mexican Americans resort to a number of devices in their relations with Anglos, particularly in the employer-employee relationship,[*] to compensate for their disadvantaged position with respect to the Anglo, and these may be construed by the Anglo as evidence of deceitfulness. The whole nature of the relationship of dominance-subordination is not calculated to make for frankness on the part of the Mexican, or to encourage him to face up directly to the Anglo in most types of intergroup contacts. With regard to the accusation that the moral standards of the Mexican family are "low", the reader is referred to the discussion of the Mexican American family and of adult sex roles[**] for the amount of truth involved. Charges of deceit and immorality serve to disqualify the Mexican American for receipt of fair treatment and consideration as an equal, and rationalize the practice of exclusion and discrimination. The claim that

---

[*] See _supra_, pp. 242-43.
[**] See _supra_, pp. 60-79.

Mexicans are mysterious and unpredictable may be in part a reflection of Anglo reaction to the Mexican's actual differences in culture and personality. Like all the other Anglo generalizations about the Mexican described here, this one is over-emphasized and exaggerated, as is evident in the quoted comments. This belief justifies unfair and inconsiderate treatment since it is useless to treat a Mexican as one would an Anglo if he is so unstable that one never knows what to expect from him. Moreover, it justifies the failure of the Anglo to make any attempt to understand the Mexican or life in the colonia, and helps to obscure the basic insecurity the Mexican feels in the majority of his contacts with the Anglo.

The Anglo fear of the colonia and of the Mexican himself is largely delusional. It is true that there is some violence in the cantinas and that this is given prominent space in the newspapers, but there does not seem to be any other realistic basis for the fear. Perhaps the best evidence of the groundlessness of the fear is that the writer lived in the heart of the Mexican colony in San Antonio for four months, visited all types of places in the course of the investigation, and was never molested in any way, either during the day or night. Although it was not always easy to strike up acquaintance with colonia residents, no one was ever unpleasant or overtly aggressive. The expectation of retaliation expressed in this belief is perhaps the result of the Anglo's own guilt feelings. It also seems to be largely a rationalization for maintaining the separateness of the two groups. If

Mexican Americans are aggressive and dangerous, it is best that they live apart in colonies of their own.

Not all the Anglo's beliefs about the Mexican American are unfavorable. Among those that are usually meant to be complimentary are the beliefs that all Mexicans are musically minded and are always looking for the opportunity to have a baile, dance, or fiesta because they love to have a good time; that they are very "romantic" rather than "realistic" (although this can have unfavorable connotations as well); that if you once make a friend of a Mexican, he will always be loyal and faithful and "will do anything for you" (but, as indicated above, they may be treacherous, resentful, aggressive); that they love flowers and plants and can grow anything because "they are close to the soil and can take a piece of land where nothing has ever grown and make it produce." All of these beliefs have their modicum of truth just as unfavorable beliefs do. It should be noted that none of them contradict the basic rationalizations employed for justifying the Mexican's subordination. They compliment the Mexican on characteristics that are not given serious consideration in Anglo society but are relegated to a lesser rank. Most of them reinforce the Anglo belief that the Mexican is "childlike" since serious, responsible adults are not primarily preoccupied with such things, and thus they provide additional support for the idea that the Mexican is fitted for his subservient role.*

---

* "All such favorable beliefs seem to have this in common, that they do not raise any question concerning the advisability or righteousness of keeping the Negro in his place in the caste order. They do not react against the major need for justification. They rather make it natural that he shall remain subordinate." Myrdal, op. cit., p. 108.

As has been indicated, the Anglo's stereotypical beliefs in almost every case take their departure from a small realistic core of fact. He has, however, a number of sources to draw on for elaborating and tailoring the facts to suit his purposes. One of these is the ample heritage of hostile beliefs about Mexicans that developed through the turbulent years of Anglo-Mexican relations in Texas, another is the repertory of beliefs about Negroes and European immigrant groups, and a third is the stereotype of lower class behavior patterns.* All of these sources have provided material for the stereotype just described. The contemporary conflicts between Anglo and Mexican, however, as these are perceived by the Anglo, provide the basic need and impulse for the development of measures adequate to cope with the conflicts and for the elaboration of a set of beliefs to rationalize these measures. The conflicts themselves are an important source for the material utilized in the elaboration process since they generate conceptions of the Mexican American that nourish the stereotype. The stereotype in turn serves to intensify the intergroup conflicts by imputing motivations and orientations to Mexican Americans that seemingly threaten Anglo American values, morality, cultural integrity, and a whole range of interests to the point where the realistic elements involved are lost in a mass of exaggerations and distortions.

---

* It should be kept in mind that the Anglo group dealt with throughout this discussion has been considered middle class.

All the beliefs considered here tend toward a common end, that of placing the Mexican American outside the accepted moral order and value framework of Anglo society by attributing to him a series of undesirable characteristics that make it "reasonable" to subordinate him and subject him to differential treatment from that accorded fellow Anglo Americans. By accomplishing this end, the beliefs provide a rationalized definition of the dominant-subordinate group relationship that makes it palatable for the Anglo, as well as a substantial support for maintaining the system as it is. Under ordinary circumstances the stereotype serves as a set of ready-made assumptions, in large part left unstated, that guide Anglos in their relations with Mexicans, and that assure them of the "rightness" of the present state of affairs, just as it lulls them into thinking of it as completely natural. Since the interaction between the two groups is confined to a limited number of spheres and is largely formal where it does occur, the discrepancy between the reality and the image defined by the stereotype rarely comes to the attention of the Anglo. If it does, the stereotyped image may be strong enough to force an interpretation of the realistic situation which in the end reinforces his beliefs, and if this does not occur, there is always the category of the "high type" Mexican into which the exception can be placed without disturbing the "validity" of the stereotype as applicable to all the rest of the Mexicans. If a positive challenge to the system arises, all the hostile attitudes, moral valuations, and sense of threat embodied in the stereotype emerge to defend the "rightness" of the system, and the stereotype comes into play as a powerful device for arousing highly emotional feelings of group solidarity and for discrediting, in moral terms, the source of the challenge.*

## Discrimination Against the Mexican American**

The discussions of occupations and politics have already demonstrated in part how the dominant group employs discriminatory devices for the maintenance of the subordination of the Mexican American group. In the occupational sphere, e.g., the dominant group's identification of the Mexican with the lowest labor role, by defining him as incapable of performing a higher one, places a serious impediment in the way of occupational opportunity for the Mexican equal to that enjoyed by the Anglo. In accordance with this definition, Mexicans are subject to differential remuneration where Anglos hold equivalent jobs, and are barred altogether from white collar employment in some cases. In politics, it was seen that Anglos oppose Mexican candidates (i.e. unless they run for office on Anglo terms) not on the basis of personal qualifications, but on the basis of group membership*** and the stereotyped definition accorded the Mexican group; and employ a number of devices for the prevention of Mexican

---

\* See supra, pp. 330 ff. for a good illustration of the stereotype in action.

\*\* For a definition of the term discrimination, see p.

\*\*\* See, e.g., pp. 332-33

American political representation and consequent access to public facilities and services not now available to the Mexican group. The disabilities suffered by Mexican Americans in the spheres of occupations and politics mutually affect each other, as has been seen. The Mexican's occupational status is so unstable and insecure that he is vulnerable to political manipulation by employers, and his political power is so weak that he has no recourse against unfair employment practices nor, as in San Antonio, access to the whole range of more attractive political jobs now monopolized by the Anglo group. Although discrimination against Mexicans will be considered here as it manifests itself in a number of individual aspects of the Mexican's group status, it should be kept in mind that all of the resultant disabilities imposed on the Mexican have mutual implications, and tend to have wider ramifications for one another. Thus, to take one example, certain of the Mexican's occupational disabilities act as impediments to equal educational opportunity apart from specific discriminatory devices employed by the dominant group in the educational sphere, just as disabilities imposed in the latter sphere make difficult the Mexican's escape from the lowest labor role regardless of the presence or absence of direct occupational discrimination.

The discussion that follows is concerned with the discriminatory devices employed by the dominant group in ordering its relationships with the subordinate group in the areas of contact already considered in Chapter IV. Whereas the previous discussion of these areas had the limited objective of delineating the distinctive patterns of intergroup contact, the present discussion will focus on the dynamic aspects of that contact, on the nature of the devices that, together with the stereotype, bring about the characteristic separateness between Anglo and Mexican and act as barriers preventing the Mexican's fuller participation in the larger society.*

## Residence

Anglos explain the phenomenon of the Mexican *colonia* in McAllen as a manifestation of the desire of Mexicans to live together and thus as a purely voluntary, "natural" arrangement. There may have been some truth in this claim in the days of the Mexican immigration to McAllen, in that the newcomers probably sought out other Mexicans who might help them in getting settled. As in the case of every immigrant group, the *colonia* type of settlement served as a means of cushioning the shock of transition to the new culture. There were a number of factors, however, that helped to determine the Mexican's choice of a home site regardless of his own volition, factors which still play an important role in keeping the Mexican within the *colonia*. The Mexican's

---

* Since all discrimination against the Mexican American is extra-legal and in certain respects neither rigid nor overt, it was not always easy for the writer to discern its manifestations, and sometimes not possible to document these when they could be discerned, given the limitations of the study. Consequently, the following presentation should not be considered a thorough, exhaustive treatment of the nature and extent of discrimination directed against the Mexican American in the communities studied. The discussion assumes familiarity on the part of the reader with Chapter    on the patterns of intergroup contact.

poverty necessitated settlement in an area where rents were cheap, land values low, and where he could be close to the sources of employment. The land in the _colonia_ was owned by a few men who divided it into lots tiny enough so that Mexicans could buy them, or built houses on them, often more than one to a lot, which were offered at a rental lower than the Mexican could expect to find in any other part of town. These practices laid the basis for the slum conditions that prevail today in the _colonia_. Since the _colonia_ area is also the site of McAllen's business and industry, it has always been the most undesirable from a residential point of view, and thus land values have been low for residential purposes. Living in the _colonia_ has insured proximity to the packing sheds where not only the shed workers are hired but also the field laborers for the harvest crews attached to the packing sheds. Thus the concentration of practically the entire Mexican population in one area of the city, and the least desirable at that, can hardly be adequately explained as a purely voluntary arrangement on the part of the Mexicans.

Apart from the matter of origins, it is evident that the concentration of the Mexican population in one area has facilitated differential treatment on a group basis with reference to the distribution of municipal facilities and services. As already indicated, the Anglo residential areas have much the better of it in this respect. Moreover, most of the substandard housing in McAllen is to be found in the _colonia_, and this is also the area of greatest population density. A proposal for zoning McAllen was made by the chamber of commerce in 1940, but it was not until 1945 that a zoning board was appointed and a zoning plan adopted. The City Commission attempted to sell the idea to the local inhabitants by claiming that zoning ordinances would contribute to "beautification, sanitation, safety, and protection of property values", and that the overcrowded and unsanitary conditions that existed in the _colonia_ would be eliminated. The zoning regulations have actually had the effect of strengthening the present arrangement and perpetuating its evils since they do not affect already established residences, and by formally placing the _colonia_ in industrial and business zones, have left it vulnerable to the continued introduction of industrial and business construction, while the Anglo residential areas have been zoned as such and are completely protected from any type of non-residential construction. The zoning plan also designated as industrial part of the area in Northwest McAllen which is the site of the northern extension of the _colonia_,* thus inviting industry into an area that had been heretofore residential and threatening the residential neighborhoods adjacent to the zone in question. Zoning regulations, impartially applied, might have prevented the development of the colonia slum if they had been initiated thirty years earlier, but present zoning regulations simply

---

\* See _supra_, p. 127.

provide another means of protecting and facilitating Anglo interests at the expense of the Mexican group, and are another instance of the differential treatment meted out to the latter by the dominant group.

No evidence could be obtained as to whether or not restrictive covenants are employed against Mexicans in McAllen. A reliable Anglo informant claimed that he had seen many deeds, usually to land located within the newer subdivisions in Anglo McAllen, which state that "this property cannot be sold to anybody of Mexican descent". The seventeen Mexican families that now live in North McAllen are scattered throughout the area, but none live in the newer subdivisions. At least four of these families are numbered among McAllen's "pioneer" families and established their present residences before this area was developed as exclusively Anglo, and practically all these families fall within the Anglo's "high type" classification. The writer did not encounter any recent cases of attempts by Mexicans to move into North McAllen. The price of land in that area is much higher than most Mexicans can afford to pay, but the rapidly increasing Mexican population will be eventually seeking residences in this or other Anglo-owned and inhabited areas since there is no room for expansion of the present colonia site, and it remains to be seen what means, if any, will be employed by Anglos in resisting this movement.

In San Antonio, the colonia population is subject to the same disabilities and unfavorable living conditions that

are found in McAllen, and on a relatively greater scale.
Here too zoning is manipulated to serve Anglo interests
at the expense of Mexican householders. In 1946, an
announcement by the city government that an area of twenty
blocks in the heart of the colonia was to be changed from a
residential to an industrial zone to permit the construction
of new meatpacking plants was met by a number of protests
from colonia organizations and residents of the affected
area, all of which were ignored. Not until the parish
priest marched on City Hall, accompanied by 750 of his
parishioners, did the City Council revoke its decision. Not
the least effective of the priest's arguments was his threat
that his parishioners would make their disapproval felt through
their voting in the next city election.[8]

A few cases of inability to purchase land or homes in
various subdivisions due to restrictive covenants were
related by Mexican informants in San Antonio. During the
period of the study, an Anglo property-owner, supported by
the real estate company from whom he had bought his land,
filed suit to prevent a Mexican American from acquiring
ownership of a neighboring house and lot that had been sold
to the latter by another Anglo, the previous owner. The
suit was based on the claim that the deed to the house and
lot in question contained a restrictive clause barring re-
sale to a "Mexican" and stipulating that in case this were
to occur, the land would revert to the real estate company

that had developed the subdivision. A local Mexican American protest organization undertook to hire Mexican lawyers and fight the case on the behalf of the Mexican involved. A number of San Antonio real estate men were called to testify during the court proceedings one of whom provided the information that the majority of the subdivisions developed outside of San Antonio's west side in the past fifteen years have had restrictions against Mexicans and Negroes.[9] As to the reasons for inclusion of restrictive clauses in deeds, the following comment by one of the real estate men is representative of those offered:

> We find in our appraisal work and mortgage risk work that real estate has the best value, the most stable value, in those neighborhoods where the people are happy, compatible, people in the same social and income group, where their children can enjoy the same advantages, where they belong to the same churches, same organizations, where they have a lot in common, and their homes mean a lot to them, and for that reason we try to provide restrictions that will insure that kind of a neighborhood. After we lose control of the land, after we have sold it, we know the purchaser will in turn have to sell it to the type of buyer we originally contemplated.[10]

When informed by one of the defense lawyers that this was discrimination against Mexicans, this man replied:

> I do not know if it is discrimination against Mexicans, but when prospective buyers go into a neighborhood, they want to know what the restrictions are, and if you do not have restrictions against Mexicans, they will buy in a neighborhood where they do have them.[11]

Shortly before this case was heard in court, the U. S. Supreme Court ruled that restrictive covenants may not be enforced in the civil courts, and the local judge followed this ruling in making his decision. Although this event represented an important step forward in combating restrictive covenants against Mexican Americans, it was of course only a limited triumph in that it did not eliminate restrictive covenants, but only deprived them of legal backing. Such agreements can still exist, based on the voluntary acceptance of both buyer and seller in a real estate transaction.

In San Antonio, the numerous areas of "second settlement" taken over by Mexican Americans are indicative of a widespread urge, at least on the part of the second generation, to leave the _colonia_ and the depressed conditions that characterize it. Most of these areas, however, are adjacent to the _colonia_ or are located far from the better Anglo neighborhoods, thus reflecting the dominant group's practice of setting up barriers that will prevent the infiltration of Mexican Americans into its residential areas. The end result is that the dispersal of the Mexican group into the general population is seriously handicapped, and Mexicans must continue to live together whether they want to or not.

## Education

The dominant group in McAllen does not deliberately practice school segregation, but segregation exists in fact for the majority of Mexican American children as a result of residential segregation. Such segregation results in overcrowding in the Mexican schools that does not exist in the Anglo schools; children who speak accented English for the rest of their lives; and a sharp drop in Mexican enrollment at the high school level because many Mexican children cannot make the transition from the Mexican grade school to the Anglo high school. Separation of Anglo and Mexican children is not regarded as a "problem" in any sense by the dominant group, and there are no indications that any changes in the present arrangement are being contemplated. At the time of the study, a new school was under construction to relieve the congestion in the _colonia_ schools that occasioned half-day classes there, but its location, on the edge of the _colonia_ furthest away from Anglo residential areas, will insure and reinforce the continuance of segregation. The placing of Anglo and Mexican children in separate classes is practiced to a small extent in those schools where both are enrolled, and the justification given for this is the "language handicap"*

---

\* "If any of you are under any illusions to the effect that segregation is being carried out for pedagogical reasons, I shall be glad to listen to a pedagogical justification that explains away a separate and inferior building, or a separate building of any kind; or that, by some sort of mental gymnastics, deems it best for children who do not know English to associate only with children who do not know English either." George I. Sanchez, "Address to Texas Good Neighbor Commission", Austin, Texas, March 26, 1948, manuscript.

of the Mexican children.* In an article in the local paper, McAllen's school superintendent explained that "if the English and Spanish speaking were mingled, the teachers would be obliged to spend half their time teaching language."[12] Since, in the words of the superintendent, "Any child in McAllen can go to the school nearest him", the dominant group feels no need for justifying the large scale separation of the scholastic population into Anglo and Mexican schools that these words overlook.

Discrimination against Mexican American children can be practiced in ways other than those facilitated by

---

* In a survey conducted by the Texas State Department of Public Instruction in 1948, of 799 school districts that returned questionnaires, 139 stated that they maintained separate schools for Mexican Americans and gave the following reasons: 106 - language handicap; 47 - only Latin American children live in boundary of school; 14 - opposition by Anglo parents to mixed schools; 7 - Latin Americans prefer separation; 6 - crowded conditions; 1 - enriched program for Latin Americans. Although maintenance of separate schools for Anglos and Mexicans for any reason other than as a result of residential concentration has always been illegal according to the State Constitution, the practice of segregation, ostensibly on the basis of language handicap, has been widespread in Texas. A suit in the federal courts to specifically prohibit segregation of Mexican schoolchildren for any reason whatsoever was brought to a successful conclusion during the period of the study. See Minera Delgado, et al vs. Bastrop Independent School District of Bastrop County, et al, No. 338 civil, District Court of the United States, Western District of Texas, Austin, Texas, June 15, 1948. This ruling makes possible the elimination of deliberate segregation practices everywhere in Texas, but does not affect school separation based on residential concentration, of course.

segregation. Most teachers, whether in Anglo or Mexican schools, are Anglo,* and in the case of at least some of these, treatment of Mexican pupils is colored by their stereotypical beliefs. In San Antonio, a Mexican lawyer said,

> I remember one teacher telling us that we had to be good and work extra hard because we were Mexicans and our parents didn't pay taxes. I think the public schools didn't help us much because the teachers made us feel we were odd specimens, that our way of living was different. They asked if our fathers were citizens, and wanted to know if we spoke Spanish at home. We'd say yes, and they'd look at us funny.

A Mexican American teacher in a <u>colonia</u> school in San Antonio said of her Anglo colleagues:

> Some of the teachers think that all Mexican children are dirty. That's a prevalent idea. All of them are lazy, and most didn't get their share of brains. And they must be taught to keep their places.

Among the unfavorable conditions to which Mexican school children are subjected are those which stem from the occupational patterns and income level of their parents. Although these have no direct connection with the nature of the school system, they are nevertheless of great importance in severely limiting the school attendance of children. The migratory cycles participated in for part of each year by many of the local field laborers often result in children beginning the school year in November or December, and in the case of those families that do not migrate, children are often taken out of school during harvest seasons or not permitted to attend at all because

---

\* The McAllen school system employs 13 Mexican American teachers as compared to 99 Anglo Americans. In two other Valley school districts where figures were available, one employs two Mexicans and 108 Anglos, and the other employs no Mexicans at all.

their earnings are needed to supplement the family income.\*
The peculiar nature of allocation of state financial aid
to schools places a premium on the non-attendance of these
children, and no truant officers are employed either in
the McAllen schools or the rest of the Valley. State aid,
amounting to $55.00 per pupil each year, is apportioned
on the basis of the scholastic population of a school
district rather than on actual attendance. The McAllen
school system had a scholastic population of 5,184 students
in 1948, but an actual school enrollment of only 3,931. A
small part of the other 1,253 children included in the
school census can be accounted for by the Catholic parochial
schools in McAllen, but the majority consist of those
Mexican children who do not attend for the reasons stated
above. The school system benefits by this non-attendance
because the additional money thereby received can be used
for whatever purpose desired, and, in view of the congestion already existing in the _colonia_ schools, additional
construction would be required if an effort were made to
compel these children to attend school.\*\*

## Recreation

The pattern of separateness between Anglo and Mexican
in the use of recreational facilities has been described

---

\* See _supra_, footnote, p. 135.
\*\* In Brownsville, the difference between scholastic population
and actual attendance is even greater and the corresponding gain
larger. In 1948 the scholastic census amounted to 8,259 and the
attendance to 4,804. If the apportionment of state funds were
to be changed to an attendance basis, Brownsville would have to
raise almost $200,000 by taxation in order to maintain the
present level of school income. See _Brownsville Herald_, April 26,
1948.

elsewhere.* Separate recreation, for the most part, is an extension of residential separation, just as in the case of education, but the few publicly-owned recreational facilities in McAllen are available to Anglo and Mexican alike. Privately-owned places of recreation are not always open to Mexicans, however. A few months before this study was begun, two incidents occurred of refusal to admit Mexican Americans to such places. In Harlingen, forty miles east of McAllen, an Anglo teacher from a nearby town attempted to enter a skating rink with her class of forty Anglo and Mexican children, but "was shocked, humiliated and very unhappy to have to tell the pupils after talking to the manager of the skating rink that he did not let Latin-Americans on the floor to skate under any circumstances." [13] In Pharr, four miles east of McAllen, three Mexican American firemen were refused admission to a firemen's ball in honor of all Valley firemen. These men were informed by their department chief that "he had been instructed by the manager of the club to tell them that no Latin Americans were allowed on the premises." [14]

In McAllen, as in other Valley towns and in San Antonio, privately-owned swimming pools open to the general public do not admit Mexicans. In San Antonio, a Mexican American, former chief of the Juvenile Office, recounted an incident he had witnessed where a group of about forty Anglo boys, armed with sticks and rocks, were driving two Mexican boys away from a public swimming pool located in a city park in an Anglo neighborhood. Informant stopped the Anglos, who

---
* Supra, pp. 137-42.

told him "that they were tired of having the damned Mexicans coming over to their park, that the Mexicans had no business there, and that they should stay in their own part of town."* The owner of the McAllen pool, in the many years he has run the pool, has never admitted Mexican Americans, regardless of whether they were "high type" or not. A Mexican American businessman in McAllen told the writer of an instance when the pool owner had refused admission to a member of the most prominent Mexican family in a neighboring county. Informant, then president of the local LULAC** Council, went to see the pool owner about the incident and was informed by him that he knew "some Latin Americans were all right, but he had to make a rule that no Latin Americans could be admitted because of the difficulty in distinguishing the better class Latins from the others." In San Antonio, the Mexican consul general was refused admission to a privately-owned swimming pool, filed suit against the owner, and lost the case. A Mexican informant, commenting on the case, said:

> In the court suit that was brought, one of the lawyers asked the manager of the pool how he even knew that the consul was Mexican. The manager said he heard him speaking Spanish and that was enough for him. He said that anyone who speaks Spanish is Mexican as far as he is concerned, and he does not have time to distinguish between better type and lower type Mexicans.

---

\* The informant went on to say that the Anglo boys soon perceived that he too was a Mexican, whereupon one of them shouted, "Why, he's nothing but a Mexican himself." They threatened to set upon him, but a policeman arrived at this point and averted further violence.

\*\* See infra, p. 537.

It is incidents of this type that force the middle class Mexicans oriented to Anglo acceptance to realize that they are subject to caste treatment by the dominant group regardless of the concessions they may receive in certain respects already indicated, that a "Mexican is a Mexican" after all.

During the period of the study, an event occurred in connection with the McAllen swimming pool that provided an unusual opportunity to gauge the strength and extent of Anglo opposition to joint participation with Mexicans, at least in the matter of swimming together. Space limitations permit only the presentation of a brief summary of the case, but a large amount of data on the event was collected by the writer in extensive interviews with most of the key figures involved. The McAllen YMCA arranged to buy the swimming pool to serve as a basis for a much-needed recreation center for McAllen youth, and undertook a community-wide campaign to obtain the down payment by means of voluntary contributions and selling YMCA memberships that included use of the pool. An announcement was made that the pool would be open to the general public subject to "health and conduct" requirements for admission. The YMCA secretary received many telephone calls and letters from Anglos inquiring if this meant Mexicans would be admitted. When it became generally known that this was the case, widespread opposition was aroused, as illustrated in these comments made by the YMCA secretary to the writer:

Some of the kids in the Y clubs asked me if they were going to have to swim with Latin Americans, and lots of people called to tell me they wouldn't use the pool if Latins were admitted. Some of our clubs have four or five Latins in them, and they participate in most of our activities, wrestling, boxing, game nights, and so on. It's funny that the Anglo kids have not objected to any of this, but they told me they would not swim with Latins. When I pointed out that they do other things with Latins, they said, 'that's different'. I received a phone call from ____ (the owner of a segregated pool in a neighboring town), and he told me if we admitted Latins, we could figure that it would only be a matter of time before we closed down. He said the Anglos would stay away if the Mexicans came, the revenue from just the Mexicans wouldn't be enough to maintain the pool, and finally we would have to close. Someone else called to tell me that if we admitted Mexicans, the pool would become a garbage dump like the one in Edinburg. The pool there admitted Latins, the Anglos stayed away, and the place went out of business. Now it's a garbage dump. You should have heard the things people told me. They said that the Latins would ruin the pool and so on. I told them all that we would maintain a rigid health check, but this didn't do any good. Some of the people who had contributed said they would withdraw their offerings if we let in the Latin Americans.

At this point, the YMCA secretary felt that the question of admission policy should be considered by his board of directors, which consisted of 23 Anglos and one Mexican. In the letter calling them together, he presented a series of alternative admission policies to be considered by the board. The alternatives were phrased unfortunately, as it turned out, and none of them expressed an explicit non-segregation policy. The alternatives, as expressed in the letter, were as follows:

   a. Absolutely no Latin Americans.
   b. The policy of the pool owner (which would admit Mexicans if they were members of Anglo organizations renting the pool)
   c. No Latin Americans Tuesday through Sunday - Pool closed Monday and Latin American groups allowed in then only - pool drained and scrubbed Monday night.

One of the board members, an Anglo merchant whose business is located in the colonia, had the letter mimeographed and distributed to all the Mexican American businessmen. This not only aroused the hostility of the colonia merchants, who heretofore had manifested no active interest in the proceedings, but created a political crisis in that one of the board members was running for office and feared he would lose the Mexican vote through his identification with the YMCA. In the face of all this, the board met hastily and voted for a complete non-segregation policy. The opposition of the Anglo community\* to this decision was reflected in the steadily diminishing response to the YMCA's money-raising campaign, which finally bogged down completely when only half the money necessary for the down payment had been collected, and not all of these funds were secure because many who had contributed threatened to ask for refunds if the YMCA persisted in its non-segregation policy. A few of the Anglo businessmen, in favor of the YMCA's stand, increased their contributions, and the deficit was made up by a bank loan underwritten by this group. One of the Anglos who participated in this told the writer, "These people are sticking with the Y, not necessarily taking

---

\* One of the reasons most frequently cited by Anglo informants as to why they objected to Mexicans using the pool reflected the Anglo fear of inundation described above. A representative comment was "You just can't make concessions like letting the Mexicans into the swimming pool. The next thing you know, they'll be wanting to take over the whole town". Another reason frequently given was that Mexicans are not clean, hence the proposal that the pool would be "drained and scrubbed" after its use by Mexicans if it were to be set aside for them one day a week.

a stand on segregation. If the Y policy involves non-segregation, they're willing to go along with it."* In the end, however, segregation triumphed. Confronted by the YMCA's intention to admit Mexicans as well as Anglos, the pool owner refused to go through with the sale. According to the YMCA secretary,

> The pool owner said that since the Y announced its decision to admit Latins he had received many phone calls and letters from Anglos all down the Valley imploring him not to sell the only pool available in the Valley for Anglos. He said that they all asked him to realize that he had a responsibility to the community not to let the pool get into the hands of the Mexicans. He also received some anonymous letters from Latins saying that now the Latins would be able to get even with him for keeping them out of the pool because the Y was going to let them in. He said that in view of all this, he decided he did have a responsibility not to sell the pool to the Y unless they could agree to maintain his operation policy.

Thus the matter was concluded, and the community slid back onto the even keel of the "natural" separation of Anglos and Mexicans. The YMCA announced its intentions of raising funds to build its own recreation center and swimming pool, which would be "open to everybody".

---

* However, a few of McAllen's prominent Anglos, some of them not connected officially with the YMCA, took an unequivocal stand against segregation from the first. The local newspaper, after the termination of the affair, published an editorial condemning those who adhere to "a worn-out belief that Latin and Anglo Americans cannot get along together", and said of the YMCA's intention to build its own recreational center that "It ought to be a monument erected by people who have had their fill of prejudice and discrimination, people who are determined that their community no longer will idly watch the growth of one of democracy's worst enemies in the form of racial dislikes or hatreds." Valley Evening Monitor, May 2, 1948.

## Commercial Services

No evidence could be found of refusal to serve Mexican Americans in restaurants, hotels, or business places of any kind in either McAllen or San Antonio.* In 1944, a Mexican American soldier in uniform, who had just returned from overseas, was refused admission to a nightclub just beyond Pharr, four miles east of McAllen.[15] The incident became well-known all over South Texas and excited a great deal of indignant comment. At the time of the study, three years later, any Mexican informant was still able to describe it to the writer in all its details, just as all of them avoided patronizing the place, apparently still under the same management. The very fact that the incident attracted so much attention indicates its atypicality, however.

There are many towns throughout Texas that are notorious for the refusal of their restaurants to serve Mexicans, and at least four of these are within a fifty-mile range of San Antonio. San Antonio has a city ordinance prohibiting discrimination against Mexican Americans in shops licensed by the city. In 1945, a bill was presented to the state legislature proposing to make illegal the refusal of service to Mexican Americans in public places of business or amusement, and to impose a fine of $500.00 and/or thirty days in jail for offenders. The bill was passed in the state senate but defeated in the house of representatives.

---

* The one exception is the refusal to serve a Mexican in a McAllen barbershop, which was described above, p. 149. It is possible that more incidents involving barber and beauty shops would occur if it were not for the fact that Mexicans invariably seek these services in the <u>colonia</u> itself.

## Religious Worship

The formal segregation between Anglo and Mexican Americans that exists in the Protestant churches is evidently taken for granted by both groups, and no attempts by Mexicans to worship at Anglo churches were encountered by the writer. In the Catholic churches there is no formal or explicit separation, but separation exists in practice, usually as an extension of residential separation. Since the dividing line is not explicitly defined, however, Mexicans will sometimes attend an Anglo Catholic church, although this is apparently rare. One type of Anglo reaction to such an occurrence, as well as the Anglo attitude regarding seperate worship, may be illustrated by a conversation between two Anglo Catholic women, a Catholic priest and the writer in San Antonio. The comments in parentheses are those of the writer.

(Are there some churches that are strictly Mexican?)
A: (the priest): Oh yes, quite a few.
B. They want to stay by themselves. I go to St. Anne's, and there are a lot of Mexicans who could come to St. Anne's because they live in the parish, but they prefer to go to San Fernando, where all the Mexicans are. They don't feel comfortable at St. Anne's.
(I have attended mass at St. Mary's and found the entire congregation to be Anglo.)
A: That's right. Most of the Mexicans know better than to come to the Anglo churches. They know the people wouldn't put up with them. Oh, it's different where you have the better type Mexican, who is clean and well-dressed, but the others know they wouldn't be welcomed.
(If one of these others wanted to go to an Anglo church, would he be refused entrance?)
B: No, he wouldn't be turned out, but he would get such a chilly reception that he would never come back.
C: That's right, he would be smoked out.
(How do you mean?)

C: Well, you know how people can do. If a Mexican comes into the church, he would get all sorts of looks. The people would just stare at him and make him so uncomfortable he wouldn't try coming back. (C then cited a case of where this had happened.)

In McAllen, a middle class Mexican couple told the writer of their unsuccessful attempt to enroll their eight year old son in the parochial school of the Anglo Catholic church when it opened in 1946.[*] The boy had attended the parochial school at the <u>colonia</u> church, but the new school was much closer to his home. The day after the parents had enrolled the boy and paid his first month's tuition, the priest notified the parents that he could not accept the boy because there was no room. The mother pointed out that a news item had announced that the school still lacked fifty students for capacity enrollment. The priest then told her the child belonged at the <u>colonia</u> parochial school because he had been baptized at the <u>colonia</u> church. Informant mentioned two other Mexican families who had had the same experience with regard to their children. Two or three top status Mexicans are members of the Anglo Catholic church, and their children attend its parochial school, but apparently a "quota" is maintained for Mexicans at this school.

It may seem curious that in this discussion of Anglo hostility toward Mexicans little mention has been made of the Mexican's Catholicism as a target of hostility, especially in a state as enthusiastically Protestant as Texas.

---

[*] A newspaper article announcing the opening of the school stated that the dedication of the school climaxed 26 years of planning, that "the event will fulfill an original hope of the parish which dates back to 1920, when Rev.____ lent aid to the cause of an Anglo American church in McAllen by calling together Anglo Americans of his parish and forming a church building committee." <u>Valley Evening Monitor</u>, October 6, 1946.

Actually, although many Anglo Protestant informants expressed general hostility toward Catholicism, none of them specifically focused this on Mexicans. Most Protestant church groups in the Valley have demonstrated little active interest in proselyting among Mexicans, leaving the missionary work to groups from the North. The largely nominal adherence and widespread indifference that have come to characterize the Mexican's religious observance in the United States[*] may have played a role in minimizing the prominence of the Mexican's difference from the majority of Anglos in this regard, allaying whatever fears the latter may have entertained that Mexicans, as Catholics, might be out to subvert their "one true religion". There is little doubt, however, that the Mexican's religion has operated to set him apart, both through exclusion by the Anglo and isolation imposed by the Mexican himself.

## Voluntary Associations

The Anglo community of McAllen has twenty women's clubs, seventeen lodges, clubs, and service organizations that have male or mixed membership, two veteran's organizations that have women's auxiliaries, and an abundance of young people's clubs. The *colonia* contains a "Latin American Businessmen's Club", three mutual aid societies, a number of religious societies sponsored by the Catholic church, and two or three young people's clubs. The Latin American business-

---

[*] See *supra*, pp. 84 ff.

men's Club serves primarily as a _colonia_ chamber of commerce, but has assumed other functions due to the paucity of organizations in the _colonia_.* A survey of the membership lists of all the Anglo women's clubs and men's service clubs yielded the following information: None of the women's clubs had any Mexican members. One of them, the Pan American Round Table (the local chapter of a state-wide organization), has as its object "to further the knowledge and interest of the members in the social life, institutions and customs of the peoples of the American nations, and to promote good will and understanding among these peoples." None of its thirty-six active and auxiliary members were Mexican American, although four of its honorary members were, and its interests are comfortably directed toward Latin America and take no cognizance of Latin life in McAllen. The American Legion and Veterans of Foreign Wars posts in McAllen accept Mexican American members, but in Mission, four miles to the west, Anglos and Mexicans have separate posts. The McAllen Chamber of Commerce had seventeen Mexican members, and no "quota" for Mexicans so far as could be determined. These Mexicans were numbered among the _colonia's_ leading business and professional men, and at various times one or another of them had been a member of the Chamber's board of directors.

Among the service clubs, three Mexicans were members of Rotary, three of Kiwanis, and one of the Lions. The fact that

---

* This and other Mexican American organizations mentioned in this section will be described at greater length in the next chapter.

these clubs contain a few Mexican members is cited by Anglos as evidence of their "democratic" practices. "We don't have any discrimination here. Why, we have Mexicans in the Rotary Club". However, more often than not, this is followed up with a qualification to the effect that the number of Mexicans admitted should be carefully limited. One Anglo informant, sympathetic to Mexicans, made the following comments on the admission policy of the service clubs with respect to Mexicans:

> They keep a pretty close watch on how many and what kind of Latin Americans they admit into any of the service clubs. In the service club I belong to, they never had any Latins until recently, when they admitted _____. _____ has been sponsored for membership a few times now, but he has been blackballed every time. There are only a few Latins in the other clubs. Naturally, they would allow in only the best (sarcastically). You know what they always tell you about the Latin Americans. They say you have to be careful how many of them you let into the clubs, otherwise it will be just too bad. If you admit a few, they'll work to get others admitted, and the first thing you knew, they'll be taking over the whole club.

The following excerpt from a conversation with an Anglo who had come from the North a few years before illustrates the same pattern:

> Informant said that when he joined a service club, he found that they considered themselves very exclusive, and kept out those they considered undesirable. Under the heading of undesirable came most of the Latin Americans. They have a few Latins, but the members feel this is enough. Some time ago they had a membership drive, and one of the Latin members went out to get members. He has a great deal of energy and soon brought in a long list of prospective members. Unfortunately, they were all Latin Americans, and the club turned them down one after another. Finally, he caught on and desisted. These people never come out and say anything about Latin Americans or anybody else, it is the expression on their faces and the

indirect references they make that give them away, and also the way they vote on admitting various kinds of people to the organizations in McAllen. When this same Latin member decided to go as a delegate to the national convention of the club, there were a lot of raised eyebrows. Remarks were passed about the idea of a Mexican representing the McAllen club at a national convention. The reason this man went was because he was one of the few who had enough money to pay his own expenses, which was a condition of being a delegate.

No survey was attempted of voluntary associations in San Antonio, but the following data are pertinent. The Pan American Round Table there had forty-five Anglo and four Mexican women in its 1943 list of active and auxiliary members. San Antonio has another organization of this sort, the Pan American Relations Council, which has a larger proportion of Mexican members. This group holds monthly meetings at member's houses and also looks beyond the local scene to Latin America. Purely social clubs abound in both the Anglo and Mexican communities, and although a few of the Anglo clubs may have one or two Mexican members, and viceversa, the dominant pattern is the usual separation between Anglo and Mexican. Of the four principal _colonia_ organizations, two, the League of United Latin American Citizens (LULAC) and the Pan American Progressive Association, are primarily protest and improvement organizations, and so of course have no counterpart in the Anglo community. The other two are the Mexican Chamber of Commerce and the Pan American Optimists. The Chamber is not a result of Anglo segregation practices since Mexicans are admitted to the San Antonio Chamber of Commerce, but was apparently developed by _colonia_ merchants as a response to the needs and demands of their subordinate situation, which could not be satisfied by participation in the Anglo organization. The Pan American Optimists Club is the Mexican counterpart of the Anglo Optimists Club, a service club, which has no Mexican members. Many Mexicans are opposed to these two _colonia_ organizations because they consider them examples of self-segregation. A Mexican informant who had been president of the Pan American Optimists had this to say of its founding:

> If I had known how the Pan American Optimists had been started, I never would have joined in the first place. The Optimists Club of San Antonio thought it would be nice to have a Latin American chapter, and suggested that the Latins form one. Theoretically, Latin Americans can join the Anglo Optimists, but membership is by invitation, and no Latin American has ever been asked to join.

### Law Enforcement

Open conflict and bloodshed were a prominent characteristic of the historic relations between Anglos and Mexicans in the border country.[16] A "joke" told by Anglo informants in McAllen states that in the early decades of this century Mexican peons used to go about with notices pinned to their clothes by their Anglo employers reading, "Don't shoot this Mexican. He belongs to me. When I get through with him, I will shoot him myself." That a Mexican's life was worth little was evidently a popular belief among law enforcement officers and other Anglos.* A few of the older

---

* "When asked how many notches he had on his gun, King Fisher, the famous Texas gunman, once replied: 'Thirty-seven - not counting Mexicans'. This casual phrase, with its drawling understatement, epitomizes a large chapter in Anglo-Hispano relations in the Southwest. People fail to count the nonessential, the things and persons that exist only on sufferance; whose life tenure is easily revocable." Carey McWilliams, **North from Mexico**, p. 98

Mexican informants in McAllen and San Antonio reminisced bitterly about a number of outrages perpetrated on Mexicans in those days by law enforcement officers. One Mexican American in San Antonio, speaking of the situation he encountered in the small towns of South Texas twenty years ago during his travels as an organizer for LULAC, said:

> The Mexican people were afraid of coming into town for a meeting because they thought they were going to be shot at or lynched if we had our meeting at the courthouse. The courthouse to them was just a medium or a means of being punished. Most of the time, even when they were innocent of what they were being accused of, somebody would just want to find a goat for something, and the goat would be a Mexican. They're no good, just kick them around. If they resist, shoot them like a dog, what difference does it make. One Mexican more or less won't make a bit of difference in the world. Another one will come across the river and take his place. That was the general attitude.

The Mexican group is poorly represented among law enforcement personnel and although there is a Mexican justice of the peace in McAllen and another in San Antonio, there are no Mexican American judges. Mexicans are now summoned for trial jury duty in Hidalgo County and in San Antonio, but in the latter city a Mexican active in politics said: "The grand juries here have always had just one Mexican, who serves a double purpose as juror and interpreter."* A Mexican American businessman in

---

* "In one Central Texas County, a Latin American was charged with killing an Anglo. He was indicted for murder by a grand jury composed entirely of Anglo Americans, although more than 30 percent of the county's population was of Mexican extraction. Upon the date set for the trial, 100 men were summoned as prospective jurors, all of them being Anglo American. The defendant's attorney filed a motion to quash the indictment on the grounds that never in the history of that county had a citizen of Mexican descent been summoned for jury service. Rather than establish the precedent of allowing a Latin American to serve on either a grand jury or a trial jury, the authorities released the accused, and he has never been brought to trial, although the alleged murder took place three years ago." Kibbe, op. cit. p. 229.

McAllen, commenting on the lack of Mexican representation among law enforcement personnel, and attributing it to the Anglo belief in Mexican inferiority, told the following anecdote:

> The deputy sheriff in Starr County (95% Mexican population) had to go to another county once to pick up a prisoner. When he got there, they saw he was Mexican and carrying a gun, so they asked him, 'Why are _you_ carrying a gun in _this_ country?' He told them he was a deputy sheriff. They asked him where he came from. He told them Starr County, that the sheriff is Mexican, the county judge is Mexican, all the officials are Mexican. So they said to him, 'You must be in a hell of a shape down there if that's the case.'

Mexican American relations with law enforcement agencies are much improved since the days when the Texas Ranger "shot first and asked questions afterward", but Mexicans still receive differential treatment in various respects. In McAllen, five Mexican informants, three of them middle class, described experiences with customs and immigration officers at the international bridge leading to Mexico where they had been subjected to discourtesy, insults, and in two cases physical violence. With regard to the police, four cases of alleged mistreatment of Mexicans by county police officers, including whipping and beating, were reported in the local paper during the period of the study. In each case, the Mexicans were under arrest and charged the officers with using violence in attempting to obtain a confession of guilt. Commenting on these cases, the editor of the local newspaper wrote as follows:

> These stories about violence on the part of peace
> officers are as old as the border. Too seldom are
> they surrounded by fact in the form of readily
> acceptable evidence. They inevitably draw denials
> from the officers involved. So the public, in
> whose hire the officers conduct their work, is left
> to its own surmises. One of the conclusions bound
> to be reached sooner or later is that where there
> is so much smoke there must be some fire ... In most
> of the incidents it is a case of taking the word of
> the officer over that of the defendant, or viceversa.
> Since most of the prisoners are unlettered and of a
> poor economic class, the tendency is to take the
> word of the officer. But here again is the confusion:
> how can an uneducated man, without benefit of legal
> or other advice, concoct down to the finest detail so
> accurate a version of mistreatment without having
> undergone it? How could he speak except from experience?
> ... If those reports of prisoner violence are only the
> bad dreams of the accused, there is no cause for
> concern. But if they are not, those responsible should
> be reminded that retribution, though often delayed, is
> seldom denied. 17

There were no complaints of lack of police protection by
Mexican informants in McAllen's _colonia_, but in San Antonio,
colonia residents did complain about the lack of adequate
policing,[*] especially in the _cantina_ areas where there are
often fights, and the writer's own observations during his
residence in the _colonia_ corroborate this. In court cases,
the sampling of court records for McAllen and its county do
not reveal any significant differences between Anglos and
Mexicans with regard to imposition of fines and sentences[**]
for comparable offences and crimes. In San Antonio, several
Mexican American lawyers spoke of the existence of a legal
"double standard", but the court records there were not
examined by the writer.

---

[*] Cf. _supra_, p. 430-31.

[**] See Appendix B, tables on Corporation Court Offences and Minutes of Criminal District Court.

## The Nature of Subordinate Status

The entire contents of this study, with the exception of the first chapter, constitute a definition of the disabilities that characterize the subordinate status of the Mexican, as well as an analysis of the factors that have been conducive to the ascription of that status. As has been shown, <u>all</u> Mexicans are subject to one or another of these disabilities primarily by virtue of their membership in the Mexican group, and so long as they are accorded differential treatment by the dominant group because of that membership, they may be said to constitute a caste in American society. However, it has also been shown that the disabilities imposed upon the Mexican group are not as permanent or severe as those suffered by Negroes, e.g., so that the caste line is correspondingly less rigid. Since the rigidity of the line drawn between the dominant status of the Anglo group and the subordinate status of the Mexican group is not absolute or unyielding in that a Mexican American may cross the line and free himself from strategic disabilities and limitations that define his subordinate status, the term "semi-caste" may be considered more appropriate in the Mexican case. Given the absolute prohibition of movement across the dividing line between the statuses of the Mexican and Anglo groups as the principal criterion of caste, the Mexican's subordinate status may be viewed as a continuum defined at one extreme by full caste and at the other by modified caste which permits crossing the line in various strategic respects. Whatever rigidity the semi-caste line possesses is derived from the dominant group practice of ascribing subordinate status on the arbitrary basis of membership in the Mexican group, but a variation between full and modified caste is induced by the dominant group's recognition of cultural assimilation as a criterion in determining the degree and intensity of caste treatment to which it subjects the individual Mexican. Concretely speaking, the assimilation criterion plays no significant role in modifying the caste treatment accorded the vast majority of the Mexican group, whose subordinate status may therefore be considered one of full caste. The Anglo feels a strong sense of difference, expressed in the stereotype, from the Mexican mass, against whom the full force of exclusion devices is exerted. Their status reveals most clearly the criteria of caste, namely, prohibition of movement, in all spheres, into the status of the dominant group, and consistent subjection, on the basis of group membership, to the most severe and permanent disabilities in access to the rewards and privileges of the society.

The status of those Mexicans who are defined by the dominant group as "high type", a definition expressing recognition of likeness to the Anglo, is less consistently characterized by the criteria of caste, since the assimilation criterion modifies the caste treatment accorded them. The "high type" Mexican is released from the caste prohibition of freedom of movement in that he may have access to one or more of the following: equal status participation with

Anglos in informal "social" intercourse, residence in
an Anglo neighborhood, membership in Anglo organizations,
and intermarriage with the Anglo group. With regard to
access to the rewards and privileges of the larger society,
there are "high type" Mexicans who have occupied high
occupational status in Anglo-owned business enterprises,
although this is more true of San Antonio than McAllen, or
whose successful businesses have depended largely on Anglo
patronage.* This freedom from caste treatment enjoyed by
the "high type" Mexican, although extremely important in
qualifying the subordinate status of the Mexican group as
"semi-caste", is neither consistent nor absolute, however,
and the correlation between the degree of assimilation attained
by the Mexican and the degree of acceptance accorded by the
Anglo is far from perfect. The role of group origins as the
sole status determinant has become modified by application
of the assimilation criterion, but it is still decisive in
that the Mexican, no matter how "assimilated" he may be,
cannot pass completely into the dominant status so long as
he does not misrepresent his origins. The middle class
Mexican defined as "high type" may not be excluded from
joint participation with the dominant group nor from
access to its rewards and privileges as consistently and
completely as is the lower class Mexican, but he is excluded
nonetheless, as this study has shown. With the important

---

* See *supra*, pp. 223-24.

exceptions just noted, the whole pattern of separation between Anglo and Mexican in residence, education, religious worship, commercial and professional services, social intercourse, and other spheres of potential inter-group contact, is as characteristic of the most assimilated Mexicans as of the least, and as the discussion of Anglo exclusion devices has just shown, the separation is largely the outcome of Anglo exclusion practices rather than of voluntary agreement between the groups. When it is a matter of refusal of service in a restaurant or of admission to a swimming pool, to be "high type" is no guarantee of immunity, and an Anglo service club that accepts one or two "high type" Mexicans as members may reject others who are just as "high type". No matter how assimilated he may be and how free from caste prohibitions and disabilities, the Mexican is never quite safe from Anglo exclusion. For example, one Mexican American in San Antonio, who is married to an Anglo, has a substantial business largely supported by Anglo patronage, and enjoys as high status with the Anglo group as any Mexican American, was unable to buy a home in an Anglo neighborhood due to restrictive covenants. As long as Mexican Americans may be subjected to such treatment solely because they are Mexicans, their status will remain different in kind as well as degree from that of the Anglo American, and they cannot escape from caste into the open class system of the dominant society. Thus the principal disability that defines the status of even the most assimilated Mexican is that he is never completely accepted as just another American, but is always vulnerable to being judged solely on the basis of his group membership. That the disability appears to be permanent and ultimately expresses the rigidity of the semi-caste line does not minimize the importance of the Anglo belief in the eventual assimilation and amalgamation of the Mexican group, but rather maximizes it. The positive role played by the belief in the present is to be seen in the dominant group's utilization of the assimilation criterion for according progressive release from caste treatment, and in the loophole it makes in the caste barrier by permitting ever greater approximation to full participation in American society. The complete fusion of the Mexican American group, or of any of its individual members, with the dominant society will be delayed, however, until either the fact of Mexican origins no longer has primary significance for the Anglo as a status determinant, or the Mexicans, attaining the necessary qualifications, are willing to pass over, one by one, into the dominant group by denying their origins.*

The importance of cultural difference and of conflicts of value in motivating the subordination of the Mexican may be observed in this tendency to gradually alleviate the caste disabilities of those who become oriented to Anglo

---
* As the next chapter will show, few Mexicans are willing to pay this price for full acceptance by the dominant group.

patterns and approach likeness to the Anglo. It is true that the conflict of interests, for power, prestige, and economic resources, is greater or potentially greater between the dominant group and the "assimilated" Mexican of the middle class than between the former and the Mexican lower class, which helps to explain why the dominant group persists in maintaining the "assimilated" Mexican in his semi-caste status.[*] However, it has been pointed out that the conflict of interests has been somewhat minimized by the fact that middle class Mexicans do not as yet represent a very serious or imminent competitive threat to the dominant group,[**] although this in itself is in part a consequence of Anglo dominance; and by the fact that middle class Anglos and Mexicans have come to share values that have enabled them to partially submerge the interest conflict in a solidary relationship across the caste line, although in many cases at the expense of the lower class Mexican.[***]

---

[*] The internal tensions and insecurity experienced by members of the dominant group that may instigate the displacement of aggression onto the Mexican group have been only lightly touched upon as a factor conducive to the ascription of subordinate status, but would of course have to be taken into account in any attempt to fully evaluate the dominant group's "need" for subordination of the Mexican. See pp. 32-33.

[**] See e.g., supra, p. 166.

[***] Supra, pp. 373 ff.

The increasing assimilation of Mexicans of all classes may eventually break down the semi-caste barrier by reducing and ultimately eliminating one of the dominant group's principal motivations for the subordination of the Mexican, but it is possible that increasing assimilation may also have the contrary effect of intensifying the conflict of interests. To the extent that the Mexican worker becomes oriented to Anglo values, he is likely to strive for greater acquisition of interests now largely monopolized by the dominant group, and by doing so threaten the advantages the latter now enjoys through access to a fund of cheap, fluid labor. Similarly, in the case of the Mexican middle class, increasing assimilation will undoubtedly improve their ability to compete with the Anglo on more equal terms. These developments may well operate to reinforce the Anglo motivations to subordination that stem from the conflict of interests, thus minimizing and perhaps annulling the rapprochement that may be achieved through assimilation. Such an outcome is not inevitable, however, since increasing assimilation would also favor the redefinition of the conflict of interests from one of Anglo versus Mexican to one of legitimate competition for interests between members of the same society oriented to common values and integrated under the same normative order.

## Chapter IX

## REACTIVE ADJUSTMENTS TO SUBORDINATE STATUS

The preceding chapters have touched upon a few of the characteristic patterns of response by Mexicans Americans to Anglo dominance in various aspects of intergroup relations, but this study would be seriously incomplete without a systematic and explicit treatment of the principal types of Mexican American reactive adjustments to subordinate status. The discussion which follows of Mexican American conceptions of subordinate status and of the dominant group, of the range of variation of modes of response, and of the ways in which these responses are reflected in patterns of leadership and organization, will serve to round out the study.

### Conceptions of Subordinate Status and Role

In one way or another, all Mexican Americans are aware that their group holds a status subordinate to that of the Anglo group, as manifested in the latter's monopoly of rewards and privileges, just as they are aware of the hostility that characterizes the dominant Anglo attitude toward them. Although all Mexicans have in common this awareness of Anglo hostility and discrimination and regard their status as constituting a frustration situation, it will be seen that the degree of intensity with which frustration is felt and the corresponding role it plays in the development of adjustive patterns varies considerably. Despite this variation, there is a dominant tendency, found in all sectors and levels of the Mexican group, to select refusal of service in public places of business and amusement as the form of discrimination that symbolizes most unequivocally the Anglo's hostile attitudes and rejection of the Mexican group. Mexican Americans are aware that many of the forms of discrimination utilized by the Anglo group to maintain its dominance are more pervasive and serious than refusal of service, but this is accorded great prominence nevertheless. Informants most frequently defined discrimination in terms of refusal of service, either as experienced by themselves or by fellow Mexican Americans; it is the theme most commonly dwelt on by Mexicans who speak and write about the "Mexican problem"; and it is the principal gauge applied in classifying Texas towns as "good" or "bad" for Mexicans. The discrimination that is practiced systematically and pervasively in more strategic spheres of intergroup life evokes direct protest or aggression from only a small sector of the Mexican group, but any incident involving refusal of service, no matter how rarely these occur and perhaps because their rarity gives them a particularly dramatic quality, has widespread repercussions in awakening Mexican American hostility toward Anglos and in stimulating protest.

The special sensitivity of Mexicans to refusal of service and other forms of personal rejection is not difficult to understand. Compared to the relatively subtle and indirect means usually employed by Anglos in maintaining dominance, refusal of service is a form of discrimination that affects the Mexican American directly and harshly, and graphically demonstrates his rejection by the Anglo. It attacks the Mexican where he is most sensitive, in his conceptions of "racial" pride, dignity, and honor.[*] For the middle class Mexican, incidents of refusal of service, when the victim is of middle class status, have an added sting because they serve as poignant reminders that Anglos ultimately consider them no better than the rest of the Mexican group. In San Antonio, Mexican leaders gave as the immediate cause for the founding of a middle class protest organization the indignation aroused when a group of top status Mexicans were refused service in a restaurant in a nearby town. As one Mexican put it, "This electrified the wealthy Latin Americans of San Antonio because they felt that if this could happen to Latins as prominent as these, it could happen to them too."[**]

The experience of subordinate status has brought into sharp focus for the Mexican the question of his own sense of worth relative to the Anglo. That Anglos are dominant in every aspect of the society and seem to monopolize all its accomplishments, at times lead Mexicans to draw the same conclusion from this evidence that Anglos do, namely, that Mexicans are

---

[*] Cf. the discussion of basic personality type, *supra*, pp. 109 ff.

[**] Cf. comment of informant above, p. 368.

inferior. This questioning of their own potentialities exists in all classes of the Mexican group, although with varying intensity, and it plays a role in every type of reactive adjustment. In interclass attitudes, its stamp may be observed in the middle class tendency to accept the Anglo's stereotype as true of the lower class Mexican and a correlative evaluation of Anglo standards as superior, and in the lower class tendency to accept the Anglo's assumption of Mexican homogeneity and conclude that all Mexicans are more or less equal. Adhesion to the belief in Mexican inferiority is reflected in such expressions as *tu sabes que asi es la raza*, you know that the "race" is like that, which is offered in explanation of the group's failure to achieve equal status, and in "don't be a Mexican all your life", which equates Mexican with inferiority. A Mexican American leader in McAllen gave the writer the following explanation for the status of his group.

> I think the biggest mistake the Spaniards made was to intermarry and mingle with the Indians. The English and others who came to this country were much wiser to try to exterminate the Indians and push what was left onto reservations. By doing that they made it possible for the United States to become a great nation. But the Spaniards felt sorry for the poor Indians, and felt they should intermarry with them. It might as well be admitted that the Indians were primitive, brutal people, and that intermarrying with them set the Spaniards who settled Mexico back a thousand years. I think it's perfectly clear that no Mexican Indian is as good as the average American.

The tendency to believe in his own inferiority is counterbalanced, however, by the Mexican's fierce *orgullo racial*, "racial" pride, and it is the latter which sets the tone of Mexican demands and strivings for equal status, although these are always colored by the tendency to slip into the inferiority belief. The informant just quoted would never have made such a statement publicly, and during other interviews often dwelt on the injustice meted out to Mexicans and condemned the Anglo's arrogance in imputing inferiority to them. The ambivalence that characterizes Mexican ideas of inferiority was expressed by a Mexican businessman in McAllen as follows:

> The trouble with the Mexican people is that fifty to sixty percent of them have an inferiority complex. The Anglo Americans think they're superior and have been telling us that for so long that half the people actually believe they're inferior. Once in awhile I believe it myself because I have heard it so often. From the time we are knee high, we hear we're inferior, so we can't help believing it. The only way to overcome it is to tell ourselves we're not inferior, and then go out and prove it.

A few excerpts from the life history of a Mexican American lawyer in San Antonio may be quoted to illustrate the insecurity and doubt involved in this ambivalence. Speaking of his childhood, informant said:

> I remember feeling that I lived in a strange land that wasn't my country. That was how we all felt at home. We weren't wanted here, we belonged to a group that was looked down on. But we didn't feel we were inferior. We felt that if we weren't accepted equally, then the hell with it. But even so I was always aware that I belonged in a niche, that I wasn't part of the big outside world around us ... When I was a kid, a teacher took us to see the Alamo, and told us all about the horrible Mexicans. There she was saying bad things about the Mexicans, and at home I was taught that I was Mexican. So I didn't know what to think.

In a later interview, informant said:

> We're not inferior, that I certainly cannot believe. There is much that is good in us. We do have to weed out the hangovers that remain from Spain and Mexico though, and I find that after going through Americanization I have an apologetic attitude toward Mexicanism. We came out second best because we were thrown against boys who knew English as their native language and who were in their native habitat. Naturally we came out second best. So even though I know I'm not, it makes for feelings of inferiority.

Referring to a position of responsibility he had held where Anglos had been subordinate to him, informant said:

> I had that feeling of insecurity and inadequacy. No matter how smart I would be, I thought, the Anglo would be smarter. I found myself wanting approval from the Anglos, and I had a fear of criticism. And if you keep that up, you may find yourself conforming to something that may not be wise, because the Anglo is not infallible although he may give the impression that he is, just as he deliberately fosters the idea that he is superior ... The Anglos look down at you through their nose, and take it for granted that they're speaking from an elevated position of authority down to a subordinate, to an inferior. Whether they feel that way or not, that's the feeling they give. I'm not the only one that's noticed it because I've heard quite a bit of comment along the same line.

The Mexican ambivalence about equality with Anglos is reflected in the constraint, lack of poise and self-assurance, and general sense of discomfort that characterizes the behavior of Mexicans of all classes when they participate in informal social situations with Anglos,* although the writer encountered a few outstanding exceptions to this generalization. The lack of experience of contact with

---
\* For some examples, cf. _supra_, pp. 159-60.

Anglos may account for this in part, but it is significant that only the Mexican, and not the Anglo, has these feelings and exhibits such behavior. One informant described how she discouraged the friendly overtures of an Anglo classmate when she was in high school because she "did not know how to behave with Anglos". A political leader in San Antonio said that he usually does not attend Anglo social functions when invited because he "does not feel entirely at ease with Anglos."

The present discussion has dealt thus far with aspects of conceptions of subordinate status that can be thought of as more or less generalized throughout the Mexican American group. Although it will not be possible to take into account all the factors that contribute to differentiation of responses to subordinate status,[*] a few of these will be inevitably touched on in the discussion that follows. However, explicit attention will be given to the class variable in the description of types of reactive adjustment, and in view of this it is advisable here to consider class differences in conceptions of subordinate status. In general, lower class Mexicans do not regard the disabilities imposed by subordinate status to be nearly as severe or oppressive as do middle class Mexicans. Primarily, this is due to the insulation that exists between the Anglo world and that of the Mexican lower class. As shown elsewhere, the lower class Mexicans are not oriented to the

---

[*] See pp. 56-57 for a list of possible variables that condition reactive adjustments.

Anglo values that place a premium on upward mobility, nor are they competing for the same interests to the same extent. Thus participation in the larger society is not conceived of as an imperative necessity and the semi-caste barrier is considerably minimized in their eyes. Since they are accorded, by default, a monopoly of the lowest roles in the occupational hierarchy, they present no competitive threat to the Anglo, who therefore need employ no preventive measures, such as differential treatment in hiring and remuneration, at this level*. The occupational nexus with the Anglos is the most important and strategic of all to the lower class Mexican, yet even here the Anglo's exclusion devices do not affect him directly and explicitly. These considerations, together with the general absence of heavy-handed dominance and lack of definition of "place" which permit a relatively wide latitude in the performance of the subordinate role, have served to largely insulate the lower class from the direct implications of subordinate status. Since the "Mexican problem" is not an urgent issue for the lower class, their principal reaction to Anglo exclusion practices has been typically that of accommodation through isolation, rather than direct aggression or accommodation through assimilation.

---

* This statement is applicable only to agricultural occupations. In some of the town occupations in the Valley, and to a much greater extent in San Antonio, there is an element of competition with Anglos so that discriminatory controls reach down to the level of lower class occupations.

Other patterns of response that are characteristic of this group display elements of indirect and displaced aggression but are often adjustments to the problems of their generally depressed condition rather than to the "Mexican problem" as such.

As should be evident from the previous discussions of the Mexican American middle class, this group is no longer insulated from the Anglo world to anything like the same extent as the lower class. Through education, improvement of economic status, the assumption of occupational roles at levels other than the labor category, and other attributes previously described, middle class Mexicans have broken through the colonia's insulation, and their orientations to Anglo standards and values as well as to the goal of fuller participation in the larger society have led them to regard the semi-caste line as an unjust and oppressive barrier to which they are highly sensitive. Their characteristic reaction has been accommodation through assimilation as a principal means of mitigating the disabilities imposed on them, but, as will be seen, there are also elements of protest, of other types of aggression, and of isolation in the patterns of their adjustments.

## Conceptions of the Dominant Group

The mutual sharp awareness of difference on the part of Anglos and Mexicans has been illustrated in a variety of contexts throughout this study. The most widespread and prominent symbolization of this sense of difference is to be found in the popular terminology used by the two groups in labelling themselves and each other. The Mexican American expresses the sense of difference in his retention of the term "Mexican" to refer to his own group,[*] and his use of the term "American" to refer to non-Mexicans. There is a growing tendency, most prominent among middle class Mexicans and reflecting their assimilation orientations, to resent the use of the word "Mexican"[**] when applied to their group by Anglos, and they insist on the use of the terms "Latin American" and "Anglo American" to eliminate the implications that they are not "Americans" too. The middle class Mexican objects most strenuously to the Anglo's use of the term "Mexican" when it is employed to set Mexicans apart from "whites", but many lower class Mexicans continue to call Anglos "white folks" or "Americans" and themselves "Mexicans". Even middle class Mexicans, despite their efforts to popularize "Latin American", usually employ the term "Mexican" among themselves,[***] although they are always careful to refer to non-Mexicans as Anglos rather than just "Americans". This inconsistency in terminology is also reflected in the names given to *colonia* organizations.

[*] This pattern will be analyzed in connection with the discussion of isolation adjustments below.

[**] The Anglo American's term "greaser" has the same insulting connotations for Mexican Americans as "nigger" does for Negroes, and is more bitterly resented than the word "Mexican". However, it apparently is no longer used as a direct mode of address to Mexicans in San Antonio and the Valley, and was used rarely by Anglo informants when speaking of Mexicans. On the possible origins of the term "greaser" see Carey McWilliams, *North from Mexico*, pp. 115-116.

[***] Those Anglos who are conscious of the Mexican's objection to their use of the term "Mexican" and wish to avoid offense employ the term "Latin American" when referring to Mexican Americans publicly or when in their presence. Amongst themselves, however, they revert to the use of the term "Mexican" just as middle class Mexican Americans do. Thus the term "Latin American" is largely reserved for formal and public occasions and for intergroup contacts by both Anglo and Mexican Americans.

In San Antonio, e.g., of the four principal Mexican American organizations, two use the term "Pan American", one "Latin American", and one "Mexican", yet all four have a large number of members in common. Despite this inconsistency within the group, resentment of the dominant group's use of the term "Mexican" is becoming more widely diffused among Mexicans of all classes, who are coming to define it as a symbol of the Anglo attempt to exclude them from membership in the "white race" and from participation in "American" society, as well as a symbol of the Anglo imputation of their inferiority. The comment of a Mexican American businessman in McAllen may be quoted in this connection:

> It doesn't make any difference if they call us Latin Americans or Mexicans, they still don't think of us as Americans. We're different. There are two kinds of people - men and Mexicans. When a robbery is committed, if the thief is an Anglo boy, the paper just says youth - a youth was arrested. They never say an Anglo youth committed the robbery. But if a Mexican did it, they always say it was a Mexican. The same thing among the farmers here. If they hire men to work for them who are Mexicans, they never say 'my laborers', they say 'my Mexicans'. And when they say Mexican, they don't think of just anybody, they think of a special kind of person, one who is inferior.

The term "gringo" has been current in the Southwest for a long time as a label applied by Mexicans to Anglos. It is occasionally used without any pejorative intent as a simple designation for Anglo Americans,* but more often it is employed

---

* Most Spanish dictionaries define the New World usage of gringo as meaning any foreigner, but "specially applied to Englishmen and Americans". It is interesting to note that to this definition, which also appears in Webster's Collegiate Dictionary, fifth edition, 1945, the word "contemptuous" is appended. Actually, the term "gringo" is current all through South America as a familiar designation for foreigners whose native language is neither Spanish nor Portuguese.

by Mexicans in a hostile although not always depreciatory way. One middle class Mexican, when asked what is meant by "gringo", said, "Just what the Anglos mean when they say 'dirty greaser'. I think the Mexicans just say it because they know Anglos don't like it and get mad when they hear it." In Starr County, where many of the small minority of Anglos live on the best of terms with the Mexican majority, "gringo" is not applied to all Anglos but reserved to designate those who manifest prejudice and hostility toward Mexican Americans. Generally, the term serves a retaliatory function and is anti-Anglo American in its implications. That it has this meaning for Mexicans is illustrated by their reluctance to use it in the presence of Anglo Americans, and their tendency to deprecate its use when questioned about it by the writer.

Estimates by Mexican Americans of the proportion of the Anglo group that feels hostility toward them range from "The Anglo Americans don't like us, none of them", to "Only 25 percent of the American people are prejudiced against Mexicans, the others are all right". Most Mexican Americans, in discussing Anglo hostility, made the qualification that not all Anglos are "bad". One middle class housewife in McAllen said:

> There are good Anglo Americans too, people who will come forward to defend Latin Americans against attacks from those Anglos who humiliate and insult Latins and who seize every chance to say something derogatory about them.

As this comment indicates, the "good" Anglo is usually one who has "proved" his sincerity by demonstrating sympathy for the Mexicans, and by condemning those Anglos who actively manifest the traditional hostility toward Mexicans. For those who are preoccupied with the "Mexican problem", there is an understandable tendency to measure Anglos primarily on the basis of their attitudes toward Mexicans rather than other bases that may be used in evaluating fellow-Mexicans. In defining the "causes" of Anglo hostility and discrimination, most Mexicans offer the explanation of "ignorance" and "lack of understanding" on the part of the Anglos, which reflects the fact that Mexicans really feel themselves to be different from Anglos. Those middle class Mexicans who feel they are assimilated and thus no longer different,* attribute Anglo hostility to "blind, unreasoning prejudice", to the "terrible picture of the Mexican created by the hopelessly distorted version of Texas history", or to "jealousy because they don't want to see the Mexicans get ahead."

As in the case of any subordinate group, those Mexicans who are preoccupied with the issue of subordinate status have to face the problem of where to place the responsibility for the Mexican American group's failure to achieve equal status with the dominant group. Reflecting the ambivalence toward their own "inferiority", Mexicans waver between the extremes of attributing the group's depressed status solely to Anglo

---

\* Cf. the comment on Anglo-Mexican differences quoted on p. 368.

machinations and injustice or to the "defects" of their own group. In their dealings with the dominant group, leaders and other middle class Mexicans attempt to maintain the former point of view consistently, but amongst themselves they often veer toward the latter. Most of them try to maintain a balanced point of view by not minimizing the severity of Anglo oppression and at the same time conceding that Mexicans can and ought to help themselves as well, but there are not lacking those who hold to the one extreme where any sort of individual or group failure is ascribed to Anglo dominance, or to the other extreme where the entire guilt lies with the Mexican group itself and the individual comes perilously close to justifying discrimination, just as Anglos do, on the basis of the Mexican's "inferiority". There is a tendency among middle class Mexicans, indicated elsewhere, that represents one variation of this latter position in that it attributes all discrimination against the Mexican group to the "defects" of the lower class with the implication that such discrimination is justified when directed against the lower class, but unjust when practiced against the middle class. As one female informant in the Valley put it:

> I hate to take part in any argument about discrimination, but when anybody says or insinuates that all Latins are dirty and ignorant, then I've had my fill. I'm not defending the low class of Latins, because I myself do not care to associate with or have anything to do with them, but I am merely defending those of us who are not in the same class with them. And we resent being placed in that class just as much as Anglos would resent being placed with the white trash, hillbillies, or any other such people.

Mexican Americans have not developed an elaborate stereotype of the Anglo group of the sort that the latter holds with regard to them, in part because Mexicans of course feel no "need" to justify the intergroup relationship in its present form, and in part because the very nature of their position forces them to view the relationship more clearly and realistically than Anglos do. Moreover, for the same reasons, insofar as Mexicans do tend to generalize their beliefs about Anglos, there is no need to hold to them with the kind of emotional intensity that has been observed in the Anglo case. As indicated above, Mexicans tend to evaluate and classify Anglos on the basis of their attitudes toward the Mexican group. The following observations, the first by a professional in McAllen, the second by a lawyer in San Antonio, illustrate this tendency:

> There are three types of Anglo Americans. The first type are those who don't like Mexicans and don't want to have anything to do with them. And they don't care who knows it. Maybe that's good because at least you know where you stand with them. The second type are those who tell you, 'I wish all the Mexicans were like you.' What he really means to say is that all the rest are trash except me. That kind of Anglo American says the same thing when he's with another Mexican, and then he includes me in the trash. That kind you can't trust at all. The third type is made up of a small group of well-meaning people who want to do something about discrimination. They hate it as much as the Mexicans do, and they want to associate with Mexican people because they like them and think they're like everybody else. Since there are Anglos like this last type, we mustn't keep to ourselves because then we're doing the same thing as the Anglos are doing, we're calling all the Anglos trash because we don't like a few of them. You know, there are good ones and bad ones in both races.

> I find myself looking at Anglos in two ways. They fall into two classes. The type which I consider friendly, warm in feeling, just, and unprejudiced, and the type that is cold, unkind, mercenary, and at whose hands I have suffered.

Other generalizations about Anglos that were encountered among Mexicans reflect the Anglo exclusion patterns and assumptions of superiority as these are experienced by Mexicans. The following remarks are all by middle class informants, the second by a woman, the others by men:

> Anglos are very different from the sensitive peoples of Latin descent, and they don't understand them. The two peoples are different in characteristics, and the Mexicans seem to sense it. As we think of it, the Anglo American is of a stolid, phlegmatic temperament, and we're different - we're warmer and more impulsive. Of course, there are cold-hearted and distant Mexicans too, but we think of the Anglos as a different race, that has a different outlook on things, that has many desirable qualities, but is snobbish and inaccessible.

> Anglo Americans think they know everything. They are braggarts. When Latin Americans talk among themselves, and someone mentions something someone else said, they ask, 'Who said that, an Anglo or a Mexican?' When they are told an Anglo, they say, 'Oh well, then there is no point in believing it because Anglos always make more of things than they actually are.' Anglos do not talk in less than millions, trillions, and jillions, yet they are often in debt, and Mexicans never are. Because they are always bragging, they think they know so much more than Latin Americans do, and they always feel they should give Latins advice. Even the Anglo women from the PTA who are friendly and sometimes visit me try to tell me how to run my children. For instance, they can't understand why I will let my older boy stay up after 7:30 or 8:00 p.m. because they believe that all children should be in bed by then. I believe that children should go to bed when they are tired and not before.

One informant accused the Anglos of inconstancy and insincerity which he illustrated by the following examples:

> Anglos will react so differently to Latin Americans at different times. When Anglos go to Mexico, for example, they find themselves very hospitably treated by the Mexicans. I don't mean the tourist relationship, but the many cases where Mexican people take Anglos into their homes and show them a wonderful

time. In such cases the Anglos are very happy to sleep in the houses of Mexicans, eat with them, and associate with them intimately. But these same Anglos will not reciprocate and will even avoid the Mexicans when they come to the United States for a visit. Another example is an Anglo I know who lives near Rio Grande City (Starr County) and has a ranch there. He sleeps and eats with his Latin American hands and with other Latin American ranchers. He really is their buddy. But when he comes to McAllen, he acts very differently. Here he does not want to associate with Latins at all, avoids them whenever possible, and even pretends not to know Latins from Rio Grande City when he meets them on the street here.

Beliefs about Anglos never impute inferiority to them, and attempts to build up a case for Mexican superiority over the Anglo are exceedingly rare. Moreover, Mexican beliefs seldom achieve the level of positive hostility that is expressed in the stereotype held by Anglos. There is, however, a latent hostility, reciprocating that of the Anglo, which was expressed somewhat peculiarly by a Mexican truck driver in McAllen. When asked to describe how Mexicans feel about Anglos, he replied:

> Well, it's hard for me to explain that. Let me put it this way. If there is an auto wreck, and some people get hurt or killed, right away the Latin American people want to know if they were Latin Americans or Anglo Americans. If they were Latins, then they say, 'Oh, that's too bad', and they feel very sorry. But if they were Anglo Americans, they don't care, and they are relieved and say, 'That's all right'. I would say that at least 90 percent of the Latin American people feel that way about the Anglo Americans. That's the only way I can express what I know about how the Latin Americans feel toward the Anglo Americans.

In the section that follows, some of the ways in which Mexican Americans express hostility to Anglos, and the conditions under which they do so, will be examined in connection with aggressive adjustments.

## Types of Reactive Adjustment[*]

The treatment of patterns of reactive adjustment attempted here is analytical, but it should be kept in mind that any particular individual may exhibit at one time or another, in different situations and on different occasions, all the various types of reactive adjustment dealt with separately here. The typology defines broad categories, and will attempt to depict the most heavily patterned variations within each category, disregarding for the most part the degree of intensity and the individual motivations involved in the process of adjustment. Wherever possible, class differences in patterns of adjustment will be indicated, but this does not mean that all middle class Mexicans are oriented to assimilation as their principal adjustment, e.g., or that no lower class Mexicans are. Background of experience, personality, age, sex, skincolor, situational factors, and many other variables may play significant roles independent of class membership in determining the individual's patterns of adjustment.

### Aggression against the Dominant Group

Compared to a subordinate group like the Negro, Mexican Americans are permitted greater freedom in the expression of

---
[*] For definitions of the types of reactive adjustments discussed in this section, see pp. 46 ff.

aggression against the dominant group. The threat of physical coercion is largely absent, and although direct protest against the disabilities imposed by Anglo dominance may be regarded as an affront by many Anglos, it rarely evokes aggressive reprisals on the part of the latter. Despite this, however, direct protest is not a prominent element in Mexican American reactive adjustments. In the case of the lower class, insulation from the direct implications of subordinate status and from the explicit manifestations of dominance techniques have minimized the urgency of the "Mexican problem" for this group, and have accordingly limited the development of motivations to open protest. There are other factors that have militated against the selection of direct aggression as a form of adjustment by the lower class. One of these is the disadvantaged occupational status of the lower class Mexican, which makes open protest in the occupational sphere unrealistic in the face of the Anglo monopoly of economic resources and power.* The extremely favorable position held by the employer is also utilized to ensure, with the aid of accommodating Mexican American leaders, lower class accommodation in the political sphere.** Another factor has its source in the Mexican's basic personality type. The Mexican's tendency to "personalize" and develop strong feelings of

---

\* See supra, pp. 251-54.

\*\* See supra, pp. 284 ff. and 308-9.

obligation and loyalty toward those Anglos who will perform the traditional role of patron, places a premium on accommodation rather than aggression in those cases where it has been possible to establish this type of relationship. The submissiveness, passivity, and fatalism that have been described as distinctive components of basic personality type, and the inhibitions to direct aggression that these involve, undoubtedly play a significant role as well in this respect.

The lack of open protest by the lower class Mexican does not necessarily signify a low degree of frustration and resentment on his part. It has been pointed out that Mexicans of both classes deeply resent their rejection by Anglo Americans as a grave insult to their "pride" and "honor". Also, the exceptionally high degree of frustration felt by the lower class Mexican that is imposed by his occupational role has been described at length. However, the response to these frustration experiences does not take the form of direct aggression but is channelled into accommodation, and, to a lesser extent, expresses itself in indirect forms of aggression or is displaced onto other members of the Mexican American group.

Open protest against the dominant group, to the extent that it exists, has been for the most part expressed by group leaders and middle class colonia organizations, which will be discussed separately below. However, it is worthwhile inquiring here into the reasons why open protest has been utilized only on a small scale even within the middle class as a means of coping with the problems posed by subordination. The explanation provided for the lack of lower class protest is much less applicable to middle class Mexicans. The middle class Mexican is neither as insulated from the Anglo world nor as helpless in the face of Anglo power as are those of lower class status. Moreover, the increasing middle class emphasis on the "Anglo" traits necessary for mobility and success[*] indicates a corresponding change in the middle class Mexican's basic personality away from the components just referred to above. There are at least two considerations, however, one of them applicable in part to the lower class as well, that help to explain why open protest has not been more prominent in middle class adjustment patterns. Many Mexican Americans have tended to adhere to a commonly encountered Anglo rationalization that discrimination is a matter of personal taste not necessarily involving a denial of equal rights and equal opportunity.[**] Although

---

[*] Supra, pp. 368 ff.

[**] "According to dominant Descanso, discrimination is just a little social quirk or idiosyncracy, an expression of personal taste which could not possibly have legal implications ... Descanso tries to place a dislike for seeing little Americans of Mexican descent in a public swimming pool in the same class as a dislike of seeing onions on the dinner table. It has not only so rationalized its breaches of civil trust for itself. It has, in the past, succeeded in convincing many a Mexican-American that fighting for equal privileges constituted a social error, a simple case of bad manners - pushing yourself in where you weren't wanted." Tuck, op. cit., p. 197.

the Mexican's extreme sensitivity may make Anglo exclusion especially painful to him, that same sensitivity, as embodied in his concept of pride, has led him to react by withdrawal rather than by protesting the rejection. Speaking of refusal of service, a Mexican informant said:

> I think a man who owns a restaurant has a right to refuse to serve anybody he wants to, and if he doesn't want to serve Mexicans, that's his business. Even if I wanted to eat in such a restaurant, I wouldn't go in because I know I'm not wanted. If you go out on the highway in your car, you don't have to stop and pick up anybody walking on the highway if you don't want to. It's your car and you can keep out or let in anybody you want. It's the same thing with these fellows who own restaurants. If they don't want to serve Mexicans, they have a right not to.

This sort of reasoning has been indulged in by many Mexicans and applied to various types of discrimination practiced against them. There has been a great deal of uncertainty and confusion in the past about the nature and extent of rights and privileges, and only now, particularly with the return of the veterans, are Mexicans beginning to understand and realize what is due them as defined by American democratic theory and the law, and to clarify the distinction between the prerogatives of "personal taste" and the denial of equal rights and privileges on the basis of their ethnic membership.

The tendency to seek approval and acceptance by the dominant group, which has been described as a middle class characteristic, also contributes toward the minimization of open protest. The fact that accommodation, in the form of assimilation, cannot help middle class Mexicans to fully

achieve the acceptance goal sends them in the direction
of protest as well, however. Actually, there is a widespread ambivalence toward accommodation versus protest
among middle class Mexicans. Middle class Mexicans often
fear that open protest, if pursued too diligently, will
endanger the progress they are making through assimilation
toward the goal of acceptance by the dominant group. In
this connection also Mexicans have allowed themselves to
be convinced at times by an Anglo rationalization, namely,
that the present pattern of intergroup relations is a natural
phenomenon mutually satisfactory to both groups and that
he who protests against it is an "agitator" bent on destroying the natural order.* To be an "agitator" or to support
one is to imperil one's efforts to gain acceptance by the
dominant group.

Some Mexican American patterns of direct and indirect
expression of aggression against Anglo Americans may now be
indicated, leaving the description of organized protest for
later discussion. Open intergroup conflict involving actual
physical violence rarely occurs either in the Valley or
San Antonio. On the part of the Anglos, the only vestige
of old patterns of violence practiced against Mexicans is
to be found in relations with law enforcement officers.**

---

\*
For an example of the middle class Mexican's fear of becoming identified with protest when it is defined by the dominant group as stirring up the "racial issue", see pp. 335-36.

\*\* Supra, pp. 466-67.

Three Mexican informants spoke of engaging in fist fights with Anglos who had made derogatory remarks about their Mexican descent. Two informants had experienced only one such incident, but the third man had three fights, all with the same Anglo. This man had worked for 18 years as a clerk in a large Anglo grocery in McAllen, and described his dispute with an Anglo clerk there as follows:

> When I first began working there, the other Mexican fellows warned me against an Anglo named Charley who worked there too. They said he didn't like Mexicans. I just minded my own business, but he tangled with me about three months later. He told me to do something, and I refused because the boss had told me to do something else. He called me a Mexican son of a bitch, and I told him to take it back. He wouldn't do it, so I hit him. He wouldn't hit me back, but he told me I was fired. When the boss came back from lunch, I told him Barney had fired me. He asked me what happened and said that I didn't have to take orders from Charley, only from him. I had two more fights with Charley about the same thing during the last 18 years. He has always run the other Mexican fellows because they're scared of him. I told them they were scared, but they never did stand up to Charley.

In San Antonio, a series of incidents occurred in 1946 involving open conflict between Anglo and Mexican youths. The Anglo boys frequenting various municipal parks gathered into gangs to drive away the Mexicans who attempted to use the park facilities. A pitched battle between Anglos and Mexicans in one of the parks culminated in the fatal shooting of a Mexican by an Anglo. At this point constant police surveillance was provided at the trouble zones, and the conflict subsided.

There are a few middle class Mexicans in McAllen and

San Antonio who engage in open protest with relative frequency. They are concerned with discrimination wherever it occurs, and their protest is directed against the injustices perpetrated against Mexicans both in general terms and with reference to specific instances of discrimination. A few of these people have written books attacking discrimination against Mexicans, but most of them voice their protest through articles which they publish in the English-and-Spanish-speaking newspapers, and more commonly through "Letters to the Editor" that appear in the local papers. Although the names of these few Mexicans appear with some regularity as writers of such letters, there are others who utilize this means of expressing protest, but the latter always respond to a specific local incident of discrimination or to an anti-Mexican letter which may have appeared in the same paper, and do not attack general issues of segregation and discrimination as do the former.

The frequency with which Mexican informants had been personally subjected to discriminatory or insulting treatment by Anglos varied considerably, just as their reactions did. Some stated that they had never felt discrimination personally, others recounted rare or frequent incidents of refusal of service to which they had reacted by leaving without protest, while a few maintained that they had always expressed direct retaliatory aggression whenever they had experienced discrimination from Anglos. One middle class woman in McAllen said, "I like nothing better than a good fight, if it is justified", and described a series of discriminatory incidents where she had retaliated with direct aggression. This is the informant who was unsuccessful in enrolling her son in the parochial school of the Anglo Catholic church.* She responded by accusing the priest of discriminating against Mexicans and told him she could have no respect for a priest like him. When the latter offered to send back the registration fee she had already paid for her son, she told him to "keep it and apply it on the tuition of some poor white trash who qualified for the school by virtue of an English name." Among others, this informant described the following incident:

> Informant attended a political rally where the audience consisted of Anglo women and a few Mexican women. In introducing the main speaker, the Anglo woman presiding advised her, loudly enough so that all could hear, to speak as though she were talking to third graders because there were Latin American women present. She said she had been a teacher in McAllen for twenty years and ought to know. Informant became incensed at this, arose and said, 'If Latin Americans do not have more than the mentality of third graders, it is because of women like you, who in twenty years of teaching have failed to better the education of the Latin Americans.' The chairwoman then apologized, said she did not mean to offend anyone. Informant said the statement was not true anyway, that Latins may not have as much culture as Anglos yet, but they are not very far behind.

The general level of active hostility toward Anglos is raised noticeably when a particularly dramatic incident involving discrimination occurs. The widespread Anglo resistance to admitting Mexicans to the McAllen swimming pool, described above, was just such an event. The colonia businessmen's club issued a public statement "condemning

---
\* Supra, p. 459.

the discriminatory practice at _____ Pool, and the needless and biased attitude of persons who make insulting remarks concerning Latin Americans."[1] A number of protest letters written by Mexicans appeared in the McAllen newspaper, and one prominent Mexican burst into the YMCA office angrily demanding a refund of his daughter's membership dues. Most informants, both lower and middle class, voiced their resentment at the incident to the writer. The following comment can stand for many:

> Who ever asked the YMCA to make any kind of a stand on segregation? That pool has been segregated ever since it was built, and I wouldn't swim in the damn thing no matter who owns it now. All the YMCA did was stir up a lot of trouble and then crawl out of it.

A number of indirect forms of venting aggression against the dominant group are also utilized by Mexican Americans, and may be considered briefly. Mexicans apparently find a release for aggression through the recounting of incidents where Anglos have been discomfited by Mexicans. The writer was told such stories when with groups of Mexicans who were already familiar with them but evidently enjoyed hearing them retold. One such story concerns a Mexican general who at one time was stationed in Reynosa, across the international border from McAllen. The general kept a list of the places on the American side that discriminated against Mexican Americans, and when he was invited to a social function in McAllen or other Valley towns, he would ask the owners of these places to stand up and be recognized. "Not as an honor, but in order to know their faces so that when they came to Reynosa he could throw them out." The hero of another oft-told story that serves the same function is a Mexican businessman in McAllen who was a pilot during the war. Once when on leave he was drinking in a _colonia_ bar about 11:30 p.m., when a military policeman, an Anglo who had been a McAllen policeman before the war and later returned to the same job, entered the bar and saw him. As one informant told the story,

> He walked up to Pete, grabbed him by the shoulder, and said, 'Hey soldier, let's get going. Pete turned around and this cop saw those bars shining on Pete's collar. Well, he just popped to attention, saluted, and said, 'I'm sorry sir'. Can you imagine? Everyone had a good laugh and the cop left in a hurry.

These stories and others like them are always followed by appreciative laughs from Mexican auditors vicariously getting the best of the Anglo American.

Another indirect means of releasing aggression, which at times borders on direct aggression, is deliberate withdrawal as an expression of protest. One such case, where the aggressive act was practically overt, was that of a group of Mexican American shoolteachers from nearby Starr County who attended a teacher's convention in a Valley town. When one of the Anglo speakers began his talk with the statement, "The problems involved in the education of whites and Mexicans ...", this group arose, left the room, and did not return for later sessions. Another instance of withdrawal with aggressive intent was that of a Mexican American member of the McAllen zoning board who resigned because he felt that changes in zoning regulations made by the board were unjust to the _colonia._ The writer collected a number of examples of such resignations, of varying degrees of overtness, by Mexicans from boards and committees because they felt they or the *colonia* was being slighted or discriminated against. One informant in San Antonio used political influence to obtain release from a summons to serve on a grand jury. As he explained it, "I was sore and didn't want to go because they always call just one Mexican and no more."

Joking or "kidding" is another indirect channel for expression of aggression. Two illustrations may be cited here. In a McAllen bar, an Anglo and Mexican were shooting dice with rounds of beer as the stake. As he shook the dice, the Mexican said to the Anglo, "The greatest pleasure in the world would be for me to beat the s--t out of you, and the second greatest would be to lose to you." At the time of the swimming pool incident, several informants were asking Anglo acquaintances if they had heard that Mexico was not going to let the Valley have any more water from a nearby reservoir on the Mexican side because some of it might get into the swimming pool.*

Finally, it should be noted that the patterns of leaving the job, idling, and lowering the quality of work, previously described in connection with the discussion of occupations,** may also be classed as forms of indirect aggression.

---

\* The Mexican government had volunteered to release water from this reservoir to alleviate the Valley's severe water shortage which occurred at this time. The story was not true of course, and was meant as a "joke".

\*\* See *supra*, pp. 242, 246 and 253.

## Aggression against other Subordinate Groups

In McAllen, Mexican Americans show little preoccupation with the question of relations with Negroes primarily because the latter group consists of only about twenty-five families. Most lower class informants either commiserated with the Negro's lot, considering it much worse than their own, or were more or less indifferent to Negroes. These attitudes are also to be found among middle class Mexicans, but their sensitivity to the issue of inclusion in the "white race" has made many of them anxious to maintain a sharp distinction from Negroes, and has been favorable to the development of a tendency to ape the Anglo's attitude of superiority.* One middle class informant said:

> It gets me so mad when people say we're not white. We're not black and we're not yellow, so we must be white. No one can say we're niggers, but that's the class we're put in if we're not white. Now, I have nothing against niggers as long as they know their place. It's like every other people, there's good niggers and bad niggers. A good nigger is one who knows his place, and a bad nigger is one who doesn't.

On another occasion, speaking of a Negro family that had lived near him in the <u>colonia</u> but had moved out, this informant said:

> I sure am glad the owner of that house ran them out. How would you like to have niggers living across the street from you? Niggers are out of their place when they live near me. They have a little section up here where they have their own church and school, and that's where they should all live.

---

\* This includes an aversion to dark skin color as well as its association with inferiority. Although there is some evidence that preference for light skin color has a history in Mexico, "race prejudice" as it is manifested by Americans is largely unknown there, and it is probable that Mexican Americans have patterned their prejudices in this regard on the Anglo model. There is a tendency on the part of Mexicans to evaluate each other on the basis of skin color, particularly in San Antonio, but this is not pronounced enough to play any significant role as a status determinant in <u>colonia</u> class hierarchies.

In San Antonio, where there is a large Negro community, the problem of relations with Negroes is of considerable importance for the Mexican American group, and is bound up much more explicitly with the question of acceptance by the dominant group and with the selection of tactics in the struggle against Anglo dominance. The anxiety to stay clear of the Negro because it might endanger Anglo acceptance and the tendency to reaffirm this by adopting the standard Anglo attitudes toward the Negro group are much more pronounced among middle class Mexicans in San Antonio than in McAllen. Nevertheless, a few Mexican leaders have perceived the potential advantages to be gained through collaboration with the Negro group, particularly in the struggle for political representation.* One of these men, describing his attempts a few years ago to persuade the Mexican leadership to this point of view, said:

> I felt that at least in politics there was a common meeting ground on which the Latin American, the Negro, and that section of the Anglo population that sympathized with our aims, objectives, and ideas could get together and elect those men to office who would naturally work toward our ends. Well, all I got at that time was just a lot of criticism. They said I was a nigger lover, that I had no right to make such suggestions, that the Anglo people were already looking down on us as it was, without getting mixed up with the Negro to make the situation that much worse. The policy of our organizations has always been against mixing or associating with the Negro people, or even talking about the Negro problem being similar to the Latin American problem in any manner.

---
\* The "white primary" is not practiced in San Antonio.

During the period of the study, Mexicans finally combined with Negroes to elect a representative of each group to San Antonio school boards,* but despite this victory, many Mexican leaders, who had been opposed to the maneuver from the first, felt that it had resulted in a substantial increase of Anglo hostility toward Mexicans and were opposed to any further attempts of this nature.

Antagonism to Jews was encountered among Mexicans, but, as in the case of the Negro, Jews are far from being a major object of the Mexican's displaced aggression. All of the hostility expressed against Jews focused on their business activities and was directed against the Jewish merchants in the colonias of both McAllen and San Antonio.** As would be expected, the hostility is more pronounced among Mexican businessmen who are in competition with the Jews, particularly in San Antonio. They complain that Jews lower prices, pay their Mexican employees low wages, and generally engage in "unfair" competition. Although there are many non-Jews who have colonia businesses, resentment against all non-Mexicans who "make their living off the Mexican people" has become focused on the Jews. However, many of these same middle class Mexicans who profess hostility for the Jew are ambivalent in that they tend to admire the Jews as a minority group that has been able to "get ahead" in spite of dominant group

---
\* See supra, footnote, p. 312.
\*\* In McAllen, two Jews have fairly large businesses in the colonia, and in San Antonio there are three Jewish-owned department stores and a number of specialty shops in or near the colonia.

resistance, and feel that the Mexicans could take some lessons from them in this respect. As one informant said, "The Jews possess those characteristics for successful assimilation that the Mexicans lack. They are aggressive, forceful, and hard working. Two Jewish merchants in McAllen and two in San Antonio have developed reputations as "defenders of Mexican rights",* and this has also softened Mexican middle class attitudes toward them, but their motives in this respect have been questioned. A prominent Mexican leader in San Antonio dismissed these activities on behalf of Mexicans as "all a dodge for getting around us."

## Aggression within the Mexican American Group

Several manifestations of aggression displaced onto the Mexican group itself have already been described in some detail, such as interclass hostility** and the exploitation practiced by political leaders in using the support of their followers to serve their own ends,*** so no further discussion of these is necessary here. There are other aspects of intragroup relations to which aggression has been attracted, and, prefaced by a few remarks regarding the extent of ingroup solidarity, these will be discussed briefly in this section.

---

\* In McAllen, one of these men, as a director of the YMCA, and the other, a large contributor to its fund-raising campaign, were among the few who adhered to a non-segregation policy for the swimming pool from the first, and were active in persuading other members of the board to this point of view. The latter Jew announced that he would withdraw his contribution if a segregation policy were adopted.
\*\* Supra, pp. 379-84 and 396-98.
\*\*\*Chapter VI.

As will be seen shortly, the idea of being "Mexican" rather than "American" is deeply rooted among Mexican Americans, and there is a very strong identification with la raza. It is expected that all Mexican Americans will retain identification with the group and will exhibit pride in their Mexican descent, and this is reflected in the Mexican's bitter condemnation as a renegade of anyone who is suspected of trying to pass as Spanish, who converts to Protestantism, or who in general manifests too obvious and eager a desire for Anglo acceptance. The feeling of ingroup solidarity expressed in this expectation is fostered, among other things, by the protective walls of the colonia and by awareness of difference from the dominant group and the other subordinate groups of the community. Mexicans often say that, based on this mutual feeling of solidarity, group members should be loyal to and help one another, but they universally agree that they are notoriously deficient in this respect, that they "can't get along with each other" and "can't stick together". One informant went so far as to say:

> If I was broke, or down and out, I would go to any Anglo American for help before I would go to any of la raza. That's just the way it is. I think an Anglo American would be ready to help me before any of the Latin American people would. The Latin American people are only out for themselves.

Mexicans of all classes tend to believe that this lack of unity has a great deal to do with their troubles and failures, and that if only unity could be achieved, most of these would disappear. The call for unity is constantly being sounded by Mexican Americans active in politics, civic work, and improvement and protest organizations, and is the most frequent theme of editorials and articles dealing with the "Mexican problem" that appear in the Spanish-speaking papers.

Given the situation of the Mexican American group, the possibilities of developing strong ingroup loyalties are severely limited. The orientations of middle class Mexicans to assimilation and Anglo acceptance place a premium on striving for solidarity with the Anglo middle class rather than for ingroup solidarity, and the rewards or fancied rewards to be obtained by selecting this road frequently appear more attractive than the often thankless, formidable task of bettering their status by attempts to "improve" the entire group in order to facilitate Anglo acceptance or to unify the Mexican group and wrest concessions in a direct conflict with the dominant group. Most *colonia* organizations are formally dedicated to working for the "improvement" of the group as a whole, reflecting the middle class conviction that ultimate acceptance by the dominant group depends on "raising" the standards of the lower class, but individual leaders often develop a dependence on solidary relationships with the Anglo middle class that may have them working against group interests rather than for them. Moreover, their situation militates against even intraclass solidarity within their own group. One finds a deep hunger for prestige and recognition among middle class Mexicans, probably because there is so little of it available. Prestige is granted very sparingly and reluctantly by the dominant group, and the narrow confines of subordinate status make for grim rivalry between members of the leadership group in their attempts to garner an adequate share within the group.* Members of all classes commonly say that "Mexicans are jealous and can't stand to see anyone else get ahead." This has a certain amount of truth in it that in the case of the middle class may be traced to the tight rivalry for prestige, which often involves belittling the achievements of others and attempting to discredit them. In the case of the lower class, resentment of another's good fortune is due in part to the expectation of equality fostered by dominant group attitudes,** and in part, when the fortunate one is of the leader group, to the perennial suspicion that a step up means a step out, that the individual is playing for Anglo favor and is thus disloyal to his fellow Mexicans.

The discussion may now turn to an examination of other outlets for aggression within the Mexican group, aside from those already described elsewhere. Paralleling the "pecking order" pattern that has characterized the adjustment of successive groups of European immigrants in the United

---

\* This point will be further elaborated below.

\*\* See supra, pp. 396-98.

States,* Mexicans have also had access to a group upon whom they could displace some of the aggression generated in response to their frustration situation. Unlike the European case, however, the target for aggression has been other Mexicans rather than other ethnic groups. The great immigration of Mexicans to the United States (1910-1928) provided the native-born Mexican American population, the "Texas-Mexicans" as they are called with a group that could serve as a suitable object for release of aggression. Although both groups had in common their Mexican descent and identification with *la raza*, the Texas-Mexicans received the "Mexicans from Mexico" with decided hostility. The Texas-Mexicans already partook of American material culture and had absorbed enough of American ideational culture so that a sharp sense of difference from the immigrants could make itself felt. Those Texas-Mexicans who were concerned with improving their status relative to that of the Anglo group viewed the influx of the "foreign" Mexicans as a threat to whatever progress they felt they had made toward this goal by "Americanizing" themselves, and all Texas-Mexicans regarded the newcomers as a competitive threat to their jobs and wage levels.[2] The immigrant's depressed condition and relative

---

* "Historically viewed, American lower class groups have always had successive groups of recent immigrants which provided both a basis for compensatory feelings of superiority and a target for release of structurally determined frustrations. Each level in the class structure could thus control and subdue those still lower by displacing its aggression on lower groups as a means of maintaining its own sense of status." Robin M. Williams, *The Reduction of Intergroup Tensions*, SSRC Bulletin 57, New York, 1947, p. 60.

helplessness as a new arrival made him a safe target for aggression. In view of these considerations, the immigrant group was peculiarly appropriate for definition as an inferior group upon whom aggression could be displaced with impunity. The immigrant reacted by ridiculing the Texas-Mexican's Anglicized Spanish (just as the Texas-Mexican ridiculed the Mexican's poor English), accused him of denying his Mexican heritage in order to curry favor with the Anglos, and asserted that the Texas-Mexican was cowardly because he allowed himself to be dominated by the Anglo American.

For a number of reasons, the conflict between the Texas-Mexican and the immigrant has lost much of its virulence,* but for many years it played an active role in the adjustments of both groups to Anglo dominance, and even today, although greatly attenuated, it still represents one of the number of cleavages that militate against the unity of the Mexican American group. At the time of the study, Mexican leaders of Texas-Mexican background in San Antonio were still accusing leaders of the immigrant generation of "waving a Mexican flag in one hand, an American flag in the other", and of being ineffective because they "still have their eyes turned toward Mexico". One female informant, a Texas-Mexican, said she still feels pressure from other women of Texas-Mexican

---

\* The acculturation and assimilation of the two groups to each other; the dominant group practice of lumping them together as "Mexicans" that made native-born and immigrant eventually realize that their differences from each other were after all minor in the face of the much greater sense of difference they both felt from the dominant group; and the rise to maturity of the immigrant group's second generation. These three factors have largely blurred the distinction between the two groups.

background because she associates with the "Mexicans from Mexico", and has been asked by them, "Aren't there enough of our own type of people here for you to associate with?" Aside from providing a convenient outlet for displacement of aggression within the group, the relations between Texas-Mexicans and immigrants have played an important role in the development of other types of adjustments to be discussed presently.

In the Valley at present, the wetback has been defined by the Mexican Americans as an appropriate object of aggression for reasons very similar to those that motivated the Texas-Mexican in his reception of the earlier immigrants. To the lower class, the wetback represents a serious threat as a competitor for jobs and in forcing down wage levels, and to the middle class, already resentful of the "low" standards of the lower class as the "cause" of Anglo hostility toward all Mexican Americans, the influx of wetbacks, whose standards are still "lower", has been no less than tragic.\* The wetback is an even safer object of aggression than was the earlier immigrant because his illegal status in the United States makes him highly vulnerable. At the time of the study, Mexican Americans of all classes exhibited a high level of hostility against wetbacks, and several informants darkly predicted "civil war between Latin Americans and wetbacks" if the latter were not prevented from crossing the border.

---

\* Cf. the informant's comment quoted on p. 381.

The _colonia_ newspaper in McAllen editorialized on the need for "better understanding" between resident Mexicans and wetbacks since both are part of _la raza_, stating that "Instead of trying to help them in some way to better their situation, we (Mexican Americans) ridicule them, brand them as "wetbacks", and if we are able to hurt them in some way, we do it."[3]

The use of physical violence among Mexicans is given a great deal of prominence in the dominant group's stereotype as well as in the evaluations made by middle class Mexicans of the lower class. As noted elsewhere,[*] violence is largely confined to a small segment of the lower class, where it is rather freely expressed.[**] Most incidents of physical aggression occur in bars, and are usually the aftermath of dissolving inhibitions in drinking, but there is some evidence that the conception of _machismo_ prevalent in this group creates a tendency toward the idealization of physical violence.[***]

A more pervasive form of interpersonal aggression within the Mexican group is gossip. Unfavorable and malicious gossip is far from rare within the Anglo American group, but it is not nearly so widespread nor prominent as that indulged in by Mexican Americans. The use of gossip may be found at all levels of the Mexican group,[#] but the principal targets are the group's leaders, who are not only attacked by the lower class and by

---

[*] _Supra_, p. 394.

[**] A count of cases involving physical violence among Mexicans as reported in McAllen's _Valley Evening Monitor_ during an eight month period for McAllen and neighboring towns yielded the following: Shootings: 15; stabbings: 15; fights: 8.

[***] See _supra_, pp. 75-76.

[#] "...all Mexicans is gossip, if they can't find some they make it." Beatrice Griffith, _American Me_, Boston, 1948, p. 174.

their fellow members of the middle class, but who also attack each other. Hostile gossip, variously referred to as "back-stabbing", "tale-carrying", and "smear campaigning", was frequently lamented by Mexican informants because "the main thing holding back the Latin American people is their habit of tearing each other down." A great deal of gossip appears in connection with personal feuds, of which there are many in the Mexican group. These feuds ordinarily begin because A has "insulted" B, as B defined it, who reacts by initiating a series of unfavorable comments about A, and a vicious circle is begun. Although the initial offence may have been very mild or inconsequential, the Mexican's sensitivity to insult will not permit him to ignore it, and the feud will begin, often to continue indefinitely with undiminished force.

In gossiping about leaders,[*] the most frequent theme is the accusation that the leader has "sold out", usually to the Anglos, for money, for special favors, or for enhancing his prestige with the dominant group.[**] Leaders are also attacked as "publicity hounds", as being "arrogant" or "superior", or a whole series of their personal "defects", real or fancied, may be seized upon to demonstrate their utter lack of fitness for the positions they hold. To a certain extent, the suspicion manifested in such accusations can serve a social control function of keeping the leadership in line,

---
[*] The following remarks are based largely on the data collected in San Antonio, where the leader group is considerably larger, but similar tendencies were noted in McAllen.
[**] See *supra*, pp. 311 ff.

but it also runs the danger of discouraging able men from assuming or continuing the difficult task of subordinate group leadership. The group leaders do have to put up with a formidable amount of injurious and destructive gossip that has made them extraordinarily sensitive, and for some, the refutation of the slander directed at them and the dissemination of gossip they themselves engage in defensively against their detractors have become a major preoccupation and activity. One such leader in San Antonio, who frequently maintained that all the other leaders were opposed to him, was extremely free in his expression of hostility toward them and was an inveterate gossiper. On one occasion, after a particularly abusive diatribe against some of these men, he offered the writer the following explanation of why he behaves that way:

> I sure am hard on those fellows, but, you know, I don't mean 90 percent of what I say. I don't hate those leaders, I just pity them. But I have to talk this way to protect myself. I have to make them afraid to talk about me and rip me up the back, so I talk about them. Then they know that they had better not say anything about me because I'll cut them to pieces if I hear they have been talking about me. They don't say anything because they're afraid it will get back to me.

### Accommodation through Isolation

As indicated elsewhere,[*] isolation and assimilation are polar types delimiting the continuum of accommodative adjustments to subordinate status. The discussions of

---
[*] See pp. 51-52.

Mexican class orientations have indicated that adjustments approaching the assimilation pole are in general characteristic of the Mexican middle class, while those approaching the isolation pole are most often selected by the Mexican lower class. Although it may thus be said that the type of accommodative adjustment selected by the individual tends to vary with class membership, it should be emphasized that isolation and assimilation are polar types, that in the concrete case no Mexican is wholly oriented to either isolation or assimilation, and that every Mexican partakes of both in varying proportions.

The isolation adjustment refers to the conscious retention by the Mexican American of orientation to his distinctive cultural and social tradition as a means of accommodation to the problems of his subordinate status. There has been a definite tendency on the part of Mexican Americans to idealize the "Mexican ways" and thus to positively sanction their retention. This idealization of his indigenous tradition has enabled the Mexican American to maintain his own sense of status despite the subordinate role to which he has been relegated, and to compensate for the imputation of inferiority that has been cast upon him.

European immigrant groups have manifested attempts to preserve the integrity and autonomy of their indigenous cultural and political orientations during the initial stages of their residence in the United States, and responded to the

hostile reception they were accorded by the dominant group
(and by immigrant groups that had arrived earlier) by redoubling their efforts in this direction. Isolation from
their countries of origin, however, and the gradual
increase of contact with American institutions inevitably
weakened the integrity of the old culture patterns and
frustrated the attempts to retain orientations to these
patterns as a significant element in the immigrant's adjustments. Moreover, the eventual decrease in the dominant group's
hostility, as well as the increase in the immigrant's participation in American life, removed the very necessity for such a
response. In the case of the Mexican, however, the isolation
adjustment has persisted, although it has diminished in
intensity and somewhat changed its form in accordance with
the changes that have permitted the development of orientations
to assimilation. This persistence has been made possible
by the continued existence of a distinctive Mexican American
subculture, which in turn has been reinforced by the isolation
adjustment. The several discussions of institutional aspects
of Mexican American society, of the corresponding basic personality type, and of value orientations have revealed at
least the bold outlines of the distinctive patterning of
the Mexican American cultural and social tradition as compared with that of the Anglo. There have been a number of
unique factors that have contributed to the preservation of
this difference, factors that were not present in the case
of any of the European immigrant groups. A principal factor

has been the unremitting hostility of the dominant group as manifested in its constant employment of exclusion devices and its insistent definition, facilitated by the Mexican's visibility, of Mexican Americans as "Mexicans" rather than "Americans" ever since the two groups came into contact. Regardless of how Mexicans might have felt about seeking assimilation to Anglo culture, this uncompromising attitude of the dominant group toward them has done nothing to persuade them to such a course, and if they have persisted in retaining the "old ways", it is in part because they have been granted few opportunities to learn any others.

The peculiar history of Mexican residence in the Southwest also helps to explain the durability of distinctive culture patterns. The "Texas-Mexican" has never been an immigrant to Anglo American society at all in the sense that his ancestors settled the Southwest before the Anglos came. Since he was "here first", the Texas-Mexican has never felt any urgent need to change his ways to fit those of the Anglo American, especially since he was rejected by the Anglos almost from the beginning of their contact. The Mexicans who immigrated into the Southwest from 1910 on settled in the colonias already established by the Texas-Mexicans, and acculturated to the peculiar Texas-Mexican variety of Mexican culture as modified by Anglo culture rather than directly to the latter, acquiring the Texas-Mexican attitude toward assimilation along with other elements of that group's culture.[4]

Finally, the proximity to Mexico has contributed to the survival of the indigenous cultural tradition by facilitating the steady influx of immigrants who have mingled with the earlier groups, and have thereby injected new vigor into the old cultural forms and have reaffirmed the identification with Mexico. Proximity to Mexico has also facilitated access to such expressions of Mexican culture as its moving pictures, newspapers and magazines, music, and popular literature, all of which are still appreciated in the colonias of McAllen and San Antonio.

Perhaps the most pervasive and striking characteristic of the isolation adjustment is the fierce pride in Mexican background and descent. The term la raza is a highly charged symbol of the group's identity and traditions that makes a stirring appeal to the majority of Mexican Americans regardless of class status or degree of assimilation. In the case of the immigrant generation, experience in the United States awakened an ardent patriotism for Mexico, a consciousness of nationality that apparently did not exist before emigration from the mother country.[5] This arousal of feelings of nationality was akin to the nationalistic awakening undergone by many immigrant groups after residence in the United States. However, in the Mexican case this sentiment led to widespread reluctance to seek naturalization since it was regarded as an act of betrayal of Mexico, although the fact that American citizenship had obviously not benefited the native-born Mexican Americans in any way was also a strong deterrent. A Mexican American leader in San Antonio, himself a naturalized citizen, said of the *colonia's* immigrant generation:

> Most of the immigrants are not citizens, and they talk their children into forgetting about their American citizenship. They feel that they are losing something very precious if they give up their Mexican citizenship when they are really not giving up anything. They think they're denying that they're Mexicans if they become citizens, but they don't get anything from Mexico and never will.

Reflecting the immigrant conviction that American citizenship could confer no added privileges in view of the dominant group attitude, a second generation Mexican explained his father's refusal to become naturalized as follows:

> My father is a man that has clung to his love for his native land. I think he has had more chance because of that than he would have had otherwise. He has maintained a dignity and a certain culture that a lot of other people wish they had because he stuck to his so-called *Mexicanismo*. In a way, it was a refuge, I guess, for the preservation of his dignity. Otherwise what would he have been here to these Texans, just another damn Mexican who didn't know English, and who should either go back to Mexico or become Americanized. To trade his heritage for a mess of pottage, to become an American when he knew that he wasn't accepted as an American, he regarded as a bad bargain.

The pride in Mexican descent and identification with *la raza* is also characteristic of the Texas-Mexican and of the immigrant's native-born children, but in these groups the nationalistic identification with Mexico tends to fade out, and only the orientation to the Mexican American cultural tradition remains. *Soy Mejicano*, I am a Mexican, is the common expression of identification with *la raza* and its traditions, and there were few informants who did not, at one time or another, utter the phrase. The pressure exerted by the group for retention of this identification has been noted elsewhere, but it may be pointed out here that the pressure is so strong that it makes for ambivalent feelings even toward the use of the term "Latin American". Although middle class Mexicans oriented to assimilation have pressed for the popularization of the term in order to eliminate the term "Mexican", due to its insulting implications when used by Anglos, many of these same people uneasily regarded their use of the term "Latin American" as somehow manifesting a desire on their part to deny their Mexican origins. One middle class informant in McAllen who often used the latter term once said vehemently:

> My father and mother came from Mexico, they're Mexican, and that's good enough for me. Anybody who calls himself a Latin American is just ashamed of being a Mexican and is trying to hide it. I'll be damned if I want anyone to call me a Latin American.

Texas-Mexicans who could trace their family residence in the Southwest back for six generations professed the same pride in Mexican descent, and even those native-born informants who insisted they were "100% American" always added the qualification that they were "Mexican too, and very proud of it."

The isolation adjustment, in its extreme nationalistic form, receives its formal sanction each year in the elaborate celebrations of the _fiestas patrias_, the Mexican national holidays, when the idealization and glorification of things Mexican and the reaffirmation of the old ties with

Mexico are ritualized for the <u>colonia</u>. These celebrations, on the fifth of May and the sixteenth of September, are fostered by the Mexican consuls, but the actual organization of the <u>fiestas</u> is accomplished by a "Patriotic Committee" composed mostly of American citizens, just as the large audiences attracted to the celebrations are for the most part American citizens. Although these expressions of <u>Mexicanismo</u> have varying appeal to Mexican Americans depending on their position in the isolation-assimilation continuum,* only those most fully bent on assimilation reject them completely as "breast-beating patriotism for a country we no longer have any connection with", as one middle class informant in McAllen put it. Another McAllen informant said:

> There are two kinds of Latin American people here. Now you take me, I have no ties with Mexico, it's just another country to me except that it's the place my ancestors came from. I think of myself as American, and feel that I owe allegiance only to the United States. Then there's the other kind of people, who even though they're born here, still think of themselves as Mexican. They feel a strong patriotism for Mexico, and celebrate the sixteenth of September and the fifth of May. They think this is the only way to be a good Mexican. It is these people who use the term <u>la raza</u>, and they think of themselves as <u>la raza</u>.

---

* <u>Mexicanismo</u> today, even for those still greatly attracted to it, is really an expression of adhesion to the Mexican American amalgam of parent and host cultures and not of political loyalty to Mexico. The splendid record of Mexican Americans in World War II is sufficient evidence of their loyalty to the United States. The fact that Mexicans seldom participate in Fourth of July celebrations is largely a function of the peculiar position they occupy in American society rather than an evidence of lack of loyalty on their part. An attempt by Mexicans to attend such a celebration in a town near San Antonio resulted as follows: "On July 4, 1941, a number of Mexicans attended a dance which was being held on one of the main streets of Lockhart. About 11:00 P.M. the orchestra (leader) made, substantially, the following announcement: 'I have been asked to make this announcement: that all Spanish people gathered here must leave the block since this is an American celebration.'" Perales, <u>op</u>. <u>cit</u>., p. 217.

A more representative and moderate attitude among those oriented to assimilation is to accept the celebration of *fiestas patrias*, but to regard it as no more than a ceremonial means of paying their respects to their Mexican background and origins. The following remarks are representative of this point of view:

> I think the *fiestas patrias* are good because there's one time in the year when we feel that our ancestors did something noble and something great, maybe not here, but somewhere else, and to me there's no realism attached to it, it's just a question of sentiment and pride, and that's about all. But as far as actual attachment to the doctrine of Mexico and all of that, I don't feel it.

The theme of *la raza* and of being *un buen y digno Mejicano*, a good and worthy Mexican, is often played upon by Mexican leaders, particularly political leaders, who find it a sure-fire method for touching off enthusiasm for a candidate or an issue,* or for obtaining support for a particular cause. However, the major preoccupation of these men is with assimilation, and the *la raza* theme is simply a device for reaffirming their identification with the Mexican group and for inducing feelings of solidarity in their followers.

### Accommodation through Assimilation

The assimilation adjustment refers to the conscious attempt by the Mexican American to orient himself to the distinctive cultural and social tradition of the dominant

---

* Cf. *supra*, pp. 302 ff.

group as a means of coping with the problems of his subordinate status. This adjustment is a direct response to the dominant group practice of rewarding, in the form of progressive release from subordinate status, acquisition of likeness to itself. For present purposes, it is useful to distinguish between acculturation,[*] as a process of mutual or one-way transmission of culture elements between diverse ethnic groups wherein the selection is ordered in terms of immediate, utilitarian considerations not necessarily dependent on mutual group attitudes, and assimilation, as a process of mutual or one-way transmission of culture elements between diverse ethnic groups wherein the selection is ordered in terms of its contribution to the synthesis of the diverse cultures and is motivated by the desire of at least one of the groups to become socially and culturally identified with the other.

In the sense defined here, Mexican Americans have undergone a considerable amount of acculturation to various aspects of Anglo American culture. The move from a folk milieu characterized by highly traditionalized patterns of social relations in which individual behavior is chiefly dependent upon immediate response and recognition to the more abstract, impersonal, and rationalized patterns of the American milieu required basic modifications of the Mexican's cultural equipment in the struggle for adaptation to the new situation. Beyond

---
[*] Cf. footnote, p. 54.

this, the Mexican has substituted American for Mexican culture elements insofar as they have demonstrated greater utility or attractiveness in relation to his changing needs and desires in the United States. With regard to material culture, Mexican Americans are hardly to be distinguished from Anglo Americans, and as a previous chapter has indicated, there have been basic changes in religion, magical and medical beliefs, and the <u>compadrazgo</u> system. There are still strong survivals from the original culture in the contemporary Mexican American diet, but the manner of preparation has been radically changed in many cases, some dishes have been modified by mixture with American elements, while all sorts of American dishes and food items have been added to the diet outright. In language, although Spanish is still retained as the primary language, it has been noticeably Anglicized, and in varying degrees, Mexicans have acquired English. Tastes in popular music are still overwhelmingly Mexican, but second generation Mexicans have adopted American music without relinquishing their own. The original family organization has persisted strongly, but here also important changes are occurring in the various familial roles with corresponding changes in the familial status hierarchy and the weakening of the chaperonage pattern.

These changes undergone by the Mexican American were made in response to the immediate needs and demands posed by the American cultural and social milieu, and represent his working adjustment to the impact of that milieu. Thus they were not necessarily brought about by the desire for cultural and social fusion and consequent identification with the dominant group. Although the changes may have provided a departure point for assimilation in that they have led to a limited sharing by Mexicans of Anglo idea and action patterns, they are primarily indicative of acculturation rather than assimilation. That such acculturation has occurred means that even those Mexican Americans most oriented to isolation have incorporated Anglo elements into their cultural heritage, and that the "old ways" they adhere to have undergone significant modifications.

Beyond this, however, in response to the peculiar position Anglo dominance has placed them in, Mexican Americans, in varying degrees, have acceded to the dominant group's demands for likeness to itself as the price of ultimate acceptance, and have thus developed orientations to assimilation. As has been seen, this is the type of reactive adjustment most consistently selected by the middle class Mexicans, who manifest a high valuation of Anglo American ways; increasing orientations to Anglo idea and action patterns with a consequent detachment from comparable aspects of Mexican American culture; and attempts at higher frequency of interaction with Anglo Americans on an equal status basis, of the sort that will symbolize greater acceptance by Anglos and eventually lead to the complete breakdown of the semi-caste barrier.* Apart from the prestige desires that provide

---
* See supra, pp. 365 ff. for this characterization of the assimilation adjustment.

motivations to assimilation, it should be noted that there are practical advantages to be gained in assumption of Anglo patterns in that this enables the Mexican to compete more effectively in the Anglo world.

Complete assimilation with the dominant group is still a long way off, however, even for those most fully bent on attaining it. Aside from the question of Anglo willingness and readiness to let down the bars, many Mexicans who have taken the road to assimilation are still uncertain as to how far they wish to travel it. Although there are middle class Mexicans who unhesitatingly advocate the complete remaking of the Mexican in the Anglo image, there are others who are not so willing to concede such sweeping superiority to Anglo ways. The latter have relinquished much of their own distinctive cultural tradition and will probably cede much more in view of their desire for integration with the dominant society, which occupies the advantaged position for demanding such change. However, they would like to see a fusion with American culture in which the "best" of the Mexican Americans ways, according to their definition, would be incorporated along with the "best" of the Anglo American, rather than a one-sided exchange in which all that is distinctively Mexican is lost completely.* Their desire for preservation

---

* Viewed historically, the Spanish and Mexican contributions to the American culture of the Southwest have been substantial. Southwestern English, architecture, diet, and property law all bear the Spanish-Mexican stamp, as do the mining, livestock-raising, and irrigated farming industries of the region. For a general discussion of the Spanish-Mexican heritage of the Southwest, see Carey McWilliams, North from Mexico, pp. 133-61.

of various aspects of Mexican American culture has little in it of *Mexicanismo* in its extreme form, although it does of course contain elements of the isolation orientation. It reflects a conflict engendered by their marginal position that significantly affects their attitudes toward assimilation and consequently the rate at which they will assimilate. The assimilation process, like that of mobility between classes, is essentially an individual affair whereby members of the subordinate group transfer themselves, one by one, to the dominant group as they acquire the necessary attributes. In the assimilation process undergone by most immigrant groups in the United States, this has involved complete repudiation of the immigrant culture, severance of all connections with the immigrant community, and "passing" into the dominant society.[6] Opposition to renunciation of identification with the group is pervasive among Mexican Americans, as has been seen, and is felt just as strongly by those who advocate the "best of both ways" as by those who adhere most completely to the isolation adjustment. Although Anglo Americans are willing to facilitate passing of Mexican Americans who can meet their definition of "Spanish", apparently very few Mexicans of those who could qualify have succumbed to this temptation, despite the frequency with which such accusations have been flung at "assimilated" Mexicans by their fellows. Insofar as this identification with the group persists, the ultimate success of the assimilation adjustment will remain problematical, given present dominant group attitudes.

The point of view expressed in the phrase "best of both ways" may be illustrated briefly. With regard to language, a premium is placed on speaking "good", unaccented English, but the retention of Spanish is valued just as highly "as a mark of culture that should not be abandoned." Mexican Americans who favor full assimilation to the Anglo American model tend to minimize the use of Spanish among themselves and attempt to eliminate it altogether by speaking only English to their children, a practice condemned by those who hold to the "best of both ways". The latter are oriented to Anglo American conceptions of mobility and favor the acquisition of behavior patterns, which they consider characteristically Anglo American, that will promote "getting ahead."[*] They favor incorporating these patterns into their own way of life, but not to the point where the drive for power and wealth would become completely dominant, as they believe it to be in the middle class Anglo, and they ridicule the efforts of those Mexicans who strive to emulate the Anglos in this regard. A Mexican American physician in San Antonio, who ardently advocated "creating a product that takes the best of both cultures", made the following comments with reference to one of the colonia's most highly mobile businessmen:

> He tries to put on the front of the big executive and affect a briskness of manner that is foreign to the Mexican businessman. The main thing is that he tries to ape the ways of the Anglo businessmen, and we think that's ridiculous. I can't help thinking that he is a little boy wearing his papa's suit. The Mexicans have a feeling for the ridiculous, and since they don't do business his way, they find it amusing to watch his antics.

[*] Supra, p. 370.

Another example of thorough imitation of Anglo businessmen is that afforded by the Pan American Optimists Club, which is modelled on the Anglo service club of that name. At luncheon meetings, the members conduct themselves in a manner surprisingly similar to that typically displayed at Anglo service club meetings, engaging in rowdyism and "wise-cracks", and responding to each announcement with boos, catcalls and whistling. A Mexican American lawyer, expressing disapproval of these antics, said:

> You know, it looks natural for the regular Optimists to relax and indulge in horseplay, but the Latin American is of a different temperament. It looks ludicrous to see them attempt to indulge in horseplay because they take themselves too seriously to relax the way the gringos do. I have seen X get sore as hell when Y threw a gibe at him.

Although there is lack of agreement as to what the nature of the end product ought to be, practically all Mexican Americans oriented to assimilation, in view of their desire for acceptance by the dominant group, favor acquisition of those Anglo patterns they regard as most essential in gaining such acceptance, and, as would be expected, exhibit their greatest divergences from typical Mexican American patterns in these respects. However, even the most acculturated and assimilated Mexican Americans still manifest idea and action patterns that are

---

\* For examples, see the discussion of middle class criteria, pp. 358ff and of middle class patterns, pp. 366 ff.

characteristic of the Mexican group as a whole, and these are at least as prominent as their divergences. Various components of the basic personality type are changing in accordance with the emphasis on such traits as independence and ambition, which are being implemented in child training patterns,* but the highly sensitive pride, the vulnerability to ridicule and insult, is to be found in the most assimilated Mexicans, as is the characteristically Mexican time conception. Although the sense of protectiveness toward children has diminished, the peculiar Mexican combination of permissiveness and inculcation of obedience and respect is still practiced by the most assimilated parents, and family life is still child-centered. There are still intimate bonds with the extended family where this is possible, and in sex roles the pattern of male dominance persists strongly, despite the pressures for change that are beginning to make themselves felt.**

## Leadership and the Association

The ambivalent attitudes of Mexican Americans toward their group leaders have been indicated at various points in this report. On the one hand, there is profound suspicion and cynicism regarding the leader's motives, summed up in the Mexican's equation of the leader with the buscon, i.e., one who tries to exploit or take advantage of a position of trust or responsibility. On the other hand, the leader, in his ideal role of serving the group, is granted top status in the class

---
\* Cf. informant's comment on p. 371.
\*\* For illustrations of the persistence and change, see supra, pp. 60-64 and 77-78.

hierarchy. The former attitude is largely born of the Mexican's long unhappy experience with venal, exploitative leaders, while the latter is mostly derived from his extreme dependency on leadership in view of the dominant-subordinate group relationship. The pervasive lack of contact between Mexicans and Anglos funnels all communication into the narrow channel accessible only to the group leaders, who are accepted as intermediaries by the Anglos in a way that no ordinary Mexican could hope to approximate. By virtue of the leaders' monopoly of accessibility to the dominant group they are defined as the only ones who can effectively work for la raza, who can perform the role of patron in obtaining advantages for the group. In the past, the Mexican masses have had little choice in selecting their leaders. Even if they had been able to choose, the range of alternatives would have been extremely narrow since there were few who had either the motivations or the equalifications to assume posts of such responsibility. The depressed condition of the masses and their dependency on those fellow-Mexicans who could serve as intermediaries to the dominant society hardly made for a situation where they were able to choose their leaders or exert any efforts to control them. Their inability to provide checks on the acquisition and use of power by leaders has been reinforced by their failure to develop leaders and improvement or protest organizations within their own lower class group, and to actively support or reject the middle class leadership when the opportunity presented itself. The constant hostility directed toward the leadership remains only at the verbal level, and although it may have some value as a means of control, may be viewed more as another manifestation of aggression displaced within the group than of positive interest in keeping the leadership in line. In practice, the lower class has left the leadership largely to its own devices, and in this sense has really not been "led" at all. This pattern is paralleled in the middle class, where the majority of those who do join improvement and protest organizations seldom have participated actively or attended organization meetings. This indifference has pushed even greater responsibility into the hands of the few who are active, and actually has forced them to assume it whether they wanted to or not. Given the indifference of the masses and the lack of checks on the leader's power, the prestige accorded the leadership role by both the Mexican and Anglo groups, and the practical advantages to be gained by "selling out", it is no wonder that there have been few mass leaders working primarily for the group interest. A more characteristic phenomenon has been that of individuals who have used the leadership role as an avenue for personal mobility under conditions that have placed a premium on accommodation rather than protest.

In McAllen, the leadership role has been dominated by one family, which established its advantaged position soon after the city's, and the _colonia's_, founding. For two generations, Anglo Americans have thought of the successive heads of the family as _the_ leader of the Mexican group, as

controlling and representing it. Actually, the present
family head can influence only those Mexican Americans
who are directly dependent upon him or can be influenced
through his associates, as the discussion of politics has
shown, and he represents the interests of his own small
middle class clique rather than those of the Mexican group
as a whole. The remarkable stability of his status as
leader has been due to the power he could wield through
possession of commercial and farming enterprises on a consistently greater scale than those of any other Mexican
in the _colonia_; to the by now traditionalized dominant group
definition of him as _the_ Mexican American to deal with in all
matters pertaining to the Mexican group; and to the mass
apathy and indifference that permitted him to consolidate
and entrench his position. As a small middle class developed,
some of its members were added one by one to form a leader
clique dominated by the B family, and those who were not
interested or objected to following the B family's lead,
remained apart and abstained from active opposition.

The B family and its clique eventually formalized their
status as the _colonia's_ leaders by the organization of the
Latin American Businessmen's Club, which acts as an extension
of the clique in dealings with the dominant group. The
policy of this organization is conservative, its stated
purposes being those of fostering and stimulating _colonia_
business, much as the city's chamber of commerce undertakes
to do for the community as a whole, and of participating

in "community improvement".* During the period of the
study, the latter included such activities as a campaign
to persuade colonia residents to number their houses in order
to qualify for mail delivery, contributing to fund-raising
campaigns for equipment for colonia schools, and adorning
the colonia's business street with colored lights for the
Christmas season. Although it is the only colonia organization capable of engaging in organized protest, it rarely
does so. During the writer's stay, its only expression
of protest was the publication of a statement in the local
paper condemning the swimming pool incident.** The Mexican
American member of the City Commission, who was also president
of the Club during the early part of the study, explicitly
formulated the characteristic attitude of the colonia leadership toward accommodation versus protest in the following
terms:

> If anything, I would say that Latin Americans have
> too much leadership, or at least all the leadership
> they can safely stand. If our leadership does more
> than it is doing now, we're liable to be considered
> too aggressive, and then the Anglos will be antagonized.

Patterns of Mexican American leadership and organization
in San Antonio have many features in common with those of
McAllen, but have developed along somewhat different lines.
The much larger scale involved in part accounts for the difference. The great influx of immigrants from 1910 on provided
the native-born colonia residents, the Texas-Mexicans, with

---
\* There are two mutual aid socieites in the colonia whose
membership is largely lower class, but they are preoccupied
only with sickness and death benefits.
\*\* See supra, p. 500-1.

a number of opportunities to serve as intermediaries between the newcomers and the dominant community, and from this group came the nucleus of a developing middle class, as well as whatever leadership the _colonia_ had. The leaders of this earlier period usually operated as individuals, without any organizational support. They maintained their positions by serving the need of both Anglos and Mexicans for a go-between, and usually exaggerated their influence with Anglos when dealing with their own group and _vice versa_. Unlike McAllen, where one family has been able to monopolize the leadership function, a competitive struggle developed in San Antonio in which each leader attempted to garner the largest share of prestige and power so that he might become _the_ leader of the _colonia_.

The first major attempt at organization for improvement and protest purposes among the Mexican Americans of San Antonio and elsewhere in South Texas was that represented by LULAC, the League of United Latin American Citizens. LULAC was founded at Corpus Christi in 1929 by a group of Mexicans from various towns and cities of South Texas, and eventually spread through four other southwestern states although it has remained most active in Texas.[7] Among other cities, councils were established in San Antonio and McAllen.* In San Antonio, although the most prominent _colonia_

---

* The McAllen council went out of existence a number of years ago. An informant who had been a member of the council explained its failure as follows: "The trouble was everyone wanted recognition and was jealous of the others. They never could agree, so the council fell apart. Everyone wanted something different. We could never have had a decent council in McAllen anyway because the B family stood in the way. If it hadn't failed by itself, they would have taken it over and used it for political purposes."

leaders became active in the local LULAC council, the old leadership rivalry persisted, as it has until the present, and reached a high point in a struggle between two lawyers for the top position not only in LULAC but in the _colonia_ as a whole. This became a famous feud that split the local council into two separate councils, a breach that endured for more than a decade. Other leaders have arisen through LULAC, as well as through other _colonia_ organizations, and at present all of them have organizational affiliation, if little mass support. Rivalry and envy are still rife among the leadership, and it has led to much fruitless dissipation and duplication of effort among the colonia's organizations. In McAllen, there are also prestige fights, but they are muted and more controlled due to the dominance exerted by the B family. In San Antonio, however, the struggle for prestige is very open, and has become one of the principal issues between leaders. A favorite method of impugning a rival's motives is to accuse him of being a "publicity hound", of wanting all the "credit". Actually, the desire for "publicity" and "credit" seems to be uppermost in the minds of many leaders, and at times becomes an end in itself. Some leaders withdraw from a particular project because they feel they are not receiving their share of credit, or will not participate at all because there is little opportunity offered for obtaining "publicity". One leader in San Antonio made the following complaint:

> There are so many people who will remain with an organization or committee only so long as it serves their own interests. They take on leadership duties expecting to get credit for what they are doing, and when they are disappointed, which happens often because no one gives them

recognition for what they've done, they drop out. The kind of leaders the people need are men who will give their time and effort with no hope of recognition or reward for themselves personally.

During a meeting of a *colonia* organization, one of the *colonia's* most prominent leaders, whose activities at the time were frequently reported in the newspapers, arose to complain that he was being attacked from many quarters as a "publicity hound", and heatedly denied this. After the meeting, another leader frankly confided to the writer:

> That's only a dodge, because I'm sure that, in all the years I've known him, he likes publicity just as much as any other man likes it. As much as all the leaders like it, as much as I like it myself, or anybody else. There's no question about it. It gives you a sense of importance, it inflates your ego when you see your name in the newspapers, and that's only natural, that's the logical reaction for any person, it doesn't make any difference who it is. Of course, some of our people have a sort of mania for publicity, but I've never had that, at least I don't think I have.

The president of one *colonia* organization, elated at encountering a complimentary editorial in a San Antonio newspaper about his activities, said that this was the best piece of publicity he had ever received. He went on to say that he had been the subject of seventeen headlines and many newspaper stories during his career, but never of an editorial before, and maintained that no other leader had ever received even one headline in all the years the other Mexican organizations have been functioning.

A closer examination of the objectives and activities of LULAC and other major organizations of the San Antonio *colonia*, although of necessity cursory, will show how they reflect the various types of aggressive and accommodative adjustments described in the previous section. LULAC was founded by the emerging Mexican American middle class in the Valley, San Antonio, and Corpus Christi, in an attempt to cope with the problems of their subordinate status.[8] Only "native born or naturalized citizens of Latin extraction"[*] have been eligible for membership,[9] and a great deal of formal emphasis has been placed on patriotism and active citizenship. The first and fifth of LULAC's twenty "aims and purposes"[10] read as follows:

> To develop within the members of our ethnic group[**] the best, purest, and most perfect type of true and loyal citizens of the United States of America.
>
> To define with absolute and unmistakable clearness our unquestionable loyalty to the ideals, principles, and citizenship of the United States of America.

In the "ritual" prescribed for LULAC meetings,[11] used at almost all weekly meetings, the first step is the reading of the official prayer, "given and said as a token of our profound love for the memory of its author, the First President of the United States. This Prayer also approaches an eminently pure expression of our devotion to America, our country." The second and third steps are the pledge of allegiance to the flag and the singing of "America", LULAC's official hymn. Five of LULAC's aims are concerned with promoting the use of the franchise, equal representation on juries and in "governmental affairs", and "social and

---

[*] In 1947, LULAC amended its constitution to permit the admission of "persons of Anglo American ancestry."

[**] Prior to 1948, the word "race" appeared here.

political unification", although it is explicitly stated that LULAC is not a "political club" and will not engage in partisan politics. This heavy emphasis on patriotism and active citizenship reflects the anxiety of the middle class to set itself off from *Mexicanismo* and to combat the Anglo's stereotype of the Mexican voter, as well as the political apathy of the Mexicans themselves. Despite the emphasis on Americanism, the identification with Mexican origins is not ignored, since one aim states:

> We solemnly declare once and for all to maintain a sincere and respectful reverence for our racial origin of which we are proud.

The learning of English is another of the aims and purposes, and LULAC is the only *colonia* organization whose meetings are consistently conducted entirely in English, although most members usually lapse into Spanish among themselves once the meeting is over. Other aims are concerned with fighting discrimination, employing legal means to obtain equal rights, and working for "education and guidance" of all Mexican Americans.

LULAC aims and purposes have been presented to demonstrate the assimilation orientations of the organization, and the extent to which it formally dedicates itself to protest. In its activities, LULAC has remained essentially a middle class organization in San Antonio, drawing most of its membership from the white collar and businessmen groups, and of course the lawyers. With a few notable exceptions, most of the top status businessmen and the physicians have abstained from active participation, and although LULAC has not discouraged lower class Mexicans from joining, relatively few have done so. LULAC's policy as a protest organization has been mild and conservative, but it has been active in improvement activities. Although handicapped by lack of funds and full-time employees, it has managed to maintain a fairly stable organization. Most of its activity has been dedicated to citizenship education among its members; to encouraging Mexicans to enter the white collar and business occupations; to registering formal protests against discrimination wherever it has come to the organization's attention; to making financial contributions to worthy colonia causes; to emphasizing the need and desirability of educating the children; to establishing scholarship funds; and to sending delegations or writing letters to the city administration requesting the installation or improvement of municipal facilities in the colonia. During the period of the study, LULAC engaged in open protest on a larger scale than heretofore by financing and actively supporting a successful lawsuit to eliminate school segregation in Texas, and by waging an active campaign against the admission of contract labor from Mexico into Texas as harmful to the interests of local labor. Both these projects were sponsored by the national organization, but San Antonio members played a central role in executing them.

Other major colonia organizations may be dealt with more briefly. The Mexican Chamber of Commerce was founded in 1928 at the instigation of the Mexican consul in order to foster trade relations with Mexico. This is still its major function, although it dabbles in "community improvement" as well by contributing to various causes. In explaining the establishment of a separate organization of this sort despite the fact that membership in the San Antonio Chamber of Commerce is open to all Mexican businessmen, informants said that most Mexicans feel lost in the larger organization, and that a <u>colonia</u> organization can look after their interests more effectively.

The Pan American Optimists Club, which follows the Anglo Optimists in being "Friends of the Boy", is composed of the <u>colonia's</u> most substantial businessmen, the most prominent lawyers, and a few of the doctors. The dues are high enough so that most of the smaller businessmen do not join. Most of its members are also members of the Mexican Chamber of Commerce, and a few are active in LULAC. The Optimists, and to a lesser extent the Chamber, represent attempts to model organizational activities on the Anglo pattern in the effort to obtain greater Anglo acceptance, but the result has been somewhat the reverse in that the maintenance of separate organizations has pushed these Mexicans further than ever away from joint participation with the Anglo group.

Shortly before this study was begun, a new organization appeared in the Pan American Progressive Association, or PAPA, as it is usually called. Founded by a number of the top businessmen and a few of the professionals, its "main purpose is to improve conditions among the Americans of Mexican descent and Mexican people living in San Antonio and elsewhere."

PAPA has attempted to raise a fund of $25,000 through donations (the minimum is $100) by businessmen who thereby become "active" members, and to recruit 25,000 Mexicans who would pay no dues and would be "associate" members. The associate members are enrolled merely by signing an application, and play no active role in the organization. The principal idea in creating this vast membership was to use the fact of such mass support as a club in fighting all types of discrimination. Thus PAPA is formally defined as a protest organization, although its aims are vaguely and generally expressed. During its first year of existence, PAPA's major achievements consisted of hiring a lawyer to fight a restrictive covenant case,[*] conducting a housing and income survey in the _colonia_, and leading a drive to obtain city water service for 600 _colonia_ homes. Although it was still too early at the time the writer left San Antonio to estimate the role PAPA could play in affecting dominant-subordinate group relations, many informants, among them active members of PAPA, had no inhibitions in attacking the organization for one reason or another. They objected to PAPA as a duplication of LULAC by businessmen who had refused to work in the latter organization, disapproved of the policy of enrolling a mass of members who would have no personal stake in the organization, and accused its leaders of participating because they had ulterior motives of a financial or political nature, or because they wanted "publicity".

---

[*] See _supra_, pp. 440 ff.

Finally, attention should be called to the School Improvement League, which is dedicated to obtaining "better educational facilities for the children of the Western section of the city". In the following respects, the League is unique among colonia organizations: It has consistently and explicitly adopted a policy of active protest; it attempts to avoid the so-called "self-segregation" tendencies of other colonia organizations by the deliberate omission from its name and aims of the term "Mexican" or a variant, claiming to serve the entire West Side rather than just the colonia; it has endeavored, although with only partial success, to obtain Anglo American support for its activities; and it has sought to reach and influence all the colonia's residents, principally by means of mass meetings. The League represents substantially the work of one man, its founder and president, who in 1934 "became convinced that bad schools make the children drop out, and as long as such schools exist, the Mexicans will never get educated." According to his own story:

> I want to the men who were then known as the Mexican leaders and tried to interest them in doing something about the problem, but they said nothing could be done, so I gave them up in disgust and started out on my own. I persuaded the fire and police commissioner and three school board members to make an inspection of the schools with me. The result was a lot of newspaper publicity and two new schools on the West Side worth a million dollars. Except for the help of a few people from time to time, I have done most of the work myself.

The League continued its active struggle until two more schools were promised for the colonia, and then became dormant until 1947, when its president undertook a new campaign for construction of schools and improvement of the physical plant of those already in existence. With the aid of a few Mexican American Protestant ministers and other interested _colonia_ residents, and the moral support of a few _colonia_ and Anglo organizations and individuals, the president's tactics consisted of presenting petitions and speeches at city school board meetings, sometimes over the heated opposition of the board members, issuing blunt statements to the newspapers attacking the board's alleged discriminatory policy with regard to _colonia_ schools, and staging mass meetings in the _colonia_. These efforts were successful in securing further commitments for school construction in the _colonia_.

Although _colonia_ leaders have been greatly impressed by the League president's achievements, they have unanimously disapproved of his methods. One of them remarked:

> He is doing good work but could do better if he didn't have a chip on his shoulder. The trouble with him is he's a fanatic. The way he's going about it he can upset the work of years. It's like putting up a building that takes years, and then have someone come along and put a stick of dynamite under it.

Aside from the League president's triumph in obtaining concrete results of a magnitude seldom accomplished by other _colonia_ leaders and organizations, he has received a great deal of attention and some eulogies from the Anglo American press, no small consideration to a group so avid of "publicity". Another leader, referring to the attitude of other leaders as well as his own, made the following representative comment:

> All the others consider him too rough and direct in his methods. They condemn him for not being diplomatic enough. Still, you have to give him credit for what he has accomplished. Actually, single-handed, whether you approve of his methods or not, he has made gains which no other group or individual can compare with.

In view of their condemnation of his methods, it is not surprising that the majority of _colonia_ leaders have offered little active support to the League's work. Their reactions to the League president and his activities reflect the ambivalence toward assimilation versus protest that has been characteristic of Mexican American leadership, in McAllen as well as San Antonio. As has been repeatedly stated, middle class Mexicans, in their attempts to solve the problems of subordinate status, have predominantly chosen assimilation, i.e., changing the Mexican group to approximate Anglo likeness, in preference to open protest, i.e., coping directly with the dominant group to win desired concessions. Although the two approaches are not necessarily incompatible and most leaders have availed themselves of both, the proportion has been heavily weighted toward accommodation through assimilation due to the belief that the use of direct aggression would endanger the progress made through assimilation, as the recently quoted comments indicate. Nevertheless, they would of course like to have the more tangible rewards that may be available through direct protest, as seen in the case of the League.

The patterns of leadership and association among Mexican reflect another conflict that has been dealt with at various points in this study, the conflict between self and group interest. The aims and at least some of the activities of the majority of _colonia_ organizations that have been reviewed here have been primarily dedicated to advancing _la raza_ as a whole, expressing the middle class conviction that ultimate acceptance by the dominant group depends on "raising" the level of all Mexicans. Such a conviction undoubtedly has its altruistic as well as self-interested elements. For the most part, however, colonia leaders who in the past have worked in these organizations have utilized them either to further the interests of their class rather than those of the group as a whole, or as vehicles for furthering their personal interests and those of a small clique of followers.

At various points in this study reference was made in passing to the Mexican American war veterans as a group who are forming the nucleus of a protest movement that is injecting a new note into the patterns of adjustment to subordinate status that have been characterized throughout this report. No attempt was made to consider this phenomenon in connection with the discussion of these patterns as it was still inchoate at the time of the study, and its most explicit manifestations had occurred in places other than McAllen and San Antonio. In general, the situation brought about by the war changed the outlook of even those Mexican Americans who stayed at home, as it apparently did in the case of other subordinate groups in the United States. Mexican Americans in the Valley and San Antonio were accepted for jobs in occupational categories they had rarely entered before, and those who did not, enjoyed more security and somewhat higher wages in their customary employment. However, the end of the war brought "reconversion" for many Mexican Americans, from the Valley's agricultural workers to the employees of the meat packing plants and military bases of San Antonio, a reconversion they found difficult to adjust to again after the glimpse of a better life and the transitory feeling of belonging to a society much larger than their insulated <u>colonias</u>. Perhaps more instrumental in sharpening their awareness of the injustice of their lot and of their rights to equal opportunity was the experience of sending their sons into the armed forces. As a Mexican American doctor in San Antonio put it:

> This war seems to have touched everyone, to have aroused feelings of unity in those who had never before thought of the United States as their country. Aliens as well as citizens were drafted, and those who stayed behind found they were called upon to participate in the war effort in one way or another.

If those at home felt that way, all the more reason for the veteran to return imbued with the resolve not to brook the disabilities of the status traditionally relegated to the Mexican American, and to positively seek integration with the larger society on an equal status basis. After their experiences in the army where, unlike the Negro, they were able to enjoy equal status with members of the dominant group and in many cases to develop satisfying relationships with them, the old dominant-subordinate group relationship was extremely difficult to adjust to. In McAllen, the father of one veteran said of his son:

> When he was in the navy he wrote that he wished he could be a human being again and not just another sailor. After he came home and found that things hadn't changed, he felt that he would rather be just another sailor than the kind of human being the Anglos treated him like. In fact, he got to thinking that he would have to be a sailor in order to feel like a human being. But he didn't go back into the navy.

In the year prior to the writer's stay in McAllen, Mexican American veterans in nearby Starr County formed a "New Party" whose candidates won the majority of the local offices from the political machine that had dominated the county for more than two generations, and in 1948, they made a clean sweep of all county offices. Early in 1948, veterans of the Corpus Christi area formed a protest organization called the American GI Forum, with a membership of 750, of which 95% was Mexican and 5% Anglo. According to the organization's constitution, its "main purpose is mutual helpfulness, striving to procure for all persons as well as veterans the equal privileges to which they are entitled under the laws of our country regardless of race, color or credd." Two months after its founding, the Forum, together with the local LULAC council, held a mass meeting to "protest segregation and discrimination against Latin Americans in the Corpus Christi area", and attacked discrimination in local school systems as well as poor living conditions in nearby labor camps, a protest that resulted in changes being made for the better in these places. By the Fall of 1948, GI Forums had sprung up in other towns of the region, all of them avowedly bent on initiating an active struggle against discrimination in their areas. In McAllen and San Antonio, no veteran's organizations had appeared by the time the study was terminated, but the "veteran protest" was evident nonetheless. In McAllen, a group of Mexican American veterans founded a Spanish-speaking newspaper for the <u>colonia</u> which soon dedicated itself to attacking the political accommodation of the established leadership.* In San Antonio, veterans were assuming active and important roles in the <u>colonia</u> organizations, particularly LULAC, and one of their number moved into a top position among the <u>colonia</u> leadership when he was elected to the city school board. In general, Mexican American veterans in McAllen and San Antonio were thinking of maintaining their independent vote, and of politics as a means of implementing their protest. As one of them said, "Latin American veterans who were prepared by Uncle Sam to be on their own are figuring to be on their own when the time comes to cast their vote in any election."

The Mexican American veterans are thus in the van of the struggle for full status and equal opportunity; they can make important contributions to their group's leadership; and they significantly represent lower class as well as middle class interests. Whether their auspicious beginning will bear fruit depends not only on how well they preserve their own determination and convictions, but on the reception they are accorded by the dominant group as well.

---

\* See <u>supra,</u> pp. 292-93.

Appendix A

A Note On Other Studies of the Spanish-Speaking Group
in the United States

Of the literature on Mexican American groups in the United States that include a large proportion of recent immigrants in their populations, Ruth Tuck's study of a southern California community,[*] and Paul S. Taylor's report on a South Texas community and his extensive studies of Mexican labor[**] have been most useful in the preparation of the present work. The work of Norman D. Humphrey on the Mexicans of Detroit[***] was also suggestive. Their relevance for this dissertation was enhanced by the fact that all of these writers have been concerned not only with the Mexican himself but with aspects of his relations with the Anglo American group. Since none of these studies were problem-oriented, they present no specific conclusions that can be compared with the findings of the present study, and a point-by-point comparison is hardly in order. However, it may be stated that there is little in their work that conflicts with this writer's findings, and much that is corroborative, as has been indicated at the appropriate places in the discussion. Aside from the researches of these social scientists, the careful work of Carey McWilliams on Mexican Americans in

---

[*] Not with the Fist, New York, 1946.

[**] An American-Mexican Frontier, Chapel Hill, 1934, and the several volumes of Mexican Labor in the United States, Berkeley, 1930-32.

[***] See bibliography.

the Southwest[*] helped to facilitate insights into various aspects of Mexican American life in a dominant Anglo community.[**]

The investigations of Spanish-speaking culture in New Mexico merit special attention in connection with the treatment accorded Mexican cultural values in this study. Of these, the most comprehensive and systematic formulation of Spanish-American cultural value orientations is to be found in Florence Kluckhohn's Los Atarquenos.[***] The writer was familiar with this study before undertaking field research in Texas, and it first called his attention to the Mexican American's time conceptions and fatalistic acceptance of life as it comes. Unfortunately, this work was not available either during the field research or during the period in which the dissertation was written, and only recently was it possible to re-read Dr. Kluckhohn's report. As has been repeatedly stated, the major problem on which the present study has focused has been that of intergroup relations, so that no consistent attempt was made by the writer at systematic formulation of cultural value orientations of the sort

---

[*] See bibliography

[**] Other research on Mexican Americans consulted in the preparation of this study will be found in the bibliography.

[***] Unpublished Ph.D. thesis, Radcliffe College, 1941.

that represents the central aim of Dr. Kluckhohn's work.
Moreover, the writer's formulations of dominant cultural
orientations and corresponding basic personality type are
not always made on the same level of abstraction as those
of Dr. Kluckhohn, nor are the as systematically related to each
other as they are in the study of Atarque. Nevertheless, with
a few exceptions, primarily in emphasis as a result of somewhat
differing interpretations, there is a surprisingly consistent
convergence in the findings of the two studies in this respect,
for the most part independently arrived at.

The principal points of agreement may be indicated briefly.
Dr. Kluckhohn's "mañana configuration",[*] which refers to the
Mexican's lack of conception of future time and emphasis on
present time, corresponds to a similar treatment in the present
study presented in connection with the Mexican American basic
personality type components of submissiveness and "primacy of
the mood".[**] Her formulation of acceptance as a sub-configuration
of the mañana configuration,[***] which refers to the Mexican's
lack of effort to change the order of events and acceptance of
life as it comes, has its parallel in the writer's treatment of
Mexican submissiveness and fatalism.[†] As in the Atarque study,
an implicit interdependent relationship between the Mexican's

---

[*]  Los Atarquenos, pp. 16-17.

[**] See supra, pp. 120-22.

[***] Op. cit., p. 19.

[†] Supra, pp. 116 ff. and 248-49.

time conceptions and the pattern of submissiveness, or acceptance as Dr. Kluckhohn terms it, is pointed out by the present writer. The "familia configuration" delineated in the Atarque study* is paralleled by the writer's formulation of familistic values and their relation to what has been called in this study the Mexican's "personalistic" sense of loyalty and obligation. Two of the principles of this configuration as defined by Dr. Kluckhohn, the loyalty to and responsibility for all family members and paternalism patterned in terms of general male dominance with the leading role accorded the father-person, receive prominent emphasis in the present study. Although there may be some disagreement as to the role these play in structuring interpersonal relations between Mexicans themselves and with non-Mexicans. The writer has some evidence that Dr. Kluckhohn's third principle, age seniority, as exemplified by the _hermano mayor_ pattern, formerly played a significant role in the system of relationships of the Mexican group studied by the writer, but the fact that little attention has been paid to it in the present study is a reflection of the weakening of this pattern due to acculturation and assimilation, as indicated above.*** Dr. Kluckhohn's "_comba_ configuration", which connotes the Mexican's "great love of a good time and his fondness for dramatizing all events",#

---

\* pp. 22-23.

\*\* Supra, pp. 109 ff.

\*\*\* p. 72.

\# Op. cit., p. 25.

converges at a number of points with the present writer's formulation of the "primacy of the mood" as a basic personality component of the Mexican American which the reader can confirm by reference to the appropriate passages in this study.*

Dr. Kluckhohn's other major cultural value configuration, "<u>costumbres</u> configuration", was not a prominent feature of the Mexican American culture in the areas studied as seen by the present writer. As in the case of the age seniority pattern, it is probable that the "thoroughgoing traditionalism", which Dr. Kluckhohn discerned as the source of legitimacy of the established order of Atarque society, has lost much of its strength and normative significance for the Valley Mexican as a consequence of his acculturative and assimilative experience with Anglo American culture. However, it still performs an important role in various aspects of Valley Mexican society, although it may no longer be considered a dominant configuration equivalent to that which prevailed in Atarque society. For example, as the writer has indicated,** traditionalism still figures prominently as a source of legitimation for status distinction in the Mexican American class structure, but is losing out in favor of the Anglo American definitions of status criteria.

---

\* See <u>supra</u>, pp. 120-23 for the explicit formulation of this component.

\*\* <u>Supra</u>, pp. 355-57.

Dr. Kluckhohn's systematization of cultural value orientations and their relation to the total culture, as exemplified in her Atarque study, which it may be repeated, was not a principal aim of the present study, has been carried a step further in her recent writings.[*] The writer had no access to these publications until after the present study had been completed, but it is possible that application of the classification of cultural orientations presented there to the findings of this study would help to clarify the relationships that exist between the value formulations attempted here as well as the perspective with which these are viewed in their relation to the total complex of Mexican American culture. Finally, it should be pointed out that Dr. Kluckhohn's classification of Mexican American dominant cultural orientations as manifesting a conception of human nature as good and evil, a subjugation to nature, a present time dimension, a "being" personality, and a combination of lineal and collateral in relational systems, are not inconsistent with the findings of this study. A review of the writer's discussion of Mexican American cultural values and personality type will show the same parallels that have been indicated in the comparison with the Atarque study, although actual convergence could

---

[*] "Dominant and Substitute Profiles of Cultural Orientations: Their Significance for the Analysis of Social Stratification", Social Forces, vol. 28, pp. 376-93 (1950), and "Dominant and Variant Cultural Value Orientations", from The Social Welfare Forum, New York, 1951, pp. 97-113.

perhaps only be definitely demonstrated by re-working the present formulations in the light of Dr. Kluckhohn's conceptualizations and with reference to her classification scheme.

The Tewa Basin Studies and related surveys of Spanish American villages in New Mexico[*] merit mention in this discussion. Although these studies were principally concerned with the play of economic forces on the Spanish American villagers, and cultural factors were only considered incidentally, they make a valuable contribution to the knowledge of Mexican American cultural orientations. The references to the Spanish Americans' reaction to the economic crises which confront them, crises brought about by overgrazing of pasture land, soil erosion, dwindling land resources aggravated by an increasing population, drought and insufficient water for irrigation, crop freezes, floods, and loss of outside markets for handicrafts, provide substantial documentation for what Dr. Kluckhohn has termed "subjugation to nature" as well as other of her formulations of Mexican cultural orientations.

Finally, a few words should be said about the Leonard and Loomis study of a New Mexican village.[**] The definition of Spanish-American value systems presented by these writers, although somewhat sketchy, places principal emphasis on familial loyalties, responsibilities, and duties as the core

---

[*] See the bibliography for the full references to these studies.
[**] *Culture of a Contemporary Rural Community, El Cerrito, New Mexico*, Washington, 1941.

of the dominant values.[*] The writers also point out the lack of a work ethic,[**] a characteristic of Mexican American orientations that has been extensively dealt with in the present study, and the "stoic fatalism" with which Mexicans accept hardship and crisis.[***]

Although the present study has been largely concerned with the significant local variations characteristic of Mexican culture and society as they are to be found in McAllen and San Antonio, this brief review of the literature on the Spanish-speaking group in other parts of the United States indicates that the broad outlines of Mexican American culture are probably the same no matter where the group's members are encountered. The filling in of these broad outlines, however, can only be accomplished by further systematic studies of Mexican Americans in the wide variety of situations in which they find themselves today in American culture.

---

[*] Ibid., pp. 17 ff., and 61.

[**] Loc. cit.

[***] Ibid., pp. 34-36.

# APPENDIX B

## Statistical Tables

## Table I

### McAllen Census

### City Directory, 1947

|  | Anglo | Latin |
|---|---|---|
| Single Male | 617 | 888 |
| Single Female | 341 | 651 |
| Married Male | 2034 | 1758 |
| Married Female | 2034 | 1758 |
| Widow or Widower | 460 | 468 |
| Children under 18 | 1925 | 4060 |
|  | 7411 | 9583 |
| Group Ratio | 43.6% | 56.4% |
| Average No. of Children under 18 per Family | .9 | 2.3 |
| Home Owners | 1256 | 1029 |
| Renters | 863 | 671 |
|  | 2119 | 1700 |
| Telephone Subscribers | 1273 | 68 |
| Non-Subscribers | 846 | 1632 |

## Table II

### McAllen

### Corporation Court Offenses

January 1947

| Nature of Offense | Latin | Anglo | Fine |
|---|---|---|---|
| Affray | 1 | 0 | $ 10.00 |
| Careless Driving | 1 | 4 | 10.00 |
| | 1 | 0 | 25.00 |
| | 5 | 2 | 50.00 |
| | 0 | 1 | 100.00 |
| Defective Lights | 1 | 0 | 10.00 |
| Disturbing Peace | 5 | 4 | 10.00 |
| | 2 | 0 | 25.00 |
| Drunk | 26 | 11 | 10.00 |
| | 0 | 2 | 25.00 |
| | 1 | 0 | 50.00 |
| Drunk-Disturbing Peace in Public Place | 1 | 0 | 100.00 |
| Left Turn | 0 | 2 | 3.00 |
| No Operator's License | 9 | 8 | 10.00 |
| | 1 | 0 | 50.00 |
| Overparking | 33 | 304 | 1.00 |
| | 1 | 3 | 2.00 |
| | 0 | 1 | 4.00 |
| | 0 | 1 | 3.00 |
| | 1 | 1 | 1.00 |
| Run Light | 0 | 1 | 3.00 |
| Run Stop | 9 | 47 | 10.00 |
| | 1 | 0 | 25.00 |
| | 1 | 0 | 3.00 |
| | 4 | 50 | 10.00 |
| Speeding | 0 | 1 | 20.00 |
| Vagrancy | 0 | 1 | 25.00 |

May 1947

| | | | |
|---|---|---|---|
| Affray | 0 | 0 | 0.00 |
| Careless Driving | 0 | 2 | 100.00 |
| | 1 | 1 | 50.00 |
| | 2 | 0 | 25.00 |

## Table II
(Continued)

| Nature of Offense | Latin | Anglo | Fine |
|---|---|---|---|
| Defective Lights | 3 | 0 | $10.00 |
| Disturbing Peace | 2 | 0 | 10.00 |
| Drunk | 22 | 7 | 10.00 |
|  | 1 | 1 | 50.00 |
| Left Turn | 0 | 1 | 10.00 |
|  | 1 | 0 | 3.00 |
| No Operator's license | 9 | 3 | 10.00 |
|  | 1 | 0 | 15.00 |
| Overparking | 51 | 438 | 1.00 |
| Petty Theft | 4 (3 fem.) | 0 | 25.00 |
|  | 1 (fem.) | 0 | 10.00 |
| Run Light | 0 | 0 | 0.00 |
| Run Stop | 0 | 4 | 5.00 |
|  | 1 | 0 | 10.00 |
| Speeding | 8 | 17 | 10.00 |
| Vagrancy | 0 | 0 | 0.00 |
| Simple Assault | 0 | 1 | 10.00 |

September 1947

| Nature of Offense | Latin | Anglo | Fine |
|---|---|---|---|
| Affray | 2 | 2 | 25.00 |
| Abusive Language | 4 (fem.) | 0 | 10.00 |
| Careless Driving | 2 | 0 | 10.00 |
|  | 4 | 5 | 50.00 |
|  | 0 | 1 | 100.00 |
| Defective Lights | 6 | 2 | 10.00 |
| Disturbing Peace | 4 (1 fem.) | 0 | 10.00 |
|  | 1 | 0 | 15.00 |
|  | 2 | 2 | 25.00 |
| Drunk | 53 | 17 (1 fem.) | 10.00 |
|  | 1 | 0 | 25.00 |
|  | 1 | 0 | 50.00 |
| Left Turn | 0 | 1 | 3.00 |
|  | 0 | 1 | 10.00 |
| No Operator's License | 16 | 5 | 10.00 |
|  | 3 | 0 | 25.00 |
|  | 1 | 0 | 50.00 |
| Overparking | 38 | 348 |  |
| Petty Theft | 1 | 0 | 25.00 |
|  | 1 | 0 | 5.00 |
| Run Light | 1 | 0 | 3.00 |
|  | 1 | 0 | 5.00 |
| Run Stop | 5 | 16 | 5.00 |
|  | 0 | 1 | 10.00 |
|  | 0 | 1 | 25.00 |
| Speeding | 11 | 60 | 10.00 |
|  | 1 | 2 | 25.00 |
|  | 0 | 1 | 20.00 |
| Vagrancy | 1 (1 fem.) | 0 | 25.00 |
| Simple Assault | 0 | 0 | 0.00 |

Table II
(Continued)

| Nature of Offense January 1948 | Latin | Anglo | Fine |
|---|---|---|---|
| Affray | 1 | 2 | 25.00 |
| Abusive Language | 0 | 0 | 0.00 |
| Careless Driving | 2 | 0 | 10.00 |
|  | 1 | 0 | 50.00 |
|  | 1 | 1 | 75.00 |
|  | 2 | 2 | 100.00 |
|  | 2 | 0 | 25.00 |
| Defective Lights | 8 | 0 | 10.00 |
| Disturbing Peace | 5 (1 fem.) | 0 | 10.00 |
|  | 8 | 0 | 25.00 |
|  | 1 | 1 | 50.00 |
| Drunk | 29 (1 fem.) | 8 | 10.00 |
|  | 1 | 1 | 25.00 |
|  | 0 | 1 | 50.00 |
| Display Deadly Weapon | 1 | 0 | 100.00 |
| Drunk and Disturbing Peace | 1 | 1 | 10.00 |
|  | 2 | 0 | 25.00 |
|  | 2 | 0 | 50.00 |
| Gaming | 6 | 0 | 10.00 |
| Indecent Exposure | 0 | 1 | 10.00 |
| No Operator's License | 9 | 4 | 10.00 |
|  | 1 | 0 | 20.00 |
| Overparking | 26 | 340 |  |
| Petty Theft | 2 (fem.) | 0 | 25.00 |
| Run Light | 1 | 3 | 5.00 |
|  | 0 | 1 | 3.00 |
| Run Stop | 5 | 12 | 5.00 |
| Simple Assault | 0 | 0 | 0.00 |
| Speeding | 11 | 23 | 10.00 |
|  | 0 | 1 | 20.00 |
|  | 0 | 1 | 25.00 |

## Table III
### Incidence of Crime
### September 1940 - January 1948, Volume 5
### Jury Cases
### Judgement of Conviction on Plea of Guilty

| Nature of Offense | Latin | Anglo | Sentence |
|---|---|---|---|
| Rape | 8 | 0 | 5 years |
| Murder | 2 | 0 | 5 " |
|  | 3 | 0 | 10 " |
|  | 1 | 0 | 15 " |
|  | 1 | 0 | 2-20 " |
|  | 2 | 0 | 25 " |
|  | 1 | 0 | Life |
| Robbery by Firearms | 3 | 2 | 5 " |
|  | 1 | 0 | 15 " |
| Cattle Theft | 1 | 0 | 2 " |
| Possession of Marihuana | 1 | 0 | 2 " |
| Murder without Malice | 1 | 0 | 10 " |

### March 1940 - March 1948, Volume 5
### Jury Cases
### Judgement of Conviction on Plea of Not Guilty

| Nature of Offense | Latin | Anglo | Sentence |
|---|---|---|---|
| Sodomy | 0 | 1 | 5 years |
| Murder | 1 | 0 | 5 " |
|  | 1 | 0 | Life |
|  | 1 | 0 | Death |
| Murder without Malice | 1 | 0 | 4 years |
|  | 0 | 1 (fem.) | 3 " |
| Accomplice to Burglary | 0 | 1 | 2 " |
| Burglary and Theft | 0 | 1 | Life |
| Murder in Producing Abortion | 1 (fem.) | 0 | 2 years |
| Burglary | 1 | 1 | 2 " |
|  | 0 | 1 (Habitual) | Life |
| Theft from the Person | 0 | 1 (2nd Of.) | 12 years |
| Seduction | 1 | 0 | 2 years |
| Possession of Marihuana | 1 | 1 | 2 " |
| Theft of Property more than $5 and less than $10 | 1 | 0 | 2 " $500 |
| Rape | 1 | 0 | 5 years |
| Passing a Forged Instrument | 1 | 0 | 2 " |
| Theft by Bailee | 0 | 1 (fem.) | 2 " |

MINUTES OF CRIMINAL DISTRICT COURT - HIDALGO COUNTY

## Table IV

### INCIDENCE OF CRIME

### February 1947 - January 1948, Volume 7

### Jury Waived

### Judgement of Conviction on Plea of Guilty

| Nature of Offense | Latin | Anglo | Sentence |
|---|---|---|---|
| Driving while Intoxicated | 1 | 1 | 5 Days, $50 |
|  | 2 | 3 | 5 " $ & Costs |
|  | 1 | 2 | 5 " " " |
|  |  |  | License suspended 6 months |
|  | 0 | 1 | 5 days, $100 |
|  | 0 | 1 | 5 " " & costs |
|  | 1 | 0 | 90 days $150 |
|  | 0 | 1 | Not to exceed 2yrs |
| Theft over $50 | 0 | 1 | 2 years |
|  | 1 | 1 | 5 " |
| Burglary | 2 | 1 | 2 " |
|  | 2 | 3 | 3 " |
|  | 2 | 3 | 5 " |
| Chicken Theft | 1 (4 counts) | 0 | 1 year |
|  | 1 (5 ") | 0 | 1 " |
|  | 1 (6 ") | 0 | 1 " |
|  | 1 (2 ") | 0 | 1 " |
| Forgery | 1 (3 ") | 2 (3) | 3 years |
|  | 1 (2 ") | 0 | 3 " |
|  | 1 | 1 | 2 " |
| Possession of Marihuana | 6 | 0 | 2 " |
| Sodomy | 1 | 0 | 5 " |
| Bigamy | 0 | 1 | 2 " |
| Robbery | 2 | 0 | 5 " |
| Cattle Theft | 2 (3 cts.) | 0 | 2 " |
|  | 1 (2 " ) | 0 | 2 " |
|  | 2 | 0 | 2 " |
| Murder | 1 | 0 | 5 " |
| Assault with Attempt to Rape | 0 | 1 | 2 " |
| Attempted Burglary | 0 | 1 | 3 " |

Table IV
(Continued)

February 1947 - January 1948, Volume 7

Suspended Sentence

Judgment of Conviction on Plea of Guilty

| Nature of Offense | Latin | Anglo | Sentence |
|---|---|---|---|
| Burglary | 0 | 1 | 2-3 years, Rel. $500 |
|  | 0 | 1 | 3 " " " |
|  | 3 | 0 | 2-5 " " " |
| Forgery | 2 | 1 | 2-5 " " " |
| Desertion of wife and children | 0 | 1 | 2 " " " |
| Murder without Malice | 1 | 1 | 2-5 " " " |
| Driving while intoxicated resulting in Homicide | 1 | 0 | 2-3 " " " |
| Sodomy | 0 | 1 | 2 " " " |

Table V

MORTALITY RATES BY AGE, SEX & "RACE"

1947

(Extracted from information compilations of the Hidalgo County Health Unit)
Not intended for publication

| DISEASE | SEX Male | SEX Female | "RACE" Anglo | "RACE" Latin | TOTAL |
|---|---|---|---|---|---|
| Infectious and Parasitic | 1 | 0 | 0 | 1 | 1 |
| Typhoid and paratyphoid | 0 | 0 | 0 | 0 | 0 |
| Plague | 0 | 0 | 0 | 0 | 0 |
| Scarlet fever | 0 | 0 | 0 | 0 | 0 |
| Whooping cough | 4 | 3 | 0 | 7 | 7 |
| Diphtheria | 2 | 1 | 0 | 3 | 3 |
| Tuberculosis | 58 | 65 | 5 | 118 | 123 |
| Malaria | 0 | 2 | 0 | 3 | 3 |
| Syphilis | 5 | 3 | 1 | 6 | 7 |
| Influenza | 3 | 1 | 1 | 3 | 4 |
| Measles | 0 | 0 | 0 | 0 | 0 |
| Typhus fever | 2 | 0 | 2 | 0 | 2 |
| Other infectious and parasitic | 8 | 4 | 0 | 12 | 12 |
| Dysentery | 29 | 41 | 2 | 67 | 69 |
| II Cancer and other malignant tumors | 30 | 30 | 28 | 31 | 59 |
| Non-malignant and unspecified tumors | 3 | - | 1 | 2 | 3 |
| III Chronic rheumatism and gout IV & V | 1 | 0 | 0 | 1 | 1 |
| Diabetes mellitus | 7 | 6 | 7 | 6 | 13 |
| Chronic or ac. alcoholism | 0 | 0 | 0 | 0 | 0 |
| Aertaminoses, other gen-diseases, of blood, chronic poisonings | 3 | 11 | 2 | 12 | 14 |
| VI Meningitis and diseases of the spinal cord | 3 | 4 | 0 | 7 | 7 |
| Intracranial lesions, vascular origin | 25 | 20 | 20 | 26 | 46 |
| Other diseases of the nervous system | 12 | 6 | 3 | 15 | 18 |

Table V
(Continued)

| DISEASE | SEX Male | SEX Female | "RACE" Anglo | "RACE" Latin | TOTAL |
|---|---|---|---|---|---|
| VII Disease of the Heart | 86 | 43 | 64 | 67 | 131 |
| Other diseases of the circulatory system | 14 | 14 | 22 | 6 | 28 |
| VIII Bronchitis | 2 | 2 | 0 | 4 | 4 |
| Pneumonia & bronchopneumonia | 58 | 58 | 10 | 105 | 116 |
| Other diseases of the respiratory system | 7 | 8 | 1 | 14 | 15 |
| IX Diarrhea and enteritis | 58 | 42 | 3 | 97 | 100 |
| Appendicitis | 3 | 0 | 0 | 3 | 3 |
| Diseases of the livery & biliary passages | 8 | 7 | 6 | 9 | 15 |
| Other diseases of the digestive system | 7 | 8 | 6 | 9 | 15 |
| X Nephritis | 16 | 15 | 9 | 22 | 31 |
| Other diseases of the urogenital system | 6 | 3 | 4 | 5 | 9 |
| XI Puerperal Infection | 0 | 5 | 0 | 5 | 5 |
| Other diseases of pregnancy, childbirth, and the Peurperium | 0 | 5 | 0 | 5 | 5 |
| XI & XIII Diseases of skin, cellular tissues, bones, and organs of movement | 0 | 0 | 0 | 0 | 0 |
| XIV & XV Congenital malformation and devility, premature birth, and diseases peculiar to 1st year of life | 73 | 56 | 12 | 116 | 128 |
| XVI Senility | 13 | 17 | 9 | 21 | 30 |
| XVII Suicide | 4 | 0 | 1 | 3 | 4 |
| Homicide | 7 | 0 | 1 | 6 | 7 |
| Automobile accidents | 17 | 9 | 8 | 16 | 24 |
| Other violent or accidental deaths | 61 | 22 | 22 | 59 | 81 |
| XVIII Causes of death, ill-defined, unknown, unspecified | 61 | 42 | 23 | 80 | 103 |
| No cause of death stated | 29 | 20 | 10 | 39 | 49 |

Table VI

RECORD OF LIVE BIRTHS 1947[*]
Hidalgo County Health Unit

|  |  |  | SEX |  | TYPE OF |  |  | OBSTETRICAL |  |  | CARE |  |  |
|---|---|---|---|---|---|---|---|---|---|---|---|---|---|
|  |  |  |  |  | Hospital |  | Home | Physician |  | Home Midwife |  | Other |  |
| Month | Latin | Anglo | Male | Female | Latin | Anglo | Latin | Anglo | Latin | Anglo | Latin | Anglo |
| January | 466 | 94 | 279 | 271 | 50 | 82 | 190 | 10 | 207 | 1 | 14 | 0 |
| Stillbirth | 5 | 2 | 5 | 2 | 1 | 0 | 2 | 1 | 3 | 0 |  |  |
| February | 493 | 84 | 272 | 253 | 38 | 76 | 181 | 6 | 200 | 1 | 19 | 0 |
| Stillbirth | 6 | 1 | 3 | 4 | 2 | 1 | 5 |  |  |  |  |  |
| March | 431 | 79 | 264 | 247 | 26 | 70 | 184 | 12 | 202 | 0 | 17 | 0 |
| Stillbirth | 6 | 0 | 5 | 1 | 0 | 0 | 4 | 0 | 1 | 0 | 1 | 0 |
| April | 428 | 88 | 268 | 247 | 40 | 71 | 151 | 15 | 212 | 0 | 26 | 0 |
| Stillbirth | 2 | 1 | 3 | 0 | 1 | 1 | 0 | 0 | 1 | 0 | 0 | 0 |
| May | 399 | 75 | 243 | 225 | 36 | 57 | 164 | 9 | 190 | 0 | 10 | 1 |
| Stillbirth | 8 | 1 | 6 | 3 | 3 | 1 | 3 | 0 | 0 | 0 | 2 | 0 |
| June | 395 | 82 | 262 | 217 | 38 | 60 | 168 | 22 | 179 | 0 | 11 | 0 |
| Stillbirth | 6 | 1 | 3 | 4 | 2 | 0 | 2 | 1 | 1 | 0 | 1 | 0 |
| July | 412 | 86 | 270 | 227 | 40 | 70 | 186 | 14 | 171 | 0 | 14 | 0 |
| Stillbirth | 5 | 1 | 3 | 3 | 2 | 2 | 2 | 0 | 0 | 0 | 0 | 0 |
| August | 503 | 96 | 331 | 270 | 50 | 85 | 224 | 8 | 215 | 0 | 13 | 0 |
| Stillbirth | 5 | 2 | 5 | 2 | 2 | 2 | 3 | 0 | 0 | 0 | 0 | 0 |
| September | 435 | 102 | 277 | 255 | 50 | 70 | 170 | 29 | 212 | 0 | 5 | 0 |
| Stillbirth | 2 | 0 | 1 | 1 | 2 | 0 | 0 | 0 | 0 | 0 | 0 | 0 |
| October | 410 | 128 | 260 | 284 | 34 | 113 | 203 | 15 | 167 | 0 | 8 | 0 |
| Stillbirth | 6 | 0 | 2 | 4 | 1 | 0 | 2 | 0 | 2 | 0 | 1 | 0 |
| November | 455 | 93 | 295 | 248 | 41 | 62 | 195 | 28 | 205 | 0 | 16 | 0 |
| Stillbirth | 2 | 0 | 2 | 0 | 0 | 0 | 0 | 0 | 2 | 0 | 0 | 0 |
| December | 485 | 82 | 288 | 269 | 56 | 81 | 204 | 7 | 208 | 1 | 9 | 0 |
| Stillbirth | 3 | k | 4 | 0 | 2 | 1 | 1 | 0 | 0 | 0 | 0 | 0 |

[*] The disagreements in this table were encountered in the original.

Selected Bibliography

Austin American, Austin, Texas.

Barker, George C., Social Functions of Language in a Mexican-American Community. Unpublished Ph.D. thesis, University of Chicago, 1947.

Brenner, Anita, Idols behind Altars. New York: Payson and Clarke Limited, 1929.

Brownsville Herald, Brownsville, Texas.

Centers, Richard, The Psychology of Social Classes. Princeton: Princeton University Press, 1949.

Cerwin, Herbert, These Are the Mexicans. New York: Reynal and Hitchcock, 1947.

Child, Irvin L., Italian or American? New Haven: Yale University Press, 1943.

City Directory, McAllen, Texas. Harlingen, Texas: B. A. Wilmot, 1947.

Corpus Christi Caller, Corpus Christi, Texas.

District Court, Bexar County, Texas, 45th Judicial District, I.N. Clifton, et al, vs. Abdon Salazar Puente, et al, case no. F-44, 264, April 27, 1948.

Dobie, J. Frank, A Vaquero of the Brush Country. Dallas: The Southwest Press, 1929.

Dollard, John, Caste and Class in a Southern Town. New Haven: Yale University Press, 1937.

-----, "Hostility and Fear in Social Life". Social Forces, vol. 17, pp. 15-26 (1938-39).

Drake, St. Clair and Cayton, Horace R., Black Metropolis. New York: Harcourt, Brace and Company, 1945.

Edinburg Valley Review, Edinburg, Texas.

El Mundo, McAllen, Texas.

Gamio, Manuel, "Cultural Patterns in Modern Mexico". Quarterly Journal of Inter-American Relations, vol. 1, pp. 49-61 (1939).

-----, Mexican Immigration to the United States. Chicago: University of Chicago Press, 1930.

-----, Number, Origin and Geographic Distribution of the Mexican Immigrants in the United States. Institute of Pacific Relations,

1929. (Mimeographed.)

-----, The Mexican Immigrant. Chicago: University of Chicago Press, 1931.

Garner, Claud, Wetback. New York: Coward McCann, Inc., 1947.

Goldschmidt, Walter, "Social Class in America - A Critical Review." American Anthropologist, vol. 52, pp. 483-98 (1950)

Gonzalez, Jovita, Social Life in Cameron, Starr, and Zapata Counties. Unpublished M.A. thesis, University of Texas, 1930.

de Grazia, Sebastian, The Political Community. Chicago: University of Chicago Press, 1948.

Griffith, Beatrice, American Me. Boston: Houghton Mifflin Company, 1948.

Gruening, Ernest, Mexico and its Heritage. New York: The Century Company, 1928.

Handlin, Oscar, Boston's Immigrants. Cambridge: Harvard University Press, 1941.

Herring, Hubert and Katharine Terrill (editors), The Genius of Mexico. New York: Committee on Cultural Relations with Latin America, 1931.

Herring, Hubert and Herbert Weinstock (editors), Renascent Mexico. New York: Covici-Friede, 1935.

Herskovits, Melville J., Acculturation. New York: J. J. Augustin, 1938.

Hoehler, Fred K. et al, Public Welfare Survey of San Antonio, Texas. Chicago: American Public Welfare Association, 1940. (Mimeographed.)

Humphrey, Norman D., "Social Stratification in a Mexican Town." Unpublished manuscript (No date.).

-----, "The Changing Structure of the Detroit Mexican Family", American Sociological Review, vol. 9, pp. 622-26 (1944)

-----, "The Cultural Background of the Mexican Immigrant". Rural Sociology, pp. 364-77 (1943).

-----, "The Education and Language of Detroit Mexicans", Journal of Educational Sociology, vol. 17, pp. 534-42 (1944).

-----, "The Generic Folk Culture of Mexico". Rural Sociology, vol. 8, pp. 364-77 (1943).

-----, "The Stereotype and the Social Types of Mexican-American Youths", Journal of Social Psychology, vol. 22, pp. 69-78 (1945).

Hunter, Monica, Reaction to Conquest. London: Oxford University Press, 1936.

Johnson, Charles S., Patterns of Negro Segregation. New York: Harper and Brothers, 1943.

Jones, Robert C., Mexican War Workers in the United States. Washington: Pan American Union, Division of Labor and Social Information, 1945.

Kardiner, Abram, The Individual and His Society. New York: Columbia University Press, 1939.

-----, The Psychological Frontiers of Society. New York: Columbia University Press, 1945.

Kibbe, Pauline R., Latin Americans in Texas. Albuquerque: University of New Mexico Press, 1946.

Kluckhohn, Clyde, Navaho Witchcraft. Cambridge: Peabody Museum 1944.

-----, "Patterning as Exemplified in Navaho Culture". In Spier et al, Language, Culture, and Personality. Menasha: George Banta Publishing Company, 1941, pp. 109-30.

Kluckhohn, Florence R., "Dominant and Substitute Profiles of Cultural Orientations: Their Significance for the Analysis of Social Stratification", Social Forces, vol. 28, pp. 376-393 (1950).

-----, "Dominant and Variant Cultural Value Orientations" from The Social Welfare Forum. New York: Columbia University Press, 1951, pp. 97-113.

-----, Los Atarquenos. Unpublished Ph.D. thesis, Radcliffe College, 1941.

-----, "The Participant-Observer Technique in Small Communities". American Journal of Sociology, vol. 46, pp. 331-43 (1940).

La Prensa, San Antonio, Texas.

Leonard, Olen and Loomis, C.P. Culture of a Contemporary Rural Community, El Cerrito, New Mexico. Washington: U. S. Department of Agriculture, Bureau of Agricultural Economics, 1941.

Linton, Ralph (editor), Acculturation in Seven American Indian Tribes. New York: D. Appleton-Century Company, Inc., 1940.

Lower Rio Grande Valley Chamber of Commerce, Reports on Planting and Maturity Dates, Population, Farm Cash Income, and Retail SalesData. (Mimeographed.)

LULAC News, San Antonio, Texas.

Lynd, Robert S. and Helen M. Lynd, *Middletown in Transition*. New York: Harcourt, Brace and Company, 1937.

MacIver, Robert M. (editor), *Group Relations and Group Antagonisms*. New York: Harper and Brothers, 1944.

-----, *The More Perfect Union*. New York: The Macmillan Company, 1948.

McBride, George M., *The Land Systems of Mexico*. New York: American Geographical Society, 1923.

McWilliams, Carey, *Brothers under the Skin*. Boston: Little, Brown and Company, 1943.

-----, *Factories in the Field*. Boston: Little, Brown and Company, 1939.

-----, *North from Mexico*. Philadelphia: J.B. Lippincott Company, 1949.

de Madariaga, Salvador, *Englishmen, Frenchmen, Spaniards*. London: Oxford University Press, 1931.

Menefee, Selden C., *Mexican Migratory Workers of South Texas*. Washington: U. S. Government Printing Office, 1941.

Menefee, Selden C. and O.C. Cassmore, *The Pecan Shellers of San Antonio*. Washington: U. S. Government Printing Office, 1940.

Merton, Robert K. "Intermarriage and the Social Structure", *Psychiatry*, vol. 4, pp. 361-374 (1941)

*Mission Times*, Mission, Texas.

Murphy, Gardner, *Personality*. New York: Harper and Brothers, 1947.

Myrdal, Gunnar, *An American Dilemma*. New York: Harper and Brothers, 1944.

Northrop, F.S.C., *The Meeting of East and West*. New York: The Macmillan Company, 1946.

Park, Robert E. and Herbert A. Miller, *Old World Traits Transplanted*. New York: Harper and Brothers, 1921.

Parkes, Henry Bamford, *A History of Mexico*. Boston: Houghton Mifflin Company, 1938.

Parsons, Elsie Clews, *Mitla*, Chicago: The University of Chicago Press, 1936.

Parsons, Talcott, *Essays in Sociological Theory: Pure and Applied*. Glencoe: The Free Press, 1949.

-----, "Certain Primary Sources and Patterns of Aggression in the Social Structure of the Western World", *Psychiatry*, vol. 10, pp. 167-181 (1947)

-----, "Racial and Religious Differences as Factors in Group Tensions." In Bryson, Finkelstein, MacIver (editors), *Approaches to National Unity*. New York: Conference on Science, Philosophy and Religion, 1945.

-----, *The Structure of Social Action*. Glencoe: The Free Press, 1949.

Perales, Alonso ., *Are We Good Neighbors?* San Antonio: Artes Graficas, 1948.

Peyton, Green, *San Antonio: City in the Sun*. New York: McGraw-Hill Book Company, Inc., 1946.

Pierce, Frank C., *A Brief History of the Lower Rio Grande Valley*. Menasha: George Banta Publishing Company, 1917.

Powdermaker, Hortense, *After Freedom*. New York: The Viking Press, 1939.

Redfield, Robert, *Tepoztlan: A Mexican Village*. Chicago: University of Chicago Press, 1930.

-----, The Folk Culture of Yucatan. Chicago: University of Chicago Press, 1941.

Rosenzweig, Saul, "An Outline of Frustration Theory". In J. McV. Hunt (editor), *Personality and the Behavior Disorders*. New York: The Ronald Press Company, 1944, vol. 1, pp. 379-88.

*San Antonio Express*, San Antonio, Texas.

*San Antonio Light*, San Antonio, Texas.

*San Antonio News*, San Antonio, Texas.

Sanchez, George I., "Address to Texas Good Neighbor Commission." Austin, March 26, 1948. (Mimeographed.)

Sanchez, George I. and Saunders, Lyle, *"Wetbacks" - A Preliminary Report*. University of Texas, 1949. (Mimeographed.)

Scott, Florence J., *Historical Heritage of the Lower Rio Grande*. San Antonio: The Naylor Company, 1937.
Sixty-ninth Congress, First Session, Seasonal Agricultural Laborers from Mexico. Hearing before the Committee on Immigration and Naturalization, House of Representatives, Washington, 1926.

Sixty-sixth Congress, Second Session, Temporary Admission of Illiterate Mexican Laborers. Hearings before the Committee on Immigration and Naturalization, House of Representatives, Washington, 1920.

Stilwell, Hart, Border City. London: Hurst and Blackett Limited. (No date.)

Sutherland, Robert L., Color, Class, and Personality. Washington: American Council on Education, 1942.

Tannenbaum, Frank, Peace by Revolution. New York: Columbia University Press, 1933.

-----, Whither Latin America? New York: Thomas Y Crowell Company, 1934.

Taylor, Paul S., A Spanish-Mexican Peasant Community: Arandas in Jalisco, Mexico. Berkeley: University of California Press, 1933.

-----, An American-Mexican Frontier. Chapel Hill: University of North Carolina Press, 1934.

-----, Mexican Labor in the United States. Berkeley: University of California Press.
----- Dimmit County, Winter Garden District, South Texas. 1930.
----- Bethlehem, Pennsylvania. 1931.
----- Chicago and the Calumet Region. 1932.

Texas Spectator, Austin, Texas.

The Pan American, San Antonio, Texas.

Thomas, W.I., "The Psychology of Race Prejudice." American Journal of Sociology, vol. 9, pp. 593-611 (1904).

Toor, Frances, A Treasury of Mexican Folkways. New York: Crown Publishers, 1947.

Tuck, Ruth D., Not with the Fist. New York: Harcourt, Brace and

Tumin, Melvin, "Reciprocity and Stability of Caste in Guatemala." American Sociological Review, vol. 14, pp. 17-25 (1949)

U. S. Bureau of the Census, Fifteenth Census of the United States: 1930. Agriculture, vol. 3. Part 2: The Southern States.

-----, Fifteenth Census of the United States: 1930. Population Bulletin, Second Series, Texas, Composition and Characteristics of the Population.

----------------, *Fifteenth Census of the United States:* 1930. Population, Color or Race, Nativity and Parentage.

-----, *Fourteenth Census of the United States:* 1920. Population. Texas. Table 12.

-----, *ixteenth Census of the United States:* 1940. Agriculture. Texas. First Series; Second Series; Third Series.

-----, *Sixteenth Census of the United States:* Census of Business: 1939, Retail Trade. Texas.

-----, *Sixteenth Census of the United States:* Census of Business, 1939, Wholesale Trade. Texas.

-----, *Sixteenth Census of the United States:* 1940. Drainage of Agricultural Lands. Texas.

-----, *Sixteenth Census of the United States:* 1940. Housing. Texas. First Series; upplement to the First Series, San Antonio.

-----, *Sixteenth Census of the United States:* 1940. Irrigation of Agricultural Lands. Texas.

-----, *Sixteenth Census of the United States:* 1940. Population. Texas. First Series; econd Series; Third Series; Fourth Series.

-----, *Sixteenth Census of the United States:* 1940. Population, vol. 2, part 6. Pennsylvania-Texas.

-----, *Thirteenth Census of the United States:* 1910. Population. Texas. Second Series.

-----, *Twelfth Census of the United States:* 1900. Population. Texas. Table 34.

U. S. Department of Agriculture, Soil Conservation ervice, *Destruction of Villages at San Marcial.* Albuquerque: Regional Bulletin No. 38, Conservation Economics eries No. 11, 1937.

-----, *Handling of a Cash Crop* (Chili). Albuquerque: Regional Bulletin No. 46, Conservation Economics Series No. 19, 1937.

-----, *Preliminary Report on Concho.* Albuquerque: Regional Bulletin No. 29, Conservation Economics Series No. 2, 1935.

-----, *Tewa Basin Study, Volume II, The Spanish American Villages.* Albuquerque: Economic Surveys Division, 1939.

-----, *Village Dependence on Migratory Labor in the Upper Rio Grande Area,* Regional Bulletin No. 47, Conservation Economics Series No. 20, 1937.

U. S. Department of Labor, Bureau of Labor Statistics, Labor Unionism in American Agriculture. Washington: U. S. Government Printing Office, 1945.

Valley Evening Monitor, McAllen, Texas.

Valley Morning Star, Harlingen, Texas.

Vasconcelos, Jose and Manuel Gamio, Aspects of Mexican Civilization. Chicago: University of Chicago Press, 1926.

Warburton, Amber Arthun, Wood and Crane, The Work and Welfare of Children of Agricultural Laborers in Hidalgo County, Texas. Washington: U. S. Government Printing Office, 1943.

Ware, Caroline F., Greenwich Village. Boston: Houghton Mifflin Company, 1935.

Webb, Walter Prescott, The Texas Rangers. Boston, Houghton Mifflin Company, 1935.

Weeks, O. Douglas, "The League of United Latin American Citizens: A Texas-Mexican Civic Organization." Reprinted from the Southwestern Political and Social Science Quarterly, December, 1929.

-----, "The Texas-Mexican and the Politics of South Texas". American Political Science Review, vol. 24, pp. 606-27 (1930).

West, James, Plainville, U.S.A. New York: Columbia University Press, 1945.

Whetten, Nathan L., Rural Mexico. Chicago: University of Chicago Press, 1948.

White, Owen P., Texas: An Informal Biography. New York: G.P. Putnam's Sons, 1945.

Williams, Robin M., The Reduction of Intergroup Tensions. New York: SSRC Bulletin No. 57, 1947.

Wilson, Godfrey and Monica Wilson, The Analysis of Social Change. Cambridge: Cambridge University Press, 1945.

Winters, Jet C., A Report on the Health and Nutrition of Mexicans Living in Texas. Austin: The University of Texas, 1931.

Wirth, Louis (editor), Eleven Twenty-Six: A Decade of Social Science Research. Chicago: The University of Chicago Press, 1940.

Young, Donald, Research Memorandum on Minority Peoples in the Depression. New York: SSRC Bulletin No. 31, 1937.

Numbered Footnotes

## Chapter I

1. Pierce, Frank C., *A Brief History of the Lower Rio Grande Valley*, Menasha, Wisconsin, 1917, pp. 128 and 132.

2. See Scott, Florence Johnson, *Historical Heritage of the Lower Rio Grande*, San Antonio, 1937, a study of the old Spanish

3. *Ibid.*, p. 165.

4. Loc. cit.

5. Taylor, Paul S., *An American-Mexican Frontier*, Chapel Hill, 1934, p. 102.

6. See Kluckhohn, Florence R., "The Participant-Observer Technique in Small Communities", *American Journal of Sociology*, vol. 46, pp. 331-43 (November, 1940), for a comprehensive discussion of the aspects of the application of the technique touched upon here. On this point, see especially p. 339.

7. *Ibid.*, p. 338.

## Chapter II

1. See Parsons, Talcott, "An Analytical Approach to the Theory of Social Stratification". *American Journal of Sociology*, vol. 45, pp. 841-62 (1940).

## Chapter III

1. Whetten, Nathan, *Rural Mexico*, Chicago, 1948, pp. 396-7, Gruening, Ernest, *Mexico and its Heritage*, New York, 1928, p. 250, Humphrey, Norman D., "The Cultural Background of the Mexican Immigrant", *Rural Sociology*, vol. 13, pp. 239-55 (1948).

2. See Whetten, *op. cit.*, pp. 398-400, Parsons, E.C., *Mitla*, Chicago, 1936, pp. 69-70 and 524-5, Tuck, R.D., *Not With the Fist*, New York, 1946, pp. 80, and Tannenbaum, Frank, *Peace by Revolution*, New York, 1933, pp. 93-94.

3. See Cerwin, Herbert, *These Are the Mexicans*, New York, 1947, p. 30.

4. On this discussion of religion in Mexico, cf. Whetten, *op. cit.*, pp. 455 ff., Gamio, Manuel, *Mexican Immigration to the United States*, Chicago 1930, pp. 108 ff., Parsons, E.C., *op. cit.*, pp. 582 ff., Brenner, Anita, *Idols Behind Alters*, New York, 1929, pp. 131 ff.

5. Gruening, Ernest, *op. cit.*, p. 229.

6. Redfield, Robert, "Folkways and City Ways", in Herring, Hubert, and Weinstock, Herbert, *Renascent Mexico*, New York, 1935, pp. 39-40.

7. Cf. Tuck, *op. cit.*, p. 155, and Humphrey, *op. cit.*, p. 251.

8. *Op. cit.*, p. 151.

9. *Valley Evening Monitor*, McAllen, Texas, August 10, 1947.

10. Cf. Gruening, *op. cit.*, pp. 239-240, and Saenz, Moises, "The Genius of Mexican Life", in Herring, Hubert, and Terrill, Katharine (eds.), *"The Genius of Mexico*, New York, 1931, p. 13.

11. "An Outline of Frustation Theory", in Hunt, J. McV., *Personality and the Behavior Disorders*, New York, 1944. Vol. I, p. 387.


Chapter IV

1. These figures are taken from "Public Welfare Survey of San Antonio, Texas", American Public Welfare Association, Chicago, 1940, p. 22, where they are quoted as findings of a 1937 San Antonio housing survey.

2. Based on information obtained from the office of the McAllen Superintendent of Schools, February 15, 1948.

3. *Valley Evening Monitor*, McAllen, Texas, April 26, 1948.

4. *Ibid.*, December 11, 1947.

5. This information was derived from an article in the *Valley Evening Monitor*, July 5, 1948.

6. These figures were derived from the marriage license records in the County Clerk's Office of Hidalgo County, Texas.

## Chapter V

1. This table is adapted from statistics contained in a mimeographed report of the Lower Rio Grande Valley Chamber of Commerce, September, 1947. The statistics were originally obtained from the Texas Bureau of Business Research Records, University of Texas.

2. Sixteenth Census of the United States (1940), Agriculture, Texas, First Series.

3. *Ibid.*

4. *Ibid.*

5. This statement is based on information contained in the Sixteenth Census of the United States (1940), Agriculture, Texas, Second Series and Third Series, and in statistics compiled by the Texas Bureau of Business Research, University of Texas, reprinted in the Chamber of Commerce report cited above. These sources indicate that in value of crops harvested, the rank order is as given here. In terms of acreage devoted to these crops, the rank order is cotton, vegetables, and citrus. The statements that follow on relative predominance of citrus and vegetable crops are also taken from these sources.

6. These dates and those that follow for vegetables are taken from information contained in Texas Agricultural Experiment Station publications reproduced in the Chamber of Commerce report cited above.

7. Sixteenth Census of the United States (1940), Irrigation of Agricultural Lands, Texas.

8. From an article published in the *Valley Morning Star*, Harlingen, Texas, February 24, 1948.

9. *Valley Evening Monitor*, McAllen, Texas, May 11, 1948.

10. See Robert C. Jones, *Mexican War Workers in the United States*, Pan American Union, Washington, D.C., 1945, p. 3.

11. See Carey McWilliams, *North from Mexico*, pp. 172 and 186-87, and Paul S. Taylor, *Mexican Labor in the United States: Dimmit County, Winter Garden District, South Texas*, pp. 353-55, for descriptions of crewleader roles in migratory labor.

12. See article entitled "The Kibbe Report", *The Texas Spectator*, Austin Texas, September 8, 1947.

13. Warburton, Wood, and Crane, *The Work and Welfare of Children of Agricultural Laborers in Hidalgo County, Texas*, Washington, D.C., 1943, pp. 14-16.

14. U. S. Public Health Service, unpublished survey data, presented in George I. Sanchez and Lyle Saunders, *Wetbacks - A Preliminary Report*, Mimeo., University of Texas, 1949, p. 32.

15. Cf. Warburton, Wood, and Crane, *op. cit.*, p. 17.

16. For a more detailed account of unionism in the Lower Rio Grande Valley, see United States Department of Labor, Bureau of Labor Statistics, *Labor Unionism in American Agriculture*, Washington, 1945, pp. 272-78.

17. See *Valley Evening Monitor*, December 31, 1947 and March 1, 1948, and *Valley Morning Star*, December 5, 1947.

18. For descriptions of this relationship in Mexico, see Tannenbaum, op. cit., pp. 188-89, and McBride, G.M., *The Land Systems of Mexico*, New York, 1923, pp. 30-31 and 58.

19. See Parsons, Talcott, *Essays in Sociological Theory: Pure and Applied*, The Free Press, Glencoe, Illinois, 1949, p. 192, for definitions of the terms "universalism" and "particularism".

## Chapter VI

1. For a brief review of the political history of South Texas, see O. Douglas Weeks, "The Texas-Mexican and the Politics of South Texas", *American Political Science Review*, vol. 24, pp. 606-27 (1930).

2. *Ibid.*, pp. 612-13.

3. *Ibid.*, pp. 613-14. As quoted by Weeks from Wells' testimony before the Texas State Legislature in hearings in 1919.

4. *El Mundo*, McAllen, Texas, May 8, 1948. (Translation by the writer.)

5. *Ibid.*, May 22, 1948.

6. *Valley Morning Star*, June 27, 1948.

7. *Brownsville Herald*, Brownsville, Texas, July 18, 1948.

8. *Valley Evening Monitor*, July 2, 1948.

9. Figures obtained from the *Valley Evening Monitor*, August 29, 1948.

## Chapter VII

1. See Redfield, Robert, Tepoztlan, Chicago, 1930, p. 68, and Humphrey, Norman D., "Social Stratification in a Mexican Town", (Manuscript), for a discussion of these and similar terms and the distinctions they sumbolize.

2. Cf. Tuck, op. cit., p. 137, for the importance of this criterion in a Mexican American community in California.

## Chapter VIII

1. Tuck, op. cit., pp. 65-66 and 133-34, and Gamio, op. cit., p. 54, report similar findings.

2. See Myrdal, Gunnar, An American Dilemma, New York, 1944, p. 58.

3. In his study of Anglo-Mexican relations in South Texas in 1930, Paul Taylor, in discussing Anglo attitudes toward the education of Mexicans, concluded that "The dominant American view is that it is undesirable to educate the Mexicans and economic, moral and religious arguments are adduced in support of it. Occasionally, the argument of biological inferiority is advanced, but even those who suggest it sometimes exhibit doubts, citing examples of very bright Mexican children." Mexican Labor in the United States: Dimmit County, Winter Garden District, South Texas, 387. See also Taylor's An American-Mexican Frontier, p. 255.

4. Valley Morning Star, October 10, 1947.

5. Ibid., November 1, 1947.

6. See Menefee, S.C., and Cassmore, O.C., The Pecan Shellers of San Antonio, Washington, 1940.

7. See article on zoning in the Valley Evening Monitor, April 29, 1945.

8. This incident is described in the April, 1946 issue of the Pan American, an English-Spanish magazine published in San Antonio.

9. I.N. Clifton, et al, vs. Abdon Salazar Puente, et al, Case no. F-44,264, District Court, Bexar County Texas, 45th Judicial District, April 27, 1948, p. 60.

10. Ibid., p. 47.

11. Ibid., p. 54.

12. Valley Evening Monitor, May 2, 1948.

13. From a letter by the teacher to the Valley Morning Star, July, 1947. Letter reproduced in Perales, Alonso S., Are We Good Neighbors?, San Antonio, 1948, pp. 235-36.

14. From a letter by the Mexicans involved to the Valley Morning Star, February, 1947. Letter reproduced in Perales, op. cit., pp. 243-44.

15. See Kibbe, Pauline, Latin Americans in Texas, pp. 212-13, for a description of this incident.

16. On the historic background of Anglo-Mexican relations in South Texas with reference to treatment of Mexicans by law enforcement officers, see Taylor, An American-Mexican Frontier, pp. 29-67; Webb, Walter Prescott, The Texas Rangers, Boston, 1935, pp. 514 ff.; Pierce, Frank C., A Brief History of the Lower Rio Grande Valley, Menasha, Wisconsin, 1917, pp. 107 ff.; Dobie, J. Frank, A Vaquero of the Brush Country, Dallas, 1929; and McWilliams, Carey, op. cit., pp. 98 ff.

17. Valley Evening Monitor, April 5, 1948.


Chapter IX

1. Valley Evening Monitor, May 2, 1948.

2. Gamio, op. cit., p. 129.

3. El Mundo, McAllen, Texas, April 24, 1948.

4. See Gamio, op. cit., p. 130.

5. Ibid., p. 128.

6. See Linton, Ralph, Acculturation in Seven American Indian Tribes, New York, 1940, p. 513.

7. See Weeks, O. Douglas, "The League of United Latin American Citizens: A Texas-Mexican Civic Organization", reprinted from the Southwestern Political and Social Science Quarterly, December, 1929.

8. For an account of LULAC's middle class origins, see Ibid., pp. 11-12.

9. The Constitution and By-Laws of the League of United Latin American Citizens, 1948, Article III, Section I.

10. LULAC's aims and purposes appear in most issues of the LULAC News, the official monthly journal, published in San Antonio, Texas

11. Ritual of the League of United Latin American Citizens.

# The Mexican American

*An Arno Press Collection*

Castañeda, Alfredo, et al, eds. **Mexican Americans and Educational Change.** 1974
**Church Views of the Mexican American.** 1974
Clinchy, Everett Ross, Jr. **Equality of Opportunity for Latin-Americans in Texas.** 1974
Crichton, Kyle S. **Law and Order Ltd.** 1928
**Education and the Mexican American.** 1974
Fincher, E. B. **Spanish-Americans as a Political Factor in New Mexico, 1912-1950.** 1974
Greenwood, Robert. **The California Outlaw:** Tiburcio Vasquez. 1960
**Juan N. Cortina:** Two Interpretations. 1974
Kibbe, Pauline R. **Latin Americans in Texas.** 1946
**The Mexican American and the Law.** 1974
**Mexican American Bibliographies.** 1974
**Mexican Labor in the United States.** 1974
**The New Mexican Hispano.** 1974
Otero, Miguel Antonio. **Otero:** An Autobiographical Trilogy. 1935/39/40
**The Penitentes of New Mexico.** 1974
Perales, Alonso S. **Are We Good Neighbors?** 1948
**Perspectives on Mexican-American Life.** 1974
Simmons, Ozzie G. **Anglo-Americans and Mexican Americans in South Texas.** 1974
**Spanish and Mexican Land Grants.** 1974
Tuck, Ruth D. **Not With the Fist.** 1946
Zeleny, Carolyn. **Relations Between the Spanish-Americans and Anglo-Americans in New Mexico.** 1974